# Introduction to Politics

## Power, Participation, and the Distribution of Wealth

○— George A. MacLean
*University of Manitoba*

○— Duncan R. Wood
*Instituto Tecnologico Autonomo de Mexico*

Prentice
Hall

Toronto

Canadian Cataloguing in Publication Data

MacLean, George A. (George Andrew), 1967–
    Introduction to politics: power, participation, and the distribution of wealth

Includes bibliographical references and index.
ISBN 0-13-913054-3

1. Political science. 2. Economics. I. Wood, Duncan R. (Duncan Robert), 1968– .
II. Title.

JA66.M324 2001                320                 C00-930431-2

0-13-913054-3

Vice President, Editorial Director: Michael Young
Acquisitions Editor: Kathleen McGill
Marketing Manager: Christine Cozens
Signing Representative: Duncan MacKinnon
Developmental Editor: Lisa Phillips
Production Editor: Sherry Torchinsky
Copy Editor: Maura Brown
Production Coordinator: Wendy Moran
Page Layout: Gerry Dunn
Art Director: Mary Opper
Interior Design: Julia Hall
Cover Design: Julia Hall
Cover Image: Otto Steininger

1 2 3 4 5      05 04 03 02 01

Printed and bound in the United States of America.

Statistics Canada information is used with permission of the Minister of Industry, as
Minister responsible for Statistics Canada. Information on the availability of the
wide range of data from Statistics Canada can be obtained from Statistics Canada's
Regional Offices, its World Wide Web site at **http://www.statcan.ca**, and its toll-free
access number 1-800-263-1136.

# CONTENTS

# Preface

One of the most difficult tasks involved in introducing students to the study of politics is the choice of an appropriate textbook. Every instructor doubtless has his or her own preferences about the material, concepts, themes, and pedagogy contained in a first-year political studies text, and there is likely no balance to be struck in any text that meets every requirement and partiality. The task of putting together an introductory text, then, is a delicate one. How might one assemble a coherent preparatory volume that addresses many disparate views on what is to be presented, and all the while posing a fresh and innovative central approach?

This book is an attempt to answer this very question. Fundamentally, its intent is to provide first-year post-secondary students with a comprehensive introduction to the study of politics. As the title suggests, this text incorporates some essential questions of politics: who has power in society, and why? How might groups participate in political activity? How is wealth distributed, and why does such inequity exist? This book deals with these questions using the political economy approach, bringing together the study of economic determinants with customary concepts and approaches of political studies. But this text does not simply merge the fields of economics and politics; rather, it is a recognition of the intertwined relationship between politics and economics as a means of organizing human activity toward the attainment of common goals. It is an innovative perspective in that it provides a historical and conceptual survey of the complex relationship between political authority and the production and distribution of wealth. Although the text is designed to prepare students for further study in the field, it is also appropriate for those with a more general interest in political studies

The focus of this book concerns the relationship between governance and the creation and distribution of wealth. Politics and economics are not exclusive fields of inquiry: after all, the study of "who gets what, when and how" is directly affected by who *has* what, when, and how. That is to say, for us to consider how resources in a political community are shared, we must also examine wealth and its distribution. The political economy approach is intensely comprehensive, and envelops all aspects of politics. Furthermore, given the eighteenth and nineteenth century roots of political studies in what was then called political economy, this approach is, in fact, quite traditional. The goal of the text, then, is to demonstrate the fundamental relationship between politics and economics and to point out how this relationship affects so many of the central questions surrounding political studies.

A final goal of this book is to help students at the first-year post-secondary level come to terms with economic ideas and processes, elements that have always been important in the world of politics, but have become increasingly so in recent years. It is hoped that, by introducing them to economics in an accessible way, students of politics will remain sensitive to this side of the political realm throughout their studies.

## Theoretical Framework

It is commonplace that most introductory textbooks begin with a survey of significant concepts (for example, the state, power, government, legitimacy, etc.), and a review of the philosophical tradition of political analysis (Plato's *Republic*, Aristotle's *The Politics*, Hobbes' *Leviathan*, and so on). Often the political economy approach is included in the broad overview of the fields of study in politics. Rather than including political economy as part of a survey of the field, this book shows how the development of this sub-field—most notably in the 1970s and 1980s—flavours the manner in which we must consider a contemporary and changing political climate, both domestic and international.

The methodology of this text is not intended to be heavy-handed or overly theoretical; theory is central to the purpose of the book, but as an introductory volume, its principal goal is to demonstrate to students the mutual and sensitive relationship between politics and economics. In short, the text does not call attention away from other perspectives, but rather seeks to provide a needed alternate view of the field of study. Linking to other approaches and methods in political analysis, this text incorporates related methodologies such as systems approaches, behaviouralism, historicism, and structural-functionalism, but retains as its central paradigm political economy. To that end, this text fulfils a crucial need in the market and sheds some light on a burgeoning field in contemporary political inquiry.

## Organization

This text is organized to introduce students to the study of politics in a comprehensive and constructive manner. **Chapter One** presents the fundamental nature of politics and the field of study in the larger context of political economy. This chapter outlines some of the major approaches, concepts, and themes related to the study of politics. The substance of this chapter is essential for the rest of the text. **Chapter Two** explores the nature and importance of political thought. It looks at both dominant and critical political ideologies, and the ideas that have driven the study of politics.

**Chapter Three** consists of an extensive survey of the nature and role of governments and governmental organizations. It covers the main forms of governments through history and today, systems of government, and the primary structures and roles of government agencies and institutions. **Chapter Four** accounts for the roles played by individuals and groups in society. It traces the formulation of ideas and information that influence citizens, and the way in which these ideas are played out on the political stage. Media, interest groups, political parties, electoral systems, culture and opinion, campaigns, decision and policy making, and lobbying are all contemplated in this chapter. In both Chapter Three and Four we have made an effort to incorporate economic concepts and elements that will help the student feel at ease with this aspect of the book.

**Chapter Five** begins a two-part examination of political economy in a comparative context. Here the focus is how political economy affects developed states. In addition to a historical and contemporary discussion of fundamental changes in political and economic life in developed states, this chapter introduces three case studies of modern political economy in action: Canada, the United States, and Japan. These three cases offer distinctive examples of how political and economic spheres influence governance. **Chapter Six** carries this discussion to the developing world, contemplating some of the significant approaches and perspectives regarding development in the so-called "Third World," and in particular, how the development process is as varied as the countries involved. By way of example, the chapter surveys the development experience in Mexico, China, and Nigeria, presenting a diverse stance on the myriad of issues facing countries in the developing world.

**Chapter Seven** is a general introduction to the study of politics on the world stage, taking some of the primary concepts and themes discussed thus far in the book to a realm beyond the boundaries of national borders. Here the nature of the international system is considered, as well as competing approaches to understanding world politics. Also, the chapter scrutinizes some current themes and issues in global politics, including globalization, foreign policy making, geography and population, global conflict, diplomacy and law, nationalism, and the environment. Capping off the text is **Chapter Eight,** which extends our view of political economy into the international sphere, covering the important dynamic of international political economy and its impact for domestic politics. This chapter complements Chapter Seven, illustrating the developments of international trade, production, and finance, as well as current themes such as world debt, leadership, and economic regionalism.

## Key Features of the Textbook: Pedagogy

Political studies, like any other academic discipline, has its own vocabulary and terminology. This text contains a **glossary** including definitions for key terms and concepts. Major themes and terms are also **highlighted** throughout the text. Every chapter contains both a **self-assessment** section and a list of suggested **further readings**. Links to important **websites** are also contained at the conclusion of each chapter. Throughout the chapters, **boxes** aid in the specifics of some themes and examples. **Images, tables, graphs, and figures** are also in each chapter to illustrate important points without interfering with the text itself. Finally, an **index** of all important terms, concepts, themes, events, and individuals is included at the end of the book.

## Supplements

In order to maintain clarity, style, and purpose, the textbook authors have written the following supplements for instructor use:

**Instructor's Manual:** This comprehensive guide provides 5 lecture plans for every chapter of the text. The authors have efficiently organized each lecture plan according to major themes, learning objectives, and lecture outlines for the instructor's convenience.

**Test Item File:** This handy resource includes a variety of questions (true/false, multiple choice, discussion questions) from which to construct tests and exams. Test questions are also available in computerized format for easy manipulation.

# Acknowledgments

There are two people at Pearson Education Canada who were responsible for getting this book project off the ground in the first place. Senior Sales and Editorial Representative Duncan MacKinnon first proposed the idea of an introductory text that incorporated political economy, and has been an unflagging advocate of the book ever since; if it weren't for Duncan, this book likely would never have seen the light of day. Acquisitions Editor Cliff Newman (now retired) was only a small step behind Duncan MacKinnon in his efforts to get us to write this book. Cliff made the early stages of proposing and writing both painless and stress-free. A number of development editors were involved with the production of this book, but Lisa Phillips took this project from its mid-life crisis to its completion. Lisa has been a constant champion of our book, and our ideas, and we are grateful to have had the pleasure to work with such a dedicated and talented editor.

This book also has benefited from the many useful comments and criticisms made by several colleagues who took on the task of reviewing it at its many stages. To these reviewers—David Black, University of Ottawa; Keith Brownsey, Mount Royal College; Mike Burke, Ryerson Polytechnic University; Joyce Green, University of Regina; Marlene Hancock, Douglas College; Michael Hawes, Queen's University; Hugh Mellon, University of Western Ontario; Chaldeans Mensah, Grant MacEwan Community College; Andrew Molloy, Ryerson Polytechnic University; Stephen Phillips, Langara College; Tony Porter, McMaster University; and Stewart Sutley, Wilfrid Laurier University—we are indebted for your time and your suggestions, which have contributed to this final work.

Several associates and research assistants were fundamental to the completion of parts of this book. At the University of Manitoba, Distance Education Area Director Bonnie Luterbach, and research assistants Shane Levesque and Jamie Rogers were instrumental in moving the project along. At the Instituto Technologico Autonomo de Mexico, Gabriela Valero, Jenni Velazquez, and Carla Hammond are to be thanked for their assistance.

We have discovered that writing a book such as this one takes more than simple authoring. It is the result of efforts both small and large by numerous people, some close friends and associates, and some we have not met. The final product is our own, however, and we alone take responsibility for any errors that it may contain.

George MacLean and Duncan Wood

# CHAPTER ONE

# INTRODUCTION: THE NATURE OF POLITICS AND POLITICAL ECONOMY

## Chapter Objectives

Chapter 1 is intended to introduce you to the study and nature of politics. After reading this chapter, you will be able to:

- describe the nature of the discipline of politics

- understand the intertwined nature of political and economic systems

- discuss the nature of, and distinctions between, politics and government

- list the various functions of government

- identify and understand the basic concepts and frameworks of political analysis.

Welcome to this textbook. This will likely be your introduction to the formal study of politics, and we hope that this book helps your broader understanding of the field, and perhaps provokes some interest on your part, as well. There are so many different fields of study available to you, and **political studies** is just one of several areas that may be presented to you as you begin your post-secondary studies. So why study politics? What can this course, and this text, tell you about your daily life, and the world around you?

Studying politics helps us understand more of our immediate surroundings, from what we see on the evening news, to our own possibility of involvement in the political process: making decisions that affect the well-being of ourselves and families, as well as the wider community. Studying politics also serves our self-interest, making us more knowledgeable of our circumstances. In brief, political studies offers a way to grasp how events and decisions that seem far removed from our lives actually affect us in ways we haven't even considered.

As a start, this chapter will introduce you to the study of politics, including some of its basic concepts and fundamental assumptions; it will also acquaint you with the principles and objectives of this text. The intent of Chapter 1 is to demonstrate the widespread features of politics in our daily lives, and to help us understand the human interaction that makes possible the pursuit of common objectives. Here we will examine the nature of political economy and government and concentrate on some of the significant terms used in the study of politics. It will also acquaint you with the importance of politics and the various methods political analysts use to study it. This introduction is a crucial basis for the rest of the text, as well as what the discipline attempts to analyze, and the several fields utilized to do so.

## What Is Political Economy?

At one time or another you may have sat down to a card or board game with some friends, only to discover that everyone has a different interpretation of the rules. In a game, this is easily remedied by either checking the rulebook, or agreeing on how it is to be played. However, imagine if everyone driving a car had a different interpretation of the rules of the road—simply deciding the rules as we drove along! Such a situation would cause chaos on the streets. Studying a field like politics is not quite the same as either of these examples, since they are extremes. Nevertheless, political studies has many different "rulebooks" used by people who study it. Indeed, every discipline has its competing approaches and methods, and the field of political studies is no different. People study politics from the perspective of political institutions, or human sociability, or ideologies. All of these methods—and many others—suggest ways to view the world, and the specific field of analysis that attempts to appreciate and comprehend these events and decisions in a way that is both meaningful and useful.

This book offers another viewpoint. It is our opinion, which we have developed in this textbook, that the fields of politics and economics are so interrelated that to study one without the other is like trying to bake a cake without an important ingredient. Consider, for instance, these questions: What do people want out of life? What do countries try to provide? How do we as individuals—and countries in the world arena—deal with others in our system? Can we truly answer these questions without examining both the political and economic realms? Answers may be found, but we consider those answers incomplete if they have not thought about or taken into account these two related spheres. We argue throughout this textbook that our modern lives are so connected to both the political and economic spheres that we must use an approach that examines them in tandem, as harmonious and mutually dependent perceptions of the world: **political economy.**

Political economy views political studies as a relationship between people, government, and the economy. It suggests that we cannot simply look at how people make decisions or interact with others without trying to understand how their way of life, and position in life, affects any judgments they might make that could affect others. What you do in life, and the conditions of your being, invariably affect your view of the political world. Political economy recognizes this as a fundamental way for us to identify ourselves, and our place in life, and that it contributes in a meaningful way towards the type of political system or surroundings we encounter. Furthermore, governments affect so many of the economic particulars of our lives, and of those around us, that we clearly cannot ignore the very important role that governments have in both the political and economic spheres of our environment.

Consider the following cases: the issue of Quebec sovereignty and Quebec's portion of Canada's national debt; Canadian sanctions in 1997 against the military government regime in Myanmar to protest human rights abuses and the lack of democratic freedoms in that country; Canadian provincial and federal government representatives at odds in 1999 over whether the federal budget surplus should be spent paying down the debt or increasing spending on social programs; the United States government shutdown in 1996 due to disagreements between Congress and the White House over the budget; 1999 North Atlantic Treaty Organization (NATO) strikes against Serbian forces in Kosovo; the United Nations Security Council provisions that allowed Iraq to sell limited quantities of oil on international markets in order to purchase food and medicine. All of these events, though highly political in nature, have at their root important economic causes.

## Approaches Used in the Study of Politics

Politics has a rich history, stemming back to the early philosophies of Aristotle and Plato. But the actual creation of departments of political studies, or political science, was a much more recent development, one that reflected a need to understand the many aspects of our social lives in a structured, formal way.

We might think of political studies as a limb on the tree of the **social sciences.** There are many "limbs" within social science, including sociology, psychology, social geography, linguistics, and of course, politics. Each discipline has its own areas of interest, and its own theories, concepts, and frameworks. Furthermore, each discipline informs us about important aspects of our lives as social beings. Politics is concerned with the governance of social units, the allocation of power and responsibility, and the relationship among political actors in society.

The study of politics was originally pursued in departments of "government," primarily in the United States and Great Britain. By the late nineteenth century, "political science" departments and faculties began to appear, driven by the convergence of interests of those studying government and economics. Not surprisingly, as this relatively new discipline developed and matured during the twentieth century, several competing approaches (or frameworks of analysis) were developed and fostered by political analysts.

| Table 1.1 Approaches in Political Studies | |
| --- | --- |
| • Analytical Approach | • Politics as empirical art; inclusion of subjective values |
| • Behaviouralism | • Politics as tangible science; use of objective variables |
| • Post-behaviouralism | • Politics as scientific study of human behaviour and values |
| • Structural-Functionalism | • Politics as study of political structures and their functions in domestic and international societies |
| • Systems Theory | • Politics as interactive systems of inputs (determinants), throughputs (decision-making), and outputs (policy) |
| • Political Economy | • Politics as a relationship of people, government, and the economy; political and economic spheres in tandem |

There are numerous different approaches to the study of politics (see Table 1.1). The most common and perhaps the oldest method is called the **analytical approach**. This perspective views politics as an **empirical** discipline, that is, one that examines evidence directly by observation, rather than a science. The basis of this approach is that politics cannot be broken down into parts, and must be viewed as an aggregate. The analytical approach, also sometimes called the **traditional** approach, becomes difficult for those of us interested in studying politics as a discipline because this method argues that it is impossible to separate facts from values: human values and convictions are just another "part" of political life that cannot be fragmented from the field. The implication is that any observer of political activity will have his or her own view and bias, which will implicate and affect their analysis. Since it is impossible—according to this approach—to observe events in an objective manner, political studies can never be a rigorous discipline.

The analytical approach had its challengers, however. The **behaviouralists** emerged in the 1950s and 1960s, particularly in American political science departments, and focused on the "tangible" aspects of political life, rather than the value-laden perspective of the analytical approach. The objective of the behaviouralists was to establish a discipline that was "scientific" and objective. Human behaviour, the behaviouralists argued, was at the heart of all political activity, so the human should be the centre of research. Behaviour-

## Politics, Political Economy, and Conflict
Box 1.1

It is often said that conflict lies at the heart of politics, and many of the political events that we see in our daily lives—such as parliamentary debates, elections, and wars—exhibit this to the full. But conflict takes place at many levels in politics and political economy, and is not always violent or obvious. Conflict can be ideological, interest-based, economic, military, or over personalities, to name just a few causes.

The key to conflict in the political and political economy realms is that a peaceful resolution is the preferred outcome. Von Clausewitz, a Prussian strategist in the nineteenth century, argued that war is the "continuation of politics by other means"; by reversing this claim we find that politics is the peaceful resolution of conflict. Of course, in studying politics and political economy we will find that war is an ever-present reality, one that fundamentally alters our assumptions, goals, and the means we choose to attain them.

Using the political economy approach to political studies is useful, indeed essential, because it recognizes that disputes and debates in the economic sphere spill over into our political lives, and vice-versa. The basic understanding of politics as the competition for scarce resources explicitly takes this into account. What's more, the competition that takes place in business and the economy directly and indirectly impinges upon the conflicts that we normally consider to be purely political.

alists concentrated on the scientific method, using "variables," theories, axioms, and hypotheses in their research.

The behaviouralist school, however, was subject to criticism for its attention to the scientific method. Many political scientists argued that in its attempt to be truly scientific, political science had neglected the fact that values were an intrinsic element of political life, because the very focus of the behaviouralist approach—the human being—was so steeped in values, opinions, beliefs, and views of the world. The **post-behaviouralist approach,** therefore, came as a reaction to the negative aspects of behaviouralism. Post-behaviouralism tried to reconcile the problems encountered by behaviouralism by allowing for values and ideology in their analysis.

Behaviouralism and post-behaviouralism, despite the problems connected with their focus on the "scientific method," have had quite an impact on our political lives. These methodologies are important because they raise **normative** (those which reflect attitudes or standards of behaviour that are generally accepted) questions about how we research political events and phenomena. Responses to questions about same sex marriages, for example, will be greatly influenced by normative views of the world. In particular, these approaches suggest that attention to the **empirical** (what can be examined) part of political life may be disassociated from the views of the examiner. One of the most common forms of political information gathering—political **polling**—rests on the assumption that properly administered polls will permit the examiner to remove him or herself as much as possible from the events to be examined. Modern polling is really a variant of the behaviouralist and post-behaviouralist approach, since pollsters are actually trying to evaluate what the broader public is concerned about, and the attitudes of citizens. Behaviouralism and post-behaviouralism, therefore, are not just discarded methodologies that have been tried and rejected. In fact, they have a profound impact on the way in which information is gathered about our likes and dislikes, and our views about political, economic, and social influences and forces in society.

Nevertheless, there were still others who continued to disagree with the "scientific" method of both the behaviouralists and the post-behaviouralists, and at the same time rejected the analytical approach as too broad. **Structural-functionalists** focused on the role of political structures and their functions in society. What, for example, is the effect and role of the legislature? How does the bureaucracy affect politics? Is the judiciary an important actor in a particular system? Structural-functionalists represent a group within a larger classification of researchers called **systems theorists**. These analysts view politics as a system of interaction, binding political structures such as government to individual action. Systems theory argues that politics is a dynamic process of information flows and responses that encompasses political institutions, groups, and individuals.

Each of these approaches has its own account of the world, and each comes with its own limitations, as well as advantages. In our view, however, the major drawback to these approaches is that they do not focus on the most important relationship in our contemporary political systems: the connection between power and wealth, between politics and economics. This book is an effort to fill this gap, and to provide you, as students of politics, with an introduction to the discipline that incorporates both fields as a coherent whole. To do this, we have compiled the most important concepts in political studies, accounted for institutions and individual participation, incorporated examples and case studies from both the developing and the developed world, and included an overview of domestic political economy, as well as the international political economy. And in all of these sections, we have tried to illustrate how the spheres of politics and economics are so intertwined that to try to separate them would result in a fragmented understanding of our world, our community, and indeed, ourselves.

## Politics, Political Economy, and Our Everyday Lives

Politics surrounds us. In our daily lives we hear of the "politics" of the family, of organized religion, of business, of sport, or of the entertainment industry. Every aspect of our common experience seems to be influenced in some form by politics or political conflict, even for those who think they don't know anything about politics. When we think about it, politics and political economy really are part of our daily lives, since they deal with any aspect of our interaction with others that involves organizing ideas, influence, or power. The "political" nature of the family unit, or religion, business, sport, or entertainment has to do with the way that these elements of our society are organized, who controls them, and how we may all benefit from, or perhaps miss out on, their collective gains.

Even though we may not be aware of it, politics affects almost every part of our daily lives, from health and social care to laws that regulate our behaviour, to the provision of goods and services made available to us. We often do not consider the political aspect of our daily lives unless we are faced with a situation that brings us directly into the political process, such as voting in elections, filling out annual tax forms, or taking part in political protests. Yet politics and political economy envelop us and influence our activities within society in a very direct manner.

## Division and Connection in a Changing World

This textbook will introduce you to the dynamic and captivating world of modern political life and political economy. It has often been remarked that the only constant force in political matters is change itself. Certainly, in our era this is true. The dawn of the new millennium has been marked by extraordinary changes in our political environment, both at home and abroad. The end of Cold War animosity between East and West has presented both new challenges and opportunities as we begin to understand the nature of this new milieu of domestic and international political affairs.

The change that so characterizes this new environment, however, is marked by both connection *and* division. Increasingly, individuals, groups, and states are intricately connected to one another through political, economic, strategic, and cultural links. Often we hear of the "globalization" of the current era, where information about other systems and cultures is readily available to us, from media sources, our educational system, and—increasingly—the Internet.

Yet at the same time, growing divisions are indicative of a complex and competitive environment for political and economic relations. Ethnic conflict, economic protectionism, and political isolationism, for example, all reflect aspects of modern political life that are divisive and contrary. Often these problems are deeply rooted in efforts by political leaders to provide goods and services to their citizens. In fact, the forces of connection and division are

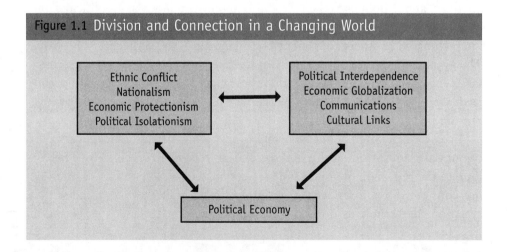

Figure 1.1 Division and Connection in a Changing World

intensely entwined: rising interaction among political players often leads to calls to reduce involvement in the affairs of others (see Fig. 1.1).

In this light, the term **globalization** is often used to depict the deepening "connection" that is felt among political communities and groups, both domestically and internationally. Globalization is more than merely a political concept, however. Simply put, globalization occurs when communities and groups become more integrated, leading to closer relations across borders. But globalization is more than just an "outcome" in political life; it is also a process of enhanced relations on economic, political, and social levels. Globalization occurs as multinational corporations stretch their influence across borders, as media and communications provide views and perspectives of the global environment that we would otherwise not witness, and as governments intensify their relations with their counterparts. In Chapter 7, we will examine the forces of globalization in greater detail, explaining how it takes place on many levels, and affects people in different countries in a variety of ways.

Politics and political economy, in simple terms, are concerned with four pervasive and encompassing questions: 1) *What* is the issue at hand? 2) *Who* is involved? Who benefits? Who is disadvantaged? 3) *How* did the events unfold? How were they dealt with? 4) *Why* did the events take place? Can we learn from them for the future?

To try to deal with these questions, there are three main and unique elements of analysis in this book. First, this text explores the intersection of politics and economics in modern life. It suggests that political decisions and events have a direct implication on economic conditions. Furthermore, economic well-being is at the heart of the aspirations and interest of all political communities. After all, a primary motivating factor for grouping together is to improve and preserve the conditions of what might be termed "the good life." Political economy, therefore, is merely an approach that seeks to demonstrate the pervasiveness of politics in economic life, as well as the deep-seated economic factors in politics itself.

Second, this book takes a comparative approach. Though it is directed towards an audience in Canadian universities, its focus is not exclusively "Canadian," or even North American. Instead, we use examples and case studies from around the world, from Latin America to Europe, to Africa, and Asia. This is done to provide a cross-examination of different political systems and viewpoints. The book places these examples in the context of the Canadian experience. In short, it is argued here that to know our own environment, we must look at various other examples.

The third element of the methodology of this text is its attention to several levels of political life. Various "levels of analysis" include that of the individual, groups, the state, and the international system. This focus on several levels complements the comparative nature of the textbook and gives you, the student, a more well-rounded introduction to this complex and ever-changing field of study.

# The Nature of Political Economy and Political Studies

Politics is a way for us to understand better how we organize ourselves in a social environment. It also teaches us how some individuals and groups benefit from society, while others do not. Since politics is an essential part of our daily lives, it is important that we try to understand the way in which humans organize themselves into communities, and the effects these communities have on society as a whole. After all, politics allows for our collective survival, because with no formal organizing structure, we would be left to fend for ourselves as individuals pitted against everyone else. So, though debate and conflict over power and authority are inevitable in human communities, so too are attempts to resolve differences, and deliberate controversies and problems, in order to allocate the benefits of social interaction.

Although politics is about conflict resolution as well as conflict, humans are by nature competitive creatures who rely—for better or worse—on larger communities to ensure their personal survival. To say that modern political life creates conditions of equality and fairness for all would give too much credit to individuals and their commitment to others. In reality, in contemporary life politics is marked by discord and controversy, rather than equality for all. This has been true since individuals began organizing themselves in political units. Nevertheless, one of the fundamental goals of politics is fairness in society, however elusive this goal may be, for politics has always involved controversy as well as cooperation, debate as well as accord, in the manner and process of human governance.

In the seventeenth century, Thomas Hobbes argued that without society and the political authority that accompanied it, humans would suffer in what he termed a "state of nature," or a state of affairs marked by an "everyone for themselves" cast of mind where life would be "solitary, poor, nasty, brutish and short." Shaping human society, or the process of socialization, he suggested, is essential for the security of life itself. Politics, then, is a means of self-

## The Basic Questions of Politics and Economics     Box 1.2

Before we understand political economy it is important to grasp the fundamental questions of both politics and economics. Though they have long been separated as academic disciplines, by simply glancing at the box above you can see that their basic issues are very similar, and certainly complementary. Politics is about the resolution of conflict and the distribution of goods (political, economic, and social) in society. Economics is about the production and distribution of material goods and services and about solving the dilemma of scarcity. This dilemma refers to the fact that human needs and desires are unlimited, whereas the resources available to us are finite. Because of this we have to work out some way of distributing goods among the members of society.

In one sense, political economy concerns the interaction between these two sets of questions. How does scarcity and the production and distribution of goods and services affect the world of politics? Secondly, how do political processes affect the production and distribution of goods and services?

preservation for human beings. As humans come together and create larger organized groups, they seek ways to allocate the benefits and responsibilities that accompany the creation of a social unit. Politics is essential for the preservation of life itself.

Perhaps the most effective way to understand the connections among society, politics, and economics is to consider how important decisions that affect a political community are made. Individual citizens voting in an election or attending "town hall" meetings on, for instance, rezoning a neighbourhood to allow for the construction of business, or the future of local school board policies, are part of the broader process that leads to decisions made by political authorities. Even not making a decision is significant, because it leaves the status quo unaffected and may be interpreted as agreement. These decisions, of course, are just one part of the decision-making process that results in policies, laws, rules, and regulations that guide and shape society. This process, in turn, is crucial to the maintenance of the state because it provides a framework for conduct within that society, enabling its members to discern what is acceptable behaviour in that collective organization. In brief, all members of a society have a role to play in the process of political decision-making, since all are part of the framework of activities that occur within that society.

In his book *Politics: Who Gets What, When, How?* Harold Laswell neatly defined the fundamental question of politics. In fact, many have come to define political science in terms of the title of his book, since it alludes to the notion of power in the political sphere and, more to the point, who has it. Laswell's book examined how the essential public goods that result from political life are allocated to members of society, since, in every civilization (historical or present), political power has been used to gain control over wealth and resources—the **public goods** of a state.

Understanding "public goods" is integral for the study of politics. Public goods are the various benefits that are made available to citizens of a political organization, including, but not limited to, social welfare, economic efficiency, security from external attack, public safety, and political freedoms and opportunity. In short, they represent what is made available by government to the people, and provided for all. Not surprisingly, the type of government that holds authority will in many ways dictate the relative access to these public goods by members of the society. For instance, political freedom is more widespread in liberal democracies than in authoritarian regimes.

It is useful to consider political and economic life, in all of their forms, as a competition for scarce resources. Whether we are concerned with immediate and tangible goods such as money, food, or minerals, or more intangible goods such as power and influence, they all represent resources that are available to a political community. Those resources are limited, and (in most political systems) the method of distributing them results in inevitable divisions between rich and poor (and within these groups), and the powerful and weak. However, even though resources are limited and competition for them is great, the most important objective of political authority is to allocate resources to members of society.

The manner in which this allocation takes place is through a system of decision-making and choice. This is when political actors, faced with the need to provide their citizens with public goods (or to protect those goods), deliberate and consider the best avenues through which their political and economic system may generate and distribute public goods. Though there are numerous specific goals available to actors in a political system, the act of choosing options is present in all cases.

Decisions, therefore, are an indispensable component of political life. We often spend our time concentrating on the outcomes of decisions, at the expense of understanding the process that actually led to the outcome. But, in order to truly understand the full extent of the determining factors that lead to such outcomes, it is imperative that we analyze the process of decision-making.

Once decisions have been made, they are restricted or enforced by the rule of law. As well, as part of the decision-making process, we expect that the choices we make will be respected and observed by others. It is the task of government to make those decisions that govern human relationships. It is important to note that, although society and choice may be considered natural consequences of human interaction, the creation of specialized agencies such as government is the product of human invention. Government, and other specialized agencies such as the bureaucracy and armed forces, are necessary to provide a means of regulating and maintaining society.

Politics is often considered in a pejorative way. We hear of how things reflect "politics as usual," or the term "the politics of the situation" is used to depict events that have a negative impact on individuals and groups. Though politics may be a negative influence, it is much more than that. Politics is about competition, conflict resolution, allocating resources and justice, the exercise of power, choice, and a means of understanding. Politics is a deliberately complex subject, and it has to be, given the wide array of issues to which it must attend.

The study of politics and political economy (which we will interchangeably call political science or political studies) is basically an investigation of political events: What took place? How did it happen? Why did it unfold the way it did? Who benefited, and who did not, from the event? The study of politics and political economy is about the description of events, the explanation of the events, as well as the prescription of how things ought to be. In this way, political studies seek to contribute to a better environment for citizens and political units. Political studies involve a systematic look at events in society. As a discipline, there is no consensus on how this should be accomplished, resulting in a rather fragmented field of study. But, as argued later in this chapter, this creates a vibrant and challenging discipline, with several important sub-fields of interest.

# Political and Economic Systems

Over 20 years ago, Charles Lindblom, in his book, *Politics and Markets*, argued that politics and economics were tightly entwined, and part of an integral social mechanism. In many ways the political economy approach is something of a return to the earliest stages of political science as a discipline. Political economy examines the relationship between governance and the generation and distribution of wealth—the allocation of the public goods in a political system. Political economists suggest that the two fields are not exclusive fields of inquiry, and the question, "Who *gets* what, when, and how" is a reflection in some way of who *has* what, when, and how. In more precise terms, the political economy approach focuses on the interaction between political authority and economic processes. Interestingly, given the roots of economics and politics in the creation of a separate "political science," the political economy approach has witnessed growing importance in the late twentieth century as we increasingly recognize the connection between political authority and markets. Political economy—the root of this text—suggests

In contemporary politics and political economy we frequently hear discussions of "the market." Sometimes it is in the context of "market forces" or even "market discipline." But what is the market? One thing we can say is that it is not merely an economic phenomenon. A useful way of thinking about the market is to envisage a real marketplace. In such a location, of course, there are buyers, sellers, and products. This is what we usually think of. But if we go beyond this first impression, we will see that a market also consists of an infrastructure (the stalls and lanes between), and rules (what you can sell and where you can sell a certain product). A marketplace is also a highly social environment in which individuals and groups interact, not only economically but on a personal level.

The "market" that we hear about and read about in the newspapers has the same attributes. In addition to the buyers, sellers, and the products they exchange, there is an infrastructure (means of production, transportation, etc.) and rules (such as health and safety standards, minimum wages, or licensing). The "market" also has a social side: it brings with it cultural aspects and consequences for human behaviour. In this book you will be introduced to some of the ways in which the purely economic side of the market interacts with its more political dimensions.

that political decisions acutely affect economic conditions, and that the linkages between the two are essential for analysis.

The main theme of this book concerns the interrelationship between political and economic systems. In fact, the main argument we make here is that politics involves the incorporation of power and wealth through measures of control and influence in society. But this text is not simply a "merging" of the fields of economics and politics. Rather, it recognizes the intertwined relationship between politics and economics as a means of organizing human activity towards the attainment of common goals. It is an innovative perspective in that it provides a historical and conceptual survey of the complex relationship between political authority and the production and distribution of wealth.

The use of the term political authority is intentional because political authority rests not only with states. Rather, it may be seen to operate at many levels: municipal, provincial, state, regional authorities and of course, international organizations and institutions. One example of the interaction between markets and non-state political authority may be seen in the regulatory dynamic between independent central banks and financial markets—clearly authority takes a political form and this interaction hits at the heart of political economy.

One element that gives the political economy approach its richness is its strong debate over the direction of the causal link between political and economic processes. Furthermore, given the interaction of political studies and economics stemming from the eighteenth and nineteenth centuries, the "unorthodox" political economic approach is in fact quite traditional. A goal of the text, then, is to demonstrate the fundamental relationship between politics and economics and to illustrate its use for identifying and addressing issues of interest to students of politics. Political economy, as an approach, has for too long been relegated as an afterthought in political studies.

## What Do Governments Do? Regulating Social and Economic Interactions

Depending on the type and needs of particular societies, government may be structured in distinctive ways and look very different. However, in all cases government is intended to provide a method of regulating the activities that take place within society, and to enforce the rules and regulations necessary to make social interaction functional and workable. Various theories have been offered to explain the tendency of humankind to organize themselves and make rules for their community. Some have suggested that political communities are created in response to the fear that humans have of isolation. This reflects in many ways what Hobbes said about the "state of nature" and its consequences. That is to say, individual freedoms, though desirable in some respects, also bring about demands in the person, as well as the fear of being conquered by another. Political organization, and the creation of political units, results in a form of "security in numbers" as individuals no longer fear isolation. In addition, as this book argues, political communities produce accumulated benefits, such as access to greater wealth, social guardianship, and the distribution of responsibilities.

In very basic terms, governments exist to accomplish two goals. The first is to provide the necessary security assurances for its citizenry: maintaining and protecting territorial integrity, national resources, and the population itself from outside attack or exploitation. The second goal, which can only be realized after securing the first, concerns the welfare goals of its citizens: providing adequate social conditions, opportunities, and benefits for its people. Of course, the provision of these welfare aspirations does not guarantee equality of access to all. But the point to be made here is that a primary function of government is to at least create the conditions that lead to betterment for its citizens. Importantly, this second goal simply cannot be obtained, or in some cases even pursued, without obtaining the first. Government must provide for the immediate security of its people before benefits and responsibilities may be distributed.

As an agency that regulates behaviour in society, then, government represents a process through which the political unit is protected and sustained. But government is not just a process; it is also a set of administrative, legalistic, and political structures that actually carry out the process of governance. The judicial structure of government, for instance, is responsible for creating and upholding the laws of the land. Similarly, legislative structures establish a forum for interaction among political actors (usually elected officials). There may be—and usually are—many levels of structures within a political unit, as well as numerous significant political representatives (politicians) that all compete and work within government.

Not surprisingly, political analysts are particularly interested in both the process and the structure of political interaction. These two dynamics are central for political inquiry because they inform us about the primary actors in a political unit and the environment in which they act.

So, while society may "pre-exist" government as a natural and evolutionary phase of human interrelationships, government is essential to create a political unit. As an illustration, consider, for instance, the differences between the game of football, and the animalistic hunt that takes place between hunter and prey in the jungle. Both are competitive environments, with the benefits of one (here either a football team, or the hunter or prey) eliminating those of the other. After all, only one team may actually win a football game, and either the hunter or the prey must prevail in the jungle. Which environment, then, is closer to that of politics? The answer lies in the *nature* of the competitive environment. Although there are similarities between the "football and jungle" illustration, there is one very important distinction: the football game involved referees. Imagine a football game with no referees: the rules could not be imposed, and disagreement and disorder would prevail. There are, of course, no "referees" judging the conduct or outcome of the jungle hunt, and the participants are left to their own devices regarding the outcome. Politics, though, does involve a form of referee. Rules are created, laws are enforced, and government acts as a legitimate authority for the activities in the political community. In one sense, governments are rather like referees: they exist to create and pattern the basic rules of the system so that order may prevail, both domestically and internationally.

Because they are given the right to exercise the legal use of force, governments are able to enforce the rules and laws of a political unit. Yet to maintain this control and power, a government must have the support of its people. Although some governments may secure the "support" of their people through fear (for example, through authoritarian rule that leaves no other options for people), they are most successful in gaining support by providing the basic requirements of government: meeting a political community's security and welfare goals.

Governments may be thought of as one of the "outcomes" of politics since, as mentioned earlier, organizing social units inevitably leads to the creation of governing bodies. Governments are considered "sovereign" bodies (discussed below) in that they alone are given the legitimate authority to make and carry out rules and regulations on behalf of the community; they are, therefore, the highest authority in a political system.

## Some Shared Objectives of Governments

Although different governments pursue these goals in different ways, the primary objective of every government is to provide for the independence, stability, and economic and social well-being of all its citizens. It is crucial to note the differentiation among government types here because some forms of government, such as authoritarian systems, consider the "well-being" of their citizens in markedly different ways than what we are used to in a liberal democracy.

Despite their differences, every state in the international system is first and foremost concerned with maintaining its national survival. This leads in part to the recognition by the rest of the international system of the **legitimacy** of the state in question. Legitimacy is thought of as the lawful and proper right of a government to have authority within defined borders, over a distinctive population, and covering the resources available to the political unit. When other states recognize the legitimate authority and autonomy of a state, then we may consider that independent state to be **sovereign**, meaning that no other political body has authority over it (see Fig. 1.2). Part of this sovereign recognition by other nations relies on the stability of the country. In turn, this stability lies in the ability of the governing authorities in the state to allow for the transfer, in an established manner, of political power to subsequent leaders. This "preserves" the state, despite significant changes to its core. Aside from allowing for the transfer of power, governments must also maintain domestic peace through the maintenance of legal systems and policing. Furthermore, governments maintain their legitimacy, especially among their own people, by creating the conditions that lead to the betterment of the way of life in that country. Governments may improve the individual welfare of their citizens through access to education, social benefits, healthcare, attempts to eliminate poverty, advances in technology, and improving the infrastructure (roads, services, and the like) of the nation.

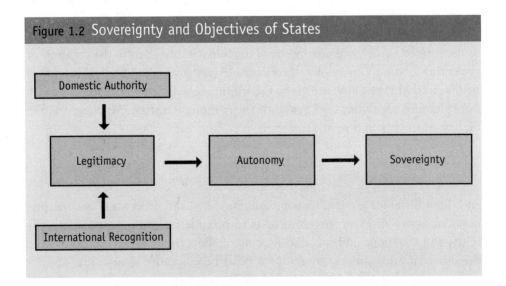

Figure 1.2 Sovereignty and Objectives of States

## Some Activities of Government

At one time the role of government was fairly simple. Immediately following the Peace of Westphalia in 1648, which came about as a result of the European Thirty Years' War and instituted our modern sovereign recognition of states, governments were largely responsible for, and concerned about, protecting themselves from external attack. In fact, even until the mid-twentieth century, governments were primarily affected by the need to preserve and maintain their own security. Since then, however, governments have grown much larger, and the emphasis on the welfare needs of citizens has occupied an increasingly important role in the latter half of the twentieth century. That is not to suggest that security from attack and war is not a great concern for governments; it still is. But population growth, challenges from foreign governments for scarce international resources, the increased complexity of decision-making, the nature of bureaucracy, and rising (and decidedly different) demands of citizens have led to growth in governments' size and power. A fundamental challenge to this growth in mandate and demands is the way in which governments may carry out these new and wider responsibilities. In broad terms, government activities fall under four main categories: economic management, government aid and subsidies, institutional and bureaucratic regulation, and program development and administration.

Economic management takes place when governments pass resources from one revenue source to other bodies without setting designated requirements as to their use. Think, for instance, of the diverse levels of economic strength in Canada, where whole sets of provinces are referred to as "haves" or "have-nots" based on their economy, relative to the other provinces. The problem that arises with such widespread and disparate levels of economic activity concerns the ability of governments to provide services at an equal level. If Canada were simply one province, the level of services, such as welfare, healthcare, education, and the like, would be based on the strength of one economy and—therefore—one source of tax revenue. However, with 13 different economies (including Nunavut, the Northwest Territories, and Yukon), the ability to provide basic services in Newfoundland, for example, is quite different than Ontario. The result is the policy of equalization payments, which redistributes revenue from wealthier provinces to the poorer ones in order to "equalize" services available to all Canadians.

Aid and subsidies represent a more active form of intervention, where monies are provided to some individuals and groups, but usually with requirements regulating their use. Alternatively, governments may wish to encourage exploration of new resources, or research and development in a particular sector that holds the promise of future employment and revenue, such as oil exploration or the microchip industry. Regulation refers to the rules of conduct imposed by government on its individual and corporate citizens in their affairs. Although traditional areas of regulation include a nation's criminal code, governments may also use regulation as a policy instrument for a number of purposes.

Program development and administration allows government to move beyond merely supervising how other people conduct their affairs, and creates opportunities for governments themselves to complete tasks on their own. Two more obvious examples of this include the government's role in its national defence and diplomacy, where government actually exercises a monopoly as the only actor with the right to carry out these tasks.

## Schools of Thought Regarding the Role of Government and the Economy

There is a wide divergence of opinion regarding how governments may best advance the economic and social well-being of their citizens. In politics, three separate approaches have been developed to help us understand the way that governments may ensure the economic benefit of the public. These approaches, or "schools of thought" are often labelled the liberal approach, socialism, and the welfare society.

The first of these perspectives, the liberal approach, is customarily associated with the writings of Adam Smith. Smith was the best-known proponent of **laissez-faire** (which means to "let act"), and argued that government is an opponent of human liberty; therefore, he suggested, the role of government should be severely curtailed in the activities of the economy. The *laissez-faire* approach holds that governments should not act as a regulatory agency within the economy, but should allow a "free market system," in which citizens could pursue their own interests, thus allowing competition and self-interest to produce the conditions where every member of the community would work to his or her own best advantage. The result would be a society where all benefited from the actions of every member. Working to each individual's personal maximum potential is referred to as "comparative advantage," where individuals' sacrifices and deeds serve the interests of the larger society. This system of free markets and *laissez-faire* constitutes what we commonly think of as a "capitalist" system.

The perspective of socialism argues the contrary. Socialist theorists argue that the possibility that every member will work to his or her own greatest potential in the interests of serving the common good is offset by the more probable reality that a few overly self-interested persons will do particularly well in a political-economic system, and the large majority of the population will do poorly. Socialism holds that government, not individuals, ought to maintain ownership and control of the modes of production and instruments of the economy in order to regulate a system that will truly serve the interests of society at large. We can see here how socialism is in reality a criticism of capitalism: whereas capitalism suggests that individuals should be left free to decide how economic benefits will be distributed in the system, socialism presents the opposite argument. Rather than yielding to a competitive environment where social welfare relies on the community concerns of individuals, socialism assumes that individuals must suppress their own interests in order to serve the greater good of the community.

The third and final approach is something of a mix of the two previous examples, and best represents the type of political system that exists in most advanced democracies today. The "welfare state" approach essentially allows for a system that is governed by a *laissez-faire* approach, but also permits governments to act authoritatively to restrict any abuses of the system (see Fig. 1.3). A "welfare state" is one that creates the means for individual protection and quality of life, such as healthcare, employment insurance, pensions, social programs for the elderly, children, and unemployed. But simultaneously, the economic system of the community is largely held in private hands, rather than government. The welfare state is exemplified in Canada, the United States, and Scandinavian states such as Sweden, for example.

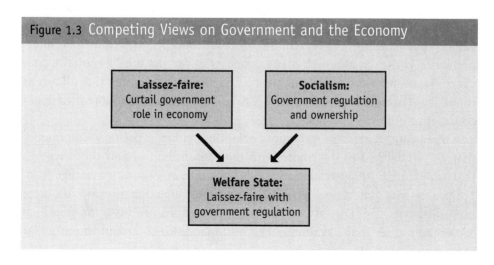

**Figure 1.3** Competing Views on Government and the Economy

**Laissez-faire:**
Curtail government role in economy

**Socialism:**
Government regulation and ownership

**Welfare State:**
Laissez-faire with government regulation

# Some Basic Concepts Used in Political Studies

The previous sections were meant as a fundamental introduction to the nature of political analysis and the necessity of government. We now turn to a review of some of the basic concepts in political studies, as well as a discussion of the various approaches or frameworks of analysis within the discipline.

Almost every field of study has its own particular vocabulary, and the field of political studies is no different. Aside from distinguishing the discipline from others, a specialized vocabulary is important because it allows us to create a "mental picture" of some of the more significant ideas that are utilized in political analysis. **Concepts**, then, are general notions or abstract ideas that are encapsulated in a specialized vocabulary. The fact that this language is specialized is crucial, for we often devise distinctive interpretations of terms in political studies that we might otherwise understand in a different sense. For instance, as we will explain in more detail on p. 33, the manner in which we consider the concept of "nation" in politics and the way we think about the term in everyday life are somewhat separate. What is important is that a word, once we settle on it, is commonly used to refer to the same aspect of our experience, even if we apply it in a more conscious manner in the study of politics. Therefore, understanding these concepts, as applied in political studies, is a most important first step.

This is not to argue that all concepts are universally regarded or agreed upon. In fact, unlike the so-called "hard" sciences such as physics and chemistry, there are no uncontested "laws" or theories in political studies. There is no corresponding political theory to that of, say, the theory of relativity, or gravity, which are accepted as a fundamental in the hard sciences. On the other hand, politics, like many of the social sciences, is marked by an ongoing debate about the utility of certain theories and concepts, as well as their interpretation. However, although many concepts in politics are "essentially contested," our important concepts can still be defined in a manner that allows us to use them in a fairly recognized way. Below are some of the more prominent concepts in political analysis.

**Organizations** refer to structured relations within a political community that are established to distribute both the responsibilities and the privileges that arise from formal association with others. Organizations may range from political parties and interest groups, to private groups that allocate resources on a different level. Directly related to organizations are *institutions*, which are organizations that have developed and mandated to attend to particular needs for society. Not simply a grouping of individuals as in organizations, institutions have strict definitions regarding their structure and functions, and set out distinct roles for members of the institutions. Institutions may or may not be organizations; similarly, not all organizations are necessarily institutions. Institutions may exist at the international level, or at the level of the national state. An example of an institution at the international level is the United Nations; at the national level, courts and political assemblies such as parliaments are also institutions.

A **system** is a connected and organized body that represents a coherent whole. A political system, for example, is a conglomerate of numerous political structures that work together to drive the political aspects of social interaction. Since the parts of the coherent whole are so interrelated, change in one part usually means a change in all, such as the way in which changes in party leadership affect the politics of a whole political system in a state. The international political system embodies the individual units—the states—as well as the functional non-state actors (such as non-governmental organizations and multinational corporations) that constitute and affect the world arena.

Many of the most important concepts in political analysis have to do with relationships of control. This is because so much of political life centres on the way in which power is distributed, whether among persons and groups in society or among all the states in the international system. What differentiates these concepts from those dealing with the relational and more active nature of power is the way that power is sought and maintained.

Power is often referred to as the principal concept in political studies because it attends to both the dynamic and static nature of political life. Thus, power may be pursued or maintained in an active manner (dynamic) through, for instance, the waging of war, or the creation of economic trade zones. Power may also be thought of as a measurement of politics (static), since we may compare actors in political life based on their access to and control of power resources, including natural attributes (oil and arable land, for instance) or influence (diplomatic expertise and respect). Power is an operative concept, in that it represents people's ability to do or act in a manner they would like. Furthermore, it allows us the opportunity to create a hierarchy of actors and interests in political systems, since the exercise of power involves the limiting or impairing of the recipient's choice. In some respect, to exercise power over someone involves controlling, to a lesser or greater extent, their freedom of action. Power, then, is an extremely important concept for political studies because it allows for the measurement of different actors in political systems, and is also what is sought through the concentration and use of resources. Power can be defined by the relative strength and influence one may have, but it is also derived from this very access to strength and influence.

Influence is closely related to the concept of power, since it refers to the effect that one person, or group of persons, has on another. Like power, influence is also an operative concept because it represents the capability of actors to persuade others to do their will. Power and influence are often referred to in tandem by virtue of their logical connection: influence is most often used to procure power, and power is an essential requirement for influence.

Understanding **authority** is essential for understanding the use of power in a political system. Authority basically refers to the "right" of a group of persons to exercise procedures that are required to regulate the community. Authority involves the granting of rights and responsibilities from the public to particular individuals and groups that undertake to govern the political unit. Because it is impossible for all the members of a political system to govern themselves directly, individuals and groups are chosen to represent the interests of the broader community in order to administer the activities and affairs of the system.

**Legitimacy** is integral to the notion of authority. Legitimacy refers to the belief of a political community that those in authority are there for justifiable and worthy reasons. "Certification" of a rightful mode of governance is thus transferred from the constituency to political authorities through the granting of the "right to rule." For instance, in most democratic states such as Canada, the legitimacy to rule is granted when individuals elect politicians to act on their behalf in the greater interest of the political unit.

**Laws** are rules that are customarily enacted in societies in order to prohibit or promote certain activities. Furthermore, laws are enforced with the imposition or threat of punishment by organized authorities in society. Laws are, simply put, a regulatory mechanism within political systems, but are not the only forms of routine activity. Norms, beliefs, customs, and ideas, for instance, also shape behaviour within political units, but none share with laws the punitive dimension—imprisonment, fines, and similar measures.

As a method of establishing the relationship among members of a social unit, political analysis is very much concerned with the quality of life. We know that we need one another to live and prosper, but we do not always find our current human situation entirely satisfactory. In response to the desire to achieve a better life, questions arise about how political authorities maintain and oversee the distribution of public benefits, as well as opportunities.

## The Community and the Individual Box 1.3

One of the most important political questions in today's world is the relationship between the individual and the community. As you will see in the chapter that follows, liberal approaches to politics and political economy hold the individual as sacred, and work towards expanding the area of individual freedom. This, of course, impacts directly on our conceptions of society and community. What responsibilities does the individual human being have to the society in which he or she lives? To what extent does that individual depend upon society and community for his or her well-being? What, ultimately, is the link between rights and duties?

As noted elsewhere in this chapter, many believe that humans cannot be separated from the societies in which they exist, that "being human" depends upon the families, groups, and nations in which we live. Certainly it is difficult to imagine life without the company of others. But where does our responsibility to the group as a whole begin and end? Should we be willing to sacrifice personal freedoms so that the lives of others are improved? Or should personal freedoms be held as sacred?

Though it may be customary to refer to the "equality" of humans, if we were to carefully study the differences among individuals, as well as the level of opportunities and benefits that are available to them, our notion of equality as "parity" in a political system would be challenged. In the real world, all persons have different qualities and strengths, and those features translate into different levels of benefits, based along distinctive areas of interest. Equality, therefore, does not always mean parity.

Political equality, for instance, refers to the right to participate in the political activities of one's society and to be treated evenly by them. Social equality, on the other hand, indicates the equal status given to everyone's basic characteristics and needs as part of a larger social conglomerate. And economic equality refers to the approximately equivalent distribution of benefits accrued from the exchange of goods and services. It is important to bear in mind that equality, in all of these senses, designates an attempt to provide parity of access to all of these public goods. Furthermore, equality is directly related to freedom, since individuals and groups must be allowed to seek out social benefits for true equality to exist.

The concept of equality has been fundamental to the development of political ideas in the Western world since the work of the modern political philosophers like Thomas Hobbes and John Locke. The ancient Greek theorists, including both Plato and Aristotle, refused to accept the equality of human individuals, seeing differences between them as more important. This is, of course, just one definition of equality, that humans are equal in terms of their capacities, both physical and mental. Hobbes and Locke changed our understanding of the word, so that it came to be seen in terms of deserving equal consideration or treatment. This is political equality. The justifications for this kind of equality are varied. Hobbes claimed that no individual was so far superior to others in terms of capacities as to be invulnerable to them, or able to permanently subdue them. Locke, on the other hand, claimed that human equality stemmed from the fact that all humans were equal inheritors of the earth. Whatever the justification, by the second half of the twentieth century it had become a standard idea in Western political philosophy that individuals should be treated equally, regardless of their physical strength, wealth, race, or beliefs.

This does not translate into equality of wealth, political influence, or opportunity. Though this may seem the logical conclusion to be reached from a starting position of equality, most philosophers have developed schemes of thought in which high degrees of economic and political inequality are justified. Locke, for example, allowed for an economic system of unequal appropriation despite his insistence on individuals' fundamental equality. Adam Smith relied on a premise of equality to justify the free market system, insisting that such economic relations would help to reinforce equality.

Equality has taken on a further meaning in the twentieth and early twenty-first centuries. Though political philosophers in the past wrote of the equality of all humans, they generally referred to one half of the human family, men. Since the suffragette movement of the early 1900s and with the rise of **feminism** as a political and social movement in the 1960s demanding gender equality in terms of pay and opportunities, this imbalance has been redressed in political philosophy. The rise of feminism, as well as demands for equal treatment for racial minorities, shows the continuing importance of the value of equality for both political theory and political practice.

**Order** is essentially the condition whereby units and interaction within a political system are marked by regularity and stability through the imposition of accepted and enforced rules, structures, and practices. Indeed, one of the basic preconditions for civilization is order, so as to provide a degree of customary activities and predictability within society. Though it is necessary for the continuance of governance and stability, order is often difficult to establish without sacrificing other desired conditions.

Social order is one of the values in political philosophy that is both necessary to secure other values, but also may contradict those values. We can understand order as the absence of chaos and the presence of a recognized structure of power, responsibility, and liberty. While many students of politics at the beginning of the twenty-first century may take this value for granted, to the political philosophers of earlier times it was one that was far from assured. Much political philosophy has been written at times of upheaval or turmoil in human society and, while that change was welcomed by many, to others it threatened to replace established political, social, and economic structures with little more than chaotic anarchy. To Thomas Hobbes, this was the fundamental issue in political philosophy. He sought to establish the conditions by which human individuals would be protected from the ravages of civil war, which would render life "solitary, poor, nasty, brutish and short." Only with order assured would human progress be possible in areas such as industry, agriculture, or the arts. As we will see in the examinations that follow, order is a value of primary importance for the ideologies of **conservatism** and **fascism**.

**Progress** is spurred by the belief that a better society is possible through the nurturing and development of a particular state of affairs that will improve conditions and advantages. The "belief" aspect of progress is significant, then, because at its core is the confidence that the goal of a better life is obtainable. Belief in progress is basically optimistic, suggesting that betterment comes through the passage of time, and is buffered by scientific knowledge, which allows us increased control over our destiny and more understanding of the human condition. Inherent in the idea of progress is a recognizably elevated outlook on the world. This is in the tradition of liberal humanism, which regards all reform and social movement as part of the effort to release humans from the oppressive nature of superstition, and seeks to create an environment of controlled improvement.

**Justice** is an issue that is intractable in political life, since the possibility of abuse always exists in the political system, given that the "many" will always be governed by the "few." A system is considered "just" where activities are sought in the interest of the community as a whole, and not just in the limited interests of the political governors. Justice ought not to be only in the interest of those in political power, but embodies the exercise of legal authority in the interests of the political community—that is, the pursuit of the equitable and legitimate aspirations of the ruled.

There are three senses of justice that require discussion here. First, the concept of justice is most commonly associated with legal affairs. We say that a legal outcome is just if we believe that fairness has prevailed, that all relevant evidence has been taken into consideration, and that the individuals or groups concerned have received what they deserve. A modern Western legal system is considered just if every individual receives equal treatment in the eyes of the law, regardless of race, wealth, religion, or social position. In that sense, legal justice is closely associated with the value of **equality**.

However, the second meaning of justice, in its political and social sense, is something quite different. It has its roots in the political philosophy of the ancient Greeks and concerns not the legal relationships within society, but rather the structure of society itself. When we talk of **social justice** in contemporary political discourse we refer to the same issue: according to what principles is society structured?

The most famous discussion of justice in this sense was written by Plato, who lived from 427–347 BC in ancient Athens. While his ideas on the division of responsibilities and duties in society seem alien to modern Western readers, Plato nonetheless put forward a convincing case as to why his model should be seen as just. His idea was that it was fitting or appropriate for each individual to carry out the role in society to which he or she was best suited by nature. Later philosophers, while developing markedly different models of justice, continued to structure these models on their understandings of what human nature is. Some, such as Hobbes and Locke, chose the concept of fundamental human equality, while others, such as Marx, built on their understanding of humans as creative beings to develop their own particular concepts of justice.

Lastly, we often hear talk of **economic justice**. In this sense justice refers to the economic system in place in a country or region—even globally. Again, economic justice can take on various meanings, based either on efficiency, equality, or equity (that is, the hierarchy of values chosen by the political authorities concerned). An idea that is commonly associated with economic justice is the notion of redistribution, the taking of economic resources from certain groups in society and redistributing them to others. Most often wealth is redistributed from the rich to the poor, but it is possible for the opposite to happen. In many developing countries over the past 50 years there has been an ongoing redistribution of wealth from society to the ruling classes, often through corruption and exploitation. Karl Marx held that capitalism was responsible for a redistribution of wealth that led to the increasing impoverishment of the masses and growing wealth for the capitalist classes. Debates about economic systems and economic justice have been one of the most important political issues of the second half of the twentieth century, both nationally and globally.

**Liberty** is one of the most important values in political studies and is often used interchangeably with the word **freedom**. In everyday usage we talk about the liberty to be able to do certain things, as long as those actions are not prohibited by law. But liberty is a more complex concept in political studies. Isaiah Berlin identified two forms of liberty, one negative, the other positive. It is important not to apply our preconceptions of what is positive and what is negative in this regard. Berlin talks of **negative liberty** as the kind of liberty central to the philosophies of Anglo-Saxon political thinkers, and this is the kind of liberty that we most commonly refer to. "Negative" liberty means the areas of activity in which governments *do not interfere*, where an individual is free to choose. An example of a negative liberty would be the liberty to choose one's lifestyle. It is obvious that this notion of liberty is closely associated with the idea of **rights**.

**Positive liberty**, on the other hand, is understood as the freedom to achieve one's full potential. This is the kind of liberty included in the political philosophy of Jean-Jacques Rousseau. It involves being free from human desires and the destructive or divisive emotions that prevent human individuals and human society from reaching their true potential. This freedom from desires could take the form of developing beyond greed, racism, or laziness, or it could involve being provided with the economic means to be able to escape such feelings. This kind of liberty reserves a significant area of activity for the state, to restrain or re-educate, or to engage in programs of redistribution, so that individuals can be free from their own harmful impulses or have the economic means to be able to fulfill their potential.

These two forms of liberty are obviously diametrically opposed: it would be impossible to maximize positive liberty while at the same time maximizing negative liberty. It is difficult to find many examples of the positive form in contemporary Western society, yet elements of both exist alongside each other in the real world. Many societies, for example, hold the freedom of expression (a negative liberty) as sacred, while at the same time promoting programs of positive discrimination (positive liberty) in the workplace. It could be argued that economic redistribution within the welfare state is an example of positive liberty, yet for more than half a century the welfare state has existed alongside the right to privacy, a negative liberty in many countries.

One last point about liberty. The modern political philosophers such as Locke made a distinction between liberty and **licence**. Liberty concerns personal freedom but it is not unlimited, whereas licence suggests unlimited freedom to do as one pleases. To exercise liberty, an individual must not compromise the liberty or rights of others. Clearly liberty carries with it responsibilities and, some have argued, **duties**.

The concept of **rights**, as mentioned above, is intimately linked to the concept of liberty. Moreover, it is a concept that is commonly used in everyday political, legal, social, and economic discourse. We hear criminal suspects on television shows claiming that they "know their rights" and that they have a "right to a fair trial." All adults over the age of 18 in Canada claim the "right to vote." United States citizens claim a "right to free speech." But what are rights? How do we know that they exist?

The first thing to point out is that rights can take different forms. There are civil rights as well as human rights. Civil rights are defined by the particular state, depending on the political and legal system concerned. Human rights, on the other hand, are considered to be universal and inalienable (that is, they cannot be given up or transferred) and are generally held to be the most precious and basic of human assets. Nonetheless, it would be difficult to say that any rights are absolute or predetermined. Rights are also defined differently in different times and places. They are essentially creations of a particular political system and age. The universal right to be free from slavery, for example, is a relatively new right, one that took shape over the course of the nineteenth century and was finally enshrined in the United Nations Universal Declaration of Human Rights (see Box 6.3). The right to vote only became universal in Western political systems in the twentieth century; until the 1930s many countries continued to deny women the right to vote.

Thus rights are intimately linked to politics. It was this realization that brought the nineteenth-century English philosopher Jeremy Bentham to claim that rights were "nonsense on stilts," that is, a meaningless idea elevated so that it appears much more important than it really is. It would be difficult to publicly defend such a position today, but Bentham's statement shows that no matter how universal we consider rights to be, they are nonetheless temporal. It is only if we believe that rights are given by a deity or nature that they take on a universal and eternal character.

Something also must be said about the matter of *duties*. Philosophies that focus on individual rights have been criticized as being atomistic, based on selfishness and destructive of the idea of community. A focus on the individual, it has been said, ignores another more important aspect of human life, namely, that we are social animals. One response to this criticism is that rights are but one side of a delicate balance in political life; along with the possession of rights goes the need for duties. It can be said that duties are the corollary of rights. Whenever an individual or group holds a right to a particular freedom or resource, there exists a concomitant duty on the part of someone else to provide or protect that right. But the relationship between rights and duties is more complex than this simple equation. It has been argued that holding rights in society carries with it a duty to respect others' rights and also to contribute in some form, either economic, cultural, or functional to society as a whole. By stressing that individual duties are inextricably linked to individual rights, it is possible to maintain a healthy respect for the individual, as well as an emphasis on human community.

As we just noted in the section on duties, many political philosophers have focused not on the importance of the individual, but rather on the social nature of human beings. To philosophers such as Plato, Rousseau, and MacIntyre, the individual was less than human when separated from a society and community. To such philosophers a political system should be so structured as to preserve, protect, and nourish the needs of the community ahead of those of the individual. To put it in Rousseau's terms, the general will must come before any particular or private will.

Related to this is the concept of **community**. First of all we must say that community is more than just a collection of individuals; the whole is more than just the sum of its parts. Community consists of the social, political, cultural, and economic ties that bind individuals to one another. To some extent tradition plays an important role, though community can be preserved, or even extended, by changing established practices. Community is a context, an environment in which human individuals develop their particular talents, capabilities, and perhaps most importantly, their identities. Without that environment, human beings cannot develop their true potential, or even their very humanity. In those philosophies that emphasize the value of community the values of duties and positive liberty play a central role.

An economic value that has take on increasing importance in recent years is that of **efficiency**. As with several of the political and social values mentioned above, efficiency can take on different meanings according to the ideology concerned, but we can take a standard economic definition to be high levels of production with a low cost per unit of output. An efficient economy is one that is able to produce a lot with a little. As we shall see later, this is one of the central elements of liberal economic theory, and one that is used to justify less government intervention in markets.

The idea of efficiency that is implied by the term **Pareto optimal** may be one that is more acceptable to students of politics. In this interpretation, an economic or social arrangement is deemed to be efficient if one individual or group in society can be made better off without making any other individual or group worse off. In other words, as long as economic activities can benefit one individual without taking away economic benefits from anybody else, then a situation is Pareto optimal.

In the late twentieth century, however, the former interpretation of the value of efficiency became central to many national governments and their economic systems as global economic competition increased. Efficiency has, in many cases, come into direct conflict with the older political and social values of justice, equality, and community. This value has come to be one of the most important elements of liberal economic ideology as it has been applied to policy-making in the real world.

**Competition** is held as a value in political economy because of its close association with efficiency. Those who argue in favour of high levels of competition in an economic system do so because they believe that it will result in higher levels of productivity and efficiency. This is a value that clearly has implications for other values held in society. By encouraging conditions that reward the most efficient or most productive elements of society, we can compare competition with the Darwinian notion of "survival of the fittest." High levels of competition will leave non-competitive groups and individuals less well off in a society, thus raising the issue of whether or not governments should intervene to guarantee a minimum level of economic welfare.

As a form of social interaction, politics encompasses the way human beings govern themselves. But governance may only take place with the existence of certain specialized agencies. Governing also requires a **polity**, which is the form or process of organized government. It can mean a state, or it can refer more generally to a collection of individuals in a community that have a political relationship with one another. This form of political grouping is commonly called a **body politic,** or a group of individuals tied together in a political connection.

There are a number of ways that we classify the body politic. Groups of people form political relationships with each other for a number of reasons, creating different types and forms of identity. In some cases, this identity is geographical. Here, the political relationship is self-evident, as groups of people that share a common territory will often create political units as a means of protecting that territory, or creating a way of regulating behaviour within the territory. Over time, the affiliations and relationships which develop among people living in that territory will be based on more than just feelings towards land, or where they live. Values, belief systems, attitudes, and images of one's world are deeply shaped by the socialization people receive in their political communities, creating a system where "identity" may be based on a multitude of reasons and rationales. How we conceptualize political communities, and the labels we place on them, are essential elements for our political analysis.

In our everyday lives we often hear about, or make reference to, our "state," or our "nation" as interchangeable ways of referring to our territorial community, or our country. But these terms actually have quite different meanings. A **nation** is a group of persons who share an identity that is based on, but not limited to, shared ethnic, religious, cultural, or linguistic qualities. Interestingly, these persons are part of a largely unacquainted group, since it is virtually impossible to "know" everyone who shares your sense of identity. Nations, strictly speaking, are not states, which are legalistic entities with sovereign authority over defined people, resources, and territory. Nation-states refer to those sovereign states that are constructed along a shared national identity; true "nation-states," therefore, are actually quite rare. However, though these three terms refer to very distinctive relationships, they are often used interchangeably in political studies, such as references to Canada as a "nation," the member "states" of the UN, or "nation-states" in the international system. Although it is generally accepted that these terms are used for the same meaning, we nonetheless should be aware of their true meanings.

## Summary

This chapter has introduced you to the study of politics and political economy, acquainting you with the broad nature of political inquiry, and the most important concepts that you will need to know in this course. The field of political studies is about the decisions about one set of values that are chosen over another. It is also about process: how decisions are made and to whose benefit; it is also as much about the resolution of conflict as it is about conflict itself.

The following chapters will explore some of the themes introduced here. Chapter 2 will provide an account of the major conceptual and philosophical approaches and perspectives in political studies. Then Chapters 3 and 4 contemplate the importance of political institutions, forms of government, and the critical role that individuals play in the participatory aspect of political life. Chapters 5 and 6 examine political economy in several different countries. Both developing and developed world examples are used in these chapters, including Canada, the United States, Japan, Nigeria, Mexico, and China.

Finally, Chapters 7 and 8 introduce you to the broader worlds of international relations and international political economy.

## Self-Assessment Questions

1.  Why, and in what way, is politics such a central component of society? How are economics and politics so tightly entwined?

2.  What is government, and why is it necessary? How does government regulate social and economic relations within a political unit? Should the level of government involvement in contemporary society be limited or expanded? Should government reduce, or increase its role in society?

3.  Without government would life truly be "solitary, poor, nasty, brutish, and short"?

4.  Is "power" the most important concept in political studies? How is it related to "wealth"?

5.  Is state sovereignty still relevant in our contemporary society? Are there other allegiances to which we may feel more closely associated? Why is the legitimacy of political authorities such an important issue in contemporary political life?

## Further Reading

Almond, Gabriel A. *A Discipline Divided: Schools and Sects in Political Science*. Newbury Park: Sage Publishers, 1990.

Easton, David. *The Political System*, 2nd ed. Chicago: University of Chicago Press, 1981.

Hobbes, Thomas. *Leviathan Or, the Matter Forme and Power of a Commonwealth Ecclesiasticall and Civil*. [1651] Edited by Michael Oakeshott. New York: Collier Books, 1962.

Laswell, Harold. *Politics: Who Gets What, When, How?* New York: Meridian Books, 1958.

Lindblom, Charles. *Politics and Markets*. New York: Basic Books, 1977.

Porter, Jene, ed. *Classics in Political Philosophy*, 2nd ed. Scarborough: Prentice-Hall, 1998.

# Web Links

### The Peace of Westphalia
http://www.fwkc.com/encyclopedia/low/articles/w/w028000570f.html

### Political Site of the Day
http://www.aboutpolitics.com/

### Newspapers from around the world
http://www.onlinenewspapers.com

### Political Studies Journals
http://www.dir.yahoo.com/Social_Science/Political_Science/Journals/

### United Nations
http://www.un.org/

# CHAPTER TWO

# THE IMPORTANCE OF IDEAS AND IDEOLOGIES

## Chapter Objectives

After studying this chapter, you will be able to:

- understand the importance and place of political and economic philosophy and ideology
- identify some of the most important concepts in political studies
- explain the relationship between theory and reality in political studies and political economy
- identify the differences between the major political and economic ideologies
- understand the history of the development of political and economic thought and their most important thinkers.

This chapter aims to introduce you to basic concepts and the most important thinkers and ideas, both political and economic, for the study of politics. Whereas traditional surveys of political thought and philosophy focus on the key figures in the political realm, this section will also introduce you to those economic thinkers and ideas whose influence has been most keenly felt in the development of political studies and whose ideas are still discussed in policy and academic circles in the twenty-first century.

Chapter 2 begins with a discussion of what political and economic philosophies and ideologies are so that you will be able to determine the significance of the ideas that follow. Secondly, some basic concepts of political studies and of political economy are included with the goal of introducing essential terminology. Then follows a survey of the most important ideologies that the student of political studies will encounter, focusing on both their political and economic aspects. Lastly, the chapter discusses the relevance of ideas, philosophies, and ideologies for the everyday business of politics and political economy.

# What Is Political Philosophy?

Before addressing this fundamental issue, we must ask one other question; namely, what is philosophy? The word itself comes from the Greek for love of knowledge. There was, of course, philosophy before there was political philosophy, and it concerned investigations in the nature, or essence, of life and its constituent elements. The early philosophers of the Western world, such as Homer, conducted theoretical investigations into the nature of Nature itself. In that sense they conducted an early form of natural science, but one that relied less on practical tests than on mental gymnastics, the forming of ideas and connections between ideas. Philosophy is thus a search for understanding.

Political philosophy can be said to follow a similar logic. It is an inquiry into the nature of politics, one that seeks understanding of things political. We must be careful here. Political philosophy is not a form of inquiry that attempts to understand the *mechanics* of politics and political systems. Instead it represents a creative process of analyzing what happens in the world of politics and constructing modes of improving that world. In this way, political philosophy seeks to understand more than just the nature of politics. In addition political philosophers attempt to explain the *significance* of political phenomena in order to improve our understanding of politics and to design better solutions for the problems that mark human life and society.

This implies, quite correctly, that there is a definite and unseverable link between political philosophy and the real world of politics. This link is two-dimensional. First, political philosophy must have some root in the realities of politics, social interaction, human nature, and ultimately, Nature itself. If this link is lost, the work of a philosopher will be useless, for it cannot be applied to the real world, and will probably be meaningless as well. Thomas Hobbes, for example (see Box 2.2), related his political philosophy to what he saw to be human nature, in both its physical and psychological meanings. Jean-Jacques Rousseau, on the other hand, held a very different conception of human nature, one that viewed humans as essentially peaceful, sentient creatures (see Box 2.8), and thus produced a body of theory that stands in stark contrast to Hobbes. What's more, political philosophies are shaped by the times in which they are created. Plato's concerns for a declining Athenian city-state (see Box 2.1), Hobbes' desire to see an end to the social and political chaos of the English Civil War, and Marx's reaction to the horrors of capitalism in nineteenth-century England each shaped their analysis of the nature of politics and of human society.

Yet political philosophy is not simply an exercise in studying political and

## Plato (427–347 BC)

The city-state of ancient Athens was a highly developed society that generated great advances not only in the areas of the arts and sciences, but also in political and social thought. Plato, a teacher in the city's academy, was the first thinker to write down his thoughts on politics and philosophy in a comprehensive fashion. He wrote his most famous work, *The Republic*, in the form of a narrative between his teacher, Socrates, and other prominent Athenians. Although this means that we are unable to decide whether the ideas conveyed in this book are those of Plato or his master, *The Republic* exists as both a work of philosophy and a record of the debates about the political future of ancient Athens. The book is as much a critique of Athens and concerns about its future as it is a work of political philosophy that transcends the particular circumstances of time and place.

The Republic is about justice, but justice in its broadest, most philosophical sense of "what is right."  Plato proposes social and political justice through a state organized according to individuals' capabilities and personalities. Those who are naturally equipped to be strong and courageous should engage in militaristic functions; those who excel at an art or craft should devote themselves to such activities. Most importantly, however, those individuals who are best equipped to be philosophical should become the rulers of the state, for they best understand the idea of justice. The image of Plato's *Republic* is of a totalitarian state, one that does not allow for much personal freedom, and is unappealing to contemporary students of politics. Yet it would be wrong to judge it by today's standards. Plato was attempting to find permanent solutions to the problem of political order, and his proposal is an ideal, a probably unachievable form of political organization. Yet in outlining such an ideal, Plato gives us the first offering in a debate about the just or good state that continues to the present day.

social realities.  It is linked to the real world in another, more creative fashion. For political philosophy not only tells us *what is*, but also *what ought to be*. This is not merely a Utopian enterprise that seeks to create a perfect world. Rather, because of its basis in the perceived realities of human nature and society, political philosophy seeks to define the political conditions that will create the best *possible* society. There are many examples of this kind of endeavour in the history of political philosophy, from Plato's *Republic* to John Rawls' *A Theory of Justice* (see Box 2.3). Each of them examines the basic conditions surrounding human life and seeks to correct the failings of the real

## Thomas Hobbes (1588–1679)

Box 2.2

Where Machiavelli brought to the study of politics a determination to see things as they really are, Thomas Hobbes developed both a scientific approach that was unrivalled in his time and a body of philosophy that addressed the most basic of political questions; namely, how to avoid civil strife and the breakdown of society. His most important work, *Leviathan*, remains an essential text for contemporary students of political philosophy.

Hobbes' overriding concern in his writings was to establish the theoretical foundations for strong and enduring government. Having lived during the English Civil War, he believed that event to have resulted from a crisis of authority in the English political system. He compared the chaos of this period to an imaginary period in history before the creation of governments. This he called the state of nature, and he insisted it would be wholly unsuitable for human life. In essence it is a state of war of all against all, where there is no room for industry, agriculture or the arts. Hobbes himself described it as a state in which life is "poor, nasty, brutish and short," and every human was at the mercy of others. Hobbes held firmly to the idea of the essential equality of human beings, in that none was so strong or clever that they could not be killed by another. The only way out of this terrible situation is the creation of a government, led by a sovereign, which would have almost unlimited power over its subjects. According to Hobbes, this would be the only way that peace would endure.

Though Hobbes granted his sovereign extreme rights, he also required the office to fulfill certain duties towards its subjects. Firstly, the sovereign must provide peace, and a system of law and order to maintain that peace, if individuals are to give up the freedom they hold in the state of nature and subject themselves to an overarching power. (It is important to note that, for Hobbes, human beings are fundamentally rational in their behaviour.) However, Hobbes goes even further, for not only does the sovereign provide peace, but must also provide for the basic necessities for the people. Hobbes is quite specific that the sovereign must ensure that there is clean air to breathe, clean water to drink, and sufficient work to keep the people employed. Hobbes is quite practical about this—unless the office of the sovereign takes care of its subjects, they are sure to rebel and there will be a return to the state of war. Hobbes' legacy was to show the importance of order before freedom, as the prerequisite for all other goods in society.

world by designing specific political structures. Perhaps the best example is the political economy theory of Karl Marx (see Box 2.11). His ideas for the improvement of society stem directly from his analysis of the social, political, and economic conditions that have prevailed throughout history. In fact, it would be more accurate to say that his understanding of the relationship between economics and politics determined the political and economic system that he proposed as a solution to the problems facing nineteenth-century capitalist society.

---

**Box 2.3**  | **John Rawls**

In the 1970s American political scientist John Rawls took an idea from the political philosophy of Hobbes, Locke, and Rousseau, and started a debate that helped to shape political philosophy at the end of the twentieth century. In *A Theory of Justice*, Rawls took the concept of the "state of nature," an heuristic tool used by many philosophers in the seventeenth and eighteenth centuries, and renamed it the "original position."

Instead of a mythical state in which humans are removed from society and subjected to the will of others and to the wilds of nature, Rawls formulated a hypothetical situation in which each individual is ignorant of everything about him or herself, including their proclivity for risk-taking. By asking what the human individual in this situation would choose in creating a political and economic system, Rawls hoped to find the basis for a just society. Rawls' answer was that each individual would likely opt for a political and economic system that is democratic and that guarantees a minimum level of material welfare.

Shortly after Rawls published *A Theory of Justice*, Robert Nozick wrote a response—*Anarchy, State and Utopia*. In this rebuttal to Rawls, Nozick argued that rather than providing the ethical and philosophical basis for the welfare state, the original position (as formulated by Nozick) would promote the choice of libertarian society in which the role of the state is severely restricted, and the individual is held sacred. The debate between Rawls and Nozick became one of the most important debates of the twentieth century, and brings to mind the contrast between the philosophies of Thomas Hobbes and John Locke.

---

How does political philosophy proceed—how is it done? Essentially, political philosophy asks questions, and then proposes answers to those questions. The questions are perennial. What is the extent of my liberty as an individual in human society? When is a government action legitimate? What would life be like in the absence of government? How can we justly divide the product of a society? The answers to these questions, however, are temporal and particular to each philosopher. The answer proposed by Rousseau, for example, to the question of what is the importance of the individual vis-à-vis the community is very different to that put forward by Locke. Rousseau emphasizes the general will, while Locke focuses on the importance of individual liberty.

It has been quite accurately claimed that political philosophy constitutes a quest for the good life, the good society, and, of particular importance, for the *just* society. Social justice is a recurring theme throughout the history of political philosophy, but its meaning and its form change from philosopher to philosopher. As can be seen from the studies included in this chapter, the Platonic or Socratic conception of **justice** is difficult to relate to the formulation of the same concept in Rousseau, just as Rousseau's conception of justice is wildly different from that of Robert Nozick. Nonetheless, though the idea of what is just varies from century to century, and from philosopher to philosopher, it remains the goal of political philosophy up to the present time. As noted above political philosophy is not merely a descriptive exercise; rather it is an attempt to establish **norms**, that is, rules or ideals for political behaviour and political reality. As a normative exercise we might expect there to be some eternal truths. However, the norms established by political philosophers depend upon their own societies, their own knowledge, and to a certain extent, their own personal experiences.

One reason behind the variations in the conception of the just society is that different philosophers have placed different emphases on moral and political values. To some, such as Hobbes, the idea of social order is paramount. To others, such as Locke, the concept of liberty, formulated as freedom from interference by authority, receives the most attention, though not to the neglect of equality. For Rousseau, liberty is again fundamental, yet he defines that liberty less as freedom from interference, and more as freedom from human passions and desires. For some philosophers, individualism is central; for others, humans are incomprehensible apart from their social setting, and this understanding of humans as social animals guides them towards philosophies that emphasize the general over the particular or private good. It is important to note that most of the influential political philosophers over the centuries have recognized the importance of more than one value; what is key in determining the political systems they outline is the priority that each gives to a series of values. Is **equality** the most important value to be respected by society? Or should equality be accorded an inferior position to **order** in the hierarchy of values?

Box 2.4

# Aristotle (384–322 BC)

Aristotle is the intellectual inheritor of Plato's philosophy, yet his work is quite different. A student of Plato, Aristotle was concerned less with proposing an ideal state than with the practical application of philosophy to the problems of everyday politics. In this way we can say that Aristotle was a philosopher who believed in the politics of the possible. In addition Aristotle can be seen as the founder of the study of politics in a scientific way, for a large part of his work is concerned with classifying and rating different political systems, trying to determine the best possible organization of the state.

However, though Aristotle's approach to political philosophy is very practical and scientific, it also seeks to establish a link between ethics and politics, to seek the "good." Aristotle's two most famous works, *The Nicomachean Ethics* and *The Politics*, examine the two areas separately, but there is little doubt that there is an inescapable link for him. Indeed, the only difference between ethics and politics for Aristotle is that ethics concerns what is right and good for the individual, whereas politics concerns what is right and good for the community. Aristotle had a clear idea that the needs of the community came before those of the individual, and for him the height of rational behaviour was public action, or participation in the running of the city-state. In his work of classification he attempts to identify the "best" political system, and he finds it in "aristocracy," a city-state ruled by a select group of men who dedicate themselves to the good life, both for themselves and the city.

It is worthwhile pointing out that Aristotle explicitly recognizes the importance of economics in the organization of political systems. A "good" economic system must allow individuals to acquire wealth, since this is a natural inclination in humans; they seek wealth because it allows them, in turn, to acquire goods that satisfy their natural needs and desires. One activity that Aristotle would forbid in a good state would be usury (money lending for profit), a highly unnatural activity that aims only at the accumulation of money, not other goods which are necessary for human survival and pleasure.

The differences between value hierarchies, and thus between political philosophies, have created a philosophical debate or discourse that stretches across not just space, but time as well. Though it should not be thought that Hobbes was responding to Plato's ideas when he wrote *Leviathan*, the existence of these contrasting and sometimes conflicting philosophies creates the

## Machiavelli (1469–1527)

Box 2.5

From Aristotle through St. Augustine and the Christian political philosophers, there had been a perennial commitment to combining ethics and morality with politics. With the work of Niccolo Machiavelli we see a dramatic break in that tradition. For Machiavelli, who was intimately involved in the politics of the Italian city-states of the late fifteenth and early sixteenth centuries, put forward a new political philosophy based on political expediency, where ethics and ideals played a secondary role to the pursuit of power and control. This philosophy came to be called political realism, and it has been one of the most important theoretical and analytical approaches in the study of politics ever since.

It should not, of course, be thought that politics had never before been based on these principles—we know that governments have done so since the time of the ancient Greeks, and probably earlier. However, Machivelli was the first philosopher to explicitly defend them as a basis for sound government. As with most philosophers, Machiavelli's work can be understood and interpreted on two levels: as an attempt to find solutions to the most important political problems of his time (in this case the internal divisions of the Italian city-states); and as a prescription for political action that would provide for sound government regardless of time and place.

Machiavelli argued that there should be a definite separation between ideals and morality and politics. Politics should instead be guided by an examination of human behaviour. If governors, or Princes, as Machiavelli prefers, understand human nature and behaviour, they will better be able to formulate policies to rule effectively and consolidate their power. He proposed that it is better for a Prince to be feared than loved by his people, though this must be achieved without inspiring popular hatred of the government. Machiavelli's approach to the study of politics can be considered the beginning of modern political philosophy, and his contribution was soon enlarged by Thomas Hobbes.

possibility for comparison and indeed cross-fertilization of ideas for the student of political studies. It is this discourse that makes the study of political philosophies so challenging and at the same time rewarding. They provide the opportunity to view the collected wisdom of history's most eminent political thinkers and to evaluate their ideas on the basis of social and political conditions, both when these ideas were transcribed and in the present day. Just as importantly, it is this discourse that makes political philosophy a vital and central part of political studies. The discourse that continues across the centuries ensures that politics is an ever-changing, always fascinating area of study.

# Ideas and Theories of Political Economy

Economic theories concern questions of distribution, essentially the question of "who gets what?" This is an issue for economists because they perceive the human condition to be governed by scarcity. Humans, economists claim, have unlimited desires but are blessed with only limited resources. The tension between these two fundamental aspects of life has guided the great economic theorists to envision economic systems that propose distinct answers to the question of distribution of material goods.

Essentially, economic theories and ideologies seek to answer three main questions, which are fundamental to both the production and distribution of economic wealth. First economics asks the question, "What is to be produced?" This question signifies choices to be made over whether an economy should be directed towards specialization or diversity of production, primary goods (raw materials, agricultural produce), manufactured goods (automobiles, refrigerators), or services (entertainment, banking). Secondly, economics asks the question, "How will production be organized?" Will it be marked by competition or by monopolies, by strict government or private control (or a mixture of both)? Lastly, economics looks to answer the question, "How will goods produced by the system, and particularly the surplus, be distributed?" What principles or values guide that distribution? Will equality be the dominant value? Justice? Or maybe competition and merit?

One of the most significant questions of **political economy** is to ask who makes the most important decisions in the functioning of an economy. Who decides what is produced, how it is produced, and how the surplus is distributed? Is it political authorities or private individuals and groups? Essentially, we are asking if it is the government or the **market** that is a guiding principle for economic decisions. If the government is making the most important decisions, we must analyze the nature of that government and the value hierarchies it promotes. If, on the other hand, it is the market that decides, then we know that the major decisions in the economy will be decided with reference to the principles of **efficiency** and **competition**.

Many of the same elements that were mentioned above with regard to political philosophies refer equally to economic ideas, but with one major difference. As economics has become more and more formalized as an academic discipline, it has increasingly taken on the aura of being "the most scientific of the social sciences." This implies a level of certainty that exceeds anything thus far achieved by political studies, and suggests that there are scientific answers to economic problems just waiting to be discovered. The reality is somewhat different. Economics, too, has its major debates and discourses that stretch throughout time and space. Interestingly enough, these debates are generally linked to political divisions concerning exactly the kind of value-based disputes discussed above.

## Adam Smith (1723–1790)

Box 2.6

In the mid-eighteenth century Scotland produced a series of important political and economic thinkers in a movement known as the Scottish Enlightenment. Adam Smith emerged as the most famous of these and it is his influence, perhaps more than any other philosopher of his period, that is still keenly felt in contemporary political economy at the beginning of the twenty-first century. For Smith incorporated a distinct economic ideology into the liberalism of Locke and introduced the doctrine of the free market into political economy.

Like the political philosophers who came before him, Smith had his own political program—he was determined to provide an ideological opposition to the doctrine of economic nationalism and particularly mercantilism, which he saw as both inefficient and conflict-causing. In *The Wealth of Nations*, Smith saw market relations as working to the benefit of all people, because everyone would benefit from more efficient modes of production. Smith introduced the concept of the invisible hand, a force inherent in economic liberalism that would ensure progress for all without any conscious direction from government.

Yet Smith wrote not only of the economic advantages of market-based economics, but also of their political consequences. He argued that economic relationships based on contracts and bargains required that individuals see each other as essentially equal. Indeed he credited market relations with ending the oppression of feudalism.

Smith believed strongly in the liberation of the economy from government interference. Furthermore he argued for free competition between firms, the free movement of goods in and out of countries, the free movement of workers and the free movement of capital. All of this would lead to progress, which Smith defined as rising real per capita income. Adam Smith fundamentally altered the way we look at economics, and it is in his work that all liberal economists find their ideological roots.

The history of economic speculation and theory is shorter than that of political philosophy, but no less divided. Furthermore, just as with political thought, economic theorists produced theories that responded to the most important questions of their time. Beginning in the early eighteenth century with the work of Adam Smith, much of whose work was designed to refute common economic practice on the part of governments in his century, the area of economic investigation and theorizing rapidly flourished and attracted new contributors. Much of this success was due to the existence of divisions between theorists, divisions that grew into the founding of separate schools of economics.

One interesting point to note is that the early economic theorists saw themselves as being political economists. To them there was not a clear divide between the two areas of investigation, a realization that has escaped the two disciplines of political studies and economics until quite recently. Adam Smith in particular explicitly recognized the political consequences of his theories, claiming that a market economy would increase both equality and freedom, as well as being more efficient and productive. However, as time went by, the two areas became increasingly divergent in their focus, each specializing excessively at the expense of a broader understanding of the fundamental issues underlying both disciplines. It is to be hoped that the student of political studies in the early twenty-first century does not make the same mistake.

# Ideologies

What constitutes an ideology? Essentially it is a set of related, generally consistent ideas and beliefs that provides a basis for political activity. Ideologies contain both descriptive and normative elements; that is, they contain interpretations of the world, and statements of how it should be. They reflect particular hierarchies of **values**, and help to shape people's perceptions and images of reality. One ideology might reflect an emphasis on the value of order over **liberty**, while another might emphasize the value of efficiency over justice. It is by examining the hierarchies of values embodied in ideologies that we can identify the differences between them, and also understand the impact they have on the world of politics.

Political and economic ideologies bear some resemblance to religions: they are based on beliefs and preconceptions, can be proved neither wrong nor right (yet often contain normative judgments and assumptions) and provide a basis for human action. Ideologies, however, generally focus on the material and physical aspects of life, rather than the spiritual, though the latter was commonly a concern for the political thinkers of Greece, Rome, and Medieval Europe, and still finds some representation in some conservative ideology in contemporary Anglo-Saxon political systems. Ideologies are a fundamental aspect of political life, for they frame the debates which dominate political and economic systems and guide political action, which in turn helps determine both political and economic reality (see the section on the relevance of ideas on p. 71).

Ideologies are commonly, but not always, based on the philosophy and thought of groups of thinkers; in that sense they can be said to follow *schools* of thought. Because of this, and because different ideologies contain markedly different ideas, perceptions of reality, and prescriptions for the just or best political system, ideologies are by their nature divisive phenomena, and exist at the heart of, or at the very least *colour* most political debates and disputes. Ideologies, however, are not necessarily mutually exclusive. An individual, group, political party, or indeed a society can be both liberal and nationalist, as was the United States during the Cold War. Similarly, a political grouping can combine nationalist economic policies with a socialist political plan of action. Ideologies are flexible things, often compromised with ideas taken from other ideologies and schools of thought. Furthermore, there is surprising variation to be found within ideologies; within one school of thought and ideas there can be individuals who appear to be completely opposed. More

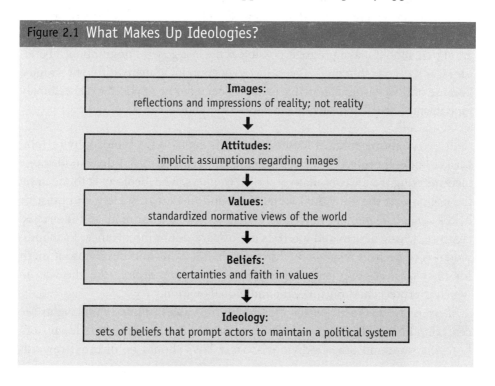

**Figure 2.1 What Makes Up Ideologies?**

**Images:**
reflections and impressions of reality; not reality

⬇

**Attitudes:**
implicit assumptions regarding images

⬇

**Values:**
standardized normative views of the world

⬇

**Beliefs:**
certainties and faith in values

⬇

**Ideology:**
sets of beliefs that prompt actors to maintain a political system

importantly, ideologies change over time and both affect and are affected by political and economic realities (see Fig. 2.1). They are evolutionary, and understanding the evolution of ideologies will in turn help us to understand progressive as well as revolutionary change in political systems.

The following selection of ideologies is by no means exhaustive, but it does give the student of political studies an introduction to the most significant political belief systems of modern times. Readers should take care to cross-reference these ideologies with the descriptions given of important political philosophers to learn more about their origins and broader implications. For the first three ideologies an attempt has been made to explain the economic as well as political tenets and applications, in order both to demonstrate the link between political and economic values and also to provide the terminology necessary for the study of political economy.

## Liberalism

Underlying both political and economic forms of liberal thought is an assumption that progress is possible and likely in human affairs. Progress, of course, can mean many things to different people, but for liberals it implies an improvement of the human condition, either materially, intellectually, or in terms of freedom. Thus it would be fair to say that liberal thought is an optimistic ideology, one that expects progress to come, and also provides a political and economic program that should make progress possible. One last general point about liberalism: it is a diverse, often divergent, ideology containing many different strands. Because of this, it is quite possible for two liberals to be opposed over seemingly fundamental issues. But such is the nature of politics.

Political    Liberal political ideology finds its roots in the philosophy of John Locke, but has evolved since the seventeenth century into a diverse ideology incorporating the ideas of many political thinkers. The ideology is founded on the notion that the individual is the basic unit of human society and must be held sacred. The human individual is believed to be a rational, self-interested creature, whose desires and interests are of paramount importance. Each individual is to be held responsible for their own actions and deserving of merit for their own achievements. Society itself takes its nature from the way in which it protects and nurtures the individuals within.

Because of this focus on the individual, the values of liberty and rights are central to liberal ideology, as they are means of protecting the individual from both the state and other individuals. State laws should be directed towards

## John Locke (1632–1704)

Box 2.7

Just as Hobbes viewed the experience of the English Civil War as a crisis of authority, John Locke saw the same event as stemming from a lack of legitimacy on the part of the English monarchy. This perspective coloured Locke's approach to political philosophy, and we have come to associate him with a school of thought that demands legitimacy from government. For in Locke lie the roots of modern liberalism, where the concept of consent is central.

In his most famous work, *Two Treatises of Government*, Locke's understanding of the state of nature was markedly different to that of Hobbes. He saw it as being more peaceful, but still inconvenient and certainly unproductive. His idea of human equality was also different than Hobbes', for he held it to be equality of right, not mere equality of vulnerability. How did human beings come to leave this state of equality and create civil societies? Locke's answer lay in the notion of consent, and he argued that for a political system to be legitimate, the consent of the governed must have been obtained, and must be maintained.

Locke also used consent as a key concept in explaining economic systems. Locke argued that all humans were equal inheritors of the earth, and therefore deserved equal access to its fruits and riches. How, then, did we reach a system of unequal acquisition and such great inequalities of wealth? He proposed that the original condition of equality was fundamentally inefficient; as time went on, and populations expanded, it made more sense to combine individual land-holdings so that more efficient agricultural methods and economies of scale might be employed. However, in order for people to legitimately transfer their equal rights to access to the land, Locke supposed that they give their consent. Being rational individuals, the only way in which they would give their consent would be if their condition was equal to or better after the transfer than before. So, for Locke, unequal acquisition is only legitimate if the poor are better off than they would be if the transfer of their equal right to the earth had never taken place. In this demand we see a philosophical justification for the welfare state and policies of wealth redistribution.

maximizing the **self-determination** of each individual, the only limit being that such self-determination does not inhibit the self-determination of others. Equality is also fundamental to liberalism, but only in the sense of equality of liberty and rights, not equality of wealth or social status. In this regard, equal-

ity also concerns equality of opportunity: the opportunity to exercise preferences, but not equality of outcomes. This is of particular importance with
regard to economic liberalism.

Here, however, it is important to identify two strands of liberalism, strands
that are directly connected with the two meanings of liberty. **Lockean** or **classical liberalism,** based on the political philosophy of John Locke (see Box 2.7),
emphasizes the idea of negative liberty, that is, the freedom from interference
by the state. This strand has developed in Anglo-Saxon societies and is very
much concerned with political rights. The second strand, that of **continental
liberalism,** carries with it the idea of positive liberty and an expanded role for
state action. This branch of the ideology developed much more strongly in
continental Europe and finds its roots in the philosophy of Jean-Jacques
Rousseau (see Box 2.8).

Because the individual is sacred in both strands of liberalism, the idea of
**consent** plays a very important role. Government is only seen as legitimate if
it carries out its functions with the consent of the governed. If a government
has the consent of those it rules, the actions it takes will not violate their
individual rights. If a government lacks the consent of the people, however,
the actions it takes will be imposed and the principle of individual self-
determination will have been contradicted.

It would be an ideal (and perhaps disturbing) world, though, if there was
unanimous consent for every government policy or course of action. Under liberal ideology governments act on principles of majority consent, in varying forms.
This means that a minority of subjects in the political system will have had their
individual right to self-determination violated. How does liberalism deal with this
problem? First, it can be argued that as long as everyone has had the chance to
express their preferences, then, under the principle of equality of opportunity (not
equality of outcomes), justice has been served. Secondly, liberalism carries with it
a commitment to the principle of **tolerance.** In liberal systems minorities are
respected and protected and even encouraged. John Stuart Mill (see Box 2.9), for
example, argued that the existence of minorities and diversity in human society
was something that benefited everyone in that society.

The need for self-determination, consent, and tolerance has linked modern
liberalism closely with **democracy,** although it is important to remember that
the classical liberals were far from being democrats, either in theory or practice. Liberals such as Locke distrusted democracy and remained highly elitist.
It was only in the nineteenth century that liberalism and democracy became
linked. The form of democracy is crucial; pure democracy will threaten the
tyranny of the masses, and the stifling of minorities. What is needed is a form

# Jean-Jacques Rousseau (1712–1778)

Box 2.8

Rousseau remains one of the most eccentric, unique figures in the history of political philosophy, and his work is markedly different from that of the English philosophers of the seventeenth and eighteenth centuries. Though Rousseau, too, used the notion of the state of nature as a beginning for his philosophy, his understanding is unlike that of both Hobbes and Locke. In *The Second Discourse* (also known as *The Discourse on Inequality*) he described the state of nature as a state of perfection where humankind lived in harmony and peace with itself and nature. What ended that paradise, according to Rousseau, was the institution of private property, which brought with it inequality, conflict, and all the evils now known to humans. For with property came power, and humans began to dominate and subject one another.

Rousseau's description of the corruption and immiseration of humankind is chilling and we are tempted to think that he advocates a return to the idyllic state that preceded civilization. However, Rousseau believed that such a return was impossible; instead he proposed a new political system that establishes a compact between government and subjects. He outlined this system in *The Social Contract*, a work which sought to establish the basis for legitimate government, that is, one that does not contradict the will of its subjects. To achieve such harmony, Rousseau invented the concept of the general will. When humans create a civil society and establish a sovereign to rule over them, they must also establish laws that reflect the general will, that is, the will of the community as a whole. This should not be misinterpreted as an extreme form of democracy. In fact Rousseau meant the general will to reflect not just the will of the people but also their true interests, that is, what is good for them.

This leaves the door open for authoritarianism in Rousseau's political thought. Should an individual's particular will not be in harmony with the general will, the government would have the right to try to reform that person's will so that it came into line with the general will. The greatest evil for Rousseau was when either a government refuses to follow the general will, or when particular wills come to dominate the general will. To prevent the latter from happening, Rousseau proposed that individuals be educated to overcome their selfish desires, to free themselves from their passions. This notion is now known as positive liberty, the freedom from our baser instincts.

of democratic government in which minorities are allowed to flourish. Democracy is important for modern liberals for it is the process by which each individual exercises the right to self-determination, gives or denies consent to government, and allows for the representation of minority views.

**Liberal Political Economy** The economic form of liberalism stems from the political and also relies on the value of liberty. What's more, there is a strong sense of cross-over between liberal political and economic theories. John Locke used his political theory as a defence of unequal, or **capitalist** acquisition. Adam Smith (see Box 2.6), on the other hand, argued that market relations between individuals would serve to reinforce notions of equality and liberty. Beginning with Smith, liberal economic ideology has been committed to free markets, that is **market economies** with minimal state intervention. Because of this adherence to market economy, the economic form of liberalism is often referred to as **capitalism**, a system that rewards competitiveness and efficiency (see Fig. 2.2). The market mechanism is held to be the most efficient way of organizing an economic system and of maximizing individual, as well as societal, welfare. As with liberalism's political form, human individuals are represented as self-interested creatures who seek personal gain ahead of, but not exclusive of, others'. In addition, humans are by their nature economic, and have a natural tendency towards trade and exchange. Because of this, markets are seen as occurring naturally wherever human communities exist.

Once again the individual is liberalism's basic and most important unit. Individual property rights are seen as one of the most basic, property being an extension of the self. Individuals are rational utility-maximizers, that is, they

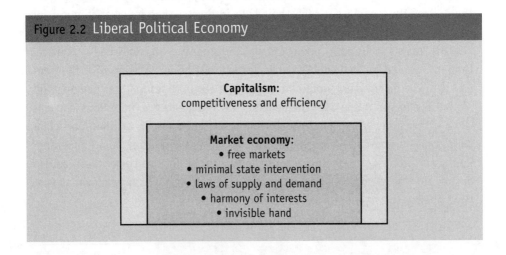

**Figure 2.2** Liberal Political Economy

**Capitalism:**
competitiveness and efficiency

**Market economy:**
• free markets
• minimal state intervention
• laws of supply and demand
• harmony of interests
• invisible hand

## John Stuart Mill (1806–1873)

One of the most important liberal thinkers of the nineteenth century, Mill strongly influenced modern economics, politics, and philosophy. Mill was the son of James Mill (1773–1836) who, with Jeremy Bentham (1748–1832), had founded utilitarianism, a philosophy that seeks to maximize the pleasure, or utility, of individuals in society. Mill took the precepts of utilitarianism and adapted them to what he saw as the main challenges of nineteenth-century British society.

Of particular importance for this chapter and this book, J.S. Mill saw himself as a political economist, and sought to combine the lessons of both politics and economics to produce a version of social science that could be applied to policy at the local and national levels. Mill argued that the lessons of political economy should be used to improve society and the lives of individuals. His thought was deeply influenced by his wife, Harriet Taylor, and it is seen as a more humanitarian doctrine than that of his father and Bentham. He was sympathetic to the ideals of socialism, and was one of the first male proponents of women's rights. Among his works, *On Liberty* (1859) is his best-known book, but Mill's *Principles of Political Economy* (1848) and *Utilitarianism* (1863) marked him as a great political philosopher and political economist.

One of Mill's central preoccupations was with individuality. This led him to advocate toleration of eccentricities and unusual behaviour and practices, as long as such things did not interfere with the freedom or well-being of others. He saw that democracy was in danger of suppressing individuality as the masses dominated minorities, and that conformity would bring about a mediocre society. This attitude towards the individual informed Mill's opinions on political economy. Though agreeing with many of the principles of socialism, he argued that the state should limit its role in the economy to the distribution, not the production, of goods.

seek to maximize their preferences. They will continue to do so until the cost of pursuing those preferences outweighs the benefit to be had from them. When the costs equal the benefits, a **market equilibrium** is said to have been reached. Equilibrium, economic liberals argue, is the natural state of market economies over the long term. Markets, therefore, are seen as **self-regulating** and inherently stable.

Under liberal ideology, economic transactions are governed by the laws of

**supply and demand.** Liberal ideology assumes that the world is one of scarcity and that there is a limited supply of all resources. On the demand side, liberalism argues that individuals, being rational creatures, will demand more of a good if its price falls relative to their income, and less if it rises in relative terms. As demand rises for a certain good it is likely to become more scarce; this will likely raise the price being asked for the good and so demand will fall. In turn the price will fall along with demand, thus increasing demand once again. It is this law that keeps the market in equilibrium.

The existence of selfish individuals, acting rationally in their own interests, serves to benefit not just themselves, but society as a whole. This principle of the **harmony of interests** is well established in liberal theory. Herbert Mandeville first explicitly made reference to the principle in his work *The Fable of the Bees*. He argued that humans acting in their own interests are like bees gathering nectar. Each bee does so because it enjoys nectar, yet it also benefits the hive in general by bringing nectar back for the production of honey. Adam Smith adapted the principle and called it the **invisible hand.** Under market economics, self-interested individuals will maximize efficiency and economic growth over time as they engage in competition against each other. This will benefit society as a whole, though it is important to realize the benefits will not be distributed equally, nor is it guaranteed that all individuals will benefit at all.

## Socialism

The roots of socialism as a political and economic ideology are not quite as long as the roots of liberalism; nonetheless, they extend back to the early nineteenth century. Socialism emerged in France and Britain in the 1820s as a term favoured by the political movements of the Owenites in Britain and the Saint-Simonians and Fourierists in France. These movements responded to the inequity created by capitalism and argued for a more egalitarian system of distribution. Although the term **communism**, which has close links to socialism, appeared earlier (in the late eighteenth century), it is appropriate to view communism as one form of socialism. The same is true of Marxism, the sub-set of socialism that has been dominant in its history.

Socialism has provided the most important philosophical, political, and economic challenge to liberalism over the past 150 years, and it should be apparent from the following description that its principles are generally opposed in both political and economic realms to the liberal tradition. Nonetheless, it shares one crucial aspect with liberalism: it, too, is diverse and

# David Ricardo (1772–1823)

Box 2.10

David Ricardo became one of the most important economic theorists of the eighteenth and nineteenth centuries due to his work on concepts such as value, distribution, wages, and profits. In one sense his perspective on economics was very similar to Smith's, for he saw the possibility of true progress through the market. But his interpretation of the economy in England during his lifetime differs markedly from his predecessor.

Ricardo looked at society not as a unified body, but as divided in the level of economic benefits received from the expansion of industry. He argued that as industry expanded, more workers would be needed to satisfy the labour demands of capitalists. This would tend to raise wage levels, but only in the short run, for as workers made more money, they would tend to have more children, which would in time create a larger workforce. A larger workforce would increase demand for foodstuffs, such as grain, and push down wage levels again. Neither capitalist nor worker had benefited much from this process. The landlord and farmer, on the other hand, would benefit because of the ever-growing demand for food. This growing wealth of the landlord would lead to growing political power, according to Ricardo, and the capitalist would be denied a fair say in government.

Ricardo's solution to this was to advocate completely free international trade. This would allow cheaper grain to come into England from abroad and thus lower food prices. This would benefit capitalists who would be able to decrease wage levels because food now cost less. Though this would harm the interests of landlords and farmers in England, Ricardo believed that it would work to the benefit of the nation as a whole.

However, the most important legacy that he left for political economy was his work on international trade and the concept of comparative advantage. Ricardo suggested that every nation would have one, or several economic activities in which it excelled. It might be that a country is blessed with large quantities of important natural resources such as oil or uranium, or perhaps has a highly skilled workforce capable of producing high-quality manufactured goods. This would give that nation an advantage in the production of these goods, relative to other countries. Whatever that area might be, Ricardo recommended that every country specialize in the production of those goods in which it held such a comparative advantage.

In several of his principles Ricardo was in agreement with Adam Smith. He believed strongly that free markets and free competition would bring economic progress for all. He saw no difference between the interest of the individual and the interest of the community or nation. And, like Smith, Ricardo held firmly to the idea of progress. If markets were allowed to govern economic relations between individuals and states, society in general would benefit.

contains many divergent strands. Utopian socialism, revolutionary socialism, reformist state socialism, ethical socialism, pluralist socialism, and market socialism have all figured as important sub-sets of socialist ideology. What follows is a description of the most important political and economic elements that can be said to constitute the heart of socialist ideology.

Political   Each branch of socialism shares with the others a concern for human community and society and order over concerns about individual rights. This can be seen in the origins of the word socialism itself. The Latin roots of the word suggest community and companionship between human individuals. Humans can only be understood as part of society, for without that common tie individuals are less than human. Human nature for socialists is inseparable from society and social life. The emphasis on the group above the individual is seen clearly in Marxist analysis, which focuses on the role of social classes in human history. Humans are identified as belonging to one class or another, and their identity and interests are defined with reference to those classes. Having said this, socialist ideology dictates that humans are rational and capable of self-development and progress, elements shared with liberalism.

Though some socialist philosophers can be seen to be critical of egalitarianism except as a final goal, socialism is fundamentally an egalitarian ideology, teaching that all human individuals, men and women, regardless of race and creed, are deserving of equal treatment. Socialism does not teach that all humans are equal in terms of their capabilities or faculties, rather it recognizes the many differences to be found among individuals. Nonetheless, it argues that these differences are less important than the underlying similarities shared among them. This does not seem much different from liberalism, yet the consequences for socialist ideology are radically different. Essentially, as we shall see in reference to the economic elements, it implies a doctrine of redistribution based upon the principle of "from each according to their capabilities, to each according to their needs." In this sense socialism attempts to satisfy human needs, rather than merely providing the opportunity for individuals to do so themselves. There is minimal talk of rights in socialist ideology, yet there is a commitment to political equality in the sense of the right to vote. Furthermore, socialism is committed to equal access to healthcare and education so that equality extends beyond the purely economic domain.

Socialism is generally seen as defending the state and its role in human society. It must be remembered, however, that for many socialists, the state has been seen as the enemy, a system of repression that represents the interests of one class over others. Marx, in particular, argued that the state had to be overthrown so that the working classes could claim the political and economic power that was rightly theirs. Nonetheless, most socialists either after, or in the place of, a socialist revolution, call for an expanded role for the state in fulfilling the economic, social, and political needs of the people. The state should represent the will of the people, a will that is assumed to be egalitarian in nature.

For many socialists science has been a central element in their ideology. Science here refers to social science, history, sociology, and economics. Marx, for example, based his doctrine on the principle of **historical materialism** and argued that human development could be understood by studying history and analyzing the economic processes within it. This scientific form of the ideology is essentially optimistic, for it argues that the truth can be known by studying the facts. Of course this suggests that there is one objective truth to be known in the first place. It also presents the problem of determinism: that things must necessarily be the way they are because of the forces of history. Despite this problem, the scientific nature of socialism has been one of its strengths, for it makes the ideology highly persuasive.

Socialist Political Economy    The economic side of socialist ideology has already been touched upon, in the sense that socialists generally hold to the principle of economic redistribution to fulfill the needs of all individuals in human society. This implies an expanded role for the state in the economy, and many socialists argue for a command economy, run in its entirety by the state. Those socialists who do not go quite this far still prefer the state to play an active role in the economy, one that works to even out the inequalities caused by capitalism. Public ownership of industry is a common theme, as is progressive taxation. The economy is to be harnessed by the socialist state, so that it adequately serves the needs of human society.

It is important to note that for socialists the economy and politics are inextricably linked. Marxists in particular argue that political relations and processes stem from and are shaped by economic relations and processes. Socialism is highly critical of capitalism, as it is destructive of the very values they seek to promote, such as community and fellowship. Furthermore, unequal or capitalist acquisition creates severe material inequalities in society which the socialist state will then have to rectify.

It is also important to point out that Marx believed that human nature itself was inherently linked to labour and to production. Human beings, he argued, were best able to express themselves through creative means, by mixing their labour with raw materials through the means of production. Capitalism as it existed in the nineteenth century, Marx's argument goes, was harmful to the workers' nature because it involved the alienation, or separation, of them from their labour and its products. This concern brings Marx to insist upon equal access to the means of production for all humans, so that they may exercise their human nature.

Marx's writing provided a critique of capitalism not only from the point of view of the working class and their exploitation by the bourgeoisie (the middle class), but also of the mechanisms and processes of capitalism itself. Marx argued that there were laws of capitalist development that would bring about the eventual demise of the system. One such law was of the increasing **immiseration of the masses,** meaning that the working classes would, over time, become poorer and poorer. This would decrease their purchasing power, which would result in **crises of over-production and under-consumption.** Faced with high levels of production and low levels of consumption, Marx predicted that the capitalist system would defeat itself.

In the twentieth century there were several states that attempted to implement the policies of a socialist political economy. The best example that history gives us is the Soviet Union (Union of Soviet Socialist Republics or USSR). After the Russian Revolution of 1917, communist governments implemented policies of state control of the economy, with an emphasis on rapid industrialization (focusing on heavy industry) and the collectivization, of agriculture (the creation of large, state-owned and managed farms). This involved high levels of state investment in these sectors at the expense of others, which resulted in severe shortages of consumer goods. Throughout the life of the USSR, the state continued to suppress private initiative and the market economy.

## Nationalism

Nationalism arose as a political phenomenon in the late eighteenth century with the onset of the French Revolution and then the Napoleonic Wars. It spread throughout Europe during the nineteenth century and was harnessed

# Karl Marx (1818–1883)

Box 2.11

Karl Marx is probably the most important political philosopher of the nineteenth century, and his ideological legacy dramatically altered the course of history. Marx's system of thought was deeply affected by his own personal experiences. Living in London, he observed with horror the way in which nineteenth-century capitalist industry treated the working classes. The working conditions and pay levels of labourers in England (indeed across Europe) at that time were not only desperately low but, seemingly, things were getting worse. These observations were confirmed by his friend, lifelong colleague, and supporter, Friedrich Engels, who had been studying the living and working conditions of the working class in Manchester.

The approach to political economy proposed by Marx had two major dimensions. First, it was materialist, meaning that it took as its starting point understanding the physical and economic basis for society. For Marx, the system of production is the basis on which any social and political system is founded. By examining the distribution of economic power, and most importantly, by determining which social groups control the means of production, Marx argued that one could then explain the nature and shape of the political system of a society.

The second key concept in Marxian thought is that it uses dialectics. This rather daunting word simply means that ideas and processes throughout history come up against each other, and from the clash of ideas, or of economic processes, a new reality is born. For Marx the whole course of human history could be explained by materialism and dialectics. As economic change took place, so would social and political change.

Applying his own approach, Marx saw the history of humankind as the history of conflict between the social classes. As the economy changed from agricultural to capitalist, society was transformed from feudal to capitalistic, and the political order became dominated by the bourgeoisie, or middle-classes, in the place of the aristocracy. This, however, was merely a forerunner to the eventual transformation of society that would take place when capitalism inevitably reached its own crises of over-production and under-consumption. At this time the working classes would overthrow the bourgeoisie in a socialist revolution.

Though these predictions about capitalism have yet to come to fruition, it is Marx's analytical approach that makes his system of thought so important to the study of politics and political economy. The way in which Marxian thought studies the interaction of politics and economics is a fine example for modern students, no matter what is thought of Marxism as an ideology.

by governments as a way to increase their political power. The economic form of nationalism, sometimes called mercantilism, had existed for much longer, however. Indeed, it was in order to propose an alternative to mercantilism that Adam Smith offered his liberal, free market model. Since the founding of the Westphalian system of nation-states in 1648, governments had used their economies as a way of increasing their power and cementing their position, both internationally and domestically.

In recent years nationalism has once again emerged as an important ideology in the world. Most commonly associated with the problems of ethnic violence in areas of the world such as the Balkans, the economic form of nationalism has also continued its ideological struggle with liberalism in both developed and developing countries. In the early twenty-first century it is nationalism, not socialism, that provides the most significant challenge to the dominance of liberal ideology.

Political   Nationalism has been one of the most powerful ideological tools employed by politicians throughout the years. It represents an appeal to human individuals to unite with other members of their nation, to recognize the ties that at the same time bind them and set them apart from other humans of a different nationality, and to create, promote, or protect political institutions designed around the national identity. It is the political form of a fundamental impulse in human nature, the need to belong. By marking ourselves as part of a heritage common to those we see as similar to ourselves, which is at the same time different to the heritage held by other groups in human society, we create a distinction that is an extension of the human family or tribe.

What, though, is a nation? Writers on nationalism have pointed to several features which must be common to a group of people for them to be called a nation:

• Language
• Territory
• Traditions, culture and history
• Race or ethnicity
• Religion

Though some nationalities do not hold the elements of race or religion in common, throughout history each has played an important part in forming nations and in marking them off from other social groupings. In the sixteenth century, for example, Henry the Eighth used religion (the Anglican Church) to pull the English people together and unite them against both the Scots and the Catholic peoples of continental Europe. Race was a central element in Nazi nationalist ideology, which asserted the superiority of the Aryan people over all others.

But what is nationalism? Essentially it is an ideology that not only seeks the separation of one nation from others, but also seeks to create and protect the political institutions and mechanisms needed to ensure the survival of that nation. Its most prominent form is seen in the demands of certain groups for independence or sovereignty. Such demands are frequently to be heard from Irish nationalists, Scottish nationalists, and Quebec nationalists. Because national self-determination is seen as being a supremely important goal, violence is not unusual in the political programs of nationalist movements. Yet the political form of nationalism is not only seen in social movements demanding independence. It is also apparent in the actions of governments that discriminate against and persecute what they consider to be alien elements in their societies. Throughout history Jewish people have been used as a target for nationalist governments trying to unite their populations. In more recent memory, immigrants have become a target in many European and North American countries as an identifiably separate and, certain political parties claim, threatening element in society.

Nationalism signifies, once again, the superiority of the group over the individual. It has been commonly used to suppress individual rights and freedoms in order to boost the strength and solidify the identity of the nation. Throughout history nationalist forces have been responsible for much of the violence, persecution, and bigotry that have plagued human affairs. However, nationalism has also been a positive tool which has united sometimes disparate peoples and has led to the creation of political and economic institutions that have proved to be more efficient than those which preceded them. The rise of nationalism marked a significant phase in political development and contributed greatly to the political landscape that persists today.

Nationalist Political Economy    Nationalist approaches to political economy set the national group above the individual as a priority, just as in the political system. They also clearly demarcate the national economy from the international economy and seek to advance the economic interests of the nation at the expense of others. Just as the focus of political nationalism is the creating and preserving of the institutions of statehood, economic nationalism takes as its goal the strengthening of the nation-state through economic means. Economic nationalism grants the state an expanded role in the economy, not just through economic policy but often through actual ownership of certain sectors. Economic nationalism can and does occur equally in democratic as in authoritarian societies, though there are deep philosophical tensions in the case of the former.

Because nationalism as an ideology views nations as separate and potentially conflicting, its economic dimension seeks to prepare the state for the possibility of competition and war. To do so it calls for both the strengthening of the economy and its competitive orientation so that it serves the broader political goals of the state. All states have, at one time or another, employed nationalist economic policies to achieve such goals and most commonly this has taken the forms of industrialization and mercantilism.

Industrialization is considered essential to boost the strength of the state, for three reasons: first, because it brings self-sufficiency; second, because an industrialized economy is able to wage war more effectively; and third, because the process of industrialization entails a domino effect on the rest of the economy which will raise productivity and efficiency. Throughout the twentieth century developed and developing states have used industry to this effect, often nationalizing the means of production to do so. Countries in Latin America in the 1930s and 1940s, in Europe from the late 1940s to the 1970s, and in Japan throughout the post-World War II era have all used nationally directed industrial policies to strengthen their economic performance and raise their profile in the international economy.

Mercantilism concerns trade. In contrast to the liberal view of international trade, which perceives a harmony of interest where every party benefits from the exchange of goods, mercantilism sees trade as a zero-sum affair in which the state must take an active interest to ensure that it benefits more than other states. This has traditionally meant the fusion of trade with foreign policy, the state guiding trading relations and manipulating them so that they serve political interests. Even in the late twentieth century, a period of liberal internationalism, powerful states in particular continued to use nationalist foreign economic policies to manage their trading relations so that national interests prevailed over the long-term harmony of interests. A prime example is the United States. At the same time as the United States government negotiated regional and global free trade agreements, it continued to have recourse to what is known as "Super 301," a piece of trade legislation that applies punitive tariffs to countries which it perceives as engaging in "unfair trading practices."

The United States, however, is but one example among many of a state which, though ostensibly liberal in its approach to economic policy, employs nationalist measures to ensure that what it thinks is a fair or adequate share of the benefits of trade comes its way. In a world of free trade, it is important to recognize the many ways in which states continue to impede the free movement of goods by the use of quotas, duties, quality restrictions, and pricing policies. Even those states that are highly liberal in their policy-making can still be nationalist by implementing policies designed to increase competitiveness and win investment, employment, and markets for their corporations and citizens.

Crucial to nationalist political economy is an understanding of the international system as highly competitive. This creates a hostile, threatening environment in which the state makes national policy, and encourages the accumulation of state power and wealth. As we will see in Chapter 8, nationalists see international economic exchange and intercourse as a zero-sum game where if one state gains, another loses. Such a perception exaggerates feelings of competitiveness and promotes policies that seek to increase state power.

## Other Ideologies

### Conservatism

When we say that someone is conservative we generally mean that they are cautious, in favour of established methods and lifestyles, and that they are resistant to change. As a political ideology and perspective, conservatism shares many of these features. It seeks to conserve the best of what has come before for future generations and is concerned with maintaining political and social traditions and customs, which are seen as being an integral part of human life. The origins of conservatism are to be found in the work of Edmund Burke, a British political writer and activist in the eighteenth century. He argued that the dramatic developments and turbulence of the French Revolution, far from improving peoples' lives, had in fact degraded the human condition and endangered social stability. This attitude towards rapid change is a marked feature of conservatism to this day. It would be wrong, however, to say that conservatives are opposed to all change; rather, they are concerned with the pace of change, and its extent.

Conservatives view society as a natural progression that is essential for human development. This is a crucial difference from liberalism. For conservatives, the individual can only be understood in relation to the greater whole of society and his or her place in it. On the other hand, the smooth and effective functioning of society depends on individuals fulfilling their own individual functions. Due to this division of labour, society is not only organic, but also hierarchical in nature. Some people perform functions in society that are more important than others, and they should receive greater rewards and be more influential than those who perform less crucial functions. In addition, conservatives believe that history has defined certain groups in society to be more important than others, and has suited them for that role. It is from this claim that the notion of social classes is legitimated in conservative ideology.

As intimated above, history plays a central role in conservative ideology, not just in defining the shape of society, but also the nature of its government and constitution. The state is seen as having evolved throughout history, not merely created from nothing as the contract theorists would argue. Traditions and customs play a key role in government, and for conservatives the constitution is not merely a collection of written statements, but also the conventions that have developed around them.

This evolutionary element in the nature of government is mirrored by conservatives' changing views towards democracy. Early conservatives were highly skeptical of giving the choice of leadership over to the masses, but latter-day conservatives in the United States and Britain have become firm defenders of the principles of representative democracy. Nonetheless, there remains a strong sense of paternalism in the conservative ideology. It is fair to say that conservatives believe that leaders are born, not made, that there is some inherent quality in some people that fits them for leadership. What's more, leaders are not just to exercise power, but also to protect the interests of those whom they lead, and such interests may just as legitimately be defined by the leaders, as by those they govern. One of the key "interests" that persists amongst conservatives is that of law and order, which for many is given preference over concepts such as equality and freedom.

At this point it is important to point out that significant differences have emerged between British and American conservatism. One such difference is concern about the concentration of power. American conservatives, in reference to their nation's constitution, argue firmly for the division of powers to avoid tyranny in government. British conservatives tend to be less concerned about the division of powers and more about the effective functioning of government. Another difference is the emphasis that each places on religion and morality. Since its origins, conservatism has been concerned with social ethics, norms, and morality, which conservatives perceive as among the most important traditions that bind society together. However, in modern times conservative ideologues in the United States have been much more emphatic about the central role to be played by Christian morals in defining the "good society."

## Feminism

The ideals of feminism began with a very simple maxim: "equal rights for women." This early feminist demand may seem unremarkable to many of today's young people, yet it was a truly revolutionary slogan in the late nine-teenth and early twentieth centuries. To understand this we only have to rec-ognize the inordinately unequal treatment to which men and women were subjected. Throughout history women have been placed at the mercy of the male gender in almost every aspect of their lives and, with few exceptions, have led an existence that can be said to be at best highly restricted. Feminism as an ideology has grown from the mere recognition of this historical reality into a set of demands concerning the status of women in every aspect of human life. Like all ideologies, there is great variance among thinkers and writers within the feminist school. As with all ideologies, there are moderates and extremists, and such labels shift over time.

The goal of equal treatment for women is, of course, a highly liberal one, for liberalism calls for equal rights and freedoms for all human individuals regardless of gender. Yet none of the classical liberal philosophers sought to apply their principles to the matter of gender, and it was only J.S. Mill who touched on the issue. It was left to female political activists of the late 1800s and early 1900s to demand rights for women which we now take for granted. In the mid- to late-eighteenth century an American woman, Susan B. Anthony, received worldwide recognition for her campaign for the right to vote (suffrage). Though the struggle was not won in her lifetime, women eventually received the right to vote in 1920 in the United States and England (although in the latter full voting rights were not achieved until 1928); and across Canada between 1916 (Manitoba, Saskatchewan, and Alberta) and 1940 (Quebec). These gains, however, did not signal the end of the feminist struggle; rather, they marked the beginning of a long fight to change the lives of women around the world. As the movement has devel-oped, so has the ideology behind it, and feminism has changed from a sim-ple claim for equality to a complex and varied collection of political, social, and economic thought.

The two main thrusts of modern feminism are concerned with justice and gender roles. Feminism's concern with justice relates to the issue of equal treatment for women in the workplace and society. The concepts of equal pay, the "glass ceiling" (whereby women are prevented from rising to senior managerial and executive positions), affirmative action, maternity leave (or parental leave, as some feminists would advocate), and sexual harassment are some of the higher profile and indeed most important issues for the feminist movement.

These are, however, only the most obvious of feminism's aims. Just as important are the ideology's concerns with the broader issue of gender, concerns that include roles in society, language, even male-constructed patterns of thought. Gender is different from the word "sex" as it refers not to the biological nature of a person (male or female) but rather to the socially constructed roles and images we have of men and women. Women's roles in society is about more than just the right to work, or to hold positions of influence. Feminism questions traditional roles for women as wife, mother or caregiver. The institution of marriage has been questioned because of the subject status that many women over the ages have experienced as wives. Motherhood is rarely questioned from a biological point of view (as yet it is only women who can conceive and bear children), but the issues of choice, timing, and who should play the primary role as caregiver to children are very much up for debate in modern society, and it is largely thanks to the work of feminists that this is so.

One of the highest profile issues of the feminist movement has been in the area of reproduction, and in particular, the right to abortion. The debate over abortion has remained hotly contested for many years in many countries, especially the United States, and, while there have been significant advances for those arguing for increased or total choice for women over their reproductive functions, it is far from being a decided issue. Neither should it be thought that all feminists agree on abortion rights; as with so many other issues and other ideologies, diversity of opinion marks contemporary feminism.

The feminist perspective on economics does not argue for either a market or a command economy. Feminism, or gender analysis as it is sometimes called in this regard, focuses on the differential costs and benefits for women (and men) of different political economic systems. This has become one of the most important of the contemporary approaches to political economy and has helped to cast new light on established economic theories, in particular, liberalism.

An interesting phenomenon to observe within feminism is the way in which seemingly radical issues have crossed over to the mainstream of public thought. The right to vote was itself considered a radical and revolutionary issue when it first emerged; the same could be said for women in parliament, equal pay for women or even the exclusionary nature of words such as "chairman" or "mankind." Whether or not the feminist issues that are today considered radical, such as those concerning female sexuality and male oppression, will one day be seen as mainstream remains to be seen.

## Environmentalism

The "green movement" that arose in the 1980s in Europe and North America and forced changes in government policy on the environment marked the birth of a new form of political thought and action oriented towards the protection of the earth's natural resources and the promotion of more simple lifestyles. Environmentalism is truly both a political and an economic approach for it identifies modern economic systems as the scourge of nature. It also shares certain ideas in common with anarchism, for it sees modern industrialism as a hierarchical system that restricts human freedom.

The ideological roots of environmentalism are several, and include romanticism, pacifism, socialism, and as mentioned above, anarchism. The anti-nuclear movement of the 1970s and 1980s produced significant political momentum which, combined with the work of non-governmental organizations (NGOs) such as Greenpeace and Friends of the Earth, helped to change public opinion and raise consciousness about the problems facing the global and local environments.

Environmentalists believe that the destruction of the biosphere, the finely balanced system that sustains life on this planet, is imminent unless radical changes are brought about. There is a focus on re-educating public opinion so that people will call for governmental change with regard to pollution and the use (and over-use) of non-renewable natural resources. The main targets for environmentalists are heavy industry and petroleum companies, and the ideology promotes alternative sources of energy (such as solar power) and alternative lifestyles that consume less.

The political economy implications of environmentalism are closely connected to this overall vision. It seeks to persuade individuals to seek natural rather than consumer pleasures, and to reduce the amount that people consume, in terms of goods and energy. This is a challenge to contemporary Western lifestyles and also to Western economic systems, since environmentalism focuses on *development* rather than economic growth. Development is a concept that embraces not only the provision of basic needs and the expan-

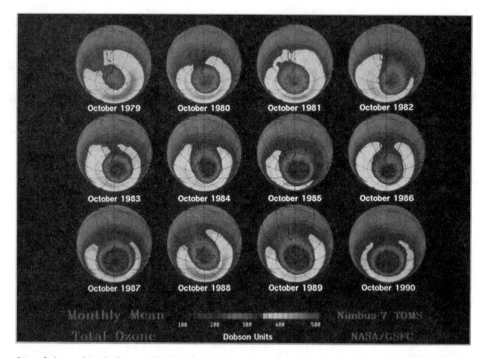

October 1979   October 1980   October 1981   October 1982
October 1983   October 1984   October 1985   October 1986
October 1987   October 1988   October 1989   October 1990

Monthly Mean
100   200   300   400   500
Total Ozone          Dobson Units

Nimbus-7 TOMS
NASA/GSFC

One of the major challenges facing our political economies at the beginning of the twenty-first century is the problem of environmental degradation. The sky, water, and earth on which we depend are gradually, but rapidly, being destroyed by our levels of consumption and the ways in which we produce both essential and luxury goods. One of the clearest challenges to our survival as a species on this planet concerns the depletion of the ozone layer surrounding the earth, particularly at the South Pole. Solving this and other environmental problems will involve action at local, national, and international levels, as well as new technologies and a willingness to sacrifice some of the economic benefits we have come to take for granted.

The impact of environmental degradation on politics and political ideas has been immense. Beginning in the 1970s environmental action groups began to increase their political influence across Western Europe, North America, and Japan. In turn, the ideological impact of environmentalism spread until ecological, or green, parties were gaining significant minorities in both local and national elections in many countries. Their impact was so great that ultimately the established political parties were forced to incorporate the green agenda into their policy platforms.

sion of economic activity, but also health, individual freedoms, education, and human longevity.

The successes of environmentalism at a practical level are many. Without the efforts of the movement we would not now have seen new policies at the national level directed towards recycling and pollution control. At the international level, the notion of sustainable development has become a maxim for international aid agencies and development organizations. Sustainable development is aimed at promoting the use of renewable rather than non-renewable resources so that economic growth can be sustained indefinitely. This longer-term perspective is not only good for the environment; at a basic level it makes economic sense.

## Fascism

"Fascist" is one of those words that has passed from politics into everyday use in English. We use the word to indicate that someone or something is dictatorial and intolerant. However, the true meaning of "fascist" is to be found within the ideology of fascism and its close cousin, National Socialism. These ideologies, close enough to be examined as one, call to mind the atrocities of the Second World War and brown-shirted skinheads threatening racial violence, but must also be examined at the level of their underlying philosophical ideas.

Fascism is fundamentally different to many mainstream ideologies in its perception of human psychology, for it rejects the laws of human reason that are fundamental to liberalism and socialism. It sees human individuals as influenced more by myths and romanticism than by logic and appeals to them in this way. One of the most important myths of fascism and National Socialism is the myth of blood, race, or *volk*. Such nationalism is central for fascism because it promotes the group (in this case the *volk* or nation) over the individual, a fundamental element of fascist thought. The individual only has his or her identity within the nation and must direct all efforts towards helping that group. Property is privately held but must be used to strengthen the nation as a whole, not for personal gain. The *volk* is to be protected from all other nations or races, and racial superiority is commonly a part of national socialist political propaganda.

According to fascist thought, the nation should be organized from within by the state, with a national leader (*führer* in German) at its head. This leader is an unquestioned authority who determines the interests of the nation and directs not only state policy, but also individual morality. The leader represents, indeed embodies, the will of the people and is seen as the only person capable of interpreting that will. The structure of the state is hierarchical, with a clear chain of command from the leader down. In practical terms this means extreme authoritarianism, and the will to use force, even violence, to ensure order and compliance.

## Anarchism

The word "anarchist" makes most people think of an individual, probably young, who is committed to the violent overthrow of government and society. The ideology of anarchism, however, is much more complex and not nearly as extremist as the popular image suggests. For anarchism is really concerned with the primacy of the individual, in which outside interference into the people's lives is minimized, especially that of government and the state. It is a form of libertarianism which stresses the sanctity of the human individual and seeks to promote the moral autonomy of the same.

Anarchism has a long history that extends back to early Christian thought and beyond. The word itself (*an-archy*) simply means the opposite of hierarchy, and thus absence of government. It is important to remember that anarchy is not the same as chaos or the absence of peace and order. Most anarchists believe firmly that human life would be more peaceful and human needs more completely taken care of in the absence of the state. It is important to note that anarchism as an ideology seeks change not through politics but through society or through overthrow of government. Having said this, some anarchists have pointed out that revolution generally leads to the installation of a new government and thus a new authority structure to struggle against. Nonetheless, throughout the late nineteenth and the twentieth centuries the most obvious forms of anarchist activity have been to strike against the representatives of authority. Anarchism has at times been a potent ideological force that has inspired direct political action, often in the form of violent attacks upon the organs of government, but also in the form of peaceful protest and propaganda.

The ideology has a rather unique perspective on political economy and in particular on industrialism. Anarchist thought blames the process of industrialization for much of the oppression of the individual that exists in modern society. This is because industrial organization requires a passive, compliant, and ordered populace from which it takes its workers. Government and industry work alongside one another to suppress individual freedoms and impose a set order upon society. Furthermore, anarchists argue for a simple lifestyle in which needs are taken care of, yet excess is not known. This marks anarchism as a deeply anti-consumerist ideology. It was Proudhon, possibly the most famous anarchist writer, who stated "Property is theft," though not all anarchists go to such extremes. One last economic element of anarchism is the desire by some to do without established forms of economic interaction. In Australia, for example, for some years there has existed an anarchist barter network that precludes the use of nationally denominated currency. Individuals exchange goods and services, one for another, without the aid of government-backed monetary notes, but rather a system of trust and credits to which the members are voluntarily committed. This small island of economic anarchy is one example of the practical applications of anarchist thought, and it helps to show that the popular conception of anarchism misrepresents its true nature.

## The Relevance of Ideas and Ideologies

Throughout history the evolution of ideas and ideologies has had a dramatic impact on the real world of politics and the economy. Most dramatically we can look to the ideas of Karl Marx as the basis for a transformation of political-economic systems at both national and international levels in the nineteenth and particularly in the twentieth centuries. In this case a new way of understanding politics and economics inspired organized social unrest, new government approaches to social and economic programs, and ultimately, revolution. As Box 2.12 indicates, the Third Way has become an important approach to political economy in the late twentieth and early twenty-first centuries, influencing government policy in several key states. Its origins lie in the work of philosophers such as Anthony Giddens (see Box 2.12), and the mental machinations that they undertook.

The interaction between ideas and ideology on the one hand, and government policy on the other, was never more clear than in the adoption of Keynesian economic and social policies by Western governments in the 1940s and '50s (see Box 2.13). By seeking to modify capitalism, to smooth its highs and lows and thus reduce its negative effects on the population, Keynesian economic policy became the norm for most of the post-war period, and the consensus only broke down in the 1970s during a prolonged period of economic stagnation. At that time the ideological approach known as neoliberalism appeared, and it in turn influenced government policies throughout the world.

It is in such transitions that we see the other side of the interaction between ideology and political practice. The movement of history and developments in the world of politics and the economy bring reform, revolution, and the creation of new ideas to the world of political and economic thought. Unless philosophical enquiry reflects the realities of the human world, it will remain separate and disconnected from it. Philosophy, remember, should help us to understand our political and economic systems before it shows us ways to

| Box 2.12 | Anthony Giddens and the Third Way |
|----------|-----------------------------------|

The idea of a middle path between socialism and capitalism is not new. It has been discussed throughout the twentieth century, as philosophers and politicians have tried to adapt capitalism so that it reflects and supports the human aspects of politics. Keynes, of course, formulated government policies that would smooth the effects of the market economy. The desire to find a workable alternative to socialism and capitalism came to be known as the search for the Third Way.

In the late 1990s sociologist Anthony Giddens revived the idea of the Third Way, and the combination of his ideas and centre-left political victories in the United States (President William Clinton), Britain (Prime Minister Tony Blair), and Germany (Chancellor Gerhard Schroeder) brought the concept into the mainstream. The Third Way proposes a middle path between *laissez-faire* and government intervention and recognizes that the values and goals of the "traditional left," such as broadly defined social programs and big government, are no longer viable given the reduced tolerance by citizens for high taxation and government economic intervention. For governments, the Third Way emphasizes fiscal responsibility (balanced budgets), the reform of social programs, and policies that promote economic growth and stability. At the individual level, the Third Way combines the liberal ideal of personal responsibility and the leftist ideals of community.

The Third Way shows the importance and relevance of theoretical approaches to politics and political economy. The governments mentioned above have each implemented policy programs that reflect the main tenets of the Third Way, although they have achieved varying levels of success. Whether or not the rise of the Third Way marks a new era in politics remains to be seen.

change them. Marx's ideas were shaped by his experiences of the Industrial Revolution and the terrible working conditions of British manufacturing workers. He explained the causes for these conditions before arguing that revolution was the only way to improve the workers' lot.

Over a hundred years later the interaction between ideology and the real world was clearly seen again. The process of globalization that marked the end of the twentieth century and the beginning of the twenty-first helped to promote neo-liberal economic ideas on a global basis. Rising international economic competition in particular forced governments to adopt policies

## John Maynard Keynes (1883–1946)

Box 2.13

John Maynard Keynes (Keynes is pronounced so that it rhymes with the word *rains*), a brilliant economist, writer, and socialite, gave the world one of the most insightful critiques of capitalism at the same time as he defended the very basis of that economic system. Unlike Marx and Engels, Keynes was not concerned with the social consequences of the development of capitalism. Rather, he was determined to find ways in which capitalism could be managed and thus made more efficient. For Keynes did not believe in the idea of *laissez-faire* capitalism, that the market would always correct itself in the event of an economic slowdown or depression, as liberal economists had traditionally taught.

In his most renowned work, *The General Theory of Employment, Interest and Money*, Keynes argued that it is precisely at the time of an economic recession or depression that capitalism is least able to help itself, for at such times investment levels drop off and consumer demand for manufactured goods is at its lowest level. This situation means that the economy will remain exactly where it is, for no improvement can take place without either increased investment or higher demand from consumers.

Keynes' solution was to advocate that government play an active role. He argued that in periods of economic slowdown, the government of a country should pump money into the economy through programs of job creation. This would increase demand as individuals found themselves with more spending power. This Keynes called countercyclical spending. It is important to note that Keynes only advocated such an expanded economic role for governments in times of economic recession or depression, when unemployment was high and consumer demand low. When the economy picked up again, the government was to withdraw from the economy and allow capitalism to provide for wealth creation by itself. Unfortunately, when Keynesian policies have been implemented by governments in the real world, politicians have not shown the self-restraint that he demanded.

based on efficiency and fiscal discipline, meaning a reduced role for the state. Democratization also became a global ideological movement, one that was clearly pushed by the policy agendas of governments such as the United States. Perhaps more significantly for the long term, however, is how ideas in one part of the world can be communicated instantly to the rest of the globe. With satellite technologies and the World Wide Web, events and political movements taking place on one continent can be coordinated with their counterparts halfway across the world. The public reaction to the Seattle Round of the World Trade Organization talks in 1999, where street demonstrations and clashes with the police helped force a re-evaluation of the movement towards free trade, was due in no small part to the unifying impact of the Internet.

Political and economic ideas and ideology, then, are an essential, living, and evolving element of political economy. It is all too easy to dismiss the importance of ideas, to classify them as mere "castles in the air." Future trends in the political economy, at both national and international levels, will be shaped equally by developments in the practical and theoretical worlds.

## Summary

This chapter has tried to show you the central place occupied by ideas, ideologies, and theories in the world of politics and political economy. As you have seen, these ideas constitute a huge spectrum of thought that extends not just from left to right, as we have traditionally perceived politics, but in many other directions and indeed dimensions. The debates and compromises that take place between ideological and philosophical positions remain one of the most vibrant and important areas of political studies.

The ideas put forward by the most important thinkers throughout history have become a basis for political debate, social movements, political change, and at times revolution. But just as importantly, though less dramatically, political and economic thought has influenced the structures of governance, their shape and level of public inclusiveness. Ideological and philosophical perspectives underlie all such structures in the real world, and it is to these that this book now turns.

## Self-Assessment Questions

1. In what sense is there "a dialogue across the centuries" in political and economic philosophy?
2. How have real events affected the development of political and economic ideas?
3. Give three examples of government policies or political parties that blend ideologies (for example, nationalism and liberalism).
4. Give three examples of the practical application of rights in politics.
5. Which concepts from political and economic ideology do you consider most relevant to today's dilemmas, and why?

## Further Reading

Heilbroner, Robert L. *The Worldly Philosophers*, 6th ed. New York: Touchstone, 1992.

Lekachman, R. *A History of Economic Ideas*. New York: Harper & Brothers, 1995.

Macridis, Roy C. *Contemporary Political Ideologies: Movements and Regimes*. New York: Harper Collins Publishers, Inc., 1992.

Nelson, Brian R. *Western Political Thought: From Socrates to the Age of Ideology*. Englewood Cliffs, NJ: Prentice Hall, Inc., 1982.

Proudhon, Pierre Joseph. *Selected Writings*. London: Macmillan, 1970.

Spragens, Thomas A., Jr. *Understanding Political Theory*. New York: St. Martin's Press, 1976.

 ## Web Links

### Thinking Politics
http://home.freeuk.net/ethos/

### Political Thought
http://english-www.hss.cmu.edu/Govt/Theory.html

### Political Philosophy
http://www-personal.ksu.edu/~lauriej/index.html

### Philosophy and Civil Society
http://www.civsoc.com/index.htm

### Cato Institute
http://www.cato.org

# CHAPTER THREE

# THE POLITICAL ECONOMY OF GOVERNMENTAL INSTITUTIONS

## Chapter Objectives

When you have finished reading this chapter, you will be able to:

- understand and distinguish among the primary forms of government systems
- recognize and apply the major compositions of government systems
- compare and contrast between the presidential and parliamentary systems of government
- recognize the significance of structures and institutions in political communities, especially the legislative, executive, judicial, and bureaucratic bodies and
- identify the most important functions and institutions of national economic management.

This chapter will introduce you to the different types of government around the world today, and the institutions and their settings that motivate and regulate government actors as well as private citizens. This chapter, you will discover, has a direct relationship to the ideologies that were introduced in Chapter 2, since they help fashion the opinions and convictions that exist within society. Government institutions are significant because their place in society often extends beyond the political to the economic and social domains. It is essential that we appreciate different forms of government and their institutions, as this will lead us to a better grasp of the widespread connection between state and society. We must remember that the state and government are social institutions like any other, and are a consequence of human desires to organize and systematize public and private relations for the political unit. This, then, is the focus of this chapter.

We begin with an introduction to the various types of political systems that exist today. Political systems are basically the important individuals and political structures that influence and make up governments and their activities. We then describe of some of the major models of government today, including totalitarianism, authoritarianism, and liberal democracies. Following this, the chapter examines how government structures are arranged, including the important divergences between federal and unitary political systems, as well as the respective roles played by municipal, sub-state, and state levels of government. Before examining the role of the bureaucracy in the modern state, this chapter also presents a comparison of the presidential and parliamentary systems of government. In a final section, the chapter addresses the most important functions and institutions of economic management, looking at the options available to governments in the modern world. The contemporary student of political studies cannot ignore the interaction between the state and the economic system, and this section provides basic information on that dynamic.

## Forms of Political Systems

The ideologies outlined in Chapter 2 are more than just a "conceptual way" of looking at the world—they represent the basis of how we envision our societies, and the manner in which they are governed (see Table 3.1). They also represent the first step in understanding the inner (and inter) workings of political structures themselves, as well as the surroundings in which they interact, which is crucial for a full understanding of how ideology affects government.

In basic terms, it can be argued that everything any political system does (or refrains from doing) is a manifestation of one of the following four purposes:

| Table 3.1 Types of Political Systems | |
|---|---|
| Liberal Democracy | Equal political rights |
| | Political participation |
| | Majority rule |
| | Political freedoms |
| Authoritarianism | Constituted authority |
| | Submission of citizens |
| | Threat/Use of force |
| Totalitarianism | Ideological re-development/thought control |
| | Restricted social interaction |
| | Tyrannical elite rule |

1. **System management**: Unless a system has a capability for persisting over time it will disappear or be overtaken by a more overwhelming form of governance. This includes, for instance, the ability of a political system to provide both political and economic goals for its citizens.

2. **Modification**: Political systems must modify to a variety of changes, including population, distribution of resources, technological advances, and challenges from within (for example, insurrection or terrorism) and without (for example, warfare).

3. **Amalgamation**: A political system has to continuously work at making a whole out of parts. To do so a system must have the political, cultural, and economic tools necessary. For example, Canada has to contend with provincialism and regionalism and uses policies of power sharing, promoting Canadian culture, and economic distribution in order to maintain its federal structure.

4. **Objectives**: Every political system must set its goals. The continued credibility of a system is in large part dependent on the feasibility of these goals.

It is important to note that these four functions of political systems—management, modification, amalgamation, and objectives—are mutually dependent, that achievement in one role usually depends on achievement within another. Moreover, notwithstanding extensive distinctions among political systems, each essentially seeks these same goals.

Plato was the first to ponder how rules and rule-making institutions influence the relationship between state and society. He offered a **typology** (a method of classification and interpretation of concepts) of government, distinguishing among the different types of governance that existed during the Greek era. In basic terms, what Plato created was a method of "rank ordering" different types of government, from monarchies to democracies. This typology is important for the way we think about politics today, because Plato essentially was arguing that political observers need to classify what exists, compare different modes of governance, and make suggestions about what needs to be done to improve circumstances for citizens. It is interesting to observe that most of those government types still exist in modern models of government today, or strongly look like current systems. The classification of government used by both Plato, and Aristotle after him, divided government according to the manner and conduct of the governing authorities, as well as the roles played by the authorities themselves.

Despite our modern fascination with **democracy**, and our widespread

## Command and Market Economies

Box 3.1

In political economy we can identify two idealized forms of economic structure; the command economy and the market economy. Though these structures never exist in an absolutely pure form, they help us to classify real world economies. Furthermore, each of these economies is closely associated with an ideology of political economy: command economy with socialism, market economy with liberalism.

In a market economy, decisions about the economy are taken in a decentralized manner by consumers and businesses. Therefore, the answer to each of the three most important questions regarding the economy is given by the private sector (the market) and there is no central planning or control. Thus:

- The issue of what to produce is decided by the demand of consumers. Because of this, producers will only be successful if they respond to consumer demand.

- The issue of how production is organized and structured is decided by the businesses that produce goods. Because of this privately owned businesses will aim for efficiency in production to survive in a competitive environment.

- The issue of distribution, or who gets what, is decided by the laws of supply and demand. Those with skills or resources that are in short supply and high demand will receive a larger share than others. Income levels will be decided by the market, as will profits.

In a command economy, on the other hand, the economic system is highly centralized, and all the important economic decisions are made by government. It can be seen as the opposite and opposing form to market economy. Thus:

- The issue of what to produce is decided by the government and the government owns all production facilities. This is known as nationalized production.

- The issue of how production is organized and structured is decided by government. Production processes respond to government needs and priorities.

- The issue of distribution, or who gets what, is decided by the government. The government sets income levels, indeed, employs the whole population.

acceptance of it as a primary form of government, Plato did not consider it to be such a virtuous system. He suspected that it would plunge to mob rule, with no curbs over authority and an unfair disbursement or allocation of **public goods**. Plato suggested that "rule by the many" required a legal context to administer the relationship between rulers and the ruled; he deemed this as mandatory in order to avert the potentially negative influences of majority rule (particularly the subservience of minority interests to majority rule). Instead, Plato offered as a better alternative what he called the **polity**, or constitutional democracy. This, he suggested, would take care of the legal context that he thought was necessary for proper government-society relations.

As legal instruments, constitutions are part of a broader legal and statutory tradition in society. Constitutions arrange the authorized proceeds within a political unit. For constitutional democracies, the "constitution" is at the heart of a country's political system and customs; it represents the fundamental law of the political community and sets the limits for political participation. In this way, a constitution provides the political "rules" for a society and establishes the design of a society's political institutions and their participation within society.

While today we often think of constitutions as a characteristic of democracies, it is crucial to recognize that many other varieties of political systems have embraced constitutions as a principal ingredient for government rule and political relationships. Certainly, in light of the many different types of relationships governments have with their citizens in modern society, most notably the rights and responsibilities we all have as "citizens" of a country, it is really no surprise why a legalistic framework such as a constitution is such an indispensable part of the relationship between governments and their citizens. The following is a list of explicit roles constitutions play in political systems:

- Constitutions reflect a country's character, its fundamental ideology, and belief system.
- Laws that are made within society, both by the courts and by legislative bodies, are reflective of, and respond to, constitutions.
- A constitution may set out the relationship between government(s) and individual citizens, prescribing what a government can and cannot do to its citizenry.
- The most important institutions of governments, and the way in which they interact, are formally outlined in constitutions.

## Liberal Democracy

Many different kinds of political thought have emerged through the ages to contribute to what we now refer to as democracy. Of all modes of political

## Sectors of the Economy

Box 3.2

We often think of the economy as a whole, as the sum total of all economic activity in a country. But it is essential to recognize that every economy is made up of different sectors, each of which performs essential functions, and responds to different stimuli. To categorize an economy we could look at very specific sectors, such as the automobile or computer sectors, but it is more common to examine three separate sectors, the primary, secondary, and tertiary.

The primary sector of an economy refers to the production of agricultural goods and raw materials or commodities, such as softwood lumber, coal, or oil. This sector is of course fundamental to the other two sectors because it is the sector that originates much of what we consume in production and our everyday lives. In Canada, for example, the primary sector has traditionally played a central role in the strength and health of the economy (see Chapter 5) and has been responsible for high levels of employment. The primary sector tends to dominate the economies of many developing countries (see Chapter 6), and they depend upon the export of commodities to world markets for their economic well-being.

The secondary sector encompasses industrial production in an economy. This sector depends on technology and consumer trends a great deal for its success. Historically the secondary sector has been seen as essential to the prosperity and strength of nations, both in economic and military terms. Though it is often claimed that countries such as Canada are currently experiencing a "post-industrial" era, the secondary sector remains an important employer and source of wealth. However, it is in the developing world, and in so-called "emerging market" economies that the secondary sector finds its greatest importance. Countries such as China, Mexico, and South Korea (sometimes referred to as Newly Industrializing Countries, or NICs) have developed their secondary sectors as a way of boosting exports and generating national wealth. It is in these countries that the developed country secondary sectors find their greatest competition.

The area of highest growth in the developed countries is recent years has been the tertiary sector. This sector of the economy is composed of the services industry, including education, sales, banking, and janitorial work, among many other areas. By the end of the twentieth century the services sector had become the largest employer in Canada, accounting for 10 million of the 13 million people employed in 1997. It is in the tertiary sector that we see the greatest innovation, and the highest levels of change. For countries such as Canada, the US, and Great Britain, the tertiary sector will determine the economic future.

beliefs, though, **liberalism** is the most influential basis for democracy. The two terms are so interrelated that they are frequently used interchangeably, though they ought not to be, given their exact meanings.

There are so many ways to think of democracy today, that we could conclude that the term means nothing, or simply suffers from overuse. While this might be the case (especially the latter), democracy has come to have almost as many meanings as there are people who use the term.

The roots of democratic thought lie in the early contemplations of Plato. It is not surprising, therefore, that the term "democracy" itself is taken from the Greek *demos*, meaning "the people," and *kratos*, which means "authority." Far from the simple conclusions about "mob" rule, democracy is a compromise between the attitude that government ought to have important checks and balances (in order to avoid the seizure of interests by the few, for example), and the acknowledgment that many interests exist within a political community. In short, democracy recognizes that rule by all is clearly impossible, but that **pluralism**—where the political system encompasses several types of interests, and politics reflects more than just the elite-driven interests of government—is integral for protection and equity.

For the Greeks, however, there was a compromise between what they perceived to be the potential deficiency of democracy (the "tyranny" of the majority) and the demand for public participation. The polity, mentioned above, created a mechanism that would allow a legal framework for democracy, and in particular, prescribed a principal role for constitutionalism and the rule of law. The expectation was that the majority—who otherwise might simply seek to override the concerns of others in their own interest—would have to accept the authority of laws created by the polity for all who lived within it. This, then, would limit the behaviour of all, including the majority.

The polity was thus the precursor to what we now recognize as **liberal democracy**, whose primary components include:

- **Equality of political rights:** Simply put, this creates the conditions where every member of society would be allowed to participate in the activities of the political unit—voting, running for office, protesting, and the like. No particular political rights are held for a select group of people; for instance, though parliamentarians in Canada alone are permitted to vote in the House of Commons or Senate, everyone has the right to seek such offices.

- **Political participation:** This is related to the notion of equality of political rights. Basically, political participation establishes the relationship between those who rule and those who are ruled. This may include direct interaction of individuals, such as in a referendum; or indirect interaction, where the political community, through voting or other democratic means, passes on proper authority to designated officials who are given the responsibility of representing the masses. As well, this also refers to the role of **interest groups** or **political action committees** (PACs) in some countries, in which decision-making is heavily influenced by groups that have a particular political agenda and seek to have decisions made in their favour. These groups may represent corporations and businesses, private interest associations, or individuals, and their most common activity is to "lobby" governments in an attempt to influence decisions and policies. More on the role of interest groups is in Chapter 4.

- **Rule of the majority**: Acknowledges that all votes must be considered equal, and that the majority of votes should determine issues.

- **Freedom**: Democratic principles hold that individual members of a political community must be allowed to participate freely in the political process, and should only be bound by the legitimate laws of the community. Interaction and representation can only be considered legitimate if individuals are encouraged and allowed to share in the political process in a free environment.

## Authoritarianism

In our everyday lives, most of the states we hear about are liberal democracies. In many ways, this is a function of where we live, our domestic political environment, and the culture in which we have been socialized. It is also a result of the interaction of our political community with others: generally, the lion's share of international activities undertaken by Canada is with other liberal democratic countries. But most political systems in the world today are not liberal democracies; most might best be described as **authoritarian** systems, those requiring absolute obedience to a constituted authority.

In short, authoritarian systems are the antithesis of liberal democracies. At their root, authoritarian systems require their citizens to submit to the consent of the government institutions. Authoritarian states are coercive in that they may rely on the use—or threat—of force to gain acceptance of the ruled and to suppress dissent. Authoritarian "regimes" (such concentrations of absolute power in government are often disparagingly referred to as regimes) are elite driven, meaning they are governed by a powerful, often wealthy, minority, and all political (and often social, economic, and cultural) activities are strictly overseen by state authorities. Authoritarian systems are not ideologically bound; they may be left-wing, right-wing, religious, military, civilian, capital-ist, or communist.

## Totalitarianism

Often used as a synonym for authoritarianism, totalitarianism is in fact a vari-ant of authoritarian rule. What distinguishes **totalitarianism** from authori-tarianism is its emphasis on **ideological control**. That is, totalitarian political systems not only control most social interaction, but also are marked by a desire by the government to force its objectives and values on citizens in an unlimited manner.

Totalitarian regimes seek to dominate all aspects of society and to subor-dinate all citizens to the wishes of the elite rulers. Governance is best described as **tyrannical** (the harsh and arbitrary exercise of authority); as there are usu-ally no rules protecting citizens, majority participation is replaced by the inter-est of the dominant political authority, and the use of strength and fear is often used to maintain supremacy. Aspects of totalitarian rule include:

- An ideological redevelopment of society, including fundamental belief systems and values
- Elite control by the few, often involving a single leader with inordinate power
- The semblance of democratic institutions (such as elections) that are maneuvred and manipulated to meet the requirements and wishes of the government
- Control of information
- The use of fear to achieve political goals.

Liberal democracies, authoritarianism, and totalitarianism represent the three primary classifications of political systems. Although there are numerous variants of governments, these three forms are the basis for most political communities. Right-wing or left-wing, secular or sacred, elitist or pluralist, multicultural or ethnically restricted, all political systems roughly fit into one of these broad classifications.

The composition of government, on the other hand, is another way of arranging political systems. Once we understand the basic ideological under-pinnings of a system, it is equally important to consider the manner in which political authority and decision-making are appropriated. This brings us to a discussion of the composition of states, predominately pertaining to federal and unitary systems.

# Federal and Unitary Political Systems

A key element for a clear understanding of the workings of different political systems is the actual physical or geographical distribution of authority. All political units, despite their ideological underpinning, must distribute the activities and functions of government within their territorial boundaries. The degree to which a political system parcels out political authority—or, conversely, keeps that authority in one place—is largely a result of **decentralization** (see Fig. 3.1).

Governments that desire to manage most of political decision-making and influence within one geographical position may seek to create a single, supreme (centralized) locus of power. On the other hand, many states seek to divide (decentralize) power and responsibility among geographical positions. The two primary compositions of government in this regard are federal and unitary arrangements. Elsewhere in this text, we have presented the concept of

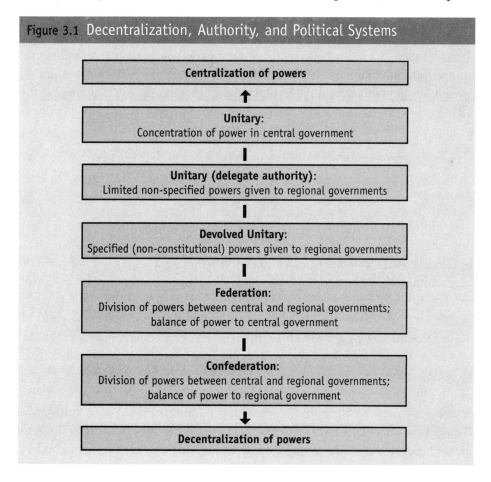

**Figure 3.1** Decentralization, Authority, and Political Systems

**Centralization of powers**

↑

**Unitary:**
Concentration of power in central government

**Unitary (delegate authority):**
Limited non-specified powers given to regional governments

**Devolved Unitary:**
Specified (non-constitutional) powers given to regional governments

**Federation:**
Division of powers between central and regional governments;
balance of power to central government

**Confederation:**
Division of powers between central and regional governments;
balance of power to regional government

↓

**Decentralization of powers**

**sovereignty,** which is the legitimate authority given to a government to rule a political unit. It is useful to think about sovereignty when we compare unitary and federal systems, and where sovereignty is "located." In unitary states with a strong central government, sovereignty is concentrated in the national government (although in some cases some powers may be given to sub-national authorities in a unitary system; this is referred to as **delegated authority**). In federal states, sovereignty is divided between the national government and the sub-national governments (provinces, states, *länder*).

## Unitary Systems

It is important to bear in mind that both unitary and federal systems are created and maintained largely as a result of the constitutional authority accorded to the geographical positions of power. Unitary political systems are those that concentrate political authority and powers within one central government. The central government in a unitary system is singularly responsible for the activities of the political unit, both domestic and foreign. Furthermore, though other "levels" of government may exist, such as city or municipal authorities, they fall under the jurisdiction of the central unitary government.

Unitary governments, then, have a single, central authority responsible for making, interpreting, and enforcing laws, and for representing the political community abroad. Examples of unitary systems include Great Britain, Japan, and France.

## Federal Systems

The opposite to the centralization inherent in unitary systems is decentralization; this is the primary factor in federal systems. At its core, federalism seeks to divide powers between the central government and regional governments. Legal authority is given to the "non-central" governments to act on behalf of citizens. Often, particular roles and capacities are given to the regional governments; for instance, in Canada education is a provincial responsibility, paid for in part from transfer payments from the central federal government in Ottawa.

Generally, federal states are territorially large, lending a functional nature to regional authorities. States such as Canada, the United States, Germany, and Australia operate under the federal system in part because powers and responsibilities are distributed to provincial, state, or *"länder"* ("states," in German) governments, which work in conjunction with the central government. Federal states are often marked by linguistic or cultural differences, making non-central governments more responsive to the individual needs of constituent parts. Furthermore, different levels of government have different powers in both political and economic matters.

## Devolution and Confederalism

There are other compositions of government, depending on the division of powers. Some unitary systems have taken steps to divide power among more than just the central government. Political arrangements where power is given to regional authorities, but is not constitutionally or legally bound, are referred to as **devolution** systems. Within a "devolved" framework, some authority is given to regional governments, but the power to oversee, dismiss, or entrench these authorities is still held by the central government. The decision in 1997 by the British government in London to give limited authority to Scottish and Welsh legislatures is an example of devolution.

**Confederalism**, on the other hand, is characterized by a group of regional or constituent governments giving some powers to a central government; in many ways, confederalism is the opposite of devolution. In a confederal system, no final authority is given to a central government to override the wishes or authority of the regional systems. Although one often hears Canada referred to as a "confederation," it is, in fact, not. At the time of "confederation" in 1867, the powers given to the provincial governments in Canada were vastly inferior to those of the central government in Ottawa. Canada was then something of a highly centralized "quasi-federal" state. Since then, Canada has further "federalized" with most final powers given to the central government. The European Union (EU), with its concentration of limited authority in Brussels, and retention of final political authority in the governments of the states that make up the EU, is an example of a confederal arrangement, where most decision-making is still contingent on the activities and will of member states.

## The Branches of Government

This section details the four most important institutions in liberal democratic systems (see Fig. 3.2). Three represent the common divisions of power in these systems (executive, legislative, and judiciary), and the other is the bureaucracy, in some ways the largest and most active (though perhaps also the most ignored) wing of government. This section also examines the difference between presidential and parliamentary systems of government, a vital dis-

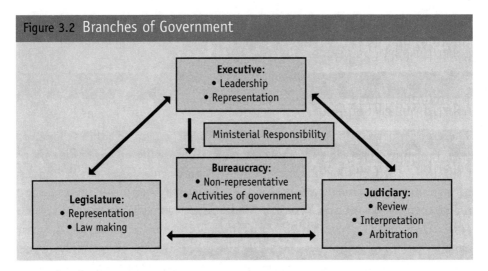

Figure 3.2 Branches of Government

tinction if we are to understand the complexities of Canada's versus other nations' political systems. Later, in Chapter 5, we provide a more detailed analysis and comparison of a parliamentary and a presidential system.

## The Executive

Modern states incorporate one of three basic types of executive systems. First, executive bodies may be a part of the legislative organization, described in greater detail later in this chapter. For example, both Canada and the United Kingdom employ this type of executive, which includes the head of government, head of state, and cabinet. Members of the executive (except the head of state, who is the Governor General in Canada and the Queen in the United Kingdom) are part of the larger legislative entity, the parliament. In this case, executive members are directly responsible to the legislature, and by means of such exercises as the "question period," they must respond to the concerns and probing of members of parliament. Second, executives may be separated from the legislature in an effort to divide powers among government institutions. An example of this model is the American presidential system, where members of the legislature (the Congress) are by law disallowed from being members of the executive at the same time. So, when members are selected to serve with the president of the United States in the executive, they must actually step down from their congressional role. Third, the powers and activities of the legislative and executive members may also be formally separated, but the concrete authority in the state may really come from the party executive of the governing class. As an example, the systems of the former communist states of Eastern Europe that existed during the Cold War were representative of this model. The differences among these systems lie in the nature of the relationship between the executive and the legislative structures.

Executives play a myriad of roles, which may come from day-to-day practice, or may be constitutionally prescribed. The executive performs distinct roles in society, in government, and in the party from which it has been chosen. In most countries, the executive, usually the leader, maintains leadership of the entire political system. Furthermore, the interests of and role played by the executive often reflect the leadership and preoccupations of the dominant political party.

One of the most consequential functions of the executive is to provide direction and supervision for the bureaucracy, which carries out the daily activities of the government. As discussed later, the bureaucracy, though the largest wing of government, has no real independent legal or constitutional function. Rather, bureaucracies are intended to be the specialized branch of the executive, carrying out the intentions and wishes of the upper levels of government. However, members of the executive are—at least in theory— accountable for all actions of the bureaucracy. In Canada for instance, the doctrine of **ministerial responsibility** means that cabinet ministers who are given portfolios by the prime minister are ultimately answerable for the actions of their ministries. It is in their own interest, then, to be fully aware of the activities of their bureaucratic members.

Two issues tend to follow any discussion of the modern executive. The first is the argument, often made, that legislatures are simply "rubber stamps" for executive decisions. This suggests that principles of democracy, meaning governance by the elected representatives of the people, are replaced by executive rule with little (if any) accountability to the parliament.

The second view goes even further, contending that it is the bureaucracy that in fact governs most political systems, creating an even larger gap between the people and their elected officials. After all, members of the bureaucracy are anonymous, frequently protected by their terms of office, and not subject to investigation by the electorate. Despite these two issues, we must bear in mind that the role of the executive includes overseeing the administrative actions of government. Members of the executive level of government may occupy the senior echelons of rule, but are also responsible—and accountable—for the daily functions of their administration.

Categories of Legislatures   Legislative groups were first formed as a means of decreasing the absolute powers held by monarchs. In the modern era, there are three main forms of legislatures. First, legislatures may function according to the principle of legislative "sovereignty" or authority. The British parliament is a good example of this model, which is couched on these assumptions:

- The highest authority in government is the legislature
- Neither the courts nor the executive may obstruct the activities of the legislature
- In terms of its jurisdiction, there are no limits to the power of the legislature
- Laws cannot be created to constrain any future legislatures; it must be permitted that all laws can be reassessed by future legislatures.

However, this is not to suggest that legislatures are totally without limitations. In fact, the "absolute" authority given to legislatures is limited by the fundamental rule of law, constitutional standards, and other customs and practices entrenched in the legal and political culture of the state.

Second, legislatures may be constrained by constitutions themselves, through the division of powers. In the United States Congress, for example, authority and responsibility is divided between the legislature and the executive in a system of what is known as **checks and balances**. Furthermore, the role of the courts in this model is important, as the respective responsibilities of legislatures and executives are restricted by **judicial review** and analysis.

Third, legislatures may also be thought of as having ultimate power within the political system, but with some limitations established by **constitutional authority**. In this case, legislatures often share powers with sub-state legislatures, such as those in provinces or states. This model, often called a **mixed system** due to the nature of power sharing among two or more levels of government, is epitomized in the Canadian situation, where jurisdictions and powers are allocated among the provinces, and the federal government. Education, for instance, is a provincial matter in Canada, though funding for education comes largely from transfer payments from the federal government. Also, provinces in Canada have the authority to carry out relations with other sovereign parties, such as other states in the international system. As an example, take the case of the recent "Team Canada" trade missions to locations such as Latin America, China, Australia, New Zealand, and Japan. Here members of the federal government, provincial governments, and private corporations travelled together to these regions to boost trade with these markets. Provincial actors often dealt with foreign government and corporate actors independent of the Canadian federal government, demonstrating the important international role that sub-state actors have taken on.

Structures of Legislatures   Legislatures generally come in two forms, based on the number of divisions, or "Houses," that make up the legislature itself. Legislatures that contain one assembly are called **unicameral** legislative bodies. An example of a unicameral body is the National Assembly of the Province of Quebec. Alternatively, legislatures may have two assemblies, or houses, and are known as **bicameral** legislatures. An example of a bicameral legislature is the federal Parliament of Canada, divided into the lower House of Commons and the upper house—the Senate. Bicameral legislative houses have two varieties. In the first case, the two houses are given approximately the same degree of influence and power. In the United States, for example, both the House of Representatives (the lower house) and the Senate (the upper house) have important, but distinct, law-making and legislative functions. As well, both legislatures in the United States are duly elected by citizens. On the other hand, some bicameral legislatures emphasize one of the two assemblies, where more power and influence is given to one of the houses. In Canada for example, more power is accorded to the House of Commons (the lower house) than the Senate (the upper house). In Canada, members of the upper house (Senators) are appointed to their posts, rather than elected, as are the members in the lower house. Finally, legislatures of both kinds operate with a series of committees and working groups that administer particular issues and items on the government agenda.

Functions of Legislatures   Legislatures were originally created to have three important and interrelated roles. First, legislatures are institutions that allow for the actual representation of individual and group concerns at the constituent level. Because it is simply impossible to envision a forum where citizens could actually represent themselves, the legislature provides a platform for elected officials to speak on behalf of their voters. This function is an integral part of the fundamental notion of **indirect democracy**. Related to this is the legislature's second function, to provide a forum for citizen representatives to interact and discuss matters of the day. Thus, the period of discussion and questioning (often called **question period**) permits opposition members to quiz the reigning government on its policies, and allows the government to state its policies and positions. Third, the legislature is responsible for law-making. This is the most important substantive role that the legislature performs, and provides an important check on the power of the executive, on the one hand, and oversees the role of the bureaucracy, on the other.

Law-making represents the real work of legislatures. In most democracies, legislatures are given the right to have final jurisdiction over issues of budgets and money matters; this is necessary to deny undue power to executives that otherwise could seek to impose their own financial interpretation on the activities of government. **Legislative proposals,** or laws, must be officially presented in the legislature, and the activities and performance of the bureaucracy are restricted and reviewed by the legislature.

## The Judiciary

The third major institution of government, the **judiciary,** is responsible for the broad legalistic aspects of government activities in society. First and foremost, the judiciary is responsible for arbitrating disputes in society. This role is crucial when we consider that individuals will at times challenge the legality of certain principles, and often these challenges will implicate the decisions of current or past legislatures. To be most effective in this role, judiciaries must be independent in order to offer the most unbiased judgments possible. Second, the judiciary is tasked with interpreting the laws created by the legislature. Finally, the judiciary—through the courts—ensures that acts and bills that are passed in the legislature meet the strict conditions of the **constitution** of the country (the basic law of any political system). Judiciaries are often called upon to clarify the legality or implications of proposed laws under consideration in the legislature.

Arbitrating Disputes   The judiciary is essential for liberal democracies because it provides a means of settling disputes or contests without resorting to the use of coercion or enforcement. We would do well to remember this point, because we often take for granted that courts are open and unbiased in their adjudication of challenges in society. However, in many states, especially authoritarian or dictatorial ones, the independence of the courts is not certain. In democracies, the judiciary is often given a separate role in terms of appointments and relationship to the government. Though judges are appointed in countries such as Canada, they are expected to act independently of the wishes or interests of the government. This is a necessary prerequisite to preserve the independence of this crucial wing of any democratic government system. The selection of members of the judiciary varies from country to country, however. In the United States, some courts have elected judges, rather than appointed ones. For the American system, this structure of elected judges is an important method of ensuring that the public views the courts to be separate from the government, and therefore cannot be used as an instrument of government.

Interpreting Laws    Anyone who has tried to read through the conditions and fine print contained in many government documents will probably agree that legalistic wording and interpretation might vary, based on the writer and the reader. Any document might be viewed by two people in two distinctive ways. Laws are no different. Often there may be inherent discrepancies in laws, regulations, or codes. The judiciary has the obligation to review laws so as to provide the proper interpretation for their use. The judiciary might be involved in the interpretation of laws as a matter of course, or in the event of a dispute. In addition, other institutions of government, such as the civil service, are frequently given the role of explaining laws, providing citizens with an alternative interpretation of laws.

Constitutional Conditions    During the process of decision-making and law-making, government actors will often call upon the judiciary to rule on the potential or real **constitutionality** of proposed laws or statutes. Importantly, the courts provide something of a legal "backstop" for the smooth implementation of laws and bills. As discussed elsewhere in this text, constitutions set the basic laws for a country, outlining the roles played by different institutions, and the interplay of these institutions. Moreover, many constitutions (such as the Canadian Constitution) contain a separate **Charter of Rights and Freedoms,** which outlines the rights and responsibilities of citizens of a country. The judiciary is often called upon to discuss the constitutionality of some decisions based on the rights and freedoms ensured by the constitution.

## The Bureaucracy

The largest and perhaps the most prominent (at least when we consider its daily activities) institution of government, the **bureaucracy** is the most familiar and misunderstood wing of any governing system. First, for those of us who have had some dealings with a government agency (and it is impossible not to have dealt with one at some time), the individuals that we talk to and deal with are bureaucrats. Obtaining a driver's licence, a passport, registering at a hospital, voting, or contacting a political representative almost always requires that we interact with a bureaucrat. Yet while these activities—getting a licence, or a passport, or voting—are essential activities, we often neglect the role played by the person that we must deal with. And, when problems arise, we often blame whomever we were dealing with.

  There is a common perception that the slow state of government affairs, high costs of government activities, or the problems we face when we try to work through government regulations are the fault of the bureaucrats themselves. Indeed, the term "bureaucratic" has negative implications in our society. To call someone's actions "bureaucratic" would be anything but generous. Bureaucracies are usually perceived to be rigid and convoluted, complicating even the simplest procedure.

But we must bear in mind that most bureaucrats actually have little latitude in the decisions they make or the activities they carry out. They often have little actual input to the decision-making system, are constrained by regulations set out by others, and do not have the authority to alter or change the rules to fit certain situations. Bureaucracies and bureaucrats are confined by the massive set of rules and conditions that are laid out by other institutions of government—the executive, the legislature, the courts—and are given the responsibility for carrying out laws and rules in a balanced and equal fashion.

Bureaucracies come in different shapes and capacities, given the level of importance that the country grants to the bureaucratic role in government. In Canada and the United States, for instance, the bureaucracy is responsible for the daily operations of educational institutions, hospitals, the armed forces, foreign relations, social organizations, the courts, finance and revenue, elections, and a myriad of other enterprises. Obviously, the more emphasis placed on bureaucracies, the more there will be a need for public servants.

However, not all bureaucrats are completely powerless in the daily operations of government. There is a small section of the public service that works at the senior levels of government, as assistants to legislators, or members of the cabinet, or judges. It is critical to remember that those people elected to serve in government ministries often are not professionals with an extensive background in their ministry. They may be lawyers, but have no experience as an attorney-general, or justice minister. It is essential, then, that elected officials not only have a team of dedicated employees working within their ministry, or department, but also that they have a select group of senior advisors and assistants whose lifelong work has been in that field. These ranking members of the public service have access to decision-makers that other bureaucrats simply do not, and also are integral to the actual decisions of government, given their expertise and experience.

Often the most neglected areas of government, bureaucracies are adaptable and malleable because of the widespread role they play. If it were not for bureaucracies, many aspects of daily life that we all take for granted might not be available: the carrying out of laws and regulations, social programs, healthcare, armed force protection, and revenue and taxation, for instance. For every incident where we have felt the seeming sluggishness of the civil service, there are innumerable examples of how our daily lives are advanced and assisted by bureaucratic organizations.

Bureaucrats do much more than just execute the laws and regulatory mechanisms of the land. They are a key element in the creation of public policy; they influence the decisions of key policy-makers; they are responsible for discharging decisions made by other institutions of government, and they operate on the "front lines" of government, working directly with citizens in society.

## Presidential and Parliamentary Systems

Presidential and parliamentary systems are the two most consequential types of political systems today. Though they are not the only types, they are the most common, and most influential. This section will outline the background to the differences between these two dominant types of systems. First, however, it should be noted that there are so many types of presidential and parliamentary systems that it would be impossible to discuss all of them in this chapter. The dominant form of both presidential and parliamentary political systems is based on liberal democracy. Hence, this section will devote most of its attention to this government type. More discussion on the particularities of these systems is provided in Chapter 5, in the description of the Canadian and American systems of government and economy.

The foundations for these two systems are rooted in the history of Great Britain. The parliamentary system is based on of the Westminster model (the name given to the British parliamentary system), while the presidential system was produced as a result of revolt in the United States against the parliamentary system in the late eighteenth century. Although some totalitarian and authoritarian states have "adopted" some features of these systems (usually in an effort to lend some degree of legitimacy to their regime), both the parliamentary and presidential configurations of government—or hybrid combinations of the two—exist in liberal democracies.

The one distinction between the two systems relates to the separation of powers, or the manner in which power is granted to the levels of government—usually the executive, the legislature, and the judiciary, but also at times the bureaucracy. The separation of powers is a crucial element of both systems because it denotes two ways in which power is protected from misuse by one wing of government.

The architects of the American system of government in the late eighteenth century were concerned that, on the one hand, power would corrupt those given it arbitrarily. On the other hand, there was also the concern that the strength of the nation would be diminished if some degree of control and authority were not given to some levels of government. The presidential system forbids anyone from holding office in more than one level of government, and each level is given a review of proceedings at the other levels. So, for instance, legislation passed in the United States Congress (the lower House of Representatives and the upper Senate chamber) must be approved by the executive—the president. However, if the president were to veto (use the constitutional right to reject) legislation, the matter could then be turned back to the Congress, where a two-thirds majority in both houses can overturn the veto. Similarly, the Congress has the right to reject bills proposed by the president, to limit appointments, or even to impeach the president. One can see, then, the emphasis in the American system is on checks and balances, the ability by one level of government to limit the independent actions of another.

In contrast to the presidential system, the parliamentary system relies on a fusion of powers, bringing together the responsibilities and rights of different levels of authority within government. In particular, the fusion of powers unites the capacity of the executive and legislative levels of government. For example, unlike the presidential system, members of one level of government in a parliamentary system—say, a cabinet minister or prime minister—are required to be members of, or seeking office in, Parliament. The fusion of powers is different from the American-style checks and balances system because it requires members of the executive (cabinet ministers and the Prime Minister) to be part of the legislative wing of government as well. This has the advantage of involving both levels of government at the same time, but is viewed by some as a disadvantage because of possible conflicts of interest.

Despite persistent questions regarding the relative benefits of one system over the other, the presidential and parliamentary systems represent the two fundamental political systems in the world today. Often states adopt elements of one or both in an attempt to create what might be termed a composite or "hybrid" system. One of the basic differences between the two systems is the emphasis on internal checks and balances within the presidential system, on the one hand, and on the other, the importance placed on representation (meaning the government is not limited by counterbalancing influences) in the parliamentary system.

## Canada's GDP

Box 3.3

A country's Gross Domestic Product (GDP) is one measure of the size of its economy. It combines several factors, including wages and income support, corporate profits, interest and investment income, and agricultural income. This does not measure the total worth of a nation, but the total output of an economy during the year.

**Canada's 1997 Gross Domestic Product ($ millions)**

| | |
|---|---:|
| Wages, salaries, and supplementary labour income | 445,924 |
| Corporation profits before taxes | 79,765 |
| Government business enterprise profits before taxes | 6,769 |
| Interest and miscellaneous investment income | 47,165 |
| Accrued net income of farm operators from farm production | 1,969 |
| Net income of non-farm unincorporated business (incl. rent) | 53,023 |
| Inventory valuation adjustment | -1,647 |
| Net domestic income at factor cost | 632,968 |
| Indirect taxes less subsidies | 114,714 |
| Capital consumption allowances | 110,428 |
| Statistical discrepancy | -1,976 |
| **TOTAL** | **856,134** |

Source: Statistics Canada, *1999 Canada Yearbook*, CANSIM, matrix 6547.

## The Institutions and Functions of Economic Management

In addition to all of its political functions, the government of a modern state is also charged with providing for its citizens' economic welfare. Of course, the strength of this commitment varies greatly from country to country, and indeed from government to government within a country, depending on ideological persuasion and resource availability. Within national economies the government is generally the largest economic actor, consuming a significant proportion of the total economic output of the country, and in some countries, producing a large percentage of that output through government-owned or managed corporations. But this direct involvement in the economic life of the country is matched or exceeded in importance by the government's role in managing the economy, making and implementing both macro- (economy-wide) and micro- (sector or area specific) economic policies. The government achieves such management through a series of agencies and ministries, which both regulate specific economic activities, and set targets for the economy as a whole.

Just as we use the terms democratic and authoritarian to describe the level of state and private involvement in the organization of a nation's political life, so we refer to command and market economies to describe the level of state involvement in the economic affairs of the nation (see Box 3.1). A command economy is one where the government takes all the most important decisions in the running of the economy, deciding what is produced, how it will be produced, and how the nation's economic wealth will be divided. In most cases a command economy implies actual state ownership of the means of production, that is, factories, banks, and services industries. The Union of Soviet Socialist Republics (USSR) was an example of this kind of economy. In a market economy, such decisions are taken by private actors, either individuals or corporations owned and managed by private citizens. Most economies in the real world fall somewhere between these two economic models, having elements of both state control and private economic decision-making and ownership.

The government can intervene in the economy in a variety of ways, but we can categorize them quite simply. First, through state ownership or nationalization, the government simply owns the means of production and of providing credit and other services, controlling productive and financial processes directly. Secondly, the government makes economic policy that helps to determine the direction and strength of economic growth, inflation, and unemployment. Thirdly, the government regulates the activities of different economic sectors, applying standards and rules to firms and corporations. Such regulation can take the form of consumer protection, health and safety standards, price levels, ensuring stability, or encouraging healthy levels of competition, among many others.

## State Ownership

One of the trademarks of socialist and social democratic economic systems in the past has been state ownership of the means of production, that is, of manufacturing, financial, and services industries. In this way the government is free to use the economy for its own purposes, increasing or reducing the supply of goods and credit whenever it deems necessary. More importantly, the government of a nation is in a position to guarantee the provision of key services, and to ensure the availability of goods essential to the economic and military security of the country.

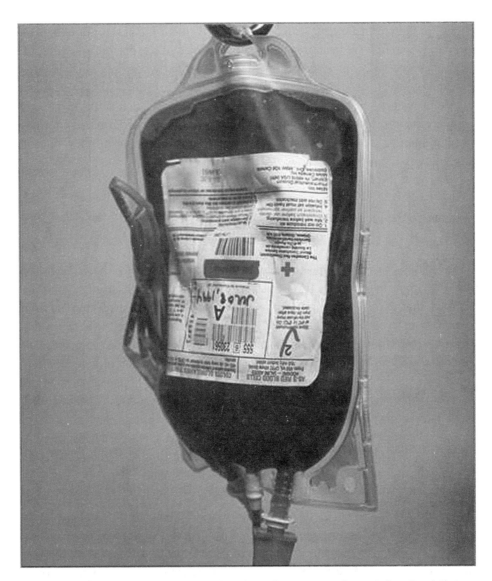

As this chapter shows, one of the central functions of governments is regulation. Regulation can take many forms, controlling economic activity, setting norms and standards for healthcare, limiting the speed of drivers on highways, or even demanding that individuals dress according to certain standards.

In the late 1980s and early 1990s in Canada, a large number of people who received blood transfusions were infected with the human immunodeficiency virus (HIV). In turn some of their partners and children were also infected. This crisis undermined Canadians' confidence in the national blood supply and was seen as a failure of government regulation in the area. Federal and provincial governments in Canada were forced to not only provide compensation to victims of the blood crisis, but also to create a new blood supply system. In September 1996 the Canadian Red Cross was replaced by Canadian Blood Services and Hema-Quebec as the organizations responsible for maintaining the national blood program.

In the nineteenth century such direct involvement in the economy by governments would have been unthinkable. However, in the period following the Second World War, many governments nationalized what they considered to be strategic sectors—those involved in the production of coal and steel and in the provision of essential services to the population, such as the electricity, water, gas, and telecommunications industries. In these countries, nationalized industries accounted for a significant proportion of total economic activity.

---

**Box 3.4**   # The Phillips Curve

The Phillips Curve is a graph that plots the relationship between unemployment and inflation. In the 1960s it was assumed that this was an inverse relationship, that is, that as the level of inflation fell, so the level of unemployment would rise. For most of the 1960s and early 1970s this seemed to hold true. However, in the mid-1970s the Western economies of the United States and Europe began to experience the phenomenon known as "stagflation"—a combination of high inflation and economic stagnation. During this period economies suffered both inflation and unemployment, changing assumptions about the relationship between the two factors. In the 1990s the United States and Great Britain have shown the other side of the relationship. Both countries have been able to achieve low inflation (in the 1-3% range) and low unemployment, with the United States claiming almost full employment (with unemployment at around 5%).

---

In the 1990s governments across the world began a process of privatization, in which ownership of nationalized industries was transferred from the state into private hands, usually through the offering of shares in the corporations concerned (see Box 3.5). This change reflected a transition from a leftist to a liberal or neo-liberal ideology in these states, and also the growing inefficiency of these economic sectors. The change was most dramatic in the states of Eastern Europe and Russia, where only a decade earlier the government had held complete control over the means of production. But the state has not yet completely withdrawn from direct involvement in the economy. In many countries in the developing world the state remains the owner of some of the largest corporations, while in Canada, crown corporations (meaning owned by the state) continue to dominate certain sectors of the economy, such as energy production.

## Economic Policy

By far the most important area of state involvement in the economy is the making of policies designed to steer the economy towards goals determined by the political process. In this section we will focus on **macroeconomic policy-making**, that is, policies which affect the economy as a whole, or at the macro-

## Privatization

Box 3.5

Beginning with the United Kingdom in the 1980s, governments around the world have made great efforts in recent years to turn over control of previously state-owned enterprises to the private sector. Such efforts have gone hand in hand with an increasingly liberal or neo-liberal approach to economic decision-making, where governments have turned to the market for a solution to problems of economic development. The arguments in favour of privatization are many, but among them we can identify three very important issues. First it is argued that governments are ill-equipped to be efficient producers or providers of services because they lack the profit incentive that drives the private sector. Second, some consider it inappropriate for political authorities to be directly involved in the industrial or services sectors because other producers or service providers will not be able to compete against corporations that have the financial strength of a national government behind them. Third, liberals argue that privatization increases economic freedom, and is thus an important step towards increasing the liberty of private citizens.

Each of these arguments has its merits, and in a majority of cases privatization has had positive economic effects. One problem, however, is that in some cases in the services sector, the quality and quantity of services has deteriorated since privatization. Take for example the privatization of national rail services in some countries, such as Great Britain. Since privatization, many train routes to and from remote areas have been eliminated because they are simply not profitable. While this development may be considered healthy by liberal economic standards, it has meant a deterioration in the standard of living of the people living in such areas. Furthermore, in some cases the prices of rail travel have gone up. Again, according to the standards of market economics this is not necessarily a bad thing. However, rising rail travel prices can mean more people choosing to travel by car, which in turn will have a negative impact in terms of pollution, traffic volume, and wear and tear on roads. Each of these negative effects will cost both the economy and the government money.

level. Within this category of policies are efforts to control inflation and unemployment or to encourage economic growth. It is important to remember that these policies emerge as a result of the political process in each country, but it is generally the executive branch that initiates a particular policy. Either the prime minister or president, in consultation with the cabinet, will determine the economic goals for the country, and then the bureaucratic branch of government will make efforts to implement these goals. However, the legislative branch of government becomes important in most democratic systems when government spending, embodied in the governmental budget, goes through an approval process in the parliament or congress.

Price stability, or low inflation, has become an increasingly important goal for government economic policy-makers in recent years. Price stability is important to the economy in order to ensure long-term confidence in investments and to provide certainty about the future value of goods. Governments try to achieve price stability by controlling the **money supply** in the economy, that is, the total amount of currency and credit in the hands of consumers, industry, and financial institutions.

This they can do by several methods. First, the government can strictly control the creation of money directly, by keeping tight limits on the printing of new money. Secondly, the government can cut back on its own spending, thus keeping more money out of general circulation. This method, of course, comes at the cost of cutting back on government services and government jobs or salaries. Thirdly, and this has become the most common method of controlling the money supply in recent years, the government, in conjunction with the central bank, will raise interest rates (that is the rate of interest offered on bank deposits). When **interest rates** rise there is less incentive to borrow money from banks and other financial institutions (because such borrowing has become more expensive), and more incentive to put money into banks (because there is a higher return on deposits). As money is taken out of circulation the money supply will decrease and inflation should fall.

These policies of reducing inflation, or of tight money, will, however, have an impact on economic growth. As the money supply is reduced, and particularly as the cost of borrowing money increases, fewer businesses will be inclined to borrow to fund new investments or to increase their corporate spending. Similarly, a rise in interest rates may dampen consumer spending, as fewer private citizens borrow money from banks or credit card companies to finance their consumption habits. One direct impact will be on the housing sector; as interest rates rise, we can expect fewer people to take out mortgages to finance the purchase of a house.

Taking this into account, a government can use the opposite strategy, that is, lowering interest rates (and thus the cost of borrowing) in order to boost consumption, investment, and business activity, with the ultimate goal of increasing the nation's level of economic growth. By reducing the cost of borrowing, a government shows that it is willing to risk rising levels of inflation to gain higher levels of economic growth. But the manipulation of interest rates is not the only way in which a government can affect the rate of growth. In some developing countries, as in many now-industrialized countries in the past, governments simply print more money when they need to either finance government spending, fight a foreign war, or provide stimulus to the nation's economy. Ultimately this will lead to a reduction in the value of the nation's currency, which will lead to inflation.

Another strategy employed by governments to promote economic growth is to increase government spending. By thus pumping money into the economy the government can provide both employment and business opportunities that should act as an economic stimulus. This approach to economic growth, however, depends on the government having access to the necessary financial resources. If the government's income from taxation and royalties does not match its intended spending levels, the government will have to borrow money. Such a situation is called **deficit spending**. If it borrows from its own citizens and national financial institutions, the government will simply be taking resources that could otherwise be used by the private sector, and so it might choose to borrow money internationally. Either way, however, the government will be incurring debt, monies that will have to be repaid over a period of time with interest.

John Maynard Keynes was an advocate of governments providing such a stimulus to the economy when the market failed to provide sufficiently high levels of growth. Keynes' idea was that when the economic cycle went into a **downturn**, that is when economic growth slowed, governments should engage in countercyclical spending, pumping money into the economy and providing employment when the private sector was unable or unwilling to do so (see Chapter 2). Such an approach to economic management became popular in the 1930s, but by the end of the twentieth century no longer appealed to the governments of most advanced industrialized countries.

Some governments use their taxation policies as a tool to control economic growth. In the 1980s, for example, in the United States, the Reagan administration proposed tax reductions as a way to encourage consumers to spend. Of course this policy approach has its limits. A government can only reduce taxes so much before it has to reduce its own spending, or increase its indebtedness through domestic or foreign borrowing. What's more, tax cuts can only infrequently be used as a tool to promote economic growth for, unless a government is willing to raise taxation levels when desired growth levels have been achieved, the policy option of further reductions will incur a drastic reduction in government resource levels.

## Regulation

The last main area in which the government exercises control over the economy is regulation. The regulatory activities of the government are more specific than the broad-sweeping macroeconomic policies that set targets for the economy as whole. For example, much regulation is sector- or industry-specific, with a government agency regulating the activity of economic organizations involved in one area of business. Banking provides an interesting example. Here the national (in some countries provincial or state) banking (or in some countries, financial) regulatory agency sets standards and oversees (or supervises) the activities of all banks within their jurisdiction. The regulator determines whether or not individual banks are following standards of good practice, of consumer protection, and of course whether or not the bank is engaging in illegal activities such as laundering money. But the regulator in this case also determines whether or not individual banks have the resources necessary to continue to borrow and lend, and whether or not the failure of one bank may lead to a wider problem in the financial sector as a whole.

Not all government regulatory agencies go so far. In the area of telecommunications, for example, the agency may limit itself to determining whether or not a telephone company is engaging in fair pricing policies, or if it is price-gouging, that is, demanding more than a fair price for its services from the public. Or the agency may study the impact of new technologies on the industry to determine if their introduction would be beneficial or destabilizing.

The other main kind of regulatory agency focuses not on a specific economic sector or industry, but on a specific economic issue, such as wages, competition, or health and safety. These agencies are particularly important because they often reflect the ideological preferences of a government more directly than industry-specific agencies. For example, an agency that regulates prices will be much more active under a socialist government that favours price controls than under a liberal or neo-liberal government dedicated to the free market. Similarly, a left-wing government is much more likely to insist upon a **minimum wage**, that is, a legally mandated minimum level of remuneration per hour, than a right-wing, liberal counterpart.

A particularly important kind of regulatory agency in the modern political economy is that which deals with levels of competition, or monopolies. A monopoly simply refers to a situation where one corporation so dominates a particular economic sector that it does not have to worry about competition from other firms, and thus is free to manipulate prices almost at will. Most states have agencies that try to prevent the emergence of monopolies and to make sure that a healthy level of competition remains a feature of the economy. While this is a highly liberal idea, it also involves government intervention, one of the few times when economic liberals feel comfortable with the idea (see Box 3.6).

## Regulating Competition                                    Box 3.6

Most governments around the world make efforts to ensure that their economies are marked by healthy levels of competition, and not monopolies, which would impede efficiency and damage consumer interests. Monopoly and anti-trust commissions or competition agencies examine patterns of ownership and market behaviour and determine whether or not there is sufficient competition in each sector of a national economy. Sometimes this function is also carried out by the national ministry of industry.

A very high-profile example of this kind of activity is the case of Microsoft Corporation in the United States. Recently the United States Justice Department and 20 individual states won an anti-trust law suit against Microsoft, charging the corporation with using its leading position in the computer software market to reduce opportunities for competitors in the Internet browser sector by including Microsoft's own browser software in sales of the company's Windows software. US regulators charged that Microsoft was trying to unfairly drive its competitors out of business, while Bill Gates, Microsoft's chairman, argued that he was being punished by the lawsuit for being too successful.

This case highlighted many of the issues that have marked other anti-trust suits in the past, as well as the new issues concerning high-technology industries. But most importantly the case highlighted an apparent contradiction within capitalism. That is, governments will refrain from market intervention and the system will reward success up to a certain point, but when success begins to interfere with the efficiency of the market by hindering competition, political authorities must intervene to control the power of dominant market players.

# Institutions

This section will describe some of the major institutions employed by governments to implement economic policy, and their functions. These institutions, most of which form part of the government bureaucracy, provide an important focal point for private economic actors to participate in and influence the policy process (see Chapter 4). They are essential to the management of the economy because they represent a concentration of knowledge specific to a particular issue area. First of all, this knowledge can be used by the government in the formation of policy, so that the most relevant factors are taken into account in its design. Secondly, the public servants working in a particular government institution possess the knowledge necessary for the successful implementation of policy, so that it can be adjusted or strengthened when necessary.

## The Finance Ministry

Perhaps the most important institution in the formation of government economic policy is the department or ministry of finance. This government department is responsible for providing the government with information on the functioning of the economy and on the impact of government activities on the economy, and advising the government on its internal finances. In some countries, such as Great Britain and the United States, this government department is known as the Treasury, or Department of the Treasury. In Canada, however, the Department of Finance is a separate institution to the Treasury Board. The Department of Finance advises the government on the economy, while the Treasury Board analyzes public finances, assigns financial resources to government departments, and assists with the calculation and formulation of the annual budget.

The importance of this government department is reflected in the position of its head, the minister of finance (known in Great Britain as the chancellor of the exchequer, in the United States as secretary of the treasury). In peacetime this minister is generally considered the most important cabinet member apart from the prime minister or president.

For example, the public servants who implement policy in the ministry of finance should ideally be experts in the area of public finances, economists with an understanding of the particular problems and implications of government spending and borrowing.

The finance minister works in close consultation with the rest of the cabinet, but also with the head of the central bank (see below), to direct the economy and to set targets for issues such as inflation, employment, and economic growth. The minister's most important job each year, however, is to formulate the government's annual **budget**. The budget states the total amount of money to be spent by the government in the coming year, how that money is to be spent, and how much the government is to receive in income from taxation. It is in this piece of legislation that the government decides which sectors of society and the economy will receive increased benefits, and which sectors will receive less or have to contribute more. The finance minister's decision will have a profound impact on the strength and direction of the economy in the coming year, either encouraging or dampening economic growth, providing or cutting government jobs, and strengthening or reducing government social programs.

If the finance minister decides to increase government spending, then he or she must either increase taxation or raise revenue from some other source, such as privatizing state-owned industries. When the budget does not allow for either of these options then it is said that the budget is in **deficit**, that is, the government is spending more than it is receiving in revenue. When this happens, the government will be forced to borrow money from banks or financial markets to finance its spending. In doing so the government will be incurring a national debt, and interest will have to be paid on this debt until it is repaid. This, of course, means that the government will have to devote money to interest payments that could have gone towards economic or social development programs. In recent years in developed economies such as Canada and the United States the tendency has been towards surplus in government finance. This has come about because of government spending cuts and increased revenues derived from economic growth.

## The Central Bank

One of the highest profile institutions of economic management in the modern world is the **central bank**. The first central bank in the world was created in Great Britain in the late seventeenth century. The Bank of England was founded to provide a source of finance for the British government, and to be financial adviser to the government and the official issuer of bank notes (the British pound) for the British economy. The functions of the modern central bank have expanded somewhat since then, though one, as we shall see, holds a more important place than the others. The nation's central bank is first a banker to the country's banks, in some countries requiring commercial banks to keep a certain amount of money on deposit (reserves) at the central bank. Furthermore, the central bank acts as a lender of last resort, extending emergency financing to banks or other financial institutions experiencing temporary cash shortages. This function provides much stability and confidence to a nation's banking system.

Connected to this role as the banks' banker, the central bank in some countries acts as the most important regulator and supervisor of bank activities (though in Canada this function is performed by the Office of the Superintendent of Financial Institutions). In regulating and supervising the banks, the central bank attempts to maintain stability in the nation's financial system, to protect private citizens who deposit their money in banks, and to ensure that the system works efficiently.

The central bank is also the banker to the government. In this regard the central bank holds the government's deposits and manages the money so that it not only sits in the bank, but actually earns interest. Complementary to this function is the central bank's role as financial advisor to the government. It gives advice to the national government on its investments, but also on how to best manage the **national debt**, that is, the money that is owed by the government to private and public actors within and outside of the country.

A fourth role for the central bank is to manage the value of the national currency relative to other currencies in the world. Though in an increasing number of countries the value of the national currency is decided by the world's foreign exchange markets, the central bank often plays an important role in smoothing out large variations in that value. The central bank can also attempt to manipulate the value of the currency upwards or downwards in the best economic interest of the nation (see Box 3.7).

By far the most significant function of the central bank, however, is a crucial management role that it performs in the economy through its most important function, the control of the nation's **money supply**, that is, the total amount of money available in the economy. In some countries the bank is in sole charge of monetary policy, while in others (such as Canada) it works in close collaboration with the ministry of finance. In almost every country there is consultation between the central bank and the government.

Determining the nation's money supply is a crucial decision. If there is too much money in the system, then the nation's economy will experience high levels of inflation (rapidly rising prices), as the value of money goes down relative to the total amount of goods in the economy. This will bring instability and a lack of confidence in the economy. If there is too little money, then a similarly problematic situation will arise, for prices of goods will fall and

## Central Banks and the National Currency

Box 3.7

Because the international economic system does not have one currency, but rather many national currencies whose relative values change frequently, a central bank may use its economic resources to manipulate the value of the nation's currency to increase the competitiveness of that country's economy. If the currency's value can be brought down in value in relation to other currencies, the nation's exports will become cheaper relative to the exports of other countries. Alternatively, the central bank may attempt to raise the value of the currency to encourage investment and confidence in the economy.

The bank can manipulate the value of the currency in several ways indirectly, but the most common method is quite direct, buying or selling the currency on international currency markets. By buying the currency in sufficient quantities (using foreign currency reserves to make the purchase), the central bank will be able to raise its value on foreign exchange (FOREX) markets. Alternatively, the central bank can lower the value of the currency by selling it on FOREX markets.

In these ways the central bank can manage the value of its national currency to the advantage of the nation's economy. In addition the central bank can use these methods to protect the currency from international currency speculators. From the point of view of political economy these actions constitute not only attempts to manage the national economy, but also a direct interaction between political authority and the market.

there will not be sufficient money available for investment and economic growth.

The central bank controls the money supply in several ways. First, in a very direct way, the central bank issues bank notes, and is thus the authority that decides on the total amount of money that is to be printed. The central bank can also invest the government's deposits in ways that increase the total amount of money available to the economy. But most importantly, the central bank sets the nation's **prime interest rate**, that is, the amount of interest that borrowers will have to pay when they borrow money from banks or other financial institutions. By manipulating the interest rate, the central bank can exercise control over the amount of money that is borrowed from banks, and thus the total quantity of money flowing through the national economy. This policy tool has become of vital importance in an era of economic management dominated by the monetarist approach (see Box 3.8).

| Box 3.8 | Monetarism |
|---------|------------|

As suggested in the rest of this chapter, the control of the money supply has become one of the most important approaches to national economic management. This approach was first formulated in the early 1950s by a group of economists whose efforts were located at the University of Chicago and by the propositions of one man, Milton Friedman. In opposition to Keynes, Friedman argued that the government should not engage in countercyclical spending to influence production and employment, but instead could exert control over the supply of money into the economy, which would influence relative prices, and in turn, production and employment.

But in what way should the government influence the money supply? Essentially, the monetarists have argued that the money supply should be allowed to increase at a steady rate (that is, without sudden jumps or decreases). This rate should be equivalent to the long-term rate of growth in the area of production. By doing so there would not be a gap between production and the supply of money that should lead to stable prices.

A standard method of controlling the money supply for monetarists is for the government, through the central bank, to raise or lower interest rates, and thus influence the supply of credit to the economy. By doing so, the rate of investment and borrowing will be affected, which in turn will influence both production and consumption.

## Other Important Economic Institutions

Though the ministry of finance and the central bank may be the most important institutions of economic management, they by no means cover all of the areas of control exercised by the government of a specific country. Government ministries and agencies regulate, direct, or interact with almost every area of economic activity, and the decisions of government institutions are often critical to new developments in national, and indeed international, markets. This section will look at two such government ministries: those relating to trade and labour.

The function of a nation's ministry of trade is, as the name suggests, to promote the interests of the country through trade relations with other states. In the late twentieth century this increasingly meant negotiating free trade agreements with other countries in order to expand export markets for national producers and to provide a wider choice of products for national consumers. But often a nation's trade ministry is also involved in the promotion of trade through providing training, information, and financing to national corporations that are seeking to export their goods. As with many other government ministries, the service that has become more and more important is the information that a ministry of trade makes available to the private sector. Such information gathering would be prohibitively expensive for many potential exporters, and the existence of a centralized database enables many firms to take advantage of foreign trade opportunities that they would otherwise miss.

The issues of employment and training, always central political as well as economic issues, are most often dealt with at the national level by a ministry

## (Un-)Employment Insurance Reform                            Box 3.9

A policy priority of many of the world's governments since the Second World War has been to provide income support for individuals who are out of work. In Canada such income support has become an integral part of the social contract between the government and Canadian citizens. However, in recent years this aspect of the social contract has come under increasing scrutiny from the federal government, which has made efforts to reform the system of income support. The reasons for this reform effort have been pressure on government finances and a perception that government unemployment payments help to create dependency on the part of the unemployed and a reduced incentive to find work. In some policy circles it has been argued that for many unemployed persons it is more lucrative not to work rather than to find employment and contribute to both the economy and to the government's finances in the form of taxes.

Though strong debate continues, the federal government has taken successive steps to reduce the level of income support to the unemployed. This has been done by reducing the amount of money paid to individuals and by increasing the amount of time that has to be worked to be eligible for unemployment insurance payments. Many of these changes were embodied in the January 1997 Employment Insurance Act, which as its name suggests, gave a new title to the system of income support. This change (from the old Unemployment Insurance system) reflected the attempts of the government to change public opinion about the system and to put the emphasis back on the individual to find employment rather than depend on government support.

of labour, or as in Canada, by a department of human resources. A ministry of labour analyzes and regulates labour markets, and also in some countries provides financial and technical assistance to those who find themselves out of work. The significance given to this work will depend very much on the ideological bias of the government in charge at any one time. A left-wing government is much more likely to provide high levels of financial assistance to the unemployed, whereas a more liberal, or right-wing, government would be more likely to reduce this aid and leave job creation to the private sector (see Box 3.9). The other function of a labour ministry, that of providing training to the nation's workforce, has become of utmost importance in an increasingly competitive and technology-based world economy, where skilled labour is in high demand. By ensuring that the national workforce is well trained, the state will be improving the competitiveness of the economy as a whole.

## Summary

This chapter has introduced you to the forms and composition of contemporary government, to the different types of governmental organization, and to the functions and institutions of governmental economic management. Each of the branches of government, executive, legislative and judicial, along with the bureaucracy, plays a crucial role in determining the political and economic future of a country, and it is their decisions and actions that form one of the principal areas of focus for political studies.

We have seen that, in many ways, the ideological roots of political systems influence their type of government and the scope of its powers. Liberal democrat, totalitarian, and authoritarian forms, and unitary and federal compositions exemplify the most prevalent patterns of governmental systems today. It is crucial that we understand and compare the various types of contemporary government, because we may then understand a bit more about our own system, as well as the distinctive nature of others.

To that end, this chapter has also introduced you to the differences between the parliamentary and presidential systems of government, the primary models of government employed by most states today. The chapter also introduced you to the executive, legislative, judicial, and bureaucratic branches of government. While power shifts have taken place within the structure of government, the basis of government, the bedrock of the governmental structure is laid out in the constitution. While all countries have constitutions, the rule of law is typical of Western liberal democratic governments.

A central purpose of this chapter was to introduce you not just to the political functions and institutions of government, but also to the economic.
Therefore we examined the importance of state ownership, economic policy,
and regulation as forms of governmental economic control. Furthermore, the
roles of the ministry of finance and the central bank were also explained.

In later chapters we will analyze the organization and functioning of different political and economic systems around the world, but one aspect of
political studies remains to be discussed. That aspect is the participation of the
public and non-governmental actors in the world of politics and the extent of
their influence over governments, and it is to this issue that the next chapter
turns.

## Self-Assessment Questions

1. What are the four primary institutions in government? What are their
   individual responsibilities? Could political systems exist without one of
   these institutions? Why is their interrelationship so significant?
2. How may we distinguish among unitary, federal, confederal, and devolu-
   tionary political systems?
3. Why are bureaucrats not elected?
4. How does ideology affect government economic management?
5. When should governments intervene in the functioning of the economy?

## Further Reading

Adie, Robert F., and Paul G. Thomas. *Canadian Public Administration:
Problematical Perspectives,* 2nd ed. Scarborough: Prentice-Hall, 1987.

Binhammer, H.H. *Money, Banking and the Canadian Financial System*, 6th
ed. Scarborough: Nelson Canada, 1993.

Brooks, Stephen. *Public Policy in Canada*, 3rd ed. Toronto: Oxford University
Press, 1998.

Jackson, Robert J., and Doreen Jackson. *Politics in Canada: Culture,
Institutions, Behaviour and Public Policy*, 4th ed. Scarborough: Prentice Hall
Allyn and Bacon Canada, 1998.

Sargent, Lynman Tower. *Contemporary Political Ideologies: A Comparative
Analysis*. Belmont: Wadsworth, 1993.

## Web Links

### Democracy.net
http://www.democracy.net

### Federalism.ca
http://www.federalism.ca

### Bank of Canada
http://www.bank-banque-canada.ca

### Department of Finance
http:/www.fin.gc.ca

### World Business News
http://cnnfn.com/

## CHAPTER FOUR

# THE POLITICAL ECONOMY OF PARTICIPATION

## Chapter Objectives

When you have completed this chapter you will be able to:

- describe the attributes of a political culture and the various stages of political socialization

- appreciate the influence of participation on the political process

- measure the significance of public opinion in contemporary politics

- describe the nature and intention of elections and differentiate between contrasting systems of elections

- recognize the significance of interest groups, media, and political parties and

- account for the concept of differential power of groups, based on wealth, organization, and the like.

You might recall the point made in Chapter 1 that the "political" surrounds our daily lives in ways that we may not always recognize. That much is true: laws and institutions are created to regulate our lives, and the lives of those around us in order to make our societies safe and functional for all. We would all agree that, though we may feel distant from the process of politics, our lives are nonetheless enhanced and more secure as a result of political institutions and governance. But how might we be involved in this process of participation? Are we truly removed from the "political" in our daily lives, or do we actually have an influence in the manner of decision-making that we all would agree affects us in a most basic manner? Furthermore, how might this involvement in the political process serve to assist our economic well-being?

The purpose of this chapter is to introduce you to the various ways that people become involved in the political process, and how this participation actually affects the lives and well-being of ourselves and our communities. Politics cannot be separated from citizens, and there are several ways in which people may affect their political community, either as individuals or as members of a group. Politics is like any other form of socialization—the process of organizing in a social manner—and we are faced on a daily basis with politics. In fact, this chapter is primarily about the political and social organizing of citizens. Participation in a political unit, we argue here, is a product of the manner in which we are socialized.

The material introduced in Chapter 4 builds on the ideological and institutional knowledge you have gained in the previous chapters. In many ways, participation is the most consequential aspect of political studies because it is only through understanding involvement in the political process that we may come to understand the larger issues of "who gets what, when, and how."

This chapter will introduce you to the study of political culture, political socialization, public viewpoints, and voting conduct. In addition, the chapter explains the functions and input of important factors in the political process where individuals may have a direct impact; for example, the media, interest groups, and political parties. Understanding the role and input of these groups in society is integral for our overall appreciation of the role of individuals in the political process, as interest groups, parties, and the media offer different ways for people to articulate their concerns and interests. Through the study of **political participation**, it is possible to gain an understanding of how different political systems allocate values in a variety of social settings with varying levels of political participation. This chapter will also introduce you to the area of business-government relations, for private economic actors are among the most influential participants in the political process.

# The Political Process and the Importance of Participation

The previous chapters in this book introduced you to some of the fundamental elements of modern political analysis. These include significant concepts for political studies, the nature of political life, the importance of political philosophy and theory for contemporary political studies, and the divisions among the important political institutions that are part of the structure of political interaction in modern society. It is important to keep in mind, though, that all of these elements of modern political studies fundamentally involve individuals and groups in political systems. This chapter, in contrast, describes how political systems are really a process of interaction among people and groups. Political participation, through a variety of means, provides the most direct and common form of direct interaction in modern political life.

## Canadian Labour Participation and Unemployment

Box 4.1

Participation by most individuals concerns their consumption and labour patterns. Consumption refers to the money we spend, and the goods and services we buy. Labour is, of course, the work that we do, whether it is paid or not, in the home or outside. In Canada, however, as in most other countries, labour participation is measured by the total number of people in paid work. Canada has a relatively high rate of labour participation: of all those people eligible to work, approximately three-quarters (75.9%) participate in the job market. However, in recent years Canada has had one of the higher unemployment rates among the industrialized economies, and this remains a serious problem for our governments, both federal and provincial, to solve.

Source: OECD, Labour Force Statistics 1976-1996, Paris, 1996.

Political participation has been compared by some observers to a sports event. While the direct participants in the event (the athletes) compete on the field, court, or track, interested observers (the spectators) cheer for their team. At the same time, however, many more people who are apart from the event (those who do not attend the event) are indifferent, or unaware of the activities within the stadium, arena, or sports field.

This analogy does bear some similarity to the process of political participation. Some members of a society may be directly involved in the political process, much like the athletes on a playing field. Alternatively, they could also be interested observers, like fans at a sports event, who place a degree of importance in the outcome of the event and wish to follow the activities at close range. On the other hand, regardless of how many people may be participating, either directly or indirectly, in the game, many more will not attend and view the event as largely immaterial to their lives.

However, politics differs from sports events in at least one very important way: the political activities of a community reflect on and affect every member of society; at times this may even occur without the knowledge of the members themselves. What's more, in a political system the spectators, to varying degrees, decide who wins. So, a number of meaningful questions are raised when considering the implications of political participation: How much participation is expected or permitted in any political system? Who participates, who observes, and who is not involved? What are the effects of citizen participation? In Western democracies, political participation is a right of citizens, but rarely is participation clearly defined.

# The Importance of Political Information and Education

Political socialization does not occur in a vacuum. Rather, individuals—all individuals—are surrounded by different and competing attitudes and desires in any political system. However, the prevailing attitudes and beliefs that emerge as fundamental to our collective political values represent the socialization process. In our families, our schools, our social groups, and among our peers and friends, we are introduced to a variety of attitudes and dispositions. How we respond to them often varies. For example, we might not agree with family members about who to support in a municipal election, based on our different views of the major issues and how candidates respond to the issues. On the other hand, some of these attitudes and dispositions may be acceptable to almost everyone in one society, but not another. For instance, it is arguable that a dominant political value in Canadian society is the importance of human rights based on the rights and privileges of the individual. Other countries, such as China, place a different emphasis on rights; in this case, China recognizes the importance of the political community or group over that of the individual. So, it is not simply a case of one country valuing rights more than the other, but a question of different values. In any case, the issue of rights brings to light the importance of how information is presented to us, and the process through which we come to agree with some information, and disagree with others. Political participation, then, is an educational process that does not end. We are constantly educated in the process of our political system, and whether we agree with our system, we nonetheless form opinions and beliefs based on what information is presented to us.

In the broadest possible terms, a **political system** is a mechanism that facilitates the process of decision-making (see Fig. 4.1). In 1953 David Easton was the first political scientist who emphasized that the political process is contained in a system of information-gathering, decision-making, implementation, and responses. The political system model put forth by analysts such as Easton suggests that **inputs** represent information that enters the system (either from sources within, or outside of, the political system, or from outside of the system). Inputs constitute the demands placed on a political community. The political system responds to these inputs based on the existing system of analysis, investigation, options, and decision-making housed in the government of the system itself (sometimes called the **throughput**). Final decisions are referred to as the **outputs** of the political process. In turn, the outputs actually become part of the inputs in other aspects of the political system, as the final decisions made by political authorities have broad implications for other political actors. This process of decision-making is part of the process of political socialization.

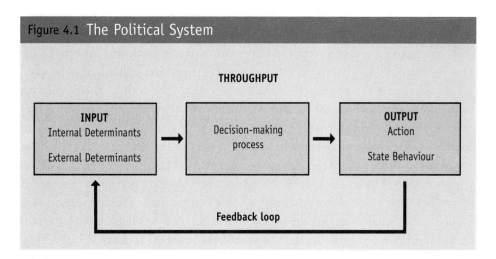

**Figure 4.1** The Political System

"Inputs," "throughputs," and "outputs," however, only demonstrate a rather rudimentary model of the real system of political education and socialization that takes place within society. In fact, we are constantly faced with opposing information within political communities, and unanimity rarely, if ever, exists. In reality, political actors may place a different degree of importance on certain activities, or view other actions as more crucial, depending on their individual perspective and viewpoint. If you think back to the introductory chapter of this book, you will recognize that this is the nature of politics—settling dissent and coming to terms over disagreements. Numerous actors are all responsible for decision-making within a society—whether they are formal members of a government system or informal participants in the process (such as interest group personnel, media representatives, political party officials, and academics). These many different groups, which are made up of all those members of a social group responsible for, or influencing, the political "approach" of the government, together form what is known as the **political community**.

But the "approach" of any government will be interpreted and construed diversely by different observers. Each of us, of course, has our own view of our environment and the world, despite the influence the process of political socialization may have on us. This is part of how we view customary behaviour in our system—our **normative view** of the world. Individuals may have a different view or opinion of what the approach of government ought to be (tax cuts? social spending? deficit reduction?), or perhaps how the approach should be changed. The focus of a political community therefore is shaped to a large degree by the beliefs and attitudes of its members, resulting in what has come to be called the political "culture" of communities.

Further, the level and significance of participation of members of any political community is a function of the information that is made available to them. Having accurate and balanced information is crucial for individual citizens to accurately assess the approach of their government, as well as their opinions of how this approach might be altered. But the process of people getting information about their government's policies is not "participation." As any good teacher will tell you, students will not learn well unless they are integrated in the material being taught. Students are involved in class discussion, they write papers and tests in which they assess issues and themes, and they are required to present their views and opinion of what is being taught. Yet, education also involves a mutual relationship between teacher and student; otherwise students could not possibly "learn" the material presented to them.

Similarly, the process of "receiving" information in society, from newspapers, political leaders, television, the Internet, or from discussions with friends and family, is not by itself political socialization. Socialization implies a relationship with others, and cannot be achieved if individuals do not participate. Participation operates on many levels, from simply forming an opinion on an issue or approach, to becoming directly involved, whether through standing for election, voting, political protest, or joining a lobby group. Receiving information, then, is not participation, because it is not truly mutual. Individuals must have a course to provide feedback, and a role to play in the decision-making process. Preventing citizens from presenting their view or becoming involved in the process violates individuals' right to affect, and concern themselves with, their political system.

One form of violation of citizen participation is the misrepresentation of information to citizens in an effort to persuade them that the approach a government is taking serves the public interest. Examples of this tactic include public canvassing intended to persuade people to agree with an "authority's" recommendations on an issue of public works, such as building roads, or publicity campaigns to influence public opinion on government initiatives, such as constitutional changes. These are examples of one-way discussions where officials educate, persuade, and advise the citizens. There is no real exchange of ideas or shared action.

Often, however, governments will refer to citizens for input on a particular issue, which permits them to play a role in the decision-making process. This input may come from polling results, political forums, official hearings, or the ever-popular "town hall" meeting that brings together public officials and citizens. Input from citizens, either as individuals or in groups, is an important way for governments to "legitimize" their decisions.

In a more organized version of citizen participation, governments will often officially work more with groups in an "associative" manner, sharing authority and control. Examples of associative relationships include joint policy boards and planning committees that include both private citizens and public officials. Importantly, the associative model will only work when citizens and private groups have established themselves into clear and informed assemblies. Furthermore, associative relationships are only as effective as the groups that are involved, so non-government officials will often be chosen based on their ability to truly contribute a particular perspective to the political process. These groups will often hire their own authorities on the issues to gather and dispense all important information.

In the rarest of cases, decisions are made by citizens, and not by public officials. Referendums, for instance, occur in circumstances where decision-makers place such importance on constituent involvement that they turn the decision-making authority over to the public. However, we can plainly see why it would not be workable to pass authority over to the public on all issues.

One reason why giving authority to the public on issues is unconventional in representative democracies has to do with the term "representative." Participation in the political process, after all, is not separated from political representation. Officials chosen by constituents are extensions of the people's expression. Elected representatives (members of parliament, congress, or other government bodies) are given the responsibility to make decisions on behalf of the people based on their office, political affiliation, personal intuition, and know-how.

Representation in the political process is a prominent element in any political system. Perspectives on the role played by the political representative vary, and have a long lineage. Fundamentally, the main issue of contention is the degree of "freedom" that elected officials have—or should have—in their capacity as constituent representatives. On the one hand is the argument that representatives ought to do just that: represent the views of their constituents, even if that means disagreeing with what their party leadership or administration would like them to do. The French philosopher Jean-Jacques Rousseau, for instance, argued that the political representative's primary role is to act on behalf of the voters; this would be the case, Rousseau argued, even if the wishes of the constituency were at odds with the feelings or disposition of the legislator. On the other hand, there are those who argue that the role of an elected official is a professional position, like any other, and that the decisions of the legislator ought to be left to the legislator him or herself. The underlying argument is twofold: first, we should not expect everyone in civil society to become fully acquainted with the inner workings or policies or government. After all, doctors, lawyers, construction workers, and the rest of us have our own jobs to do in society, and legislators, who are elected to act on behalf of the voters, should do just that. Second, this argument suggests that the electors might not know what is best for them, and may act impulsively, without due regard for the potential implications of a particular policy. Thus, legislators, whose job it is to know about and deliberate on such decisions, must be allowed to act independently, it is argued. The English philosopher Edmund Burke was one proponent of this view. For more on both Rousseau and Burke, see Chapter 2.

In fact, though, legislators today act neither completely on the whim of their constituents, nor on their own behalf. Politicians are indeed professional, and like any professional, they certainly recognize the importance of a balanced approach: seeking advice and input where necessary, and using their own judgment as well.

As we said previously, political participation operates on several levels. Individuals, for instance, may become involved in the activities of their political units directly, through protest, voting in elections, attending political conventions or seminars, or some other activity. Interest groups, political parties, and non-governmental organizations are examples of group behaviour affecting the political process. States and international organizations (both governmental and non-governmental) represent other forms of participatory bodies in the political process.

# Political Culture

Though we may not be fully aware of it, there is a set of attitudes, beliefs, and values that underpins any political system. These attitudes, beliefs, and values may come in a variety of forms—religious, cultural, linguistic, or class-based— but they all contribute to our general outlook as citizens regarding our political system and our relations with each other and the rest of the world. These attitudes, beliefs, and values are referred to as our **political culture**. Our political culture—any political culture—is an integral part of the process of political socialization. Think about the views you might have about the role of your government, and your rights and freedoms that are constitutionally guaranteed as part of your citizenship. These rights and freedoms allow you and others to freely group with others, to express your views without persecution, to pursue your own religious beliefs, and to have an open and free system of information and communication. Now imagine life in an authoritarian state where these rights and freedoms are not reality. The political culture of an authoritarian state will be necessarily different than your own, largely because of the type of system in which the culture exists. Political culture, then, is an important element of our community, our tradition, and our identity as citizens.

Political culture is also activated by and influences political activities. For instance, the relative freedom of the media, the role of interest groups and political action committees, the influence of parties, collective bargaining among unions and corporations, and the relationship between constituents and elected officials are all seriously affected by the prevailing political culture in a political system. Just as different political systems exist, whether they are liberal democracies or authoritarian states, presidential or parliamentary systems, federations or unitary countries, capitalist or command economies, so does a distinctive political culture in every state that affects the desires and hopes of its citizens. The North American Free Trade Agreement (NAFTA), the future for Quebec in the federation, and aboriginal rights and land agreements are examples of contentious areas of public policy in Canada. But most issues of governmental policy in Canada are not so contentious because of the prevailing political culture in Canadian society that concedes a legitimate role to the federal government in decision- and policy-making.

## Public Opinion

Participation can also mean expressing an opinion in public discourse. This is a way for citizens to proclaim their views regarding the activities of their government in a sanctioned and legitimate manner. Often, our public opinions

The process of liberalization of Canada's trade has brought with it costs as well as benefits. Some national economic actors have complained that they are unable to compete in a completely liberalized Canadian economy and thus will be forced out of existence by foreign competition. In the 1990s the magazine industry has been at the centre of a controversy as free trade has changed established practices. Until the North American Free Trade Agreement (NAFTA) the Canadian government insisted that some US magazines (such as *Sports Illustrated*) create separate versions of their product for the Canadian market, including content on Canada. Under NAFTA rules, this form of restriction was challenged, so that US magazines can be sold in their original forms, without sensitivity to Canadian content. This is seen by some as an attack on Canadian culture, and there are fears that Canadians' sense of distinctiveness will be diminished.

might seem to be so straight-forward and accepted that we do not even recognize them as opinion. For instance, our attitudes towards our system of tolerance, economic openness, and free expression may simply be seen as accepted attitudes regarding our relations with our government, but they are actually part of the opinion we hold about our entire political system. Our public opinion might be quite constant, depending on the issues involved. On the other hand, our opinions might be changing, depending on our age, where we live in the country, our economic status, or level of education. Thus, someone who is recently unemployed will no doubt form a very different opinion regarding job creation, benefits, and unemployment benefits than they would when they were employed.

Public opinion is also influenced by the strength of the views held.

Religious beliefs, for instance, are a strong indicator of public opinion, which is why pollsters and public opinion firms ask respondents to indicate their religion, to identify the views held. Attitudes towards issues such as abortion and church schools, for example, are heavily influenced by the relative strength of the individual's religious views and beliefs. Other issues, such as public works projects and the creation of national parks, are not likely to be affected by the intense opinion that influences other issues.

## Media and Political Systems

Perhaps the most pervasive information provider in our modern society is the media. In 1993, when American Navy SEALs (Sea, Air, Land) forces landed on the beaches of Somalia as part of the international peace-building force, they were met not by other soldiers, or even by Somalis, but rather by members of the American media. CNN, ABC, NBC, and other major media outlets had news crews on the beaches waiting for the SEALs to land. What transpired was a surreal episode of American troops carrying out their peacekeeping role while being photographed and filmed by cameras, and questioned by reporters at the scene.

The modern media has become the most organized purveyor of information in our society. Twenty-four hour news channels, international correspondents, and a seemingly endless barrage of newscasts, print media, and Internet dispatches allow us, as ordinary citizens, a view of the world that was simply not available to previous generations.

But with the advent of all this information, there are drawbacks. News reporting, like any other information outlet, is competitive. It is expensive for media organizations to maintain correspondents around the world, and to employ the technicians and professionals to produce and transmit the broadcasts. News reporting requires advertising revenue, and revenue operates in a very aggressive market, with several options available. As a result, news organizations must constantly be aware of the share of viewers, listeners, or readers that they attract, in order to lure advertisers and their funds. Thus, newscasts are often not as informative or as inclusive as they might be. In order to capitalize on a relatively small market, given the number of media outlets offered to potential viewers, listeners, and readers, news organizations "package" their news much like a network television program in order to lure and captivate an audience. This means that some stories, and particularly those deemed uninteresting or tedious, are given short shrift, while even the most riveting issues of the day are bundled into a summary piece with titles, graphics, and main players.

Dealing with the media also is a two-way street. Political decision-makers take note of what is being reported in newspapers, television, and on the radio in order to recognize and anticipate the concerns of citizens. And, by making decisions about what gets reported principally, what is left to the margins, and what is not reported at all, news organizations actually affect the course of public debate and participation in society. We citizens, after all, can only respond to what we hear about.

The modern media represents an exceptionally important actor in our modern political systems. News organizations contribute to the substance of public debate, influence the story line in which the story is reported and, ultimately, give us the opportunity, however limited, to learn about events in our nation and abroad that previous generations would not have had access to.

Box 4.2

## Gender and Employment

Gender, as we have already seen, refers to the roles performed by men and women in society and the economy. It has a very real impact on the kinds of jobs men and women do. As you can see from the chart below, while the largest source of employment in Canada in 1997 for both men and women was the services sector, it employed a larger percentage of women than men. One of the reasons for this is that the services sector tends to offer more flexible hours of work, but also offers more part-time labour, which makes it more accessible to women who also perform functions as homemakers and primary caregivers. It also means that women tend to earn less than men (see Box 4.3).

**Employment by Gender and Sector**

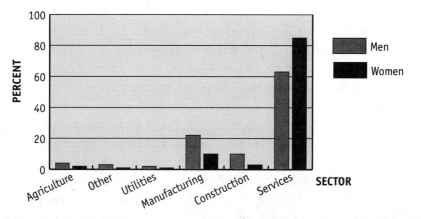

Source: Statistics Canada, *1999 Canada Year Book*, Catalogue no. 71F0004-xcb.

# Electoral Systems

More than any other form of political participation, **elections** are the most direct forum through which individuals in the political system may affect the decisions made for society as a whole. Elections decide who will be given the authority to make decisions on behalf of the entire political grouping. Since it would be impossible for every member of a society to be a direct part of the decision-making process (the life of a politician is, after all, a full-time job), indirectly having one's opinion and position defended and articulated by an elected representative creates what is referred to as **indirect democracy**.

In modern liberal democracies such as Canada, most citizens who have reached the age of majority (adults) take part in an array of elections. Elections represent that aspect of the voter-government relationship where individual citizens have the opportunity to choose politicians that best meet their interests and preferences. Although the most direct way that we might affect the political system, electoral systems do not come without conditions. Every electoral system, whatever its composition, sets out formal restrictions on this choice, indicating who may vote and through what means.

Josh Beutel, ATLANToonS

It is notable that electoral systems, though generally considered open and liberal today, were once highly restrictive. Most conspicuously, the right to vote (**suffrage**) was not always an open affair. Historical systems discriminated based on gender (usually only males were allowed to vote), on age (often only certain age groups were given the right), economic status (requiring, for instance, individuals to be employed or own land, or other valuable resources), or even literacy (thereby eliminating people who were not educated from the class of voters). These restrictions were slowly relaxed over time, but for women and some minority groups, it was still impossible to partake in the voting process. Some provinces excluded Native Canadians and some ethnic groups from voting as recently as the early 1960s, and women were only given the right to vote in Quebec in 1940, and in Newfoundland in 1948. On the other side of the coin, restrictions were put in place governing who could legally run for election. Most of the time the laws regulating who was allowed to vote also pertained to who was allowed to stand for election; often the laws surrounding election candidacy were more stringent than those for voting.

Every country also has its own laws applying to candidates who run in constituencies. Membership in political parties in some countries governs whether an individual is permitted to stand for election; if he or she is not a member of a party, they may not be allowed to run. On the other hand, states such as Canada do not have party requirements, so **independents** may run in elections.

Elections take place in constituencies, the geographical units in which the voters are separated and within which candidates compete for votes. Most political systems try to create an equitable system of **constituencies** to accurately match where the majority of the population lives, thereby giving more elected representatives to densely populated areas (cities), and fewer to sparsely populated regions (rural ridings). Electoral systems furthermore set out the rules regarding where voting occurs, who is given authority in ridings, and for ballot collection, ballot counting, **enumeration** (surveying who lives in the riding), and how votes are actually converted into seats.

## Types of Electoral Systems

There are two main systems of voting that allow for the conversion of votes into seats. The **simple plurality** system, used in Canadian elections, involves the election of the individual who obtains the greatest number of votes. Also called the **first-past-the-post** system, it is compared to a horse race, where the winner is simply the first one to cross the finish post. The major, and common, result of a simple plurality system is the election of a **minority government**,

## Gender and Earnings

Box 4.3

One of the key goals for feminism, and one of the most interesting areas of research for gender analysts, is to compare the level of income of men and women throughout the economy. We often assume that men and women earn about the same amount of money. But when we look at the figures, we see a surprisingly high differential. Although the earnings ratio between men and women has improved since the 1950s (when it was 59.7%), even in the late 1990s women in full-time work only earned less than 75 percent of their male co-workers. This has been a source of great dissatisfaction among female workers, and of calls for change in labour legislation.

**Earnings by Gender**

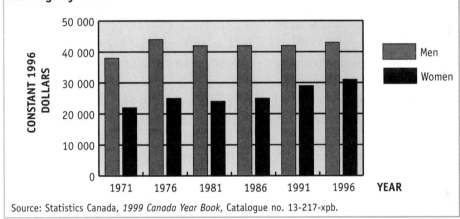

Source: Statistics Canada, *1999 Canada Year Book*, Catalogue no. 13-217-xpb.

where the party that receives the most number of seats might still not win a majority (more than 50 percent) simply as a result of the number of parties involved. The party that wins the "most" seats, then, might not win the "majority" of support. Alternatively, it is quite possible for a party to receive a majority of seats (more than 50 percent) but not more than 50 percent of the overall vote, or the majority of the vote. In this case, though the governing party may in fact be in a majority situation, it cannot say that it drew the majority of votes. Finally, a winning and majority government might not receive any seats at all in certain regions, given the peculiarities of individual riding preferences. For instance, in the Canadian federal election of 1997, the dominant party in Quebec was the Bloc Quebecois, and in Alberta, the dominant party was Reform. In both cases, these parties won both a majority of votes, and seats, yet neither formed the federal government; that title went to the Liberal party. These two parties, then, have been referred to as **regional parties** due to their strong provincial strength, but weak national presence.

The other basic type of electoral system is called **proportional representation,** where seats are designated according to the parties' popular vote. These systems use the country as a whole in order to determine proportions between votes allotted for all the parties. The percentage of party vote, then, counts across the entire nation. Proportional representation may also use a preferential ballot system, or a "two-stage" election. In this case, electors vote for candidates, and also for parties. This form of electoral system is used in Israel, France, Germany, Australia, and Ireland.

Proportional representation is a better assessment of the likes and dislikes of voters. It also makes room for minor parties that otherwise would be ignored or eliminated in a simple plurality system of voting. On the other hand, proportional representation downgrades the relationship constituents have with their individual representatives because so much in the election rides on the weight and influence of the parties involved. Yet proportional representation—despite its flaws—is often used as an example of what the Canadian system of elections might aspire to in an effort to overcome the problems associated with the simple plurality system.

No doubt the most critical problem facing election systems today is voter apathy. Apathetic individuals simply decide not to vote, or even bother to follow the election process, because they believe that elections do not affect or influence them. In some countries, like the United States, voter turnout is a major challenge, where it is considered a "good" turnout if over half of registered eligible voters actually cast a ballot. It is easy in modern society to discard the role that casting a ballot plays in our systems of government; the multitude of issues facing individual citizens often seem overwhelming, and the real role that we might play in the political process frequently seems small indeed.

Still, voting is an essential part of living in a liberal democracy. Studies show us that voting preference, and the tendency to vote itself, is highly determined by one's position in society, level of education, family background, and chosen profession. But aside from the issues revolving around actually getting individuals out to vote, there are a host of concerns about awareness of issues and platforms taken by the candidates themselves. In an environment where candidates recognize that they will only be given a short sound-byte in the media, and where voters are literally inundated with information, it is difficult, if not impossible, to truly have a meaningful discourse about the issues or on the stands taken by candidates.

As a result, the process of electioneering in modern society takes on a paradoxical dimension: candidates reduce what they say into digestible commen-

## An Aging Population

Box 4.4

Canada, like many other developed nations, faces a problem in the twenty-first century: its people are getting older. As birth rates drop and lifestyles and healthcare improve, Canadians as a nation are gradually getting older. As you can see from the chart below, the percentage of people of working age declined between 1976 and 1996, and that trend will continue. This will have a large impact on the economy. First, fewer people will be productively participating, and more people will be using either private or public pensions to pay for their everyday needs. Secondly, more people will be using the healthcare services provided by the government, while fewer people will be paying taxes to support the system. Canada, then, faces a dilemma. One of the potential solutions is to increase levels of immigration, particularly of young people and those in the 18–39 age bracket who are considering having children.

**Canada's Population by Age Group, 1976-1996**

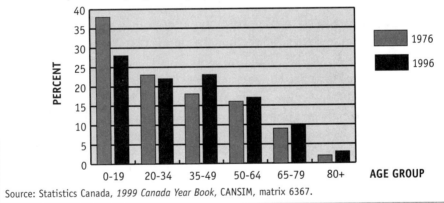

Source: Statistics Canada, *1999 Canada Year Book*, CANSIM, matrix 6367.

tary and pursue marketing strategies to appeal to voters. Voters, on the other hand, complain of not getting the information they need, but also of not having the time to absorb what is presented to them! Increasingly, elections become rather superficial contests that focus on personal qualities and presence, rather than issues, platforms, and policies.

## Political Parties

Unlike interest groups, political parties are first and foremost absorbed with the attempt to control government through the election of members of their group. While interest groups may be concerned with a particular issue or sector of a political system, the function of political parties is to present a clear perspective on how a political system is to be administered. In brief, political parties are organized groups that place members as candidates for election with the expressed goal of governing the political system.

Earlier in this chapter we discussed suffrage, or the process of gaining the right to vote. The rise of political parties was directly related to suffrage, since the growing number of groups of people being given the right to vote coincided with the need to organize the interests of these new voters in some institution. Parties, then, developed as a result of the need to represent the views of different sectors of public interest.

For many voters, political parties seem to emerge only when there is an election. This is not surprising, given that political parties first and foremost exist to coordinate and organize the opinions of party groups in a formal and institutional manner. However, parties do have a broader role in the political process. Aside from their organizational role in society, they also have a direct role to play in the legislative setting. Parties allow for the grouping of elected members into coherent clusters, and provide for governmental direction, as well as opposition in the daily activities of the legislature.

Parties are created and operate based on a set of beliefs or attitudes; these are referred to as **ideologies**, or the underlying ideas for a political and economic system. And, just like electoral systems, or as we will see regarding interest groups, political parties and their level of influence in society and government vary from country to country. In many states in the international system, for instance, only one political party is allowed to form the government. These are called **one-party systems**. Most of the former communist systems that existed under the Soviet era are representative of this form of government. There are still examples of one-party states today—Cuba, North Korea, Iraq, and Myanmar are all illustrations of this form.

In liberal democracies, on the other hand, political parties are permitted to compete with one another for support from the electorate. These are referred to as competitive party systems, and there are a number of varieties. These systems may be composed of two competing parties—a two-party system, or more than two—a multiparty system.

However, these classifications tend to be alterable, depending on the prevailing interests in society. The United States, for example, is often described as a two-party system, but in recent years the relative influence of the traditional parties—the Republicans and the Democrats—has been challenged by the upstart Reform Party (not to be confused with the Reform Party of Canada, which is a separate party). Similarly, the United Kingdom is often characterized as a two-party system, dominated by the Labour and Conservative parties. Yet this portrayal does not take into account the role of many other parties, including the influential Scottish National Party, or the Liberal Democratic party. There is no guarantee, after all, that either of these two parties, or the Reform Party in the United States will not gain sufficient influence and strength in their respective nations to seriously contest the term "two-party system" in those countries.

In a similar vein, the role and influence of some parties in multiparty states is not always clear. In Canada, for instance, there are several significant political parties—the Liberals, New Democratic Party, Reform, Bloc Quebecois, and the Progressive Conservatives. Yet only two of these—the Liberals and Progressive Conservatives—have actually formed a federal government. Should this mean that the other parties are not as significant? Should the fact that the New Democratic Party has formed provincial governments, but not a federal government, give that party a different level in the Canadian party system? In fact, developments in the Canadian political party system are really no different than in any other state. Political parties tend to rise and fall in their level of support among the public based on a variety of societal concerns, and the major issues in the civic debate.

There are several types of political parties. **Cadre parties** refer to those parties that are created and directed by a small elite group, and tend to control much power within legislatures. The history of cadre parties extends back to the initial process of suffrage, as powerful elites sought to maintain the control over government that they stood to lose with the influx of many more voters in the political system. By forming parties that they controlled, the relative influence of huge masses of voters in society was offset by the continuing dominant role played by elites in party organization. **Mass parties**, on the other hand, were formed partly to combat the influence that cadre parties had in government. Mass parties are organized in society at large, rather than within government. They exhibit a large public influence by placing a great degree of power in the membership, rather than in the hands of a small minority elite. Militia parties are a third example, and are often found in military governments or communist systems. These party types have an extremely centralized leadership system, and place great requirements on members. **Militia parties** often are led by martial leaders, and are frequently found in one-party systems.

Political parties have many prominent functions in society. Parties create a link between government and the people, since government members are usually members of parties that also include private citizen participation. Therefore, in theory at least, party leaders and government members will be attentive to the concerns of other members of the party. Parties are also a way of arranging and categorizing interests in society, as individuals that choose to join—or at least support—a party are essentially making an ideological choice, as well. The level of party support, then, is an indicator of how the electorate feels about the role of government in society, and the approach that administrations should take. In a more functional way, parties are a basic way for private citizens, even if they do not support a party at large, to register their backing for individual potential representatives. Related to this is the role that political parties play in the education and instruction of future politicians and political actors. As institutions, parties embody established structures that might be used to train party workers and upcoming leaders. Once parties are elected to power, they are crucial in creating and upholding the direction, approach, and organization of government. In this way, parties determine not just the immediate bearing for an administration, but also a "template" for future ones, and future supporters.

## Interest Groups

So far in this section, we have discussed the more formal and direct links that people might have to government—voting and political party involvement. There are other ways that individuals may affect the process of decision-making in their societies. One of these examples is the role played by **interest groups**. Increasingly in our society, interest groups affect decision-making and the "approach" taken by government. In many ways, interest groups are similar in their effect to political parties; for that reason, this section of the chapter will examine both. However, interest groups may be distinguished from political parties in that they are not concerned with controlling who runs for election as representatives of certain parties. Rather, interest groups are primarily concerned with influencing the decision-making process, though not through direct means, as politicians may. Therefore, interest groups are an integral part of the "political community" of policy-makers discussed earlier in this chapter.

Interest groups are also called **pressure groups**, or **political action committees** (PACs). These groups seek to either alter or maintain the approach of government without taking a formal role in elections or seeking an official capacity in government. Just as political parties differ from country to country, interest groups have varying degrees of importance depending on the country in which they exist. In some countries, like Japan, interest groups are not usually given a substantial role in decision-making by government leaders. Though there may be some attention paid to the concerns raised by the groups, the more traditional form of government in that country—which places a high degree of importance on the customary and formal delineation of authority in society—limits the influence that these groups might have. In the Japanese decision-making process, greater attention and value is placed on the opinions and interests of formal corporate and business interests in Japan (more attention is given to this in Chapter 5). On the other hand, various other countries, such as the United States, place such high relevance on the role played by interest groups in the decision-making process that there are even laws regulating the formal role that the groups might have in the pattern of government-society relations.

There are a number of different types of interest groups. Political action committees are conglomerations of several groups that have combined their resources to more effectively influence the decision-making process. Associational and non-associational interest groups, respectively, are closely related to, or not connected with, particular political objectives. Ad hoc interest groups are called anomic interest groups, and do not have a standard organized composition. Instead, these groups are formed to deal with short-term issues and concerns.

Interest groups attempt to convey their point of view primarily through **lobbying**, which refers to those activities undertaken by groups in order to get their perspective and views across to political decision-makers: petitions, meetings, hearings, demonstrations, and so forth. Often, interest groups will hire professional "lobbyists" whose job it is to carry on these activities on behalf of the group. Later in this chapter we will return to the issue of lobbying, and the important function it performs in the articulation of citizen views in government decision-making.

There are competing views regarding the presence and role of interest groups in liberal democracies. Interest groups, it must be kept in mind, are not inclusive; that is to say, they do not represent the views of all, or even a majority, of citizens. Rather, they are in place to bring attention to concerns that some sectors of the public find important. This tends to draw criticism from those who view interest groups as the voice of an elite in society, and not representative of all. Not all groups in society, after all, have the means or are capable of forming organized groups and hiring lobbyists to try to alter the approach of government. So, there are those who view interest groups as corrupting the true purpose of democracy, which is to represent and account for the views of all.

Yet there are those who consider interest groups to be an integral part of democratic society. They argue that there are not enough formal avenues for individual citizens to vocalize their concerns or views in the governmental process. Voting is a relatively infrequent event, and does not allow citizens to do anything more than simply choose a representative. And joining a political party may not be satisfactory for others. According to this view, then, interest groups allow for a more informal role in the approach of government. Those who view interest groups as a positive force in society argue that true democracy is pluralist, where a number of groups and concerns are expressed; interest groups, then, are a functional and indispensable arena for citizen action.

To take the view of this latter group (those that consider interest groups as essential in democracies), let us assess the broader function of interest groups a step further. Whereas it might be true that interest groups are created to deal with the particular concerns of members of the group, we should recognize that interest groups play a bigger purpose in society. Interest groups are a basic means of tying the function of government to that of groups in society. In this way, interest groups are a "bond" between the formal and informal segments of our society that influence the approach of our political systems. Interest groups provide a "feedback" loop for government, as they funnel information back to their members and the public at large. Furthermore, given their level of expertise, these groups provide essential information to decision-makers themselves. Interest groups can be particularly important for members of the public service, who are responsible for accounting for the views of the public, and providing all necessary information to decision-makers in the legislature and the executive.

When we stop to consider the real impact interest groups have on the political process, substantial contrasts to voting behaviour and political party involvement emerge. Unlike the immediate consequence that voting or parties demonstrate in the political domain, interest group influence is not as easy to measure. There are, after all, many different interest groups competing for attention and influence, and the opinions that they put forward may be changed substantially by the time governments sit down to make decisions. However, there are some factors that help define the relative success and sway that these groups have. First, if the opinion of the group tends to match that of government in some way, the level of importance placed on the group will rise. Second, an interest group will have more influence if there is an absence of a real contending perspective. Finally, the stability of the group is important. Groups that have experienced lobbyists, plentiful resources, and an organized structure are more likely to have the ear of government at any level.

In sum, interest groups are one of the most important means of real influence that citizen groups have in the governmental process. Interest groups are becoming increasingly influential in democratic societies, largely as a result of their level of organization, as well as the considerable expertise and substance that they bring to the process itself.

## Campaign Contributions

One area in which private interests seek to influence the political process is through their financial contributions to electoral campaigns. By the late twentieth century successful campaigning had become an incredibly expensive endeavour, requiring television, radio and newspaper advertising, extensive travel, and appearances at high profile events by the candidate to ensure the widest possible media exposure. Because of the high costs of election campaigning, candidates seek contributions from a diverse array of sources, both from individuals and from groups, as well as from corporations. These contributions raise the spectre of wealthy groups or individuals buying political favours in exchange for substantial contributions to the campaign coffers. Of course such a trade-off is vigorously denied by both politicians and those who contribute to their campaigns, arguing that contributions merely reflect the desire of a particular group or individual to see a candidate (re-)elected.

Because of this problem many countries have put in place legislation that limits the amount of money an individual or group can contribute to a campaign, and demands transparency and accurate and detailed accounting of all contributions and spending. In other countries the state provides financing to political parties proportional to the number of candidates they intend to run and provided they achieve a certain minimum percentage of the popular vote. Canada's system, embodied in the Elections Expenses Act and the Canada Elections Act, provides state subsidies for candidates who achieve 15 percent of votes and allows candidates to raise private funds, but places limits on total spending and requires candidates to provide detailed accounts of all monies received and spent. These regulations came into operation in response to problems experienced by political parties in generating enough funding and also public outrage over scandals involving just the kind of influence-buying behaviour discussed above.

Nonetheless, elections provide an opportune moment for private interest groups and corporations to buy the support of candidates. Any aspiring officeholder who intends to seek re-election at some time in the future will be tempted to exchange political support for sizeable campaign contributions.

Though this is hardly the rule in the political systems of most democratic states, it remains a serious concern.

One way in which some interest groups circumvent limits on contributions is to organize their own campaigns on behalf of a candidate, buying press space or media time in which they express their support for an individual, independent of the official campaign. Some such television, radio, or news-paper commercials do not even feature the name of the candidate in question, choosing instead to negatively influence the public against the opposing can-didate(s). Because such media exposure is often the most expensive element of an election campaign, doubts must also be raised about the legitimacy or eth-ical nature of such assistance.

An important distinction to be made in the area of election campaign con-tributions is that between "soft money" and "hard money." The former refers to funds given to the party as a general, or non-specific contribution, whereas the latter refers to monies donated to the party or candidate specifically for the purposes of fighting an election campaign. This distinction has come to be of particular importance in recent years in the United States, and it has become clear that the line between the two kinds of donation is very often blurred, a problem that makes the issue of campaign financing that much more complex.

# The Participation of Economic Actors in the Decision-Making Process

In this section we will discuss the interaction between political authority and private economic actors in the formation of policy. An understanding of this interaction is vitally important if we are to get a comprehensive grasp of the dynamics of political participation and of the policy process itself. Governments clearly need the involvement of non-state economic actors, such as corporations, business associations, and labour unions if they are to make policies that are not only politically acceptable to key groups, but also func-tionally viable.

In contemporary political systems in Europe and North America, govern-ments and bureaucracies do not simply formulate their economic policy in a vacuum. Instead there is an often intense system of consultation and collabo-ration with important economic interests and actors within the nation. Governments rely on the expertise of private economic actors so that policies can be designed and implemented so as to be more efficient, and more broadly accepted. Such consultation takes place in all levels of government and with all areas of economic policy-making, both macro and micro. In Canada this is most clearly seen in industry consultations in the area of regulation. In the banking industry, for example, banks are closely consulted before any new regulations affecting their activities are applied. This can, of course, become a problem if the industry concerned attempts to skew regulation so that it increases profitability yet sacrifices other goods such as safety and soundness, or public welfare. In areas such as finance, or high-technology industries, there is often a serious inequality in the level of expertise relevant to regulation between policy-makers and industry representatives. This can make it extremely difficult for governments to design efficient policies without the help of the actors they seek to regulate. In this case concerns can be raised about the independence of government policy-makers and also about the effectiveness of economic policy.

These concerns are particularly important in the area of environmental regulation, where large corporations such as oil companies can afford to hire expensive lawyers and teams of scientists to "prove" that their economic activities will have only a minimal impact on the environment. Because governments rely on information in the policy process, and because specialized information is expensive, such large corporations have an advantage over environmental protection groups in their influence over government.

The issue of expertise in the policy-making process is of particular important in developing countries. There, governments are especially handicapped in their ability to negotiate with corporations because of the extra financial constraints they face. Large multinational corporations in particular are able to dominate the governments of poorer countries in negotiations over investment and regulation because they are able to utilize both the best personnel from that particular country and indeed expert personnel recruited from all over the world.

A final point that must be made here is that different states allow different levels of business and other interest group participation in the policy process. As we have seen, some political systems encourage more citizen participation than others, and the same is true of business involvement. Peter Katzenstein, in a 1978 work entitled *Between Power and Plenty: Foreign Economic Policies of Advanced Industrial States*, examined the domestic political structures of six states and asked how they impacted upon the shape of their foreign economic policies. The key determinant that emerged from the study was that states' foreign economic policies were shaped to a significant degree by the amount of access they allowed major interest groups (most importantly those representing industry, trade, and finance) to the policy-making process. Katzenstein's study found considerable variance between the six states, not just in the amount of access but also in the way that access was organized. Such examinations of the role of economic actors in the policy process remain an integral part of political economy to this day.

## Policy Communities

As should now be clear, policy is not made in a vacuum. Politics and policy-making involve a variety of actors, both within and outside government. If we are to fully understand the ways in which policy is made, particularly in the economic realm, we have to identify the group (or groups) of actors who participate in that process. William Coleman and Grace Skogstad, in their 1990 book, *Policy Communities and Public Policy in Canada*, employed the concept of a **policy community** to understand the making of policy. A policy community can be understood as the collection of actors who have a direct or indirect interest in the issue area. These actors will have different levels of influence over the policy process, but they each play a significant role, even if they do not apply pressure directly to policy-makers.

This useful concept it allows us to identify key actors in political economy, and encourages us to include individuals and groups that we would not normally take into consideration. So in the formation of government policy concerning road safety, we would not only include insurance companies and automobile associations, but also groups such as MADD (Mothers Against Drunk Driving) and, on the other hand, civil liberties action groups.

There is, of course, no natural limit to the size of a policy community or to the kind of actors that get involved. Policy communities are of particular importance in open political systems, but we can also use the idea to examine closed or authoritarian systems. Policy communities exist even within a military dictatorship, as the armed forces governing the country consult with industry and other elites to smooth the business of government.

## Corporatism

A significant challenge for capitalist countries this century has been to avoid direct clashes between what may be seen as, and sometimes are, opposing interests. What makes sense to the owners and controllers of industry may be anathema to those who work in their factories and corporations. The idea of price controls and the minimum wage, for example, will be more popular with the representatives of labour than with producers and employers. Increasing the maximum number of hours to be worked in one week, on the other hand, may be favoured by industry but vigorously opposed by labour unions. Such controversial policies provide ample opportunity for conflict and economic disruption, strikes, or maybe even the departure of private industry to other countries where the business climate is more favourable. It may be preferable, therefore, for government policy to be formulated so as to minimize the level of conflict between opposing interests.

In several countries of Northern Europe and Scandinavia in the 1970s an alliance developed between government, business, and labour which came to be known as **corporatism**. This approach to governance entails close cooperation and coordination between these three sectors, in the expectation that such activity will bring more stability to the political economy and also that it will produce a larger degree of consensus, making economic and social policies more acceptable to important constituencies in society.

## Unions and the Economy

Box 4.5

Canada has a tradition of active trade unions, but their influence is not evenly spread across the economy. Some sectors are dominated by unions, while in others, a majority of workers are not union members. As the following graphic shows, just under 35 percent of all Canadian workers belonged to a union in 1992, but that rate of participation went as high as over 65 percent in the construction sector. The services tend to be less influenced by trade unions, while financial and agricultural workers are extremely unlikely to belong to a union.

**Unionization Rate by Sector**

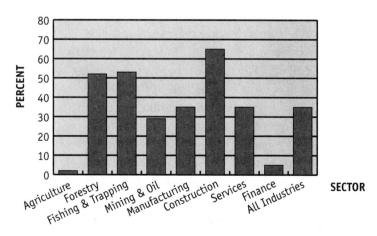

Source: Statistics Canada, *1999 Canada Year Book*, Catalogue no. 71-202.

One of the most powerful arguments in favour of corporatism is that it will include and benefit a broader section of society than more traditional pluralist systems, where elites tend to dominate the policy process. However, that self-same criticism can be levelled against corporatism itself, since selected agencies of business and labour are chosen to represent the views and interests of the wider business and labour communities. There is a tendency for business representatives to favour big business in the demands they place on government, while the representatives of labour have tended to favour the larger, more powerful unions. Perhaps more worrying has been the accusation that both business and labour representatives "climb into bed" with each other and the government, and tend to compromise the interests of those they represent. Of equal concern is the issue of corruption, the danger that the leaders of business and labour will seek individual rather than collective gains, sacrificing the interests of their members in return for personal reward.

In the 1980s and 1990s the corporatist approach to economic and political management fell into disrepute in some European countries, particularly Great Britain. This was largely in response to the feeling that organized labour had gained too much power and was jeopardizing the long-term economic interests of the nation. However, as we shall see in a later chapter, quasi-corporatist arrangements still exist in Japan, and other Asian countries. Indeed, such close cooperation between government, labour, and business has been regarded by many as one of the fundamental reasons for Asian economic success since the 1950s.

## Lobbying

One of the most important and increasingly common ways in which business/interest groups interact with the policy process is through lobbying, where they apply direct pressure to the executive, legislative, and bureaucratic branches of government. The roots of the word "lobbying" are disputed, some arguing that it derives from the hallway of the House of Commons in the British Parliament, where constituents could meet with their representatives and demand their support for legislation. Others have suggested that it came into use in the early nineteenth century with reference to the lobby of either the New York State Capitol building or the Willard Hotel, both places where private citizens and interest groups could directly pressure legislators. Whatever the word's origins, lobbying has become an integral part of the reality of modern politics in democratic and even non-democratic systems.

How is lobbying carried out? First, it can be an activity in which the interested party, either an individual or a group, directly meets with those involved in the policy process and attempts to secure the support of these individuals. Secondly, and increasingly this is the norm, individuals or groups hire as their representative a professional lobbyist who understands their issues and has contacts within the political process. Lobbyists do not always go by the title itself, often preferring to label themselves public relations experts, lawyers, or consultants.

Earlier in this chapter we described information as a crucial element in the area of political participation, since private citizens need access to information so that they can make informed choices. With lobbying the process is reversed. Here, it is the legislator who needs access to information before deciding how she or he will vote on an issue. Similarly, bureaucrats often find themselves under pressure from lobbyists when they are drawing up legislation or deciding how to implement it.

Lobbying has a mixed reputation. First, it can be considered a vital part of the policy process, ensuring the representation of diverse views, and that relevant information is taken into account in decision-making. On the other hand, lobbying can be seen as an example of the undue influence of some groups at the expense of others, where well-organized, often wealthy or economically powerful groups buy the support of influential members of the policy process.

A key word here is expense. Lobbying is not a cheap business, and groups may pay upwards of tens of thousands of dollars to engage the services of a professional lobbyist for one issue. Some large corporations keep a lobbying firm on contract full-time, so that the firm's interests are continually represented in the political process, an enterprise which can cost them hundreds of thousands of dollars annually. This expense puts lobbying out of the financial reach of most individuals and groups in society, and thus we have to ask whether or not lobbying is truly compatible with the pursuit of democracy in modern political systems. Does lobbying allow certain groups to have a disproportionately high level of influence over the political process? Or is this simply the best way for decision-makers to take the views of interested parties into account? Here we have to ask whether political favours are being bought in exchange for material rewards, either financial or in kind. If so, then lobbying certainly crosses the line between acceptable and unacceptable behaviour. But what about the personal relationships that are built up between lobbyists on the one hand, and legislators, bureaucrats, and members of the executive branch on the other? Does this contravene the principles of democracy? Can lobbying be seen as a mere extension of corporate hospitality activities, where one corporation courts another, offering tickets to sporting and cultural events in an attempt to secure a business contract? Or do we have to draw a distinction between the world of business and the world of politics?

Directly related to these questions is the issue of the "revolving door" between the world of politics and lobbying. Insiders who have learned the inside workings of a national political system and who have built up a network of contacts are in great demand with professional lobbying, consulting, or public relations firms. Their influence is an invaluable addition to the tools used by consulting firms in the struggle to be heard in the policy process. In addition, governments (and certainly political parties) can benefit from the expertise of individuals who have experience in the world of public relations and communications. Doubts can be raised about the benefits of such a revolving door, however. Is inside knowledge of government business a commodity that should be traded like any other form of specialized knowledge? Or is it something different, special, because it confers such an advantage on those who can pay for it?

One last point about lobbying that ought to be made clear is that governments employ lobbyists themselves. This occurs when authorities at one level seek to influence policies at another—for example, municipal or provincial governments seeking to influence federal policy. Perhaps even more important is national governments contracting lobbyists to represent their interests in another country. Most commonly this occurs when foreign governments seek to influence policy in the United States, but the phenomenon exists around the world, with foreign governments taking advantage of local expertise to lobby the national government. A very important example of such lobbying took place in the early 1990s when the Mexican government employed Washington-based lobbyists to secure congressional approval for the North American Free Trade Agreement.

## Summary

This chapter has introduced you to the issues surrounding political participation, the level of politics that involves all citizens. We are all socialized in a particular political culture that embodies certain values and ideals about politics. Our attitudes and disposition to the world of politics is shaped by the socialization process of our society, the exposure to family, community, institutions, government, and the media. In addition, you were introduced to various methods and avenues of political participation, including types of electoral systems and political representation. Finally, this chapter presented interest groups and political parties as two contrasting and yet complementary methods of aggregating individual interests and concerns into large public forums. While political parties are primarily created in order to seek political power, interest groups are created to influence the decision-making process with respect to interests of a specific group of people.

The remaining, and vital, purpose of this chapter was to introduce you to the area of business-government relations. In the policy process, lobbying, and election campaigns, organized economic interests are central players, wielding considerable influence. Though this influence varies from country to country, from government to government, and from industry to industry, the interaction between governments and business interests has a major impact on the shape of politics in all states. Nowhere is this more evident than in the advanced capitalist democracies (ACDs), where, as we will see in the next chapter, business and other economic interests play a central role in politics, though each country organizes this involvement in its own way.

## Self-Assessment Questions

1. In what ways is citizen involvement different in political parties, interest groups, and the media?
2. Does corporatism allow too much involvement for business and industry in decision-making?
3. Which is the more effective means of expressing citizen concerns in an election: the plurality system or a proportional representation system?
4. How important is political culture in the forming of public opinion and the approach or focus of government? Are values still important in contemporary society?
5. Is lobbying a legitimate form of interest articulation?

## Further Reading

Archer, Keith, Roger Gibbons, Rainer Knopff, and Leslie Pal. *Parameters of Power: Canada's Political Institutions*. Toronto: Nelson, 1995.

Almond, G., and S. Verba, eds. *The Civic Culture Revisited*. Boston: Little, Brown, 1980.

Berry, J.M. *Lobbying for the People*. Princeton: Princeton University Press, 1977.

Easton, David, *The Political System: An Inquiry into the State of Political Science*, New York: Knopf, 1953.

Tanguay, A. Brian, and Alain G. Gagnon. *Canadian Parties in Transition*, 2nd ed. Toronto: Nelson Canada, 1996.

Pross, A.P. *Pressure Group Behaviour in Canadian Politics*. Toronto: McGraw-Hill Ryerson, 1975.

## Web Links

### Electoral Systems Index
http://www.aceproject.org/main/english/es/default.htm

### Democracy and Electoral Systems
http://worldpolicy.org/americas/democracy/democracy.html

### Canadian Lobbyists
http://strategis.ic.gc.ca/cgi-bin/lobbyist-bin/bin/lrs.e/lrsmain.phtml?

### Angus Reid
http://www.angusreid.com/

### Pollara Research
http://www.pollara.ca/new/POLLARA_NET.html

# CHAPTER FIVE

# POLITICAL ECONOMY IN THE DEVELOPED WORLD

## Chapter Objectives

When you have finished reading this chapter, you will:

- have a clearer idea of the practical application of politics and political economy
- be able to compare and contrast the political and economic systems of Canada, the United States, and Japan
- be able to explain the interaction between economic and political processes in these three countries
- understand the links between domestic economy and foreign economic policy
- be able to identify some of the most important issues facing developed nations today.

In previous chapters in this book, you have been introduced to several important aspects of contemporary political economy, governance, and the nature of politics and markets. Introductory concepts in political studies, government structures and roles, and the importance of citizen and group participation in the political process all have demonstrated the fundamentally intertwined state of affairs of politics and economics. The intent of this chapter is to apply some of the concepts and ideas introduced in earlier chapters of this book in the more specific context of how political economy works in some selected advanced industrialized nations.

Chapter 5 begins with a presentation of some of the major themes and issues facing the political economies of advanced industrialized states. This section will provide an overview of the development of advanced economic interaction after the end of the Second World War. These years, often referred to as the **post-war order**, were crucial in the development of institutions and regulations governing the global economy. Interestingly, though there are several areas of mutual concern and interest for a diverse set of industrialized nations, the experience of these states, and the relative importance placed on disparate elements of economic development and emphasis, is strikingly unique. Our three country study cases in this chapter bear this out. In general terms, however, the chapter introduces the nature of political economy in developed states in terms of broader concepts: the pursuit of justice, equality, economic growth, and stability within industrialized economies. In Chapter 6, you will note that the same broad concepts are applied to the political economy in the developing world

In order to apply these concepts, this chapter examines in greater detail the political economy of three selected states in the developed world: Canada, the United States, and Japan. At first blush, it may appear odd, or even a bit redundant, to include both the United States and Canada in this chapter. But there is a wider goal here. You will recall that earlier chapters explained the important distinctions between parliamentary and presidential forms of government, and used the Canadian and American systems as examples of each. We learned in Chapter 3 that the political structures in these seemingly similar countries are actually very different, though the broader goals and objectives of the two states may in fact be quite the same. In the economic sphere, as we will see here, the two countries are greatly entwined, and the economic dimension is the most significant element of their mutual relationship. In addition, these two examples demonstrate two different levels of development and economic focus in the post-war environment.

On the other hand, Japan represents a distinctive and important example of an alternative trajectory for economic development. Due to specific circumstances (explained later) that constrained the activities and development of the Japanese economy, its shift from a decimated system to a global economic powerhouse is particularly striking. Besides being a different mode of capitalist development, Japan maintains a rather individual democratic experience, leading to a very separate level of growth and prosperity in the international economic system. Because Japan has not been given as much attention as the United States or Canada in previous chapters, we will spend more time here on the matter of Japanese political and economic history and development.

# Political Economy in Developed States

Let us reiterate that attention to the political economy of advanced nations is still a relatively recent phenomenon. As we will explain later in greater detail, the physical security of states was once the predominant sector of interest for analysts of state affairs. Indeed, it was not until the mid-twentieth century that the economic welfare of states became a major arena of analytical examination in political studies. The rise of the **welfare state**, in which governments sought to increase the efficiency and development of their countries through social spending and programs, undoubtedly became the single most important development in industrialized states after the end of the Second World War. Thus, at the close of the twentieth century, the level of attention paid to economic affairs in state politics should not surprise any observer of domestic or international politics. Economic interaction among political actors has become the normal, routine activity of states in the international system, due largely to the development of national economies in the states themselves.

But it was not always thus. Before the end of the Second World War, it seemed that the dominant form of state interaction was not economic interchange, but war, or at least conflict among political actors. The lack of routine economic interaction among political actors had a direct effect on the physical well-being of states and their governments. In the **interwar period** (the years between the First and Second World Wars, 1919–1939), a state of **autarky**, or non-interaction and isolation among states, was the defining feature of political relations. It might seem odd in an environment like ours to envision a system where rules or normative behaviour were not agreed upon, resulting in a general state of economic confusion in regards to exchange, yet that was the situation in the interwar period. Making matters worse for states was the state of general non-interaction in an economic sphere that—coupled with a confusing and ever-changing array of rules implemented unilaterally by different governments at different times—did not limit itself to the apparently benign realm of economics. In fact, this autarkic system was a major contributor to the more widespread suspicion and distrust that existed among states in the international system. Furthermore, a lack of coordinated economic relations was one of the major contributing factors leading to the Second World War.

Not surprisingly, world leaders at the close of the Second World War sought a mechanism to avoid the state of autarky that had contributed in such a major way to the First World War a decade earlier. The resulting agreements (and there were many, dealing with a variety of spheres, ranging from finance, banking, and international loans to currency stability and trade) first and foremost sought to avoid the conditions that all agreed had had such a serious part in the Second World War.

The development of advanced industrialized economies after the end of the

Second World War took a variety of forms. Some nations, like Canada and the United States, were largely protected from the direct effects of damage from the war, such as the sheer devastation felt in Europe and Asia. Thus, by the end of the war, the United States was responsible for over 80 percent of global production. While this number is shocking, it is not altogether surprising, given the level of reconstruction that was required in Europe and Asia. Because the United States did not have to rebuild its industries and infrastructure as European countries did, it enjoyed a high level of immediate strength in the economic arena. Yet this very high level of relative productive output in the United States declined as economies in Asia and Europe began to rebuild and re-establish their pre-war capabilities. Nonetheless, the United States maintained the world's largest productive output, and remains the world's largest economy today. The fact that the United States and Canada were largely insulated from the direct effects of the war's devastation allowed these two countries to very quickly establish a foothold in the world economy, and indeed, in all spheres. Other states, such as Japan, had to deal with the cost of rebuilding, in addition to the challenges of the new international economy.

Before turning to the case studies, it is helpful to briefly review some of the macroeconomic shifts that have affected industrialized political systems in the world today. Therefore, in the following sections, we will turn our attention to "revolutions" in political economies, the growth of the modern welfare state, and other issues pertinent for countries like the ones studied here.

## Revolutions in Political Economy

The eighteenth-century sociologist Auguste Compte argued that human societies create institutions in response to needs (that is, for the benefits they will bring us) and discard them when they are no longer of use. As argued in earlier chapters, human economic and political development has not occurred in a single wave of development. In fact, economic and political change in human history might be separated into what we refer to as "revolutions" of thought and practice (see Table 5.1). These "revolutions" are not the familiar violent episodes that seek to replace wholesale existing systems. Rather, theses revolutions refer to the manner in which we think and apply our existing practices. For instance, anthropologists tell us that early human societies were nomadic out of need—groups of humans were unable to secure the necessary conditions of life in a static environment. Hence, early societies were mobile, in search of more appropriate climates and access to food. The advent of early agricultural advancements, however, allowed societies to form semi-permanent and permanent communities and to survive in a stable environment. This **Agricultural Revolution,** therefore, allowed human societies to abandon their earlier nomadic modes of interaction, and to form rudimentary political communities.

| Table 5.1 Revolutions in Political Economy | | |
|---|---|---|
| Name | Period | Characteristics |
| Pre-Agrarian | pre-4000 BPE | Nomadic |
| | | Non-static political system |
| | | Limited political development |
| Agricultural | post-4000 BPE | Organized agriculture |
| | | Rise of ordered civilization |
| | | Semi-static political system |
| Industrial | 18th century | Industrialized advances |
| | | Urban development and concentration |
| | | Static political system |
| "Post-Industrial" or Technical | Late 20th century | "Web" of enterprise |
| | | High-tech/high-value over high production |
| | | Non-static political system (regions and economies) |
| | | Capital concentration |

In the early eighteenth century, the Agricultural Revolution was surpassed by industrial advances, starting in Great Britain, and moving rapidly through the rest of Europe. The **Industrial Revolution** made possible not just the concentration of a great number of humans within designated political communities, as the Agricultural Revolution did, but also permitted large communities to live in densely populated areas where previously it would have been impossible to sustain large numbers of people, given limited land resources. The Industrial Revolution managed this by creating the conditions for the modern mass city, allowing for the more efficient allocation of goods within society. This was an important change in human development, and ultimately contributed to the conditions that permitted the rise of the welfare state, where the state is able to provide the services and programs necessary to improve the daily lives of citizens. This exchange is in the nature of a two-way street, in that the logic of the welfare state extends to the interests of government as well: a well-provided for public, it is reasoned, is more capable of providing an efficient and competitive environment for economic development.

More recently, much has been made of the transfer from an industrial economy to a **technological** or **innovative economy**. Briefly, this means that developed economies have come to focus increasingly on the necessary components of a high-technology, or high-value, economy. In order to demonstrate this, take, for example, the automotive industry. Cars today are built with what is known as **mature technologies**, which are technologies that are generally known to a wide number of people, and as a result, are not necessarily "protected" (under patent law, or as a proprietary technology) by individual manufacturers. In addition, it is assumed that a mature technology contains few obstacles for those who would like to obtain this knowledge; anyone, in theory, can learn what makes an internal combustion engine work, and related aspects of automotive manufacturing, such as drive trains and chassis, are relatively easy to access. For automobile companies today, then, the key to gaining market share is not necessarily in unique attributes in the mature components of their industry, but rather in the marketing, reputation, and unit cost of their products. Car companies today, therefore, are eager to reduce costs in the factory-line production of their vehicles, and to concentrate capital—their profit—in research and development geared towards innovations in their products that might capture a market that has shrunk as a multitude of automotive manufacturers compete for a relatively stable consumer market worldwide. This research and development might be concentrated on innovations in existing mature technologies, such as engine developments, but also might be geared towards the new aspects of the established industry—new developments in computer technology and other high-technology evolutions in the industry. These are known as **infant technologies**, and are carefully guarded and protected from others in an effort to secure market share. The upshot of all this is that automobiles once considered to be "American" are in fact not that at all; all American vehicles today have at least some component of their production originating in another state. Importantly, labour for factory production is often removed from the developed states and off-loaded to another country where workers work for less.

The future effect for the political economy of developed states will be an increasingly shrinking industrial output—heavy production, such as factory construction—and an increasing concentration of corporate capital in high-value industries—innovation and research and development—at the expense of employment and worker benefits. This is not to suggest that industries in developed states such as Canada, the United States, or Japan are now nonexistent; this is clearly not the case. Rather, the important development here is that the legacy of the Industrial Revolution and its accompanying emphasis on the productive state is now undergoing a degree of change as economic actors in developed nations (such as multinational corporations) spend more of their capital in the developed states on high-value production, and labour costs are often incurred in other states, where expenses are lower.

## The Jutan Corporation                                           Box 5.1

The Jutan Corporation is a prime example of the proliferation of multinational corporations in modern political economy. Jutan is a Japan-based manufacturer of electronic consumer goods, with several different name plates under its corporate identity. Citizen and Candle, for instance, are both names of electronic product lines offered in Canada, often competing with one another in the same stores for the same customers. However, both are managed and run by the same larger corporation, which has a series of manufacturing plants throughout Thailand, Malaysia, Singapore, Taiwan, Korea, and China. Having several names under the same corporate banner allows Jutan better access to consumer markets by covering more market share with different "brands"; this gives shoppers the feeling that they are competitively buying, when in fact a decision to opt for another brand may still yield profits for a company like Jutan. As a multinational corporation, the manufacturing is farmed out to less expensive labour markets in the Asia-Pacific Rim.

This is particularly evident in Japan, where high production has dramatically shifted to other nations in the Asia-Pacific Rim. Japanese companies that were once entirely national are now multinational, with enterprises in countries such as Thailand, Malaysia, Singapore, Korea, and even mainland China. In this economic climate, there are serious concerns for those states that do not maintain a high level of national ownership of industries. In Canada, for instance, over 50 percent of industry is controlled by non-Canadians, mostly Americans and Europeans. The fear of many in the labour movement in Canada is that the interests of Canadian workers are not as likely to be upheld by foreign interests as they would be if ownership was held by Canadians.

Neither do we want to suggest that some form of widespread "de-industrialization" has taken place in advanced economies such as those in these case studies. Rather, we are witnessing a transitory period where the benefits and elements of an industrialized society remain, but increasingly the emphasis is placed on the technical side of production in domestic affairs. This has resulted in the development of what has been termed the **technical state,** where countries do not completely discard their industrial roots, but have grown to focus on the increasingly important economic goals of technical leadership and expertise.

The development of a technical emphasis within advanced economies like Canada, the United States, and Japan is part of what has been identified as a movement towards a **post-Industrial Revolution**. What must be pointed out, however, is that unlike the Agricultural and Industrial Revolutions, the post-Industrial evolution of economies necessarily is limited to a select number of countries. So, in order to become a technical state, others must remain focused on continued industrialization in order to pick up the slack that has been off-loaded from the rising post-industrial states. Yet this is not always a decision with a lot of choice for the countries that are industrializing. In short, many of the so-called **newly industrialized countries**, or NICs, such as Thailand, Mayalsia, Singapore, and Mexico, have benefited from surplus labour markets that have been removed from costly environments in the industrialized wealthy states, yet likely do not stand to gain from the post-industrial emphasis on innovation and technical expertise that now serves as a foundation for market economies.

As the case studies will bear out, Canada, the United States, and Japan have had their own distinctive experiences with regard to technical advances. In all cases, however, there has been a recognition that innovation and technical advances form the basis of the new economy of advanced states. Competitiveness in advanced economic countries, then, has witnessed a new emphasis on high-value (innovative) output, rather than the previous mode of high production that marked so much of the twentieth century.

# Post-Industrialization and Political Authority

As you learned in previous chapters, governments have two very simple goals in the contemporary world. First, governments seek to ensure the physical security of their borders and people. Security has always been the central objective of any political unit throughout history, because a community that is not secure cannot seek a better way of life. Once security is ensured, states may pursue goals that benefit the welfare of constituents. Programs that we have come to expect in our day-to-day lives, such as employment benefits, healthcare, and government funding for social policies are impossible for governments to pursue without being able to first secure the state against possible attack or incursion from foreign parties.

It is important to keep in mind that the growth of the modern social welfare state—political units that seek to provide benefits to their citizens in order to improve efficiency and competitiveness—is a relatively new development. In fact, if we were to study the major policy questions facing nations before the Second World War, we would find that issues pertaining to physical security, concerns of alliances and possible conflict with foreign parties, and internal stability would fill the daily docket of governmental mandates in advanced industrial nations.

The growth of a modern global economy, and the post-war creation of a set of institutions and organizations to help govern peaceful economic relations (for example, the **Bretton-Woods Agreement**, detailed in Chapter 8) allowed states to concentrate not only on the security of their people and territory, but also on the benefits that might be allocated to citizens in order to improve their way of life. This is not to suggest that governments suddenly became altruistic for no cause: there was a perception that supplying these programs and benefits would improve the general ambitions of governments in a growing environment of economic mutual dependence and openness.

The pressure to create a welfare state, then, was understood to be in the best interest of national governments. Industrialization facilitated the allocation of social benefits in advanced states, leading to the globalized economy we experience today. Yet the current environment that focuses so much on technical innovation and diversified markets no longer permits the previously accepted nationalistic modes of identification. In other words, economies are not as "national" as they once were perceived to be, and economic actors are far more transnational and apolitical than they were in the past. The roots of this development are not too hard to recognize: the leaders of the post-war order sought to create an open and liberal environment for national economies to flourish. Yet the same openness, coupled with the creation of international regimes (which are essentially structures that guide rule-making and decision-making) and institutions that were not simply agents of single national governments, led to a distinctly *non-national* international environment of transborder relations. Major corporations, once considered the "national champions" of the states in which they were situated, were now multinational, with interests that straddled or sometimes ignored national concerns. Furthermore, private corporate actors began to control an increasingly significant portion of the global economy, as national governments began to remove themselves as major players in international economics.

International circumstances have domestic effects. The growing lack of control over the global economy by national states and the rise of non-governmental corporate and business actors led to a new agenda at the domestic level at the close of the century. Governments sought to ensure a continued environment of social welfare and internal benefits for citizens, while at the same time losing a degree of control over the mechanics and dynamics of the global economy, which was now the single most important arena of domestic strength.

So, the close of the twentieth century has brought with it a mixed bag of effects for the political economy of advanced states. While unimagined growth and wealth exists in some sectors, the number of those sectors is decreasing, with obvious effects for societies. Governments struggle with the expense of social welfare programs in states that are de-industrializing as a result of a global economy and major decision-makers that are not held by a constituency of citizens, but by shareholders or directors. The next revolution in political economy, therefore, is not nearly over, and presents serious challenges for the governments of advanced states. With this in mind, we now turn our attention to the individual political economy of three case studies: Canada, the United States, and Japan.

# Canadian Political Economy: The Challenge of Strategic Alliances

Canada's is neither a command, nor a pure market economy, since it contains elements of both government and free market control (see Chapter 3). Canada's economy is mixed in another sense, too, since it produces primary or raw materials, manufactured goods, and is also heavily influenced by the high-technology and services industries. Furthermore, the dominant ideology behind the management of Canada's economy has shifted over the last 15–20 years, moving from a strong belief in state management intervention to a growing commitment to the free market. Lastly, the Canadian economy is one of the largest in the world, and is highly competitive in several areas. The combination of these factors makes Canada's political economy an ideal case study.

But it is the interaction between the political and economic worlds in Canada that makes it a fascinating example for political economy. Although Canada's economy is advanced and competitive, and although it is dominated by the principles of the free market, Canada's commitment to the welfare state and to social justice means that the government remains an important actor in economic management and intervention. As mentioned above, Canada's economy is a mixed, or "mixed free enterprise system." This means that although most production and employment is located in the private sector, healthy levels of competition and incentives exist in the economy, and the profit motive is fundamental for most Canadian enterprise, with the government playing an active role in the economy.

What levels of government involvement do we see in the Canadian economy? The provision of goods and services to the public by the government accounts for 25 percent of Gross Domestic Product (GDP), making the state the single largest economic actor in Canada. Of course this includes activities at both federal and provincial levels, so we should not see this activity as monolithic. The state participates in the economy in several ways. First, the state regulates the economy, guaranteeing a minimum wage, regulating pric-

As noted in this chapter, Canada still depends on nature and natural resources for a large part of its wealth as a nation. Though the share of Gross Domestic Product (GDP) accounted for by natural resources has declined dramatically since the early twentieth century, as a sector it still employs huge numbers of people, both directly and through natural resource-based industries. Furthermore, Canada derives a large amount of its foreign income through natural resource-based exports. All of this means that Canadians as a society have to recognize the link between their natural environment and their prosperity.

ing, and providing standards for quality, health, and safety. Second, the government engages in income redistribution, transferring money taken from taxes and giving it to the poor and unemployed. Last, the government participates directly in the economy through crown corporations (state-owned enterprises) such as the Canadian Wheat Board, Canada Post, and Via Rail.

Canada's taxation system can best be described as progressive, in which the level of personal contributions to the government increases with the level of personal income. Some see this as highly equitable, while others (in particular, such organizations as the Fraser Institute) claim that such a system punishes individual success and provides a disincentive to ambition and working harder. Either way, the Canadian government's tax revenues are essential if it is to continue providing services at the level to which Canadians have become accustomed.

Much of Canada's tax revenue goes to sustaining the welfare state, that is, the system of income support, healthcare, and education paid for by the government, both federal and provincial. Though a relatively recent phenomenon in historical terms, the welfare state has become part of Canadian political culture. Despite recent attacks claiming widespread abuse of the system, Canadian people continue to name health and education spending as priorities for governments.

In earlier chapters you were introduced to the idea of budget surpluses and deficits. In the 1990s the Canadian national deficit and debt became a central topic in discussions about the country's political economy. Canadian public indebtedness had increased from 9 percent of GDP in 1977 to 71.9 percent of GDP in 1996. As governments at both federal and provincial levels continued to spend more than they brought in the form of tax revenues and royalties (from natural resources—see below), the state was forced to borrow more and more from capital markets. Interest payments on this debt became a serious drain on government financial resources, accounting for 5 percent of GDP in the 1990s. Critics also argued that high debt loads impeded Canadian competitiveness, as interest rates remained high to attract funds to cover the debt.

The Liberal government of Jean Chretien, pushed by the rising popularity of the Reform Party (which had made debt and deficit reduction a central political platform) and growing awareness of the consequences of high levels of indebtedness, began reducing public spending, laying off government workers, reducing federal-provincial transfer payments and business subsidies, and cutting back on military spending. This program resulted in a balanced budget by the fiscal year of 1997–98, with balanced budgets for the remaining years of the century also planned.

The Canadian labour market has undergone dramatic changes in the past half-century. Since 1950, the share of employment between manufacturing and services has shifted in favour of services. In 1951, 56 percent of Canadians were employed by the goods-producing sector, with 44 percent in services. Today that figure is 26 percent in the goods-producing sector and 74 percent in services. Such structural change has been matched by the rise in part-time work as a feature of the modern Canadian economy. Between 1975 and 1993 the proportion of all jobs that were considered part-time rose from 10.6 percent to 18.3 percent.

These changes have meant shifts not only for those people seeking work, but also for the labour unions that represent them. Union membership in Canada reached a high point in the 1970s, when 31 percent of all workers belonged to a union. Since then union membership has declined slightly, but it is important to remember that a union represents all workers in a bargaining unit when it negotiates with the employer over wages, benefits, or working conditions. Unions remain an important actor in the Canadian economy, particularly in debates with the government and employers over globalization (see Chapter 7).

Structural change in the Canadian economy in the late twentieth century meant high levels of unemployment. Unemployment reached a high in 1992 with 11.3 percent of the workforce out of a job. A startling aspect of this statistic was that 71 percent of all job losses in manufacturing in the 1990s were permanent—that is, jobs that would not return when the economy recovered. Since then, unemployment has fallen to below 8 percent, but it remains high in comparison with the United States, and many of the newly created jobs are in the services sector (which often means lower wages) or part-time, often meaning that an individual will have to work in two different places to make ends meet.

The economic recovery in Canada at the end of the twentieth century demonstrated the high level of competitiveness of the national economy. For the past hundred years Canadian competitiveness has been based on its high levels of productivity, stable social and economic systems, and its geographic proximity to the United States. The Canadian government has tried to maintain that competitiveness through policies aimed at reducing corporate tax rates, reducing national indebtedness, keeping inflation low, reforming labour markets by reducing income support to the unemployed, and by promoting Canadian exports, particularly in the region. These policies have achieved a certain level of success, keeping Canada close to the top of international rankings.

One last point about Canada's economy relates to both its origins and its

Box 5.2

# Canadian Competitiveness

We hear a lot in the press about the problems facing the Canadian economy and how Canada is relatively uncompetitive compared to countries such as the United States and emerging market economies such as Mexico. In fact Canada has managed to maintain a high level of competitiveness in the international economy, for reasons that are both political and economic. Canada's competitiveness for the past hundred years or so is attributable, not only to its geographic proximity to the United States, but also to its highly stable political system and the skills of its workers, which have increased Canadian productivity.

**Canadian GDP Growth, 1988–1997**

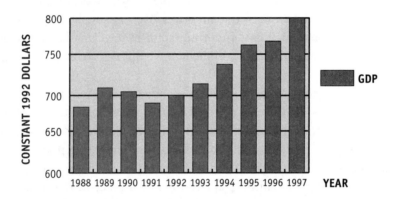

Source: Statistics Canada, *1999 Canada Year Book*, CANSIM, matrix 6549.

future. It is commonly noted that natural resources have been central to the Canadian economy throughout the country's history. Indeed, the exploration of Canada's territory was led by the search for natural resources such as fur and timber. The east coast of Canada was settled by people who exploited the huge supplies of cod in the eastern fishing banks. By the nineteenth century commodities such as gold, wheat, and minerals had grown in importance, and in the twentieth century a combination of natural resources such as oil, natural gas, water, agricultural products, fish, and forestry products all contributed to Canada's wealth.

However, we tend to think of Canada today as dominated by manufacturing industry, the high-technology sector, and the services. By the 1990s natural resources accounted for only 6 percent of total GDP and employment. But we would be forgetting that the natural resource industries provide the basis for other industries in Canada, for example, industries related to forestry and wood and pulp products, which are the largest employers in Canada. What's more, natural resources account for a sizeable proportion of total national exports (e.g., wood and paper, which make up 14.27 percent of total Canadian exports). In the future, Canada's natural resources will continue to play an important role in national economic development, particularly with the export of hydroelectric power and water to the United States.

The central place held by natural resources in the Canadian economy means that debates over the environment, renewable resources, and sustainable development (see Chapter 6) have a special resonance. Canada depends on what nature can provide for its wealth and employment; therefore nature must be protected so that such resources will be available for generations to come.

Canada's political economy represents an interesting confluence of several competing forces. Canada is a developed state, yet is dependent on trade for its affluence; it is a wealthy donor nation, yet has one of the world's highest per capita rates of debt for its citizens; it maintains close trade and commercial links with the largest economic actor in the world, the United States, yet is vulnerable to the decisions and policy-making of that state; it is a resource-rich country with abundant natural assets and a diverse population, yet faces the challenge of regionalism and provincialism; it holds close economic and political relations with Europe and the Asia-Pacific region, yet an inordinate amount of its real day-to-day relations are with one country—the United States. Canada, then, is an intriguing example of a modern industrialized political economy due to its resources, its international setting, and—most importantly—its history of strategic alliances and relationships.

## The Canadian Political System and Societal Factors

Canada is a federation, with a parliamentary democracy. This means that the Canadian political system of authority has divided responsibilities, with some powers given to the ten provinces and three territories, and other powers given to the federal government in Ottawa. Canada's basic law—its constitution—was originally the British North America Act (BNA Act) of 1867, which housed ultimate power and authority in the United Kingdom. The **repatriation** of the constitution in 1982 brought authority for decision-making to Canada, though the Queen, represented by the governor general in Canada, remains the official head of state. The head of government is the prime minister, who is leader of the dominant party in parliament, and is responsible for creating and leading the federal cabinet. Parliament is split into two houses, the Senate (with 104 members) appointed by the governor general on the advice of the prime minister, and the House of Commons, with 301 members based on a representation by population allocation grounded on a popular vote system in the constituencies.

It will not be surprising to readers of this text to learn that much of Canadian politics and economics is driven by its close relationship with the United States. Indeed, though we may recognize the importance of this bilateral relationship, we may not give it the attention that it deserves. Canada's relations with the United States stem back to the establishment of independent political systems in both states (though the American system was born through violent revolution in the late eighteenth century, and Canadian independence was won over a longer period of time and through peaceful political means), but the crux of what we know now to be Canadian-American relations came about in the early twentieth century as Canada found its independent role in domestic and foreign affairs, and the United States rose to global power status. Canada's relations with the United States grew with the American move from relative isolationism in the early twentieth century to its current more internationalist role.

| Box 5.3 | Canada's Geography and Politics |
| --- | --- |

Canada, unlike the European nations from which most of its early settlers originated, is a vast, sparsely populated land. Canada's population is just under 30 million people, making it larger than most European nations, but these people are spread out over a huge geographic area. It is true that most of Canada's population is concentrated within 500 miles of the United States border, but Canadians grow up with a feeling of space. That feeling helps to shape political and social attitudes, and to provide economic opportunities, particularly in the natural resource sector.

As mentioned earlier, Canada is a resource-rich country, with easy access to air and space, as well as the high seas. These geopolitical attributes give Canada a comparative advantage in economic relations, thanks to both access to needed resources, as well as the infrastructure to trade these resources with the outside world. Consequently, Canada has maintained strategic economic alliances with the United States and the American hemisphere, Europe, and the Asia-Pacific Rim. Economically, Canada is part of the **North Atlantic triangle** of Canada, the United States, and the European Union—so named because these three partners represent the most significant and strategic modes of interaction for each other. Canada's economy is diversified, which means that it not only benefits from import-export trade with its partners, but also from high-technology trade, foreign direct investment (both by Canadians abroad, and from foreigners in Canada), and membership in crucial economic organizations. Fully one-third of Canada's GNP comes from its foreign trade, which means that its overall economic health very much depends on a favourable international trade and commercial environment; Canada is by no means an "independent" economy, and requires continued and consistent relations with its partners in order to maintain its welfare state programs and quality of life.

The welfare state in Canada extends back to several programs that were instituted by the federal government in the early twentieth century, but really took hold in the post-war years as provinces in Canada undertook a larger

## The Nuclear Family                                      Box 5.4

Most of us are brought up in a family with a mother and father who live in the same household, but a growing number of us experience a less traditional upbringing. It is increasingly common for families to be constituted, not by mother, father, and children, but by a single parent of either sex (though more commonly female), or of two same-sex individuals living together and raising children. Between 1986 and 1996 there was significant growth in single-parent families and in common-law marriages. The changing structure of the Canadian family is important because it is there that most of us receive our most elementary political and cultural socialization. Indeed, it is fair to say that the family is the primary agent of socialization. What will changing structures do to Canadians' political, economic, and social assumptions? Unfortunately it is not yet clear how this new reality will affect politics, but it is just one of the many changes in society (along with growing immigrant communities and advances in communications, for example) that will challenge our assumptions in the years to come.

role in social support programs for Canadians, and the federal government strove to institute standardization across the country. In Canada, the modern welfare state is financed largely through a **progressive taxation system** that is based on income.

Canadian power and influence in domestic and foreign political economy is largely a function of its influence among and with greater powers as well as its emphasis on group membership. On the first point, Canada is most commonly considered a **middle power** due to its influence and close relations with the United States; unlike other comparable economic powers such as Australia or the Netherlands, Canada has an inordinately close and strategic relationship with the world's only remaining superpower. However, despite what we might commonly think of as Canada's reliance on the United States for its economic vitality, Canada is neither a satellite nor a dependent state. In fact, Canada retains a great deal of autonomy in its policy-making, and is often at odds with the United States on key issues, such as west-coast fishing or economic relations with Cuba. Canada's middle power status, then, is not just a measurement of Canadian power, but is representative of Canadian attributes in policy-making, as well as its style and history of domestic and foreign relations.

On the second point—group membership—Canada is a world leader in its emphasis on the importance of international organizations and institutions to help guide political and economic relations (see Table 5.2). Canada is a member of many diverse organizations, ranging from cultural and linguistic groups such as *la francophonie*; economic associations such as the North American Free Trade Agreement (NAFTA), the Asia-Pacific Economic Cooperative (APEC) body; the Organization for Economic Cooperation and Development (OECD) and its constituent body the Development Assistance Committee (DAC); political organizations such as the United Nations (UN) and its component bodies, the Organization of American States (OAS), and the Organization for Security and Cooperation in Europe (OSCE); strategic alliances such as the North Atlantic Treaty Organization (NATO), and the North American Aerospace Defence (NORAD) partnership with the United States. Canada does not join and stay with these organizations lightly. There is a much higher purpose for membership in such groups. Though respected in the international community, Canada, as a middle power, is simply unable to create and alter the rules and regulations that pertain to nation-states and their interaction. This has particular resonance for political economy, given Canada's dependence on foreign trade for its prosperity. However, being a member in larger organizations allows Canada a voice among states that otherwise might be overlooked, or even ignored. Institutional membership, therefore, allows

## Table 5.2 Canadian Membership in International Organizations

The "Agence de Coopération Culturelle et Technique (ACCT)"

Arctic Council

Asia-Pacific Economic Cooperation

Bank for International Settlements (BIS)

The Commonwealth

Group of Eight (G8)

Food and Agriculture Organization (FAO)

*La francophonie*

International Atomic Energy Agency (IAEA)

International Bank for Reconstruction and Development (IBRD – The World Bank)

International Chamber of Commerce (ICC)

International Center for Genetic Engineering and Biotechnology (ICGEB)

International Civil Aviation Organization (ICAO)

International Committee of the Red Cross (ICRC)

International Fund for Agricultural Development (IFAD)

International Institute for Democracy and Electoral Assistance (IDEA)

International Joint Commission (IJC)

International Labour Office (ILO)

International Monetary Fund (IMF)

International Organization of Securities Commissions (IOSCO)

International Telecommunication Union (ITU)

Investment Promotion Agency (IPA)

North American Aerospace Defence (NORAD)

North American Free Trade Agreement (NAFTA)

North Atlantic Treaty Organization (NATO)

Organization for Economic Cooperation and Development (OECD)

Organization for Security and Cooperation in Europe

Organization of American States (OAS)

United Nations (UN)

World Health Organization (WHO)

World Intellectual Property Organization (WIPO)

World Meteorological Organization (WMO)

World Trade Organization (WTO)

Canada a degree of *independence* in its policy-making, since it is able to assert its views and opinions in groups, and often is able to affect the international agenda and decision-making of other states. This has real repercussions for Canada's economic affairs.

On the issue of societal considerations that drive the Canadian political economy, Canada is best described as a liberal plural state with a diversity of interests that reflect Canada's regional, cultural, and socially plural population, as well as its linguistic duality (English and French). Canada is a parliamentary democracy with a great deal of concentration of power over political and economic affairs at the level of the executive. The prime minister is responsible for powers of appointment in the Canadian government, which includes the major organs of economic affairs. Cabinet ministers, appointed by the prime minister, are the individuals in government with the most real power over the state, with support bureaucracies responsible for goal articulation and the implementation of policy.

## Canadian Political Economy: Branching out by Necessity

Canada's economic position—both domestic and foreign—is in many ways curtailed by, and a function of, its alliances with other powers. Canada's "place" in the international system, in other words, determines much of the relative success and deficiency in the Canadian political economy, since Canada is by no means an independent economic actor. It has been said that to understand Canadian politics on any level requires an understanding of international affairs, given the level of exposure that the Canadian economy has in the context of the wider global economy. To illustrate, Canada's exports in goods and services composed over 35 percent of Canada's total GDP; Canada is the most globally integrated economy of all the G8 (Group of Eight: Canada, the United States, Great Britain, France, Germany, Italy, Japan, and Russia) nations. This means that Canada's economic strength depends on its trade with the rest of the international system.

Of this international exposure, none is more evident than that to the United States. Canadian interest rates, central bank policy, import-export trade, corporate ownership, and multinational activity, as well as the lion's share of foreign investment, is dependent on Canada's bilateral relationship with the United States. Canadian exports to the United States amount to 75 percent of total export trade in Canada, and imports from the United States exceed 70 percent of all Canadian imports. The Canadian-United States trading relationship is the largest in the world; in fact, if all the remaining provinces and states were deleted from the equation, Ontario and Michigan would still remain the largest trading relationship in the entire world, thanks in large part to the massive amount of cross-border trade in automobiles and automotive parts by Ford, General Motors, and Chrysler. Whereas Canada is the largest trading partner for the United States, the high Canadian reliance on the American economy is much higher, and constitutes approximately 30 percent of Canada's total GDP.

Furthermore, the kind of trading relationship Canada has with its foreign partners, as well as issues pertaining to ownership and investment in Canada, present some future problems for Canada's political economy. Although Canada is the world's seventh largest exporter, and the eighth largest importer, Canada is both trade and investment-dependent. Because of its relatively small population and high resource base, Canada is a trading state out of necessity. Additionally, partly because of the type of goods Canada imports (high-technology) and exports (high-production or resource products), Canada experiences a trade imbalance with its partners. Canada, then, is not a self-sufficient state, and is tightly linked to global technical and industrial shifts.

## Pollution and Government Spending                    Box 5.5

As we discovered in an earlier chapter, awareness of environmental degradation has increased dramatically over the past 20 years and has become an issue of political significance, with green parties and environmental pressure groups lobbying governments across the world to protect the environment. In Canada, environmentalists have been relatively successful in pressuring the federal government to improve upon existing environmental regulations and their enforcement. The federal government increased its spending on pollution controls over a 10-year period, from under 450 million dollars to over 800 million dollars. This is still, however, only a tiny portion of the federal government's budget, and environmentalists constantly lobby for more financial resources to be devoted to this issue, particularly when government spending declines, as it did in 1994–95.

## Canada and Free Trade

Classical liberal theory would have us believe that everyone in a society should perform those duties and functions that they are best capable of fulfilling.

And, for nation states operating in an international environment, this standard holds as well: countries operating to their best purpose would do what they do best. This is the theory of **comparative advantage**. Since all states have very different capabilities, and these capabilities often mean serious deficiencies for some and great benefit for others, comparative advantage may not appear to be realistic. Yet in broad terms this is how states manage in the international economy: some are resource states, others are technologically proficient, and others capitalize on changing industrial markets.

Increasingly, developed states have been moving towards the regional trading bloc model to supplement the weaknesses they may experience in their national economies. Trading blocs, or **free trade zones,** may come in different forms, and have different objectives. Ordinarily, free trade zones seek to eliminate or greatly reduce the stumbling blocks to better trade among nations: tariffs, customs duties, trade legislation, national programs to protect industries and sectors, and impediments to commercial relations and investment across borders. More frequently now, smaller groups of states are binding together to create limited access to free trade among a select group of states, usually in a defined geographical realm. Mercusor, in South America, APEC in the Asia-Pacific Rim, the EU in Europe, and the NAFTA all are illustrative of the tendency by industrialized states to seek out specialized relations with a designated group of states in their regions.

NAFTA is much like the other free trade arrangements. As early as 1983, the governing Liberal party proposed that Canada consider sectoral free trade with the United States. Brian Mulroney was elected as prime minister in 1984, and though he had argued against free trade in the election campaign, his government began negotiating with the Americans on a comprehensive free trade agreement in 1985. Building on the original Canada-United States Free Trade Agreement (the CUFTA, or FTA), which was implemented in 1989, NAFTA added Mexico, and was set in motion in January 1994. NAFTA eliminates most of the barriers to trade and investment among the three states. It is the largest free trade area in the world, comprising over 350 million people and US $6.2 trillion in goods and services every year. NAFTA was in many ways a response to the increasingly successful model in Europe, which had transformed from a general agreement on coal and steel in the 1950s to the world's most integrated free trade zone in the 1990s. Conceding that harmonized economic relations in Europe would come at the expense of trans-Atlantic commerce, Canada, the United States, and Mexico pursued an agreement to reduce tariffs in the northern hemisphere, some of which were as high as 29 percent. The resulting NAFTA sought tariff elimination and the reduction of trade tariff barriers, as well as compatible rules on investment, services, intellectual property, competition, and the cross-border movement of business persons.

It is important to point out that, for Canada, membership in the NAFTA free trade zone was not a function of comparative advantage, but rather the matter of access to larger markets in the American economy. Since 1994, Canada's trade with both the United States and Mexico has grown, and Canadian trade with its NAFTA partners came to over $388 billion. Despite Canada's growth in trade with both of these states, Canada is still very much a follower of the United States in the NAFTA, which reflects the overall Canadian position in regards to its bilateral commercial relations with the United States (see Fig. 5.1).

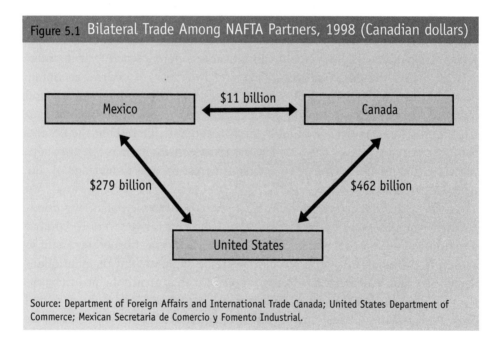

**Figure 5.1** Bilateral Trade Among NAFTA Partners, 1998 (Canadian dollars)

Source: Department of Foreign Affairs and International Trade Canada; United States Department of Commerce; Mexican Secretaria de Comercio y Fomento Industrial.

# The United States: A Leader in Search of a System

The US is commonly seen as the "home of capitalism," a place where the market reigns supreme. Understanding US political economy, however, is much more complex than comprehending the operation of the free market. For though the rules of the market are dominant in the United States economic system, it is vital to remember that, in addition to the formation of economic policy, the state plays two important roles in the US economy, those of consumption and regulation. The United States economy became the world's largest in the first half of the twentieth century, and since then the combination of private initiative and effective government management has kept it far ahead of other national economies.

The nature of political economy in the United States is intimately linked to the American political tradition of keeping the state out of the lives of its citizens. This has created a concern to minimize the role of the state in the functioning of the economy, and of keeping levels of taxation low. Throughout the twentieth century debates over taxation stressed maximizing individual freedom by allowing US citizens to keep as much of their earnings as possible. Debates over state regulation of the economy have followed a similar logic.

Government management and regulation of the economy in the United States involves a variety of agencies at the federal and state levels. These different levels of government create multiple access points where private interests can affect the policy process. First and foremost, of course, economic management emanates from the United States congress and presidency and lobbying impacts directly on the management of the political economy (see Chapter 4). The importance of lobbying by economic interests in the US creates a system which gives privileged access to those with money, but also, supporters argue, to those who have a direct interest in, and knowledge of, the issues concerned.

At the end of the twentieth century, US macroeconomic policy was dominated by the obsession of the central bank (the Federal Reserve) to combat inflation and keep it suppressed. The Federal Reserve was hugely successful in achieving this goal, raising interest rates at the slightest hint of inflationary tendencies, and it remains a priority. One factor that greatly helped this policy goal was the fact that the US economy experienced an unprecedented period of growth and very low levels of unemployment, reducing resistance from trade unions and workers. This combination of low inflation, low unemployment, and high levels of growth contradicted the predictions that we might expect from the Phillips curve (see Chapter 3). Low inflation helped maintain the confidence of both investors and consumers, which contributed to US growth.

In addition to regulating and managing the economy, the US government is also a consumer of enormous dimensions. Each year the US federal budget involves over US$1.5 trillion in spending. This gives the government enormous influence over the economy, and again raises the possibility for lobbying and pressure over the awarding of government contracts. It also gives the United States government the option of providing a large stimulus to the economy, if it should choose to. In the 1980s the government of President Ronald Reagan stimulated the economy through massive spending on a military build-up for the Cold War (see Chapter 7).

Of course, the economic dominance of the United States is not merely the product of effective government policies. The United States economy is also the world's most advanced, committed to the production of new technologies and products. Though we tend to think of Asia as the home of high-tech, the United States spends more than any other nation on R&D (Research and Development). This investment in the future has allowed the US to stay ahead of the product cycle (see Chapter 8), and to maintain control of key technologies.

Another element that is key to US economic dominance has been the spread of American multinational corporations (MNCs) throughout the world (see Chapter 8). Beginning in the 1950s, US corporations took advantage of the strength of the United States dollar to invest in Europe, Asia, and Latin America, buying existing industries and setting up new production facilities. Such "multinationalization" of production allowed these corporations to take advantage of economies of scale and exploit markets across the world.

## The United States Political System and Economy and the International System

The United States is a democratic republic, with political powers divided among the 50 states, one district (District of Columbia, DC), and the federal government in Washington. The United States was founded after a revolt against British rule in the late eighteenth century. Official independence was achieved in 1776 after the United States won the revolution. The American judicial system still retains vestiges of the British legal system, but with a strong tradition of judicial review of legislative acts.

The American political system is not anything like the British parliamentary model, however. In a form break with the Westminster parliamentary system, the United States political system was based on a definite separation of powers among the levels of government, with a firm role to be played regarding the review of each others' actions—the "checks and balances" system. The American executive is headed by the president, who is both head of government and head of state, and the cabinet. The legislative wing of government is bicameral, with an elected upper house (Senate, with 100 members), and lower house, (House of Representatives, with 435 members).

To speak of political economy in the United States and not to include an account of its role in the international system of trade, commerce, and financial relations would be to leave out an essential part of power and wealth in that state. Henry Luce, publisher of the American magazine *Life*, suggested in 1941 that the twentieth century was the "American century." As we will see later in this section, Luce might be forgiven for this comment, though it might seem a bit domineering for our contemporary sensitivities. In fact, in hindsight, Luce's statement sums up much of what made the United States such an economic leader in the twentieth century, and—ironically—what brought about its relative decline.

Before exploring in greater depth the conditions that led to Luce's statement, and the international system itself, we will examine briefly elements of the American domestic political economy that contributed to its pre-eminent role in our modern international political economy. For the American and international systems, the linkages among levels of analysis are deeply entwined, and fundamental for our understanding of modern political economy.

## Building on Strength: The Domestic Context of the American Economy

It is important to review some domestic background regarding the American system. As you probably are well aware, the United States is an open democratic political system, with a capitalist economy. From a political standpoint, the American system relies on the input and involvement of all citizens in a form of indirect democracy, which denotes the representation of views of citizens by elected officials. The United States is a federal democracy, meaning that decision-making and authority are divided among different levels of power—national, state, and municipal. American politics divide executive (or presidential) power from that of the legislature (the bicameral congress, which is separated into the House of Representatives and the Senate), and the judiciary (the courts). Separate from these levels is the bureaucracy, which could well be referred to as the fourth level of government, given its important role in the definition of policy-making and implementation. More on the role of bureaucracies may be found in previous chapters on the roles of levels of government.

From an economic standpoint, the American capitalist economy means that the production and distribution of goods and services in the American

## Lobbying

Box 5.6

In the first six months of 1998 in the United States of America, a coalition of insurance companies spent over US$60 million lobbying members of Congress in the struggle to prevent the passage of the Patient's Bill of Rights, a piece of legislation that would reform healthcare. This staggering figure gets even bigger when we factor in the US$11 million spent by the industry on advertising and the millions spent in campaign contributions. In opposition to this campaign, a coalition of medical organizations, consumer groups, lawyers, and unions spent over US$14 million. Why this massive expense? Because insurance companies feared that the new legislation would lead to higher claims and thus adversely affect their profitability. How did they spend so much money? By employing the most successful and influential lobbyists available, individuals who have access to the most important Representatives and Senators.

It is estimated that each year US$10 billion is spent on public relations in the United States, and a significant proportion of that amount is spent on lobbying, though it is difficult to tell exactly how much. Many of the largest and most successful public relations firms are owned by advertising agencies, which creates a powerful concentration of communications expertise and understanding of the political process. It also raises an issue: should social, political, and economic issues be packaged and sold in the same way as breakfast cereals, automobiles, or hair-care products?

system relies on private, rather than public or government, profit-making and capital. Though this might seem rather obvious when we speak of the American political economy, they are really elemental properties of the system of accumulating and distributing public goods in the United States.

The American economy is a prime example of a diffuse economy, where trade and commerce are dependent on diverse arenas of exchange, ranging from production, innovation, and technology, **portfolio and direct investment**, and tight trade relations with economic allies. The American economy is based on a classic **laissez-faire** approach, whereby the marketplace is permitted to operate relatively freely within a set of legislated rules. So, though we often think of the United States as a country where the economic environment is open, this is not to suggest that there is no role for government. Indeed, given the sheer size of the United States economy, as well as its integration with the world economy, a role for the American government is a necessity.

Characterizing the American economy is a daunting task. On the one hand, the United States system might be defined in fairly tight and simple terms. It can be said, for instance, that the American economic system is predicated on three elementary factors: upholding internal and international capitalism; the government's protective and relatively passive (rather than domineering) role in the marketplace; and, the protection of public order and private property. In turn, these basic economic principles are essentially integrated with the basic political system of the United States. On the other hand, however, the American economy is one of the most complex in the world, given its sheer size and role played in international markets.

The magnitude of the American economy is only matched in the international system by regional trading *blocs*, or groups of trading nations. In fact, the United States economy is only slighter smaller than that of the entire European Union; no single state in the world can claim to rival the United States economy on the same level. As the most diverse, powerful, and innovative economy in the world, American per capita earnings are over US$30,000, which makes it the richest state in the industrialized world—gross domestic product (or GDP, the total value of goods and services produced in the country) is over US$8 trillion each year. Based on the aforementioned principle of *laissez-faire*, the American economy leaves most of the day-to-day productive, trade-related, and capital-related activities to private individuals and actors. Governments at all levels rely on private actors in the domestic marketplace for supplies and services, and private business and corporate interests in the United States are given a wider degree of flexibility in regards to microeconomic decision-making on a number of levels: production, trade, labour, and research and development. Aside from having the most important (while not always the most stable) currency (which spontaneously makes the United States the most important player in international capital markets—see below for more on the role of the United States currency in international markets), the United States is a leader in the most important economic sectors in the world today: computers, automotive technologies, medical, aerospace, and military equipment. The United States is a leader in most other major economic areas as well: petroleum, steel, telecommunications, chemicals, electronics, food processing, consumer goods, lumber, and mining. Though the United States has seen its global share decline in the late twentieth century (described in greater detail below), it still retains an absolute advantage over others.

The increased focus on technological development has resulted in a splintering of the labour classes in the United States, as major corporate and busi-

## Election Campaign Financing

Box 5.7

In recent years a growing number of questions have been raised by lawmakers and the public over the nature and implications of contributions to election campaigns. Nowhere has this been more true than in the United States of America, where the scale and intensity of election campaigns exceeds any other country. During the presidential election campaign of 1996 the Democratic party came under increasing scrutiny because of questionable methods used by fund-raisers and also because of the sources from which large contributions came.

First, a highly controversial issue emerged relating to foreign donations to the re-election campaign of President William Clinton and Vice-President Albert Gore. Evidence emerged that John Huang, a leading fund-raiser for the Democratic National Committee, had travelled to Taiwan to solicit contributions to the Clinton re-election campaign. Furthermore, he had close ties to a wealthy Indonesian family responsible for huge donations (measuring in the hundreds of thousands of dollars) to the Democratic party. Republicans charged that Clinton had promised preferential trade deals in exchange for such contributions.

Second, questions were raised about the actions of Vice-President Albert Gore, who used the White House to solicit contributions from individuals and groups. Gore argued that he was using White House phones but charging the calls to a Democratic National Committee telephone charge card, and that, more importantly, he was soliciting financial support for general party-building efforts and not specifically for the re-election campaign that he and President Bill Clinton were about to undertake. In other words the money he was soliciting was "soft," not "hard money."

Though Gore was cleared of any misconduct by United States Attorney General Janet Reno, the issue was sufficiently controversial to warrant an extension of the 1998 presidential impeachment hearings to include issues of election finances. More significantly these events led the US Congress to consider a ban on soft money, a form of political funds which brought in more than US$173 million for the Republican and Democratic parties between January 1997 and November 1998.

ness actors focus more on technological innovation and less on heavy production, which was the bedrock of the growth of the American economic development in this century (and largely contributed to Luce's comments about an "American century"). This has generated a "two-tier labour market" in the United States, with stark distinctions between professionals and factory or service labourers. This is also a consequence of the American links to global markets: severe financial crises in East Asian markets in 1998, for instance, put heavy pressure on American manufacturing, exports, and investment from emerging markets in that region.

The American **budget**—the annual estimate of national government revenue and expenditures—is the largest in the world; the United States collects over US$1.5 trillion a year, and spends about that amount as well. The budget is the basis of American **fiscal policy**, or the balance between spending and taxes as set out by the American federal government. In the United States, fiscal policy is produced by the combined efforts of three main economic actors: the Office of Management and Budget, the Council of Economic Advisors, and the federal Secretary of the Treasury. This conglomeration of powerful economic counsellors makes suggestions and recommendations to the United States president, who is ultimately responsible for making a yearly budget proposal to the American Congress, which must then agree to its terms, or make submissions to the president for agreement. Often, however, this agreement is not forthcoming, as in December 1995, when the United States government effectively shut down because the President and Congress could not agree on a suitable budget formula for that fiscal year.

The other macroeconomic factor at the basis of the American economy is **monetary policy**, or the management of the money supply and interest rates. This is managed by the Federal Reserve Board. Monetary policy in the United States is perhaps the economic sector that has the largest global impact, given the level of interaction other currencies in the international system have with the American dollar. It must be remembered that the flow, and the value, of currency (the "money markets") make up the two most important elements of any political economy, domestic or international. It will be seen later just how important the American dollar was (and still is) to the entire global economy.

## Leadership and Linkages: The United States and the Global Economy

As explained in greater detail in other sections of this text (see, for instance, Chapter 8), the international economy as we know it today is a tightly entwined dynamic that relies tremendously on the relations of many different actors. However, there is no doubt that the most significant actor in the modern global economy is the American one, both for its leadership role, and lead economic position. Of all the economies in the international system, the United States is most intertwined with the rest.

You will recall the emphasis on exports in the Canadian economic system. Unlike Canada, example, the United States is not trade-*dependent*, but a large share of its economic health is a consequence of international linkages. The economic relationship between the United States and Canada is a symbiotic, or mutually dependent, one, as each is the other's most important partner. However, where Canadian trade with the United States counts for around 80 percent of Canadian imports and exports, it only counts for around 20 percent for the United States. Nonetheless, given the immensity of the American market, Canada is not an unimportant trade partner—trading over 20 percent of the world's largest economy is no small feat. On the other hand, United States foreign economic relations are more equitably diversified than Canada's, as Western Europe constitutes a close second to Canada in both imports and exports (approximately 20 percent), and Japan and Mexico are currently almost even in terms of their relative importance to American foreign trade.

In order to understand the importance of the United States in the global economy, let us refer again to the remarks of Henry Luce. His comment that the twentieth century belonged to the United States was made at middle of the century (1941), when the United States was quite clearly the undisputed leader in the international system in both military and economic power. At the close of the Second World War, the United States had the world's largest military force, and was responsible for over 80 percent of global production. Unlike most of the rest of the industrialized world, the United States had not witnessed most of its economic and military infrastructure destroyed by the war. As a result, the Bretton Woods Agreement, which is explained in greater detail in Chapter 8, sought to create a series of international institutions, organizations, and regimes (rules and decision-making procedures) that would guide the decisions taken by states. The plan was not to strip countries of their sovereign power, but to give an important role to international institutions so as to provide peaceful ways of alleviating potential conflict. Importantly, the new international system of institutions needed a leader to uphold the system, and to provide a military and economic guarantee. That leader was the United States.

It was significant that the United States was chosen to be the leader of the international economic system at the close of the Second World War. Most of the former international leaders—the colonizing powers of Europe such as Great Britain, France, Belgium, and Germany—were simply so weakened at the close of the war that they were unable to uphold their position in the global order. And, while it might seem clear to us that the United States would be chosen to act as the leader of the new system, the decision was not taken without some resistance. As part of what became known as the **Trans-Atlantic Bargain,** the former great powers of Europe conceded to American leadership in exchange for an agreement that the United States would uphold the economic and military stability of Europe, as well as the rest of the Western world.

In turn, the global political economy at the close of the Second World War quickly began to reflect dominant American interests. From a relatively closed and autarkic environment grew an open and liberal system, predicated on economic freedom, partnership, and cooperation. For a time, it appeared as though Luce's reflections on the role of the United States in the global system was correct—for almost two decades the United States remained the unquestioned leader in the international system, retaining the position of **hegemon,** or principal power among states.

As we suggested earlier, money is really the basis of all economic systems. Therefore, managing the value and international flow of currencies was essential for the stability and strength of the post-war order. Part of American hegemony included the agreement that all currencies in the international system would be tied to the United States dollar, which was undoubtedly the strongest currency at that time. Under a rather convoluted, but sensible, system, state currencies were hitched to the American dollar, which in turn was linked to gold, at $35.00 an ounce. It might seem rather odd today to think of tying currencies to gold, but the idea at the time was perfectly sensible: locking the dollar to a tangible substance such as gold would mean that governments would not be able to overvalue or devalue their currencies, and all currencies would ultimately be linked to a hard unit of measure. One facet of this mechanism was the prohibition against individual citizens trading or speculating in gold; people could have gold jewellery, or gold fillings, but were prevented from buying or selling large amounts of gold for fear of destabilizing the values of international currencies. In addition, one of the Bretton Woods international institutions—the International Monetary Fund (IMF)—was responsible for evaluating the currencies of all member nations each year, to ensure that the currency value of each state did not fluctuate too greatly and derail the entire system. The gold standard system was an effective method of linking currencies and maintaining stability in international markets so as to avoid the autarky and lack of interaction that marked the pre-war years. But, in order to work, it needed a benchmark currency on a continual basis.

By the 1960s, a variety of factors led to the beginning of the end of

American hegemony. The rise of countries such as Germany and Japan, growing economic regionalism in Europe and Asia, the high costs of waging an unpopular war in Vietnam, the strengthening of multinational corporations (MNCs), and the rising costs associated with leading the international system and its component institutions put a huge strain on the economic viability of the United States. Had it not been for the immediate concern about warding off the perceived threat of the Soviet Union (this was, after all, the height of the Cold War), the United States might not have been considered such an inordinate leader at this time. By the early 1970s, nevertheless, these economic costs had simply become too great, and in August 1971, the United States announced unilaterally that it no longer could maintain the system as it had in the past. Then President Richard Nixon declared that the United States would no longer permit its dollar to be rigidly linked to other currencies, and to gold, and that the conditions of the Trans-Atlantic Bargain (for instance, acting as the lender of last resort for debtor nations) would not be preserved by the hegemonic power of the United States. This **New Economic Policy** (NEP), as it was called, in many ways signalled the end of the classic hegemonic period of the post-war era, and brought about the beginning of the end of real United States economic leadership in the international system.

Indeed, by the 1970s, the American political economy, as well as its position in the international system, looked very different than it did in previous decades. The closing of the gold standard in 1971, coupled with the oil shocks of 1973 and 1979 (where the price of a barrel of sweet crude oil quadrupled, resulting in the single most consequential price rise in the world's most critical natural resource), left the United States in an economic downturn. The result was a global economic **recession**, or a serious decline in economic activity, productivity, and prosperity. Making matters worse for the United States was the onslaught of domestic **stagflation**, where prices were inflationary, but employment was also down. The two most influential elements of a domestic economy—prices and wages—were both experiencing a decline. It appeared to many that the "American century" was in fact now in crisis. Political analyst Felix Rohatyn observed that the "American century" was more appropriately a "quarter century."

By the early 1980s, the economic climate in the United States began to change dramatically. The election of Ronald Reagan in November 1980, and his inauguration in January 1981, signalled a massive shift in American foreign relations. On a political level, Reagan's administration again raised the Cold War rhetoric against the Soviet Union, returning to a more traditional viewpoint of American relations with its adversary, and a more hard-line approach. It was Reagan, after all, who publicly declared the USSR an "evil empire," and sought to reclaim international military American dominance over the Soviet Union. On an economic front, Reagan pursued a reduction in the role of government in the national economy. Reagan's economic mantra was called **supply side economics**, in which the fundamental expectation is that decreasing the government's function in economic relations and reducing taxes will cause private investment to rise (along with consumer procurement, given the rising levels of personal saving thanks to reduced taxes), stimulating growth and—it was believed—ultimately lead to more taxes (but not necessarily *higher* taxes, since people and corporations would simply be making more, and paying more in taxes). The underlying logic to supply side economics (which then President George Bush once referred to as "voodoo economics") is that reducing the role of government in the economy will in fact raise revenue for government by allowing individuals and corporations to retain—and likely spend—more money than they otherwise might have.

The real upshot of the Reagan era was a mix of political success and economic troubles. While the rhetoric in Washington against the Soviet Union was met with the eventual warming of relations between the former superpowers, the supply side mantra of two successive Reagan administrations, combined with great military spending as part of the American effort to outweigh the Soviet Union in the world arena, left the American economy with the largest **deficit**, or an excess of liabilities over assets in a fiscal year, in its history. The United States deficit rose from just over US$73 billion in 1980 to over US$290 billion in 1992.

One of the interesting circumstances of the modern American economy is the seeming contrast between two fundamental forces—openness and protectionism. On the one hand the United States stands for the preservation of open liberal markets in the international system, with little impediment from national governments. This is the benchmark, after all, of the Bretton Woods system created after the Second World War. Yet on the other hand, the United States is a protectionist state, seeking to maintain its domestic stability and security in the global environment. This tendency of the American state to protect its own economic interests, even at the expense of external relations, harkens back to the strategy of **mercantilism**, or government control of national wealth in an effort to dominate the accumulation of power within a political unit. The former colonial states, Britain and France, for instance, practised mercantilism during the age of empire as they controlled the political interests of their colonies in order to command total access to wealth. While it is impossible to be either a completely free and open trading state, content to never allow governments to interfere even to protect their national interests, it is also impossible to be a completely protectionist state in a global climate of interdependence and openness. For the United States, a nation founded on openness and liberalism, reconciling its proclivities to shelter its economy, while at the same time ensuring international competitiveness is still a constant struggle.

In recent years, the United States economy has been challenged by a variety of forces, some at odds with one another. While the international system may be characterized as increasingly interdependent, states in the developed world have begun to shift their economic focus from global cooperation to cooperation within a regional sphere. Additionally, states continue to place great emphasis on the role of international institutions while at the same time they are wary of the role of non-governmental actors such as multinational corporations. The United States is one of the very few states in the international system today that can lay claim to a global sphere of influence, coupled with a regional leadership role in the Americas.

# Japan: Managing a New Leadership Role

Japan is located in the North Pacific, in one of the most volatile and robust regions in the world. One the one hand, Japan is surrounded by potentially belligerent countries such as North Korea, India, Pakistan, Taiwan, and China. On the other, Japan's emergence in the latter half of the twentieth century as the world's second largest economy has given that nation a clear economic, if not political, leadership role in this growing region.

Japan's well-being relies on close and amiable relations with its partners. Slightly smaller than the American state of California, Japan's terrain is mountainous and rugged. Its arable land comprises only 11 percent of total land mass, and permanent crops in Japan total only 1 percent of its territory. Of necessity, Japan is a trading nation. It is also an almost ethnically pure state, with over 99 percent of its population ethnic Japanese. It is impossible to become a Japanese citizen unless one is Japanese; others may work or live in Japan—many ethnic Koreans do, for example—but citizenship is reserved for Japanese only.

Japan is a constitutional monarchy with a bicameral legislature. The monarch—the Emperor—has played a largely symbolic role in Japanese politics since the modern Japanese constitution was implemented in 1947. Although this role is not unlike the Canadian governor general, the Japanese Emperor still commands a high degree of reverence in Japanese society as a result of his links to the imperial system, where he was considered a deity on earth. The Diet, or Japanese parliament, is divided into the House of Councillors and the House of Representatives. Though the Japanese political system is a multiparty one, it is nonetheless dominated by the Liberal Democratic Party, or the LDP, which has dominated domestic politics for most of the Cold War and post-Cold War eras.

Unlike the United States or Canada, Japan's domestic political economy, as well as its global position, underwent severe changes and alterations in the latter half of the twentieth century. From regional great power, to defeated nation, to global economic presence, Japan has seen its power and influence shift drastically in a short period of time. What is particularly remarkable is the short timeframe within which the Japanese political economy became such a global forerunner, second only to the United States. Partly because we are not as aware of Japanese history, and also partly because earlier sections of this book provided more details about the Canadian and American political and economic histories and systems, the following section provides more historical background than for the other two case studies.

## A Brief Political History of Japan

Japan has one of the oldest and most sophisticated political and economic histories among the advanced industrialized nations (see Table 5.3). Early written historical records in Japan, which date to the eighth century AD, relate the story of the emergence of the Japanese state, which took its first steps to nationhood in the fifth and sixth centuries. For two centuries prior to that Japan was ruled by the Yamato tribe, which had divided the island chain into hereditary units called *Uji*. (It is worth noting that the belief system of this early civilization served as the foundation for *Shinto*—or "the way of the gods" which, as Japan's traditional religion, emphasizes the need for humans to live in harmony with nature and the environment.) By the seventh century some aspects of the political system of the Chinese T'ang Dynasty (618–907) were also introduced to Japanese civilization.

Throughout this early period the Japanese political system was highly centralized. As often happens with such a system, particularly when it is able to remain relatively isolated and unchallenged, the political leadership weakened and power was decentralized. Feudal Japan emerged as a result of the decadent rule of the Fujiwara, whose political system borrowed heavily from that of China. Throughout the tenth and eleventh centuries the power of the central government declined as the prominence of provincial powers grew.

| Table 5.3 Major Periods in Japanese History | |
|---|---|
| Paleolithic period | pre–8000 BC |
| Jomon period | ca. 8000–ca. 300 BC |
| Yayoi period | ca. 300 BC–ca. AD 300 |
| Yamato period | ca. 300–593 |
| Asuka period | 593–710 |
| Nara period | 710–794 |
| Heian period | 794–1192 |
| Kamakura period | 1192–1338 |
| Muromachi period | 1338–1573 |
| Azuchi-Momoyama period | 1573–1600 |
| Edo period | 1600–1868 |
| Meiji era | 1868–1912 |
| Taisho era | 1912–1926 |
| Showa era | 1926–2989 |
| Heisei era | 1989– |

With the attainment of independence from the direct influence of the Chinese in the eleventh century and a simultaneous surge in population growth, the Japanese feudal economy began to prosper. As in the West, the mounted warrior aristocrat was a key element of this society. By the twelfth century these aristocrats were responsible for the management of tax-free estates called *shoen*, and were charged with the defence of their territories from marauders.

Although power was decentralized to provincial authority, the imperial court at Kyoto was still generally recognized as the governing authority for judging land claims and awarding government positions. However, the aristocrats were responsible for their own security, unlike European feudalism where the nobility could always appeal to the king or any other higher authority for assistance. This requirement of self-protection encouraged several groups to band together, and two became particularly powerful. The *Taira* and *Minamoto* were both composed of branches of the imperial family and both managed to garner the support of a strong military following. In the mid-twelfth century the central authority, even as limited as it was, came to be called into question. Wars started to become the commonplace way of settling various disputes among groups of nobles. When the imperial succession became a question Taira Kiyomori took advantage of his military strength to assume power in Kyoto. This action set the stage for the rise of military governance in Japan, as the *Minamoto* and other groups were not prepared to settle for *Taira* rule. This culminated in the introduction of the shogunate in 1192. The almost constant warfare made this an extremely unstable period in Japanese history.

It took until the late sixteenth century before national unity was finally restored, though in the *Tokugawa* shogunate, rather than in the imperial court. In the new *Tokugawa* period peace was maintained from roughly the mid-seventeenth to the mid-nineteenth century. Reunification and the peace that came with it fostered change, growth, and the mobilization of the Japanese economy. The *Tokugawa* period also witnessed the start of the decline of the prominence of the warrior class in Japanese politics and society.

During this time deeper relations were being forged with European states. Towards the end of the eighteenth century both the Russians and the British tried to increase their economic activity with the Japanese. Japan was also recognized as a useful water and coal replenishment station for American whaling ships and ships involved in the trade with the Chinese province of Canton. However, the Japanese of that period remained highly isolationist and resisted all attempts by the United States, Britain, and Russia to coax them into a trade deal. They were largely successful, too, at least until the mid-nineteenth century.

In July 1853 an American fleet under Commodore Matthew C. Perry entered Tokyo Bay. Perry presented a letter from the president of the United States to Japanese officials demanding that Japan open itself to trade with the Americans. The steam power and big guns of the American fleet awed the Japanese, who were given the opportunity to deliberate over their "invitation" throughout the winter. The next spring Perry returned to find that the Japanese had agreed to open two small ports to US ships and establish an American consulate. Many conservatives in Japan were vehemently opposed to this concession, but the *Tokugawa* leadership saw that it had few alternatives. Other treaties were soon reached with Britain, Russia, France, and the Dutch. By the 1860s it was becoming increasingly clear to most Japanese that their country was fast approaching the same semi-colonial status as China. With Japanese isolationism dead and the acceptance of an externally imposed policy change, domestic unrest grew to significant levels.

Many samurai declared themselves *ronin* (masterless), thus contributing to the decline of the *Tokugawa* shogunate and the re-emergence of centralized authority in the imperial court at Kyoto. In an effort to assuage some of the public discontent, the Emperor's court demonstrated a strong opposition to the adoption of Western ways in general and Western military technology in particular. The Emperor came to be revered in Japanese society, as a symbol of adherence to Japanese tradition in the face of imposed change. Everything was done in his name, including the expulsion of the "barbarians," which became the number one priority of the people. The new government, which was actually driven by a small elite consisting of samurai and court nobles, abolished the feudal system and set out to redefine Japan with the motto *fukoku kyohei*, meaning "a rich country and strong military." This effectively marked the end of the *Tokugawa* period and the introduction of the period of the *Meiji*, or "enlightened rule."

In 1871 the class system was abolished, effectively dissolving the status and power of the samurai, and a declaration of equality was made. Furthermore, all land became centralized under the empire. The finance ministry soon became the core of the government, and a banking system was created. Japanese banks were initially decentralized like those in the US, but were later redesigned and centralized based on the model of Belgian banks. The unification of Japanese currency also occurred in 1871 with the development of the yen.

Then in 1873 universal conscription was declared in an effort to ensure that Japan would have the military resources to resist foreign occupation in the early stages of its approaching period of growth. In the same year a cash tax, which replaced the feudal tax on agricultural or other produce, was levied, and those who paid a land tax were deemed the rightful owners of their land. Though the peasants were finally able to own their own land, they still revolted occasionally against the imposed taxes and conscription.

The government also recognized the need to industrialize and develop a comprehensive communications system in order to keep the West from stifling Japanese growth. Consequently, a railway, postal system, and port facilities were all developed. The Japanese were also quick to develop their own mining and munitions industries in order to fulfill their mandate for a strong military. Another important step was the recognition of the need to develop an education system and to learn about technology and industrialization from other countries. Students were sent abroad to study the navy and merchant marine of Britain, the army and medical sciences in Germany, local governmental systems and law in France, and business methods in the US.

It is worth noting that during this period of growth and modernization reliable foreign aid was not available to Japan. Where loans were made available, interest rates were extremely high. In any event the Japanese were extremely mistrustful of the West and preferred self-sufficiency as a development model anyway. The fortunate circumstance of a European silk blight in the 1860s served as the foundation for the emergence of Japan as a regional and global player. Japan seized the opportunity to increase its own exports during this period by basing its economy almost completely on the export of silk. Japan then reinvested in its own agricultural development. From this investment soon emerged the Japanese cotton industry, which became another staple in the economy. By the 1880s Japan had grown strong enough to resist most attempts by Western states to throw their weight around and dictate terms of trade. In essence, then, the Meiji revolution was a successful response to the threat of foreign domination.

Political development took another step forward in 1881 when Okuma Shigenobu suggested that Japan adopt the full British parliamentary system. For this radical suggestion he was expelled from the government. The leaders of the Meiji restoration favoured a more cautious approach, promising the establishment of some sort of constitution by 1890. A great deal of effort subsequently went into researching the constitutions of various Western governments. Preference was given to the conservative German and Austrian models in the drafting of the Japanese constitution, which was completed just before the 1890 deadline and with a great deal of German consultation.

One of the most important aspects of the Japanese constitution was that it reinforced the sovereign authority of the Emperor. This was balanced somewhat by the establishment of a House of Peers, in 1884, made up of the old court aristocracy, former *daimyo*, and new political leaders. Within a year a modem cabinet system, through which central executive control could be exercised, was also established. At the same time a civil service system that borrowed heavily from the German model was established. Both the cabinet and civil service system have remained largely unchanged since their establishment.

The Japanese constitution included a bill of rights of sorts; however, the rights of the people remained subordinate to the rule of law, which was aimed at preserving the state and, more specifically, the Emperor. It also introduced limited democracy to Japan, as a House of Representatives was established in 1890. Voting was limited to adult males who paid at least 15 yen per year in direct taxes. This only accounted for 1.26 percent of the population and 6 percent of Japanese families. It was generally believed that the efforts of the Japanese leadership to modernize and develop Western forms of government would earn the respect of Western states and help place Japan on more even footing with them. This was in fact the end result of these changes. By 1899 the British had given up their extraterritorial claims in Japan, and other

Western states soon began to do the same. By 1911 even the "unequal treaties," which prevented the Japanese from exercising control over their own tariffs, had been removed.

The result of the Meiji experience was that the Japanese came to be a strongly unified people. This was facilitated by its status as an island nation that had previously been isolated for over 200 years, as well as by the people's strong, shared sense of self-identity. These factors, combined with the absence of any significant ethnic or religious tensions among the Japanese, contributed to a highly nationalistic sentiment among the people. It may also be possible that Japanese nationalism stemmed in part from an inferiority complex involving China. The need to borrow from Chinese culture in the past created the sense in the region that Japan was a small, backward country in competition with the larger, older, and more advanced China. However, the realization that much of their culture was borrowed anyway made it somewhat easier for the Japanese to accept the need to adapt to Western encroachment. In fact, this willingness to adapt is still an important part of Japanese (and Chinese) culture and is expressed in the philosophies of Taoism (mostly Chinese), Zen Buddhism (Chinese and Japanese), and Budo (Japanese), among others.

This sense of nationalism contributed to the creation of the Japanese empire throughout the 1880s and 1890s. In addition to consolidating control over the entire island chain, the Japanese government also managed to take control of the island of Taiwan and the Korean peninsula. Competition for control over the Liaotung Peninsula and Manchuria, where the Russians already had a strong presence, was the initial source of conflict in the Russo-Japanese war of 1904–1905.

Japan took advantage of the alliance it had established with England in 1904 by declaring war on Germany in 1914 and seizing control over German colonies in the East. Throughout the interwar period Japan began to distance itself somewhat from the West in an attempt to fall back into its isolationist cocoon. Perceptions of Western racism, especially in the US and Britain, were particularly offensive and contributed further to the nationalist sentiments nascent in Japanese society. These perceptions were derived largely from the marginalization of Japanese concerns and perspectives at international conferences such as the Versailles Peace Conference of 1919 and the London Naval Conferences between 1930–1935, among others.

Japanese militarism began with the swift and total conquest of Manchuria in 1931. Japanese policy rapidly shifted from one of isolationism to one of expansionism on the continent. This period of heightened nationalism and expansionism, which obviously continued into World War Two, serves as the basis for much of the mistrust and animosity on the part of other Asian states towards Japan today. Economic development reflected this militaristic trend with a developing emphasis on light and heavy industries and chemical production.

## Japan and Post-War Political Economy

Japan was devastated at the end of the war. For seven years, from 1945–1952, the Americans occupied Japan and played a significant role in rebuilding the country, both economically and politically. For their part, the Japanese were surprisingly accepting of the Americans, particularly once they saw that the Americans had a genuine interest in helping to rebuild the country. Much of this acceptance may also be attributed to a certain degree of resentment towards the Emperor's government for leading the country to such failure. In the aftermath, concepts such as nationalism became taboo, and the Japanese had little interest in rebuilding their military, regardless of the fact that they were prevented from doing so. Instead, Japanese and American energies were focused on the redevelopment of the economic and civil infrastructure of the country.

When Japan finally achieved full independence in 1952 it also inherited the struggle against communism that much of the rest of the world was also facing. During the 1950s Japan went through a period during which much of its domestic politics was taken up by the struggle between its socialist and conservative political parties. At the same time it was experiencing an economic boom. American involvement in the Korean War necessitated an increase in trade with Japan. This increase in Japanese exports was capitalized on and has continued to the present. With its newfound economic prosperity Japan was able to make its war reparations in relatively short order.

The post-war years represent the most remarkable period in modern Japanese economic history. As a result of the redrafting of the Japanese constitution—the foundation for its basic law—and its tight alliance with the United States (the Japan-United States Mutual Security Treaty), Japan was restricted from organizing or budgeting for an offensive armed forces. An important factor that allowed Japan to appear not to have taken sides during the Cold War was its efforts to normalize relations with the Soviet Union and China. By steering clear of involvement in major international conflict and relying on its relations with the US, Japan has been able to focus its developmental efforts almost exclusively on domestic government and civilian industry.

Furthermore, though permitted to maintain a defensive security force,

Japan was not allowed to rebuild its large pre-war military arsenal. Though some may consider this to be an infringement on Japanese sovereignty, it must be borne in mind that the framers of the United States-Japanese relationship were worried about Japanese military resurgence, on the one hand, and the perception from the Asian regional sphere, as well as the rest of the globe, that Japan would again seek its former imperialist role.

However, the restrictions placed on Japan regarding its domestic military ability actually permitted a large degree of independence in economic matters. Given the opportunity to concentrate on matters of a non-security nature, the Japanese government began a strategic effort to rebuild its domestic economy and industry, and to strike out in sectors of the international economy that would aid in its redevelopment efforts. Perhaps the most significant medium for this development was the creation of the federal Ministry of International Trade and Industry (MITI). This ministry was, and still is, responsible for the orchestration of domestic economic ventures and targeting within the international environment. It was MITI that was responsible for the strategic marketing of Japanese technology and consumer electronics worldwide. Partly because of the **corporatist** model of government in Japan, which allows for the integration of business interests and government officials in decision-making, MITI was very successful in both identifying emerging consumer and corporate markets in the industrialized world, and distributing its goods globally. For instance, MITI was integral to the international efforts to market microelectronic goods such as small transistor radios at a time when established American and European manufacturers (Zenith, Emerson, and Philips, for example) were still producing larger vacuum tube units. It only takes a quick look around any electronics store today to see the influence of the Japanese manufacturers on our buying habits.

The broad policy implemented and followed by the Japanese in the postwar years was a combination of three basic decisions: to establish a non-interventionist role in international affairs; to support the United States as hegemonic in the global system and to deepen links with the Americans; and to focus on the domestic economy of Japan as a means of reassembling power and influence. This came to be known as the **Yoshida Doctrine**, and was a largely successful policy of domestic attention and international interaction. It was also a firm break from the more entangled and involved role Japan had played, particularly in the Asian sphere, in previous eras. The post-war order, then, saw the role of Japan in a far different light.

| Box 5.8 | Business-Government Relations in Asia |
|---------|---------------------------------------|

In many Asian countries the relationship between business and government is very close, with a high level of interaction between the state and large corporations. The goal of this cooperation is to produce both economic stability and higher levels of international competitiveness. In South Korea such a relationship existed and appeared to work very well until the financial and economic crisis of 1997–98. The largest industrial and business conglomerates, families of corporations known as *chaebol*, worked closely with the government in the formation of domestic economic, trade, and investment policies. Many analysts saw this as being one of the great advantages of countries such as South Korea, allowing them to harness the power of the national government to assist in the development of competitive industries, and also ensuring the collaboration of big business in achieving the goals of the government, both domestic and international.

When the deep financial and economic crisis of 1997 hit South Korea, these longstanding assumptions were rapidly reconsidered, for it emerged that the relationship between government and big business had been, perhaps, too close.

## Japan's Contemporary Political Economy

It is ironic, therefore, that Japan became such a leading international participant in trade and commerce. Though its economy and national infrastructure were obliterated as a result of the Second World War, Japan quickly came to challenge the United States as a regional economic forerunner in the Asia-Pacific rim, and became the second largest single national economy after the United States; by the early 1990s, Japan was responsible for 11 percent of global exports and 8 percent of global imports. In addition, since the end of the Vietnam conflict in 1974, Japan has consistently been the world's second largest source of investment and development aid in the Asian region, again, after the United States. Given the relatively recent colonial history of Japan, this move to regional supporter is a consequential shift in Japanese regional political economy. As evidence of this, Japan is a serious proponent of the two main economic bodies in the region—the Association of South East Asian Nations (ASEAN), and the Asia-Pacific Economic Cooperation (APEC) body.

The reasons for Japanese economic success in the post-war and post-Cold War eras are numerous, but several are particularly irrefutable. First, Japan's careful planning and strategic marketing have contributed to its long-term objective of regional and international strength. Rather than attempting to immerse itself in existing sectors—such as primary resources or heavy manufacturing—Japan instead targeted future and emerging markets that were not already inundated with existing actors.

Second, self-imposed regulations on international investment, for instance, kept credit and wealth at home, and discouraged the foreign ownership of domestic enterprises. Later in the 1960s, as the Japanese domestic economy began to benefit from the tremendous effects of growth in international markets, the government began to relax laws on domestic and international investment at a time when investment opportunities—both for Japanese interests and foreign interests—were exceptionally sound. Investment laws were again loosened in 1986, leading to another period of growth in Japanese multinational interests abroad, as well as international investment in Japan.

Third, Japan made critical assessments of its domestic abilities and needs. For instance, Japan must import over 80 percent of its domestic energy needs, even though it has a small oil production and refinery industry. As well, Japan has negligible mineral resources, meaning that many of the primary goods for daily life in that country must be imported. Strategic assessments, then, allowed the Japanese government to set objectives in regards to goods and services that needed to be imported, versus those in which Japan held a crucial pre-eminence, such as manufactured goods and high technology. Due to the nature of the value of primary, secondary, and tertiary goods, a country such as Japan that exports final—tertiary—goods such as automobiles is able to hold a favourable balance of trade with a country that relies on the export of primary goods, such as timber or ore, and in turn must import final goods. Japan is an excellent example of successful strategic economic assessments: its trade surplus in 1992, for instance, was US$107 billion. Obviously, this is a fortunate position to be in, but it does pose problems with trading partners who may feel as though states such as Japan take advantage of rules of international trade and commerce.

This relates to the fourth reason for continuing Japanese economic success. As mentioned earlier in this chapter—and also explained in other chapters—the post-war order, or the Bretton Woods period, was framed by the international liberalization of markets, openness in trade and commerce, a reduction in tariffs, and the careful integration of national modes of economic interaction and interdependence. So what happens when a country plays just outside the rules—normative or legal—of an open system? One possible result is a position of predominance and success based on ensuring that others adhere to the rules, while maintaining domestic rules and regulations that take advantage of the system. This is, in a nutshell, what many have argued Japan has been able to do in the post-war environment. Previously we introduced and discussed the concept of mercantilism, where countries seek to control and contain wealth in an effort to gain power and influence. As already argued, European states during the age of empire sought to control the accumulation of wealth as a means of securing power and influence in the international system. Japanese "mercantilism" is a little different. The Japanese government does not completely control the economic activities within and outside of its borders, but through the aforementioned corporatist structure of decision-making, the Japanese government sees the direct involvement of private interests in the public realm of government policy-making. Though there are clear benefits for private businesses and corporations here (after all, having a direct say in the process of decision-making may only be seen as an advantage for private interests), there are also gains for government in this mechanism. Government actors have a direct input in and observation of private economic players in the Japanese system, giving them a better understanding of and more efficient relationship with these actors. Here is an unveiled example of true *political economy* whereby the political and economic sectors of a system are deeply entwined and it is impossible to analyze one without the other. However, it is important to note that this new form of national mercantilism employed in Japan relies on an international system that is open, free from tariffs, and competitive, rule-driven, and liberal. It also relies on the dominance of a single actor, and the substantial involvement of international regulatory institutions. Finally, a modern mercantilistic state such as Japan cannot be entirely prosperous if others follow its lead, or if the openness in the system is challenged or threatened. Herein lies the potential stumbling block for the Japanese: the likelihood that other actors in the international system would seek to punish Japan for its machinations of a liberal, open trading order.

Fifth, the Japanese economy has been successful in the contemporary era in part as a result of its distinctiveness. It is, after all, a very different state in terms of political history, culture, and domestic economy, than states in North America or Europe. Japan's ability to continually enjoy a favourable balance of trade means that it sells more valuable final goods and products than it needs to import. This has been characterized by some observers as "one-sided globalization" whereby Japan reaps the benefits of international openness, institutions, and world markets, yet does not position itself on the import side to the same degree that other trading nations do, or must (see, for example, the case of Canada above). Though a strong player in an international environment of openness and liberalization, Japan has often been criticized as being a **protectionist** state that would seek to uphold its domestic interests at all times over the health of the international economy—even though it benefits greatly from the international economy. There are many details of the Japanese political economy that lead analysts to apply the protectionist label to Japan. Perhaps most broadly, Japanese culture and history is vastly different from other trading states in the international system, often resulting in confusion and misinterpretation about Japanese practices and conventions. For instance, high-level actors, usually government officials, are essential for laying the groundwork for future economic interaction with Japanese participants. Cultural mores that require deep and respectful relations before the nuts and bolts of economic relations may be applied are often confusing to Westerners attempting to do business in Japan. As a result, Japanese officials and executives are often misunderstood as not interested in immediate joint ventures or collaboration with Westerners.

On a more substantive level, government procurement practices, legislated administrative regulations, restrictive standards, and government policies to safeguard national industries are often perceived as protectionist to foreign observers. For example, the before-mentioned sectors of the Japanese economy that are not capable of strategic global positioning (such as agriculture and mineral extraction) are supported by government subsidies in order to safeguard against their deterioration in the face of foreign competitors. As a result, foreign exporters are often frustrated at the discriminatory environment in which they must compete for Japanese market share.

Further to this is the Japanese tradition of *keiretsu*, which is the vertical integration of large industrial groups. "Vertically integrated" means that the essential independence and autonomy in decision-making and production is retained by individual industries and businesses through the practice of permitting like-minded groups to bind together to influence the policy process in Japan. In addition, smaller or medium-size industries and enterprises may not just be protected by governmental subsidies, but may also be linked to the larger *keiretsu* that are so influential in the corporatist political operations in Japan.

In contrast to the United States and Canada, Japan's political economy today is the result of short- and long-term strategic economic planning after the Second World War. With a ruined national economy and relatively few close bilateral or multilateral partners, the Japanese government made a series of important policy decisions regarding the future and focus of economic relations in that country. The direct involvement of business and corporate actors in policy development in Japan, coupled with a targeted approach regarding sectors of the international economy and protection of domestic economic interests, has created one of the most powerful economies in the world, second only to the United States. For the immediate future, one of the most significant issues that must be faced by the Japanese government is the matter of Japan's place in the international system beyond its leadership in the Asia-Pacific region. Will Japan begin to focus more directly in its regional sphere, or will it continue to broaden its scope to the globalized economy? In addition, the continuing question of Japanese mercantilism and protectionism plagues relations with the United States, which has come to view its Japanese counterpart as shielding its own economy at the expense of the global economy.

In the 1990s, however, the Japanese government was faced with a more pressing problem. A deep financial crisis struck the country in the early part of the decade, breaking several banks that had earlier ranked among the largest in the world. This banking crisis was matched by a crash in the real estate market, which had become hugely inflated in the 1980s. For the first time since the Second World War, the Japanese economy began to shrink as corporations and individuals faced bankruptcy. For many Japanese this crisis challenged the assumptions they had come to take for granted concerning Japan's economic dominance and efficiency. Political instability followed, and for the first time in a decade the Liberal Democratic Party lost power, albeit temporarily.

Japan's recession did not only have economic and political consequences at home. As the world's second largest economy, the crisis exacerbated a deep economic crisis in Asia (in Thailand, Indonesia, and South Korea in particular) in 1997 as the Japanese market for Asian exports shrank. The two crises combined to slow down global economic growth and brought the prospect of a global recession to the attention of policy-makers in the United States, Europe, and the International Monetary Fund (IMF). Since then Japan's government has been under pressure from the United States and the IMF to stimulate the Japanese economy by deregulation, tax cuts, and government spending. In mid-1999 the Japanese economy began to pull out of recession, and the future for Japan looks relatively bright.

This crisis, however, underscored the importance of Japan in the international economy, and highlighted the fact, already apparent to some, that Japanese (and Asian) approaches to political economy may not be as efficient and effective as we had long assumed. Indeed, some analysts claimed that the close relationship between government and business, long praised for increasing the efficiency of economic policy, was in fact partially responsible for the crisis. As the Japanese recovery continues, important questions are being asked about the future of Japan's political economy.

## Summary

Chapter 5 has introduced you to some of the major issues facing industrialized nations today. Economic stability and growth is a key element of a modern state's political stability and international reputation. Increasingly, countries have focused on the welfare goals of their citizens as the need to concentrate entirely on military and defensive security has been less important than in the past. As we will see in the following chapter, developing states have their own set of concerns, which are often quite different from those of the developed world. Yet one of the lead themes that binds both developed and developing nations in their political economy is the entwined nature of international and domestic levels of analysis. Indeed, it is impossible to fully comprehend the intricacies of any nation's political economy if attention is not given to both levels.

## Self-Assessment Questions

1. What is meant by the "revolutions" in advanced political economies? What are the implications for industrialized states?
2. Why has the rise of the welfare state placed such strain on industrialized nations?
3. Compare and contrast industrial and economic development in Canada, the United States, and Japan since the end of the Second World War.
4. What is meant by "post-industrialization?"

## Further Reading

DiClerico, Robert D., and Allan S. Hammock. *Points of View: Readings in American Government and Politics.* Toronto: McGraw-Hill, 1995.

Landes, Ronald G. *The Canadian Polity: A Comparative Introduction.* Scarborough: Prentice-Hall Canada, 1998.

Oliver, Thomas F. *The Political Economy of Trade Integration.* Heildelberg: Physica-Verlag, 1996.

Richardson, Bradley. *Japanese Democracy: Power, Coordination, and Performance.* New Haven: Yale University Press, 1997.

Rohatyn, Felix G. *The Twenty-Year Century: Essays on Economics and Public Finance.* New York: Random House, 1983.

Roskin, Michael G. *Countries and Concepts: An Introduction to Comparative Politics.* Upper Saddle River: Prentice-Hall, 1998.

 Web Links

Government of Canada
http://www.gc.ca
Government of United States
http://ciir2.cs.umass.edu/Govbot/
Government of Japan
http://dir.yahoo.com/Regional/Countries/Japan/Government/
NAFTA
http://www.nafta-sec-alena.org/
Japanese MITI
http://www.miti.go.jp/index-e.html

## CHAPTER SIX

# POLITICAL ECONOMY IN THE DEVELOPING WORLD

## Chapter Objectives

After reading this chapter you will be able to:

- define the terms *development* and *developing*
- differentiate between national and international development paths
- compare and contrast the political and economic challenges facing developing countries in the early twenty-first century
- assess the importance of democratization
- identify some of the links between political and economic development.

Countries in the process of political and economic development face many of the same problems and challenges as those we consider to be "developed." Issues of justice, equality, economic growth and stability, and inflation, all feature in the political debates and conflicts of states in Latin America, Africa, Asia, and Eastern Europe. Governments, citizens, and corporations in developing countries, however, confront a wide range of challenges that the nations of Western Europe, Scandinavia, North America, and Japan have already overcome, or are unique to political and economic development in the early twenty-first century. These problems include overpopulation, disease control, capital flight, environmental degradation, democratization, public order, and the creation of a viable infrastructure.

In Chapter 6 we will examine the political and economic systems of three **Less Developed Countries** (LDCs), Mexico, Nigeria, and China. These three countries face many different challenges among them, but also some that they share in common. Each has chosen, or had chosen for it, a markedly different development path, and the road to development has presented each of them with obstacles both large and small, short- and long-term, national and international.

Such problems at the beginning of the twenty-first century pose a strong challenge to the stability and well-being of the world's developing countries, but they also provide the student of political economy with a myriad of interesting research cases. As we will see in this chapter, the dual challenges of political and economic development are linked, though exactly how we are not yet sure. Many developing countries face a difficult situation in which they must stabilize their economies, an often painful process for ordinary people in economic terms, at the same time as they try to consolidate democratic practices and the legitimacy of their regimes. The interaction between political processes and economic adjustment and stabilization can teach us much about the nature of political economy, about the problems of applying abstract theories to the real world, and of the dangers of formulating economic policies without taking political factors into consideration (and vice-versa).

A word should be said about the terminology used in this chapter. During the Cold War students of political studies and political economy referred to poorer countries in a number of ways, labelling them the **Third World** (after the First World of Western industrialized states and the Second World of the communist bloc). Others (quite inaccurately in geographic terms) have divided the world into **North** (the wealthy countries) and **South** (the poorer states). Financial analysts and economists today talk of **emerging markets**, poorer economies with potential for future growth. This chapter, however, prefers to use the terms LDCs and developing countries.

# Political and Economic Development

For many years development was seen in a purely economic sense, implying growth and industrialization of the economy and little else. Slowly students of political economy came to see the problems of development in a multidimensional manner, accepting that progress could be understood in more than one way and that truly developed societies must provide more than just economic benefits for their members. Citizens should be involved, for example, in the decisions that affect their futures, either through group representation, direct democracy, or perhaps decentralization of power. The governing of society should be less arbitrary and more rules-oriented, guaranteeing due process of law and security of person. Of course economic growth should be a priority, but it has become obvious to political economists that the issue is far more complex. Questions of distribution, stability, and government involvement versus free markets all complicate the goal of growth.

## Political and Social Development

In the early twenty-first century, the issue that has come to dominate discussions of political development is that of democracy. Since the end of the Cold War democratization has been considered a priority for underdeveloped countries by both national and international authorities and organizations, a political liberalization to go hand in hand with the progressive (and in some cases rather rapid) liberalization of their economies. But the spread of democracy throughout the world is but one feature of political and social development. LDCs are often young states, many having been created since the end of the Second World War and the retreat of **colonialism** (see below), and lack well-established government institutions (see Table 6.1). What they seek in their development paths are essentially the political values and goods (justice, order, freedom, etc.) described in Chapter 2. One of the most common goods sought by developing country governments is legitimacy. In many cases the short history of their countries as independent states makes it difficult for governments to achieve true legitimacy in the eyes of the people. In others it is not the brevity but rather the turbulence of their history that makes legitimacy an elusive goal.

Democracy, of course, is one way to achieve legitimacy in the eyes of both

### Table 6.1 Decolonization and the United Nations: Years of Admission

| Year of admission | Countries |
|---|---|
| 1960 | Benin |
| | Burkina Faso |
| | Cameroon |
| | Central African Republic |
| | Chad |
| | Congo |
| | Côte d'Ivoire |
| | Cyprus |
| | Democratic Republic of the Congo |
| | Gabon |
| | Madagascar |
| | Mali |
| | Niger |
| | Nigeria |

*continued*

| | |
|---|---|
| | Senegal |
| | Somalia |
| | Togo |
| 1961 | Syria |
| | Mauritania |
| | Mongolia |
| | Sierra Leone |
| | United Republic of Tanzania |
| 1962 | Algeria |
| | Jamaica |
| | Rwanda |
| | Trinidad and Tobago |
| | Uganda |
| 1963 | Kenya |
| | Kuwait |
| 1964 | Malawi |
| | Malta |
| | Zambia |
| 1965 | Gambia |
| | Singapore |
| | Maldives |
| 1966 | Barbados |
| | Botswana |
| | Guyana |
| | Lesotho |
| 1968 | Equatorial Guinea |
| | Mauritius |
| | Swaziland |

national and international societies. By including all adult citizens in the electoral process, by allowing voters to choose their government rather than having it imposed upon them, a democratic political system helps to guarantee its own survival. As we shall see, however, in two of the three countries studied in this chapter there have been serious problems to overcome before Western-style democracy could be achieved, and in the third, democratization is not even an option made available to the Chinese people. Democracy is difficult to institute in society, as the experience of democratization in Western Europe in the eighteenth, nineteenth, and twentieth centuries demonstrates. It requires the overthrow of established power elites and the creation of strong institutions that guarantee democratic representation. Primarily, of course, it requires the presence of a liberal ideology that will drive individuals and groups to fight for democracy.

It should not be thought that democracy acts as a cure-all for the political challenges faced by developing countries. Democracy, on its own, cannot rectify deep social divisions for example, nor can it guarantee justice. It cannot eliminate the use of violence as a means of exercising power, nor the political advantages conferred by wealth. Democracy does not imply stability or even security. Neither should it be thought that it is necessarily the best system for all societies. Most of human political history has been un- even anti-democratic. The norm throughout history has been repression of the many by the

---

## The Human Development Index

Box 6.1

Instead of focusing exclusively on the size of a nation's economy, or even on the size of the economy per person, the United Nations decided that it would use a broader indicator of national development that took into account a wide range of relevant factors. The United Nations Human Development Index (HDI) uses a combined measurement of income, life expectancy, and literacy to determine the level of individual development granted by national economies. These factors are chosen because they increase individuals' freedom to direct and control their own lives. The index gives a rating to each country, and the closer that number is to one, the more highly developed it is according to the HDI. Countries such as Canada and Japan frequently appear at the top of this list with ratings of around 0.90–0.95, but most of the world's LDCs fare less well. Countries such as China feature in the middle of the list, but Nigeria comes in at number 141 overall, with an HDI rating of only 0.41.

few, of might equalling right. Even those societies (tribal or otherwise) which have been egalitarian in nature have been based on the group or family rather than the individual. Many societies today still hold the group in higher regard than the individual and may thus not be ideally suited for democracy as practised by European and North American states.

On the other hand, liberal democracy appeals to us for the reasons we saw in Chapters 1 and 2. Morally it makes sense to us as North Americans to accord every individual member of our society the same right to decide their political future. A commitment to democratic values means seeking peaceful resolutions to conflict before resorting to violence. Democracy, when applied in its Western form, means including groups and minorities, not excluding them, a quality that leads to a higher probability of stability and sense of community. Just as importantly, the history of many developing countries demonstrates that non-democratic regimes find themselves unable to hold on to power either sooner or later, even if they are not then replaced by democratic regimes.

As we saw in Chapter 5, democracy works in developed countries such as Canada, the United States, and Japan because of the political institutions that enforce and implement the principles of democracy. Institutions such as a competitive party system, parliaments, or congresses where elected representatives may not only voice the concerns of the electorate but also meaningfully influence the policy process, and electoral commissions that ensure that elections are run according to universally accepted rules and regulations all encourage the use of democratic and non-violent means of resolving political conflicts. As we shall see in the case of Mexico, an independent federal elections commission is essential if elections are to be free and fair, as is the involvement of observers from other countries and from international organizations.

If democracy is going to work and become embedded in a country's political culture, it is surely crucial that the electoral system functions effectively. This means choosing a system that adequately represents the views and interests of significant minority groups and parties, while at the same time ensuring stability and a government's ability to both pass and implement legislation. Here the choice is usually between a plurality system with single-member constituencies and a first-past-the-post (FPP) method of determining winners on the one hand, and some form of proportional representation (PR) on the other. Both have their advantages and disadvantages for stable democracy.

FPP systems tend to favour large, universal parties, tending to produce either two- or three-party systems. This generally means greater stability in the short- and medium-term as governments find themselves with considerable freedom of action to develop and implement policy initiatives. However, FPP systems tend to exclude smaller parties, leading in the longer term to a problem of legitimacy as minority views are not taken into consideration. If these minorities are sufficiently powerful, and sufficiently alienated by the system, then there is the risk of violent resistance as they try to protect their interests.

PR systems tend to represent the views of important minority groups much better than those using FPP methods, particularly those employing large multi-member constituencies. In these systems smaller parties can generally garner enough support to win a limited number of seats in the legislature, where they can form coalitions with each other or with larger parties, and thus exercise influence over the legislative process. But such coalition-building can cripple the effectiveness of the same legislative process. Governments are often held hostage to the whims and interests of their minority partners, forced to modify policy initiatives in exchange for continued support. Worse, a government can find itself losing support from its coalition partners if it does not represent their interests and preferences, and in such a situation can rapidly become a **lame-duck,** lacking sufficient support in the national legislature to have its policies passed into law.

The choice of electoral system is particularly important in those states which have deep ethnic and social divisions, as we will see in the case of Nigeria. In much of the developing world, and in particular in Africa, national borders were drawn arbitrarily by the colonial power, without respect for existing forms of social organization or even natural and geographical boundaries, and many different ethnic and linguistic groups share the same geographical territory, government, and institutions. An electoral system in such situations must recognize the differences between different groups but also help to unify them and encourage cooperation rather than conflict as the guiding principle of their relations. In many African countries this has been exceedingly difficult, and in some cases so far, impossible to achieve.

A free and independent media establishment is one of the private institutions that is desirable if democracy is to function effectively, yet in most LDCs this has remained an elusive goal. Television, radio stations, and newspapers are directly controlled by governments in some countries with little viable competition, while in others there are severe restrictions on reporting, with censorship regulations that allow the government to control the flow of information. China is a perfect example of this. Not only does the Chinese government control the flow of information, it also censors the arts to prevent criticism of its own activities (see Box 6.2). For many developing countries there is still a shortage of access to reliable information and independent evaluation of the government and political system. However, as technology has become cheaper, and televisions and radios more commonplace, there has been a positive effect on both the spread and consolidation of democracy.

But of course not all political institutions are concerned with democracy, though they can help to consolidate its place in society. The structure of political parties greatly influences the ability of the state to formulate and implement policy. Other institutions help governments to rule. A well-run, professional, and independent bureaucracy will grant the government the expertise it needs to govern a country efficiently and effectively. A mature, rules-based, and egalitarian legal system will ensure equal and predictable treatment for a country's citizens and help to resolve private conflicts peacefully.

This last institution is essential of course for the achievement of legal justice. The achievement of justice is a vital element of political and social development, for without it the government will face constant opposition from those treated unfairly by the system. Increasingly the search for justice in

**Box 6.2**

# China vs. Richard Gere

China's record on human rights marks it as a politically under-developed country, despite the immense progress made in the economic realm. In recent years there has been a spate of Hollywood movies about Chinese repression, particularly over China's occupation of Tibet, which the Chinese government claims is a part of China. Actor Richard Gere has made a personal quest out of campaigning against the Chinese government on this issue, and in 1997 made a movie titled *Red Corner* which focused on the unjust nature of the Chinese legal system. Such movies as *Red Corner*, *Kundun*, and *Seven Years in Tibet* have been banned from China, and censorship extends into many other areas of the media as well. China is one of the most enthusiastic countries in the area of censoring the Internet, though this is not, of course, in order to protect young people from the effects of pornography, but rather to prevent the spread of status quo-challenging ideas and anti-CCP discourse. The long-term viability of such policies of censorship is dubious, however. With satellite television getting cheaper all the time, increased and cheaper access to the Internet, cell phones and, of course, good old-fashioned radio, such attempts to restrict the free flow of information seem destined for failure, particularly among a population which is getting wealthier every year.

LDCs is focused on the respect for human rights as understood by international society and the United Nations (see Box 6.3). A high level of **human rights abuses** is a strong signal that a country is socially and politically underdeveloped (though developed countries also commit such offences from time to time). Each of the three countries studied in this chapter has recently been under international scrutiny for its human rights records, and it is a constant embarrassment that their respective governments try to smooth over and cover up as best they can.

The legal system of a country is also an important weapon in the defence against corruption. This particular problem has come into high profile in recent years as international aid agencies have linked their programs to efforts to reduce the influence of corruption in national political and economic systems. There is an important connection between anti-corruption policies and democracy, of course; a system's benefits cannot be universally shared and enjoyed if they are reserved for those with economic, social, or political influence. The legal system must be seen to apply equally to all if all are to have respect for that system. Likewise government and the bureaucracy; without free and equal access to these institutions they will not be seen as legitimate.

## Universal Declaration of Human Rights          Box 6.3

### Preamble

Whereas recognition of the inherent dignity and of the equal and inalienable rights of all members of the human family is the foundation of freedom, justice and peace in the world,

Whereas disregard and contempt for human rights have resulted in barbarous acts which have outraged the conscience of mankind, and the advent of a world in which human beings shall enjoy freedom of speech and belief and freedom from fear and want has been proclaimed as the highest aspiration of the common people,

Whereas it is essential, if man is not to be compelled to have recourse, as a last resort, to rebellion against tyranny and oppression, that human rights should be protected by the rule of law,

Whereas it is essential to promote the development of friendly relations between nations,

Whereas the peoples of the United Nations have in the Charter reaffirmed their faith in fundamental human rights, in the dignity and worth of the human person and in the equal rights of men and women and have determined to promote social progress and better standards of life in larger freedom,

Whereas Member States have pledged themselves to achieve, in cooperation with the United Nations, the promotion of universal respect for and observance of human rights and fundamental freedoms,

Whereas a common understanding of these rights and freedoms is of the greatest importance for the full realization of this pledge,

Now, therefore,

The General Assembly,

Proclaims this Universal Declaration of Human Rights as a common standard of achievement for all peoples and all nations, to the end that every individual and every organ of society, keeping this Declaration constantly in mind, shall strive by teaching and education to promote respect for these rights and freedoms and by progressive measures, national and international, to secure their universal and effective recognition and observance, both among the peoples of Member States themselves and among the peoples of territories under their jurisdiction.

## Article 1

All human beings are born free and equal in dignity and rights. They are endowed with reason and conscience and should act towards one another in a spirit of brotherhood.

## Article 2

Everyone is entitled to all the rights and freedoms set forth in this Declaration, without distinction of any kind, such as race, colour, sex, language, religion, political or other opinion, national or social origin, property, birth or other status.

Furthermore, no distinction shall be made on the basis of the political, jurisdictional or international status of the country or territory to which a person belongs, whether it be independent, trust, non-self-governing or under any other limitation of sovereignty.

## Article 3

Everyone has the right to life, liberty and security of person.

## Article 4

No one shall be held in slavery or servitude; slavery and the slave trade shall be prohibited in all their forms.

## Article 5

No one shall be subjected to torture or to cruel, inhuman or degrading treatment or punishment.

## Article 6

Everyone has the right to recognition everywhere as a person before the law.

## Article 7

All are equal before the law and are entitled without any discrimination to equal protection of the law. All are entitled to equal protection against any discrimination in violation of this Declaration and against any incitement to such discrimination.

## Article 8

Everyone has the right to an effective remedy by the competent national tribunals for acts violating the fundamental rights granted him by the constitution or by law.

## Article 9

No one shall be subjected to arbitrary arrest, detention or exile.

## Article 10

Everyone is entitled in full equality to a fair and public hearing by an independent and impartial tribunal, in the determination of his rights and obligations and of any criminal charge against him.

## Article 11

Everyone charged with a penal offence has the right to be presumed innocent until proved guilty according to law in a public trial at which he has had all the guarantees necessary for his defence.

No one shall be held guilty of any penal offence on account of any act or omission which did not constitute a penal offence, under national or international law, at the time when it was committed. Nor shall a heavier penalty be imposed than the one that was applicable at the time the penal offence was committed.

## Article 12

No one shall be subjected to arbitrary interference with his privacy, family, home or correspondence, nor to attacks upon his honour and reputation. Everyone has the right to the protection of the law against such interference or attacks.

## Article 13

Everyone has the right to freedom of movement and residence within the borders of each State.

Everyone has the right to leave any country, including his own, and to return to his country.

## Article 14

Everyone has the right to seek and to enjoy in other countries asylum from persecution.

This right may not be invoked in the case of prosecutions genuinely arising from non-political crimes or from acts contrary to the purposes and principles of the United Nations.

## Article 15

Everyone has the right to a nationality.

No one shall be arbitrarily deprived of his nationality nor denied the right to change his nationality.

## Article 16

Men and women of full age, without any limitation due to race, nationality or religion, have the right to marry and to found a family. They are entitled to equal rights as to marriage, during marriage and at its dissolution.

Marriage shall be entered into only with the free and full consent of the intending spouses.

The family is the natural and fundamental group unit of society and is entitled to protection by society and the State.

## Article 17

Everyone has the right to own property alone as well as in association with others.

No one shall be arbitrarily deprived of his property.

## Article 18

Everyone has the right to freedom of thought, conscience and religion; this right includes freedom to change his religion or belief, and freedom, either alone or in community with others and in public or private, to manifest his religion or belief in teaching, practice, worship and observance.

## Article 19

Everyone has the right to freedom of opinion and expression; this right includes freedom to hold opinions without interference and to seek, receive and impart information and ideas through any media and regardless of frontiers.

## Article 20

Everyone has the right to freedom of peaceful assembly and association.
No one may be compelled to belong to an association.

## Article 21

Everyone has the right to take part in the government of his country, directly or through freely chosen representatives.

   Everyone has the right to equal access to public service in his country.
The will of the people shall be the basis of the authority of government; this will shall be expressed in periodic and genuine elections which shall be by universal and equal suffrage and shall be held by secret vote or by equivalent free voting procedures.

## Article 22

Everyone, as a member of society, has the right to social security and is entitled to realization, through national effort and international co-operation and in accordance with the organization and resources of each State, of the economic, social and cultural rights indispensable for his dignity and the free development of his personality.

## Article 23

Everyone has the right to work, to free choice of employment, to just and favourable conditions of work and to protection against unemployment.

   Everyone, without any discrimination, has the right to equal pay for equal work.

Everyone who works has the right to just and favourable remuneration ensuring for himself and his family an existence worthy of human dignity, and supplemented, if necessary, by other means of social protection.

Everyone has the right to form and to join trade unions for the protection of his interests.

## Article 24

Everyone has the right to rest and leisure, including reasonable limitation of working hours and periodic holidays with pay.

## Article 25

Everyone has the right to a standard of living adequate for the health and well-being of himself and of his family, including food, clothing, housing and medical care and necessary social services, and the right to security in the event of unemployment, sickness, disability, widowhood, old age or other lack of livelihood in circumstances beyond his control.

Motherhood and childhood are entitled to special care and assistance. All children, whether born in or out of wedlock, shall enjoy the same social protection.

## Article 26

Everyone has the right to education. Education shall be free, at least in the elementary and fundamental stages. Elementary education shall be compulsory. Technical and professional education shall be made generally available and higher education shall be equally accessible to all on the basis of merit.

Education shall be directed to the full development of the human personality and to the strengthening of respect for human rights and fundamental freedoms. It shall promote understanding, tolerance and friendship among all nations, racial or religious groups, and shall further the activities of the United Nations for the maintenance of peace.

Parents have a prior right to choose the kind of education that shall be given to their children.

## Article 27

Everyone has the right freely to participate in the cultural life of the community, to enjoy the arts and to share in scientific advancement and its benefits.

Everyone has the right to the protection of the moral and material interests resulting from any scientific, literary or artistic production of which he is the author.

## Article 28

Everyone is entitled to a social and international order in which the rights and freedoms set forth in this Declaration can be fully realized.

## Article 29

Everyone has duties to the community in which alone the free and full development of his personality is possible.

In the exercise of his rights and freedoms, everyone shall be subject only to such limitations as are determined by law solely for the purpose of securing due recognition and respect for the rights and freedoms of others and of meeting the just requirements of morality, public order and the general welfare in a democratic society.

These rights and freedoms may in no case be exercised contrary to the purposes and principles of the United Nations.

## Article 30

Nothing in this Declaration may be interpreted as implying for any State, group or person any right to engage in any activity or to perform any act aimed at the destruction of any of the rights and freedoms set forth herein.

Restraining the non-legitimate use of violence is a further political challenge for developing countries. Around the world national governments fail to control all of their territory or face significant challenges from rebel or guerrilla groups. In Africa, Asia, and Latin America such groups threaten not just the sovereignty of states but also their survival in their present forms (see Box 6.4). The existence of rival military factions in a country may signify military weakness on the part of the government but, more importantly, it denotes a lack of universal legitimacy. The same can be said of governments that fail to keep public order in their cities and towns. When there is rioting and widespread disrespect for the rule of law, governments must take measures (through either reform or suppression tactics) to ensure that the social and political systems survive.

A perennial issue for many LDCs has been the role of the military in politics. Where the military has not been placed under strict civilian control in a state's constitution, and thus restricted to a legitimate and restrained role in national affairs, it has tended to intervene in the political life of developing countries, especially during times of political, social, and economic crisis.

Most such interventions claim to be in the broader national interest, and often military leaders argue that such actions are necessary to restore the right conditions for democracy to be successful. Many military coups are carried out on the principle that military rule will be temporary, yet most have retained control over politics much longer than they first promised.

Another concern involving the issue of force is territorial integrity. While almost all developed countries have held their present geographic boundaries for extended periods of time, many developing countries are involved in border disputes and conflicts with neighbouring states. Peru and Ecuador only settled their border dispute in 1998, a conflict that had continued for over 40 years. India and Pakistan continue to come to blows periodically over the region of Kashmir over which they both claim sovereignty. Partially this is the result of the complex and often messy situations left behind by withdrawing colonial powers. Partially the problem arises as national leaders seek to consolidate their domestic power and influence by unifying the electorate and important domestic constituencies behind a national cause involving conflict with a neighbouring state. As long as a state's territorial boundaries are disputed, there will probably be an enhanced role for the military in the political life of the nation. What's more, it is likely that a developing country will be forced to divert valuable resources away from other, more deserving and productive purposes.

One such productive purpose that has unfortunately remained a secondary goal in a large number of LDCs is public education. The majority of developing countries have failed to develop effective systems of public education and this hinders not only economic development but also the development of mature political and social institutions. The problems of instituting a comprehensive system of public education are enormous; not the least of them is the fact that in most LDCs child labour is very common, and indeed necessary for many families if they are to generate sufficient income.

Another social issue is that of healthcare. Modern healthcare systems are incredibly expensive to run, absorbing more than 10 percent of the GDP of countries such as Canada. LDCs, which have much smaller economies and tax bases, and generally much larger populations, are in no position to provide comprehensive healthcare at the level found in the developed world. This means that the majority of LDC citizens face a life plagued by the worry of ill-health and disease, which in turn has an enormous cost for the economy. To compound the problem there is the fact that Sexually Transmitted Diseases (STDs) and insect- and water-borne diseases such as AIDS, malaria, and cholera are much more common in the developing world. As we shall see with the case of Nigeria, AIDS has become a threat, not just to individuals and families, but to the strength of the country as a whole (see Box 6.9).

One last issue that has risen in importance in recent years concerns questions of gender. Whereas women in the developed world made many important strides towards gender equality in political, social, and economic spheres in the twentieth century, in most LDCs women continue to face a far more difficult future than men. Not only do women earn much less than men for similar work (which of course also remains the case in most developed countries), but many women are denied reliable access to education, healthcare, and the vote. Recent studies have shown that it is women who pay a disproportionate amount of the costs of economic adjustment during times of crisis. Perhaps more worrying is that with the rise of Islamic fundamentalism in many countries of the Middle East and North Africa, there is a tendency for women's rights to be curtailed even more severely.

## Economic Development

The economic development of poorer states is a highly contentious issue, and no sure path to economic development has been found. While some LDCs, in particular the **Newly Industrializing Countries** (NICs) of Asia experienced high levels of growth from the 1960s to the late 1990s, developing countries in other parts of the world were unable to repeat that particular development path. In the 1980s and 1990s the dominant philosophy of economic growth has been liberal, but its results are as yet uncertain. Debates continue to rage in most developing countries about the wisdom and benefits of free markets, open economies, and less government involvement in the economy. The future of economic development still seems to lie in liberal models, but questions continue to be raised about their sustainability (see below).

Nor should it be thought that economic growth is enough to secure economic development. A number of other conditions must be met if economic growth is to have a positive impact on living standards. The first and most obvious of these is that the economy should grow at a rate higher than that of the population. If the population grows faster than the economy, the benefits received by the individual will gradually decline. Furthermore, benefits and costs of economic development should be perceived to be divided equitably among society's members, if widespread support for the program of development is to remain.

Just as important for the long-term economic development of a country is the concept of sustainability. Sustainable development, a term that came into widespread use in the 1990s, marked a wholly new approach to the dilemma of development (see Box 6.6). Sustainable development recognizes that many models of economic growth result in severe environmental degradation and the depletion of non-renewable resources. While such models may succeed in kick-starting economic growth and the process of development, they are unsustainable in the longer term. Sustainable development seeks a model of economic growth that uses renewable resources and does not destroy the environment in which human beings have to live. This is, of course, a very simple and logical calculation—in theory. The application of the principle of sustainable development has proven much more complex, for strategies based on this concept have tended to be more expensive and produced tangible gains much more slowly.

Economic development has to be sustainable in other ways. First it must be sustainable in the sense that it does not produce cycles of boom and bust, as the history of Mexico's economy demonstrates. Economic growth should ideally be more steady and progressive, producing smaller gains in the short term but greater benefits in the medium and long term. The chosen path of economic growth should also be politically sustainable. This generally means ensuring that the benefits of economic growth are widely dispersed and that the population in general experiences an improvement in its standard of living. Connected to this issue is the commonly observed Kuznets Effect. This economic formula demonstrates that, as a country develops economically, income distribution will become more unequal before it becomes more equal. This means that in the short to medium term developing countries are likely to experience a widening gap between rich and poor. This has been one of the main criticisms of Mexico's liberal model of economic development, and as the country becomes more democratic, it will become a greater problem for the Mexican government. China, too, faces this problem, and it may become a political problem in the twenty-first century as the gap between rural and urban populations widens.

The debate between liberal and alternative models of economic development is connected to the debate between national and international development paths (see section below). Since the Second World War, the developing world has attempted both integration with and isolation from the wealthy countries and the international system. Purely national development proved too slow and inefficient for most LDCs in the post-war period, and this was one of the factors that propelled them to attempt liberalization and opening of their economies in the 1980s. However, the international financial and economic crises that hit many LDCs in the second half of the 1990s have caused a re-evaluation of openness and, though the dominance of liberal economic policies seems certain to continue, LDC policy-makers are currently seeking greater insulation from the damaging effects of global economic processes.

# Theoretical Debates about Development

The issue of political and economic development has been marked, as with so many other areas of political economy, by an ongoing debate between left and right. While democracy has been widely regarded as a worthwhile and legitimate goal for LDCs, at times authoritarianism has been accepted as a necessary evil in order to achieve stability. Both socialism and liberalism have in turn dominated the field of development studies, and the twentieth century saw a progressive swing back and forth between proponents of the market, of the state, of nationalism, of internationalism, of autarky, and openness.

The most important debate over economic development has been between those who argue for an expansion of market forces, and those who favour an interventionist state which tightly regulates the economy through capital, price, and wage controls. This debate hits at the heart of political economy as it concerns the freedom given to the market to determine economic processes and outcomes. Often it takes the form of a debate between left and right, but restricting the role of the market has also been a preferred policy tool of many right-wing, nationalist regimes in the developing world.

The debate here revolves around the question of how to achieve rapid, but sustainable development. Economic liberals argue that by far the best way to achieve such growth is by allowing the market as much freedom as possible, to allow the principles of competition and efficiency to guide economic development. As much as is feasibly possible the government should withdraw from the economy, privatizing state-owned industries, removing regulations and controls, and opening up the country to foreign imports, capital, and competition. Contained within liberal economy is the theory of the dual economy, which argues that in every national economic system there are two elements, the modern industrial and traditional agricultural sectors. According to this theory, when left to its own devices the industrial sector serves to modernize and transform the traditional agricultural sector. This will lead to higher levels of efficiency and real advances in productivity and in the national standard of living.

Nationalists, on the other hand, tend to favour an expanded role for the state in economic development, encouraging state intervention and sometimes ownership. They argue that the state should foster a process of industrialization, investing in this sector so that the traditional economic reliance (seen in many LDCs) on primary products and raw materials (such as agricultural products or commodities such as copper or tin) is reduced. The industrial sector, it is argued, will have a more dynamic effect on the rest of the national economy, and will make a significant contribution to national economic power. Trade should be regulated by the government so that it benefits domestic producers more than foreign producers; similarly, capital should be regulated so that it is invested in those sectors which the government considers most important to national development.

Marxists, of course, favour state-ownership of the means of production so that the fruits of labour can be shared equally by all classes of society and not reserved solely for the capitalist class. They argue that, left to its own devices, the market would bring about crises of over-production and under-consumption, increasing immiseration of the masses, and eventual breakdown and revolution. Marxist economies tend to be closed to the outside world, with the state carefully managing foreign economic relations with other friendly states.

Mirroring this debate over the role of the state in economic development is that over the level of openness of an economy and the most suitable level of integration with the rest of the international system. In the nineteenth century there was very little debate in this area, as the dominant liberal economic theory dictated free flows of trade and private capital and operated in terms of comparative advantage, with each national economy seeking the productive process to which it was most suited. For most developing economies this meant the extraction and export of raw materials, which they held in abundance and which could be produced at low cost because of the presence of huge reserves of cheap labour.

This consensus on internationally oriented development strategies, however, ended with the onset of the Great Depression following the New York stock market crash in 1929. As economies in the rich nations of Europe and North America went into depression and production slowed, demand for the raw materials and primary products from the developing world contracted sharply. Latin America in particular was hard hit by the world's (and especially the United States') economic crisis. There policy-makers began to turn away from internationalism towards more nationally led economic development strategies. Latin American governments began to use policies of **Import Substitution Industrialization** (ISI) which aimed at developing a domestic industrial base by keeping out imports of certain manufactured goods and investing in their production on a national level. This substitution of imports required the selective but widespread use of **tariffs** (a tax or custom payment on imports) and non-tariff barriers (such as imposing national content requirements on certain products or applying quotas to their import). By thus closing their economies off from competition from foreign producers, governments hoped to develop their own industrial bases to the point where they would one day be competitive at the international level and the restrictions on imports could be removed.

Underlying this approach to economic management was a perception of the international system as being essentially biased in favour of the advanced industrialized economies. This view suggested that, rather than seeking further integration with that system and those economies as the liberal theorists of the nineteenth century had argued, it was preferable for LDCs to approach development on a national basis. This new theoretical perspective came to be known as **structuralism** which, as it became better defined, argued that the structure of the international economic system was such that close integration into that system would not benefit the economies of the developing world. Instead, LDC governments should close off their economies from the rest of the world and use the domestic market as a springboard for industrialization. Foreign capital would still be needed for this process where government revenues were insufficient, but governments themselves could borrow the money or at least strictly control where foreign direct investment would take place.

The hold of structuralism, and its close relative, **dependency theory**, continued for several decades in the middle of the twentieth century. From the 1930s to the 1970s many LDCs used ISI as a development strategy, and refused to become closely interdependent with the system as a whole. Those countries, however, which used ISI strategies for a short time until national industries had become competitive and then opened up their economies to international competition have been by far the most successful. The Asian NICs, including Taiwan, South Korea, and Indonesia are prominent among these. With the onset of the debt crisis in the 1980s, though, ISI and dependency theory quickly became discredited in policy circles, and there began a rapid process of liberalization in many LDCs. By the 1990s there was no longer a serious debate at the governmental level in the developing world over internationalization, though the economic and financial turbulence that marked the end of the century (especially in the countries of Asia and Latin America) once again raised doubts about the benefits of full-scale openness.

## The Link between Political and Economic Development

One of the most perplexing and challenging aspects of development studies is the analysis of the connection between political and economic development. Often the argument is made that sustainable economic growth and stability cannot be achieved without stable democratic institutions. Almost as often we hear that workable democracy cannot be achieved without first obtaining high rates of economic growth. Certainly the connection has often been made between economic liberalization and democratization, particularly in the aftermath of the end of the Cold War and the dual transitions in Eastern Europe.

Yet the relationship between these two spheres remains elusive. There does appear to be a connection between economic development or progress and more stable democratic institutions and in those countries where socioeconomic inequality reaches high levels, democracy is often under threat. But some analysts have argued that undemocratic regimes may actually be better suited to the business of reforming and modernizing an LDC economy, most often making reference to Chile's experience under General Augusto Pinochet, or as we will see in this chapter, in China since the late 1970s. The argument here is that economic liberalization and reform incurs high levels of social and political costs, and an autocratic or authoritarian regime is better equipped to deal with the pressures arising from these costs. These two examples, however, do not seem to be representative. A more thorough examination of LDCs demonstrates that democracy actually contributes to stability, and stability to the prospects for economic growth, and therefore the maxim often heard in the 1960s, that LDCs should forget about democracy and concentrate their efforts on economic development, does not seem to hold true.

One area where the link between economic and political spheres is particularly interesting is that of **structural adjustment** and economic reform. Structural adjustment refers to the dramatic reorganization of a national economy along liberal lines, involving programs of liberalization and privatization, greatly reducing the role of the state in the economy. This kind of program is most commonly imposed by the **International Monetary Fund** (IMF) and **World Bank** when they lend money to struggling LDC economies. Democratic practices and institutions can both complicate this process and help it along. In Mexico, as we will see, since the economic crisis of 1994–95 there have been increased calls for democracy; a similar situation can be seen in Indonesia since the onset of the economic crisis there in 1997. Widespread consultation

## Terrorism and the *Sendero Luminoso* in Peru

Box 6.4

Peru's multiparty republic has in recent years been forced to face up to threats to political stability stemming from terrorist groups. The largest of these groups is the *Sendero Luminoso* (SL) or Shining Path, among the world's most ruthless guerrilla organizations.

This left-wing revolutionary group was formed in the late 1960s by university professor Abimael Guzman, who proclaimed the goal of destroying existing Peruvian political structures and replacing them with government by a peasant revolutionary regime. The SL in the 1980s and 1990s attacked almost every political institution in Peru, often in the most brutal and violent ways imaginable. Having proclaimed itself against the presence of foreign governments and businesses in Peru, the SL has bombed the embassies of several countries and many private foreign interests, too, particularly those belonging to US citizens. Though the arrest of Abimael Guzman in September 1992 was a major success for the government's security forces, the SL continues to be a threat. What's more, another Peruvian terrorist group, the Tupac Amaru Revolutionary Movement (MRTA) achieved international notoriety in December of 1996 when they took over the Japanese Ambassador's residence in the country's capital, Lima. The siege lasted for over four months until the nation's anti-terrorist forces eventually stormed the building, killing all of the MRTA terrorists in the process. Though both the MRTA and the SL are responsible for loss of life and serious infringements of human rights (particularly among indigenous populations), Peru's security forces have used the situation as a cover for widespread human rights abuse as well. In order to maintain control, the government declared certain sections of the country security zones, and within them some constitutional protections are suspended and the military is in charge. In those areas, and to a lesser degree in the country as a whole, the police and military have been involved in political repression and human rights violations.

with the public over the shape of economic reform in developing countries can help the legitimacy of these programs, but if the costs go on too long such democratic practices can make the programs more difficult to sustain. During the Latin American debt crisis of the 1980s, the Costa Rican government found itself in exactly this situation, struggling to implement effective economic reforms before public tolerance of the costs associated with reform wore too thin. What helped the Costa Rican government in this situation was the public's perception that the costs of reform were being relatively evenly shared throughout society and the economy.

---

| Box 6.5 | # The Brundtland Commission Report and Sustainable Development |

In 1987 the World Commission on Environment and Development (the Brundtland Commission) issued its report, entitled *Our Common Future*. In this report the Commission prescribed a development path for LDCs that did not "compromise the capacity of future generations to satisfy their own needs." The report outlined the concept of sustainable development, that is, a form of development that does not rely upon the use of non-renewable resources and which does not destroy the environment, which we need to survive as a species.

Though this seems an uncontroversial proposal, many developing country governments have seen it otherwise. They have argued that the notion of sustainable development is another way that the wealthy countries have tried to pass the costs for environmental protection onto the poor in the international system, while those same wealthy countries long ago destroyed their own forests and have pumped billions of tons of pollutants into the earth, oceans, and atmosphere.

Population Growth     One of the perennial challenges for most developing countries is the size of their populations and, more importantly, the rate of population growth. Many LDCs experience a doubling of their populations every 30–35 years—and that is with an annual growth rate of around 2 percent. If the population growth rate is closer to 3.5 percent, then the population will double every 25 years. This can cause immense strains on the economic system. If the standard of living of the average citizen is to improve, the economy must grow at a rate faster than that of the population. New jobs, new housing, and education must be provided for all of these new people. The issue of population control is, of course, a highly contentious one. The use of barrier methods of birth control is still limited in many countries (particularly in Africa and Latin America) for cultural and religious reasons, and overcoming these obstacles has proven incredibly difficult. China, as we shall see, achieved considerable success in limiting population growth in the latter part of the twentieth century, but this was only done with the use of policies that were repressive and highly intrusive into the private lives of its citizens.

One of the costs of population growth is government services. Providing healthcare for a rapidly expanding population is hugely expensive. So is providing public utilities such as potable water and electricity. Rapidly expanding populations also lead to high levels of migration, both within a country and outside, in the form of emigration. As can be seen in the case of Mexico, this leads to strains on government services and also on Mexico's relations with its northern neighbour, the US.

As much as population growth is a problem, it can also eventually become a strength, too. China's enormous population will constitute the world's largest national market at some point in the first half of the twenty-first century, and this will give China increased economic influence in the international system. India's population will surpass that of China during the same period; if the government can secure high levels of economic growth, then India, too, will be a force to be reckoned with.

The Role of International Organizations     One final word that must be said about development in general concerns international aid and development organizations. More will be said about such organizations in Chapters 7 and 8, but here it should be noted that the international aspect of development has become more and more important to LDCs in recent years. Most prominent have been the World Bank and IMF, whose lending activities have been essential to the rescue of developing country economies in Asia, Africa, and Latin

America. Though the IMF is not officially a development organization, its financial facilities are used almost exclusively by LDCs.

A strong and credible criticism of international development organizations in recent history has been that they try to impose liberal and neo-liberal policies on LDC governments. Another, more contentious accusation is that they act as agencies of wealthy country governments, in particular the US, to make LDC economies more dependent on the developed world. This raises serious questions about the sovereignty of LDCs and the impartiality of these organizations.

# Mexico: Stable Democracy or One-Party Authoritarian State?

Perhaps more than any other developing country, Mexico highlights both the problematic link between political and economic development and the divorce between the theory and practice of political economy. Mexico is a democracy in which only one party has ever held power during the 70 years of its existence in its present form (though this may soon change). Mexico has a presidential system which on paper is almost identical to that of the United States, yet in practice the Mexican Congress has acted as a mere rubber stamp to presidential policy initiatives. Mexico is an NIC and an emerging market, yet every time it appears to be getting close to achieving its goal of developed country status it seems to fall into an economic crisis and has to begin the long climb back. Mexico, it is claimed, has the highest number of billionaires per capita, yet it is also a country which has regions where over 50 percent of its people live in extreme poverty.

## History

Mexico was one of the first areas of the New World colonized by the Spanish in the fifteenth and sixteenth centuries, and the turbulence of conquest was followed by an equally turbulent birth and adolescence as a nation. Mexico's early history saw the assimilation of indigenous and imperialist cultures, with much intermarrying between Spanish and native peoples. This is not to say that indigenous peoples fared better than their counterparts in Canada and the US; disease, war, and episodes of genocide all took their toll on the country. Unlike Canada and the US, however, Mexico was an incredibly rich colony for many years, promising unimaginable reserves of gold and silver to the conquering nation. As has seemed to happen throughout Mexican history, this wealth failed to produce lasting benefits for Mexico itself or for its people.

Mexico's history as an independent country began in 1821 with the end of the war of independence against Spain. Chaos and deep political instability followed, with a succession of weak presidencies. A disastrous war against the United States in 1848 and the secession of the state of Texas left Mexico with only half of its original territory, and the country found itself in an impoverished and uncertain situation. The solution to a part of these problems was found in the autocratic, authoritarian rule of Porfirio Diaz, who became president of Mexico in 1876. However, though he was highly successful in stabilizing the country and attracting foreign investment into Mexico, Diaz headed a gravely repressive regime that was arbitrary in its rule and severely limited individual rights.

The reward for Diaz's repression came in 1910 when several groups rose up in revolution against his regime. Most notable among them was the band led by Emiliano Zapata, a peasant of both indigenous and Spanish heritage who sought to defend farmers and native rights against the central government. The revolution proved a long and bloody affair that resulted in the coming to power of the *Partido Revolucionario Institucional* (Institutional Revolutionary Party) or **PRI** as it is most commonly known in Mexico. This party has ruled Mexico for over 70 years and, like the Diaz regime, has provided considerable stability to Mexico. Unfortunately it has also shared some less desirable features with Diaz, such as repression of political opposition, a sometimes authoritarian style of governance, and limiting the freedom of the media.

## Mexico's Political System

Mexico has, in theory, a highly democratic and inclusive political system that closely mirrors that of the United States, at least at first glance. The Mexican constitution sets up a federal system in which the powers of the President are balanced and checked by those of the Congress. Individual states (of which there are 32, including the *Distrito Federal*, or Federal District of Mexico City) are given considerable powers, which is reflected in the official title of the country, *Estados Unidos de Mexico*, or United States of Mexico. Each state has its own elected governor and state legislature (the *Distrito Federal* having its own mayor, elected since July of 1997). As with many elements in Mexican political economy, however, the theory is far divorced from the reality of everyday politics. In reality the country's political system is highly centralized and has been since the Revolution. Most spending (over 85 percent) is controlled by the federal government, with state and municipal governments (*municipios*) sharing the rest. To make matters worse, *municipios* depend on the upper levels of government for over 80 percent of their income, having very few independent sources on which they can draw.

This centralization in fiscal terms has been compounded by one of the most enduring, yet now changing, aspects of the Mexican political system. The dominance of the PRI has meant that the governing party has been able to limit the independence of the states through **patronage**, or the awarding of key government positions to favoured and loyal supporters. In recent years there has been a weakening of this form of control as the PRI's grip on power has been gradually reduced, but it continues to play an important part in the evolution of Mexican politics.

The Mexican Presidency   The Mexican presidency has traditionally been the focal point of power in the system. As chief executive and head of state, the President is given wide-ranging powers under the constitution, which creates the potential for presidential dominance of the other branches of government. In the past the extent to which this has been the case has largely depended on the personality and strength of the individual holding presidential office. In recent years we have seen one very strong President, Carlos Salinas de Gortari, replaced by a much weaker one, Ernesto Zedillo Ponce de Leon. The President has traditionally been responsible for almost all of the important legislative initiatives that are passed into law by the Congress. Thanks to long-running PRI dominance of both the Presidency and Congress, this has meant that legislation initiating in Los Pinos (the Mexican equivalent of the White House) has rapidly become law. Up until the 1980s this power was used by many Mexican presidents to alter the constitution, though since that decade the PRI has been unable to obtain the two-thirds majority needed to effect a constitutional amendment, due to increased electoral competition.

The President in Mexico is popularly elected but limited to a single six-year term (or *sexenio*). This limitation was created as a response to the Mexican experience of dictatorship under Porfirio Diaz in the late nineteenth and early twentieth centuries. Every Mexican president since the Revolution has been from the PRI (or its predecessor, the PNR, or National Revolutionary Party), but the way in which the candidate has been chosen gives us an insight into a central feature of Mexican politics. Aspiring young Mexican politicians and bureaucrats move up the political ladder by attaching themselves to one or more patron-client relationships, called *camarillas*, and working with that patron in order to advance. Most of these relationships begin at university, where established political figures seek out new disciples among their students. Because many of these relationships are interlinked, Mexico's political system up till now has to a large degree been structured as a complex web of patron-client relations. This patronage system is continued right through the political system, to the point where a sitting president in effect names his successor, a process Mexicans call the *dedazo* (or finger). The current President, Ernesto Zedillo, had the former President, Carlos Salinas, as a patron, and was "fingered" by Salinas when the leading presidential candidate, Luis Donaldo Colosio, was assassinated in 1994. The patronage system means that there has been a significant level of continuity in the Mexican presidency, as each candidate has been able to trace his (there have been no female presidential candidates) political heritage back to a former president or other leading figure. But of course this also means that the level of democratic input into the process of selecting a president has been limited, particularly as one party has held such dominance of the system for so long.

The Mexican Congress    Like the United States of America, Mexico's Congress is divided into upper and lower chambers, the Chamber of Deputies and Senate, respectively. Unlike the United States, however, there has until recently been very little division and conflict between the legislative and executive branches of government in Mexico. This is, of course, because of the PRI's dominance of both branches. The power of the Congress has been further limited by the fact that all PRI congressional candidates have needed presidential approval and, due to their one-term limit, rely on the President to grant them opportunities to continue their political careers. In practice this has meant that the Congress has played a rather insignificant role in Mexican politics, which is reflected in the very low number of important politicians who have begun their careers there.

Nonetheless, with increased electoral competition at the end of the 1990s, the Congress finally seems to be taking on its prescribed role in the Mexican constitution. The Mexican electoral system is a strange one that, since 1979, has been structured to allow disproportionate representation to opposition parties to encourage the development of democracy. Until 1988 this system brought about very little real influence for those parties, but in the 1990s this has changed. The congressional elections of 1997 brought an end to PRI majority control of the Mexican Chamber of Deputies, and now the presidency has been forced into a process of collaboration and negotiation with the legislative branch. This has meant that Mexican politics are finally beginning to resemble the process suggested by the country's constitution, with Congress taking on real influence and power.

Though this change in the 1990s was most positive in terms of democratic representation and accountability, it did create certain problems of **gridlock** and uncertainty. An important example of this was the 1998 financial reform bill, which was delayed until the end of the year because of partisan struggles within the Congress and between the legislature and executive. This delay was expensive, as it damaged the image of Mexico in the eyes of international investors. Current and future debates over the federal budget will no doubt create similar problems.

### The *Partido Revolucionario Institucional* (PRI) and Party Politics in Mexico

Though Mexico's political system went through considerable change in the twentieth century, one element seemed to be constant. The country's ruling party, the PRI, governed Mexico from the end of the revolution to the end of the century, providing much stability but also limiting the level of democracy and political and economic innovation. The PRI has traditionally been a **catch-all party**, meaning that it has sought to include all important political and economic constituencies and a broad cross-section of the ideological spectrum. Over the years it has represented the interests of both business and labour, the left and the right, and the public and private sectors, often at the same time. The most stable element of PRI support has traditionally been government employees and the rural population, but the Mexican political landscape is now changing so rapidly that this is no longer guaranteed.

It is true that nationalism has been a recurrent feature of PRI policies and public statements over the years, but the guiding principle of the party has been political pragmatism and the drive for re-election, rather than any ideologically driven manifesto. Nonetheless, it must be noted that the PRI itself has gone through several phases of transition. For many years following the revolution it was largely left-leaning, adopting populist policies designed to consolidate its hold over the country. Key among these policies was agrarian reform, transferring control over the land from the wealthy to the poorer, peasant classes, and government support for organized labour that resulted in significant increases in working-class salaries. From the 1940s to the 1970s this was replaced by a shift to the right, a period during which the Mexican government set industrialization and economic growth as policy priorities ahead of redistribution. Having said this, it must be noted that the government did not begin liberalizing the economy and opening up to foreign competition until the 1980s, as we will see in the next section.

The structure of the PRI is complex and can tell us a great deal about the nature of politics in Mexico. Nationally it is organized in a hierarchical manner, with a National Executive Council at the top and local committees at the lowest level. Internally it is organized into three main groupings, the labour, agrarian, and popular sections. The largest and most powerful of these has traditionally been that of labour, and the PRI has maintained a close relationship with the country's largest union, the CTM (*Confederacion de Trabajdores Mexicanos*).

In recent years the most important division in the PRI has been between the older, more traditional elements (the dinosaurs) and the modernizing, liberal sections (the technocrats) in the party. The dinosaurs have for several years been fighting a rearguard action against the technocrats, trying to halt the shift to the right within the PRI, and holding fast to traditional PRI policies based in nationalism and anti-US statements. Their power, however, has been significantly reduced by the rise to prominence of the technocrats, a group of politicians and bureaucrats educated mostly in US universities and favouring neo-liberal economic policies. The struggle between these two groups will continue to define Mexican politics into the twenty-first century.

Party politics in Mexico are vastly different to those in Canada and other advanced capitalist democracies. Each of the major parties in Mexico, the PRI, PRD (*Partido Revolucionario Democratico*) and the PAN (*Partido de Accion Nacional*) offers a wide range of free services to its supporters, including healthcare, dental treatment, and help with finding work. This remains one of the most high-profile ways of attracting support for political parties, though its effectiveness has not really been tested. Another obvious difference is that the opposition parties have never held national control. Up until now they have been restricted to control of several gubernatorial (governor) posts, and the mayor of Mexico City (Cuahtemoc Cardenas of the PRD).

The PRI's hold over the country, however, is in doubt, and the 2000 election will be the first presidential contest in which the outcome is unclear. Having said this, the 1988 presidential election is widely thought to have been fixed by the PRI to prevent victory by opposition candidates. With one-third of the votes counted in that election, the FDN (*Frontera Democratica Nacional*) coalition presidential candidate, Cuahtemoc Cardenas (before he joined the PRD) held a clear lead over the PRI candidate, Carlos Salinas. At that point the computers tallying the votes lost power. When power was restored, Salinas had gained the lead and went on to win the election, though by the smallest presidential victory margin ever. Though the PRI denied tampering with the election, and though post-election opinion polls suggested that Salinas would probably have secured victory regardless, the 1988 election highlighted the very real problem of corruption in Mexican politics. Since then the Federal Elections Institute (IFE) has greatly improved its elections monitoring, thanks in no small part to support from international and foreign national agencies, both governmental and non-governmental. The role of IFE is crucial in Mexico, as its work is the only way that elections have come to be seen as legitimate. In many ways IFE offers an example for other LDCs seeking ways of securing **free and fair elections**.

## The Mexican Economy

In terms of natural endowments Mexico is one of the world's richest lands. The country has vast oil and gas reserves, huge forests, access to the ocean's resources on both sides, both Atlantic and Pacific, and tourism opportunities that would make any country jealous. Yet because of mismanagement, exploitation, and corruption, Mexico has been unable to take full advantage of these resources. Ask any taxi driver in Mexico City what they think of the economic prospects for their country and they will answer you, "*Tantos recursos, pero tantos problemas*" (so many resources, but so many problems).

In the twentieth century national economic development was driven by the state for long periods. Between the Revolution and the 1980s Mexico went through a period of rapid industrialization which raised expectations among Mexicans that they would one day join the ranks of the First World or wealthy nations. The Mexican government acted not only as economic planner and manager, but also as owner and director of many of Mexico's most important industries, most significantly and symbolically of PEMEX (*Petroleos de Mexico*), the nation's oil company. The nationalization of such industries during the middle of the century went along with a high degree of state intervention in the economy as a whole, regulating both wages and prices. In this period Mexico experienced high levels of growth, particularly as a result of the policy of stabilized development in the 1960s.

In the 1970s, however, economic development became much more complex in Mexico, despite the discovery of huge oil reserves in the Gulf of Mexico in 1976. The governments of Luis Echeverria (1970–76) and Jose Lopez Portillo (1976–82) dramatically increased government spending and borrowing, mostly from foreign banks. This money was not spent wisely, however, and was used up in unproductive projects and public sector wages.

With the onset of the Latin American Debt Crisis (see Chapter 8) in the mid-1980s, the billions of dollars owed by Mexico created a national financial and economic crisis, which required the intervention of the IMF and World Bank to stabilize and later resolve. For Mexico, as for much of Latin America and the developing world, the 1980s were a lost decade, where very little positive economic growth was seen, living standards and real wages declined, and the enthusiasm and optimism of earlier decades evaporated.

Economic Liberalization and Openness    Beginning in 1982 with the Miguel de la Madrid *sexenio*, Mexico gradually opened and liberalized its economy, allowing foreign competition into the country and slowly removing the state from direct involvement in the economy. A key factor in this liberalization were the demands made by the IMF that the Mexican government improve the efficiency of its economy through policies of structural adjustment. From a largely closed and state-run economy, Mexico has transformed itself into an open and relatively dynamic one. The role of the private sector has increased and foreign investment, both **portfolio** (short-term capital able to come into and leave a national economy with ease) and **foreign direct investment** (FDI) have grown dramatically, and Mexico has become an active proponent of free trade. On this last point, Mexico became the first developing country in the world to join a free trade association with developed countries when it signed the North American Free Trade Agreement (NAFTA) in 1992. Studies seem to indicate that this has benefited Mexico, guaranteeing the country access to the markets of Canada, but much more importantly, the United States. In the second half of the 1990s, Mexico became the second largest trade partner of the US, after Canada.

The NAFTA was an important event for Mexico as it signalled once again that the country was close to First World status. President Carlos Salinas de Gortari, who pushed for Mexican membership in this organization and signed the treaty for Mexico, was determined to bring Mexico into a true partnership with the US, and the NAFTA marked the high point of that effort. Mexican hopes, however, were dashed at the end of 1994 when, less than 12 months after the NAFTA came into force, Mexico went into deep economic and financial crisis. Fortunately, this crisis took much less time to stabilize and resolve than the Debt Crisis of the 1980s, but its effects on the general population were just as keenly felt. Since the crisis, which again required massive borrowing from the IMF to resolve, Mexico has continued with its liberal economic policies, examining privatization of many national industries, including PEMEX, and signing a series of free trade treaties.

Economic Crisis and the *Sexenio*    A key feature of the political economy of Mexico has been the interaction between economic development and the electoral cycle. In many countries, developed and developing, governments seeking re-election tend to spend freely towards the end of their terms of office, in an effort to buy votes. This is known as the **political business cycle** and can result in temporarily high levels of economic growth, but also problems of inflation and boom and bust periods. In Mexico, where the presidency and all elected offices are limited to one term, this problem would appear to have been avoided. In reality the opposite is true, however. Presidents who are limited to one term find themselves at the end of their *sexenio* without any political future and often give out economic and political favours in exchange for future considerations and influence. What's more, with no possibility of re-election, Mexican presidents are forced to care little for the long-term economic performance and stability of the country. In the last year of a *sexenio*, it has become customary for Mexicans to expect an economic and financial crisis, as the outgoing administration engages in widespread economic mismanagement and doling out of favours. Whether or not this will remain a feature of Mexican politics now that elections have become truly competitive is unclear.

## The Future of Mexico

As Mexico enters the twenty-first century its future is far from certain. Major problems endure, such as political and economic corruption, economic mismanagement, and human rights abuses, but there is much reason to be hopeful at the same time. Democratization and economic liberalization are beginning to bring perceptible benefits to Mexicans, and the country appears to be handling the transition to a multiparty electoral system well, without sacrificing too much of its stability. So what does the future hold?

On the political side of things Mexico still has to deal with several major issues. The first of these is the growing political awareness of Mexicans. Instead of passively accepting PRI rule as they have done for so long, individual Mexicans are learning more and more about the past and present abuses of power, and learning to be more critical and demanding of their politicians. While this is in many ways a positive development, there is the danger that Mexicans will become overly skeptical of politicians in general, especially as opposition control of key constituencies such as the *Distrito Federal* has shown the political alternatives to be almost equally incapable of resolving the deepest problems facing the country. The real challenge here is for the oppo-

sition parties to prove themselves to be different from the PRI, not just in their
professed beliefs, but in their actions and in the ways in which they provide
real benefits for the Mexican people.

The political future of Mexico will certainly be complex. The days of pres-
identialism may be at an end in Mexico and the government, no matter what
its political hue, will be forced to develop modes of cooperation with the
opposition and, more importantly, with the Mexican Congress if political
stalemate is to be avoided. To complicate things further, the internal struggles
within the PRI, and within the other main parties, will continue to influence
national policy debates.

Another ongoing issue is that of the region of Chiapas. A poor southern
state, Chiapas, where over 50 percent of the people live in extreme poverty, witnessed an armed uprising in 1994 of a left-wing *zapatista* (followers of Zapata)
rebel group led by a charismatic figure known as sub-comandante Marcos.
Though this rebellion has since calmed down considerably, the success of its initial stages shocked the Mexican government and embarrassed it in international diplomatic circles. The Chiapas rebellion is important because it has
focused national and international attention on the issues of human rights,
indigenous peoples' representation, and land reform. Although the negotiations
between the government and *zapatistas* seem to have reached an impasse, there
is hope that eventually the lives of the region's people will be improved.

Population growth remains a major economic, social, and political challenge. Though the official population of Mexico sits at around 92 million,
more realistic estimates put it at 95–97 million. By the year 2050 it is predicted
that this number will reach 170–180 million. To achieve any substantial
improvement in income per capita, Mexico is going to have to sustain economic growth rates of over 4 percent per year for this period. Government
expenditures on healthcare and education will become astronomical, and
unless there is wholesale reform of the taxation system and a significant rise
in the price of oil (on which the Mexican government depends for so much of
its income), Mexico will be forced to either cut services or go further into debt.

Population growth is also leading to long-term problems with the environment. Nowhere is this more clearly seen than in the *Distrito Federal* where,
some estimate, more than 22 million people now live. The city lacks adequate
public utilities (particularly in the area of water and sewage systems) and has
been unable in recent years to control the dangerously high levels of toxins in
the air. Mexico City remains one of the most dangerous places in which to live
on the planet. But the environment is under threat elsewhere in the country.
Fish stocks in the Gulf of Mexico have reached ominously low levels, and soil

degradation and erosion continue to threaten the future of agriculture. Unless the Mexican government can obtain substantial foreign funding for environmental projects, however, it is difficult to see how it can afford to devote more public money to such issues when there are so many other pressing concerns.

One last issue that Mexico will face in the future is the sustainability of neo-liberal economic policies. During the global financial crisis of 1997–99 some Mexican politicians began questioning the wisdom of continuing to liberalize the Mexican economy. This was a natural and expected response to the economic and financial problems being transmitted to Mexico from other developing countries in Latin America, Eastern Europe, and Asia. Nevertheless, it highlighted the fact that the dominance of neo-liberal policies depends to a large degree on sustained economic growth and real improvement in living standards. Should Mexico fall into crisis at the end of the present *sexenio*, such doubts will be reinforced.

# China: The Political Economy of Reform in a One-Party State

China is the world's most populous country, with (depending on the estimate), anywhere from 1.3 to 1.6 billion inhabitants. China will, at some point in the twenty-first century, have the world's largest economy. China is a nuclear power, and occupies one of the five permanent seats on the United Nations security council. Yet for all of these qualities, China remains a largely impoverished, underdeveloped country facing serious and deep-rooted problems. China's political system remains highly undemocratic, and there appear to be few signs of it becoming so in the near future. China's economy, though greatly liberalized in recent years, maintains a very high level of state involvement and ownership.

This section studies the political economy of China and addresses the major challenges lying ahead for the Chinese people and their government. It shows us a country that is indelibly marked by its history, and in which reform of the economic system has not been accompanied by real political change.

## Chinese History: The Heritage of Imperialism and Revolution

Long before the countries of Western Europe had organized themselves into coherent nation-states that we would recognize today, the Chinese empire had united a huge territory and many disparate peoples under one system of government, using the strong arm of military force to bring them peace, prosperity, and innovation (see Table 6.2). During the more than two thousand years of imperial rule, China developed a mode of government that was highly authoritarian, willing to use violence to suppress dissent and which stressed the value of the group over the individual. This governmental and cultural tradition continues to exert a strong influence on modern China, though at the dawn of the twenty-first century the pervasive values of Western culture are knocking hard at China's door.

The end of China's imperial history came with an armed uprising in 1911 and 1912, ushering in a long period of civil war in China. During that time regional warlords struggled for supremacy, as did the two main political parties, the **Nationalist Kuomintang Party** (KMT) and the **Chinese Communist Party** (CCP), a party committed to Marxist revolution. During a brief alliance in the late 1920s, the KMT turned on the CCP and slaughtered hundreds of thousands of its supporters. After that the CCP split into two competing factions. The more successful faction, led by **Mao Zedong** (sometimes written as Mao Tse Tung and also known as Chairman Mao), turned away from the traditional focus on the working class and towards the rural peasant class, a group that made up over 85 percent of the Chinese population. Mao created the People's Liberation Army (PLA), a guerilla army made up of poorly equipped peasants which was at first unable to withstand the KMT's professionally trained soldiers, but which in time became the country's dominant military force.

Before and during the Second World War China was occupied by Japanese forces, and this invasion of Chinese sovereignty discredited the KMT in the eyes of the Chinese people. With the close of that war, the civil conflict resumed, and this time the CCP defeated the nationalist forces. By 1949 the KMT and its supporters withdrew to the nearby island of Taiwan, and the People's Republic of China was born with Mao as its leader. Communist ideology governed policy in the People's Republic, with Mao developing his own branch of communist thought, one based on constant vigilance against the forces of capitalism and the bourgeois or middle-classes. In practice this brought a turbulent and bloody post-Revolution history to the country.

China's economy grew rapidly in the period from 1949 to 1976, an achievement brought about by a series of policies in which the government played a central role. From 1949–58 the government used Soviet-style policies of industrialization that had been employed in Stalinist Russia, but which were ultimately not well suited to China's mostly agrarian economy. From

| Table 6.2 Major Periods in Chinese History | |
|---|---|
| Xia | ca. 2100–ca. 1600 BC |
| Shang | ca. 1600–ca. 1100 BC |
| Western Zhou | ca. 1100–ca. 771 BC |
| Eastern Zhou | 770–256 BC |
| Spring & Autumn | 770–476 BC |
| Warring States | 475–221 BC |
| Qin | 221–206 BC |
| Western Han | 206 BC–AD 24 |
| Eastern Han | 25–AD 220 |
| Three Kingdoms | 220–280 |
| Western Jin | 265–316 |
| Eastern Jin | 317–420 |
| Southern Dynasties | 420–589 |
| Northern Dynasties | 386–581 |
| Sui | 581–618 |
| Tang | 618–907 |
| Five Dynasties | 907–960 |
| Song | 960–1279 |
| Liao | 916–1125 |
| Kin | 1115–1234 |
| Yuan | 1271–1368 |
| Ming | 1368–1644 |
| Qing | 1644–1911 |
| Republic of China | 1912–1949 |
| People's Republic of China | 1949 |

1958 to 1962 Mao instituted the **Great Leap Forward,** a program of economic policies designed to revolutionize rural production by replacing private ownership of land with communes, in which all agricultural production was to be sold to the state. The chaos that ensued from this program resulted in the loss of, in some estimates, 25 million lives from starvation and malnutrition.

As horrific as these figures are, they represent only one of the more unpleasant features of Mao's rule over China. Up until his death in 1976 Mao and his followers used terror tactics to maintain control and to weed out dissident factions. Most infamous was his program of the Cultural Revolution, in which Mao oversaw the creation of Red Guard units throughout the country, which were aimed at eliminating any subversive bourgeois or capitalist elements in Chinese society. During this program of repression between 3 and 20 million people were killed.

## The Origins of Modern China

Like Mexico, China's politics have been dominated by one political party, the CCP. Unlike Mexico, there is no pretence of political opposition and there are few prospects of a viable opposition emerging from outside the ruling party. Politics as they transpire in China can only be understood if one understands the internal struggles and processes within the CCP. Even before the death of Mao Zedong in 1976, Chinese political and economic development was determined and shaped by such divisions, especially the struggle between the Red faction, a radical Marxist group led by Mao himself, and the Expert faction, a more pragmatic grouping led by the Chinese president, Liu Shaoqi, and the future leader of China, Deng Xiaoping. Though the Red faction was victorious in this struggle and Mao imprisoned or executed many of the leading members of the Expert faction, it was the ideas of the latter group that would come to dominate Chinese development at the end of the twentieth century.

When Mao died in 1976 his passing was marked by a power struggle within the CCP for leadership. Mao's widow and three of his most radical supporters, known collectively as the Gang of Four, were held up as scapegoats and blamed for the horrors of the later years of Maoist rule. Mao's immediate successor, Hua Guofeng (who had been responsible for the arrest of the Gang of Four), was soon replaced by **Deng Xiaoping**, and much of the old CCP cadre was weeded out. Maoist policies and ideology were officially discredited, and the modernization of China proceeded apace.

Yet the internal divisions within the CCP did not end there. Chinese development since the early eighties has been defined by the struggle within the Communist Party between those, like Deng, who favour a rapid transition towards a market-oriented economy, and those who prefer to see a slow and gradual movement in the same direction. A radical return to communist production has long since ceased to be a viable alternative for the CCP and China, and adherents of such Maoist policies have no voice in the politics of modern China.

How is the CCP organized? First of all it must be noted that the party is massive in size, with over 50 million members, so that it reaches down through every level of Chinese society. It is organized hierarchically, from the national level down through provincial and local levels, with the Politburo and Standing Committee at the top of the CCP's structure. It is in these two bodies that the major policy directions and important day-to-day decisions are determined. Though the National Party Congress (NPC) officially serves as the highest authority in the CCP, it plays a relatively minor role in legitimizing rather than directing government policy. The only other body at the national level that performs an important function is the Central Committee, which serves as a representative body for the members of the CCP and votes on major policies. Having said this, the NPC has at times played a role in displaying popular discontent with government policies, as happened in the debate over the Three Gorges dam in 1992 which took place shortly after the Tiananmen Square massacre (see Box 6.6). Though the government is not directly accountable to the NPC, it is the organ which elects the Central Committee and the government will face pressure from that body to respond to discontent manifested in the Congress.

This last example points to an often neglected fact of Chinese politics, namely that pluralism exists in the system, albeit in a very different form to that which we find in democratic systems in Canada and other advanced capitalist nations. Though the most important officials in the CCP do not depend on popular re-election for their mandates, they must always be mindful of their power bases in other areas, such as the military and important sections of the Communist Party. In her 1994 study of the liberalization of the Chinese economy, *How China Opened Its Door*, Susan Shirk[1] demonstrated this point by examining the way in which the success of economic reform depended on support from within the government and party structure, as well as upon China's quite decentralized federal structure. The role of internal party support for economic reforms was of particular importance during times of political instability and especially during leadership struggles, she found. As we learn more about the internal workings of the CCP, we should expect that this way of explaining Chinese politics will take on increasing importance.

## Chinese Economic Reform

We tend to think that the emergence of a market-oriented economy in China only really began in the 1990s with the end of the Cold War. In fact the

[1] Susan L. Shirk, *How China Opened Its Door: The Political Success of the PRC's Foreign Trade and Investment Reforms* (Washington, DC: The Brookings Institution, 1994).

## The Tiananmen Square Massacre

Box 6.6

The economic boom that China experienced since Deng Xiaoping began his program of economic reforms brought not only increased wealth to the country but also new political problems. These problems involved calls for democratization and greater choice in the political arena, but also complaints brought on by a growing income gap between rich and poor, and between rural and urban populations. The result of this growing discontent was a mass protest in the summer of 1989 in Tiananmen Square in the heart of the nation's capital, Beijing. For several weeks the square was occupied by protestors, whose most vocal demands concerned the opening up of the Chinese political system. Coming as it did at the same time as the end of the Cold War in Europe, many Western observers predicted that this would mark the beginning of a similar political transition in China.

The reality, as it turned out, was quite the opposite. On June 4 Chinese tanks rolled into the square, destroying protestors' barricades and killing several hundred of them. International condemnation of the massacre was immediate, yet the Chinese government expressed no remorse or any intention of reforming the nation's political system.

process began long before the fall of the Soviet Union was ever envisaged. The reform of the centrally planned Maoist economy of the 1970s began in earnest almost as soon as Mao had died. Deng Xiaoping, who had proposed economic reform in the 1960s and been imprisoned for his audacity, led a steady process of introducing market-oriented practices to economic management in China. From the late 1970s onwards the Chinese government began decentralizing production and economic decision-making, giving more power to the provinces, which served as an incentive for them to increase productivity. A further step in the early years of economic reform was the institution of rural enterprise reform in 1979, when the system of collectives was gradually replaced with a system giving responsibility to household farms. These households were entitled to hold onto the profits they received from their agricultural production. Though they still had to sell their required quota to the state, these farms were allowed to sell any surplus goods at free market prices, thus giving them the incentive to increase productivity. This incentive appears to have worked well, as productivity increased rapidly in the early 1980s.

Following on from rural reform the Chinese government in the 1980s focused on expanding the non-state sector and increasing inter-firm competition in the economy. This program resulted in large increases in private sector employment and in productivity and competitiveness. Throughout the later eighties and 1990s there were further market reforms and the gradual opening up of China's economy to foreign trade and investment with the implementation of the **Open Door** policy and the creation of **Special Economic Zones**. By the end of the century China was experiencing the highest levels of foreign investment in the world, and was seeking membership in the World Trade Organization, the global trading regime.

The Chinese government, however, maintains active involvement in the economy. In addition to its role as economic planner and manager, the government also acts as banker and entrepreneur, continuing to control many state-owned industries. Large-scale privatization of Chinese industry had still not occurred by the end of the 1990s, but mergers and joint ventures with foreign multinational corporations (MNCs) had dramatically changed the shape of the Chinese economic landscape.

China has also been highly successful in controlling one of the most important areas of growth for most LDCs: population. By limiting its citizens to one child per couple, the government has been able to contain population expansion to within reasonable limits. The methods used by the government, however, go against most Western conceptions of the right to privacy and freedom of choice. They have severely limited the individual rights of many Chinese men and women, and may in the future be unsustainable. On the positive side, real income growth throughout history has resulted in lower reproduction rates, so this problem may in time solve itself.

The results of China's economic reforms are that the country has consistently experienced the highest rates of economic growth in the world, surpassing even the Asian Tigers, with annual rates of growth around 10 percent. China's economic strength and sound management ensured that China weathered the Asian economic crisis that began in 1997 without having to devalue its currency or experiencing high levels of capital flight.

## Future Challenges for China

Entering the twenty-first century, China's prospects may at first look promising, but the country faces many challenges in both the political and economic spheres. Politically the government must face international condemnation of its human rights record at the same time as an increasingly wealthy middle-class will likely demand greater freedom of choice in the political sphere. The issue of human rights continues to be a problem for the Chinese government, and it faces significant international opposition to its policies concerning political prisoners, labour camps, and freedom of expression. The political protests that culminated in the Tiananmen Square crackdown are also likely to resurface, and the government will once again be faced with the choice between tolerance and repression. A policy of tolerance would be more popular with foreign governments and human rights groups, but it may encourage further questioning of the Chinese political system as a whole, threatening the hold that the CCP has over the country.

In the economic realm, the challenges that face China at the end of the 1990s are still considerable. The reform of the Chinese economy must be seen as a work in progress that must continue to bring tangible benefits to key constituencies in China if it is to remain sustainable. The government must increase agricultural prices and public investment in agriculture, if production levels are to rebound to the levels they reached in the 1990s. Rural poverty also remains a problem, and the government of Jiang Zemin should not forget Mao's lesson that the key to Chinese political power lies with the peasantry. The government must also continue to modernize the country's infrastructure, building roads, bridges, and electrical networks to support a modern economy. However all of this costs huge amounts of money, and the government will be forced to find additional sources of revenue by reforming the nation's tax system, a move that could prove highly unpopular.

China as a country will also have to face other growing pains. As some regions grow faster than others, political tensions will emerge, and calls for redistribution will either have to be ignored, thus further aggravating these tensions, or placated, risking the alienation of wealthy provinces. Ethnic problems have already reared their head in the western provinces, particularly in those with large Muslim populations. The government will either have to provide sufficient economic benefits to these people or use the PLA to suppress rebellion. Lastly, China has to face the responsibilities of becoming a regional power and decide if its future lies in encouraging regional cooperation or trying to dominate the weaker countries on its borders. It must decide what to do with Taiwan (see Box 6.7) and how to define its relationship with the United States, which continues to be the most important force in the Pacific.

Box 6.7     **Taiwan**

The exile of Kuomintang forces from mainland China in 1949 led to the birth of a new state in the international system, Taiwan, or Chinese Taipei. The United States and its allies immediately recognized Taiwan as the legitimate government of the whole of China, denying recognition to Mao's communist regime. Since then the mainland Chinese government has campaigned successfully to have itself recognized as the legitimate voice of the Chinese people. However, it has also campaigned continuously to limit the recognition of Taiwan by other states in the international system, and has used the threat of force to attempt to destabilize and weaken the strength of the government in Taipei. In recent years these threats reached new heights, with the Beijing government firing missiles towards the island. This brought about an immediate response from the US government, which has committed itself to the defence of Taiwan.

Taiwan is more than just a cause of tension in the China Sea, however. Since 1949 it has become a highly successful economy, industrializing at a rapid rate and dramatically raising the standard of living of its people. However, it has done so with the help of an authoritarian political system that has consistently limited political freedoms. Ironically, the Chinese government itself has looked to Taiwan as an example of how to implement a capitalist economic system without democratization.

# Nigeria: The Political Economy of an African Nation

In many ways Nigeria encapsulates many of the most difficult and frustrating problems in the political and economic development of African states. A potentially rich nation, Nigeria has wasted much of its wealth through corruption and mismanagement. When the British colonial forces withdrew from Nigeria in 1960 it appeared as if Nigeria had a very bright future and would emerge as one of the leading nations of the African continent. Since then, however, the country has fallen into chaos and disarray, experiencing deep-rooted ethnic and regional tensions that have resulted in a leading role for the military in politics, and a squandering of the opportunities for development. As much as any other country, Nigeria shows the close link between political and economic development, and what can go wrong if national unity is not achieved.

## Colonial History

The Nigeria that became independent in 1960 had been shaped by British rule since 1914. As with so many other African nations, the external and internal boundaries of the country had been determined rather arbitrarily, without a full understanding of the underlying ethnic and tribal divisions. In Nigeria this meant that the British seemed to apply a uniform administrative system for the entire country, but in fact divided it into northern and southern regions. Different political rights were accorded to native peoples in the north and south of the country (southerners being allowed to vote for members of the Legislative Council, an advisory body to the British governor, long before their northern counterparts), and education was encouraged in the south at the same time as access to schools was limited in the north. This internal division served to reinforce and aggravate differences between the wealthier, well-educated southerners and the poorer, Islamic northerners. Before independence the British further split the south into two regions, east and west, creating the potential for heightened regional tensions.

During the later years of British rule the country was split once again, this time into three regions. While this reflected the dominance of the three major ethnic groups (see below), it failed to take into account the interests of the smaller tribes, which found themselves forced to live in predetermined regions dominated by the large tribes. The 1951 Nigerian Constitution, imposed by the British, placed the three regions at the centre of Nigerian political life, and it was this legacy that would mark the country's transition to independence.

## The Political System

Nigeria's political landscape has been largely determined by its major **ethnic and tribal groupings,** of which there are 10. The three most important are the Igbo (Eastern Nigeria), Yoruba (Western Nigeria), and Hausa-Fulani (Northern Nigeria), and the country's post-colonial history has been scarred by the conflicts emerging among them. Traditionally the Hausa-Fulani have been the largest ethnic group in the country, but also the poorest. The fact that the cultural and religious values of each of these groups are so different has exacerbated tensions. Political parties in Nigeria are based upon these tribes, and successive attempts to create national parties that cross ethnic boundaries have consistently failed. The three main parties at independence were:

• the National Council of Nigeria and the Cameroons (NCNC), an Igbo-dominated party that nonetheless sought to become a national party in the early years of independence

- the Action Group (AG), a Yoruba-dominated party from the west of Nigeria, and
- the Northern Peoples' Congress (NPC), the party representing the interests of the Hausa-Fulani in the north.

When Nigeria gained independence on October 1, 1960, it was constituted as a parliamentary democracy, with upper and lower houses and a division of powers between executive, legislative, and judicial branches. A federal system was created, with considerable powers reserved for each of the three regions. All adults in the east and west of the country, and all male adults in the north (a concession to Islamic tradition), were accorded the right to vote. The First Republic seemed at first glance to be a healthy, workable system, but it soon became clear that each of the three dominant regional ethnic groups was willing to use its power to suppress opposition and claim overwhelming power for itself. Though the three major parties, one for each large ethnic group, competed on the national stage, at the regional level one-party rule soon became the order of the day. This resulted in severe problems of favouritism and oppression, and in the perversion of justice and legal procedure.

The First Republic was marked by a succession of crises at both national and regional levels. The AG was eliminated from the national political scene after its leader, Chief Awolowo, pushed for a redefinition of Nigeria's political boundaries to reduce the tribal nature of politics and the dominance of the three major parties. As conflict intensified between the regions (a fourth was added in 1961, the mid-western), **election fraud** became commonplace, and the legitimacy of the political system disintegrated. Ethnic tensions and divisions were further exacerbated by a controversial census in 1962 and another the following year (see Box 6.8).

The conclusion to this opening period of Nigerian independence came with a **military coup** in January of 1966. This overthrow of the national government by the army received widespread support from all sections of society, as the existing system had simply ceased to work. The group of army generals who took over the country promised to restore it to civilian rule as soon as the basis for democracy was assured, but they never managed to fulfill their promised goal, for they were rapidly replaced by an Igbo military leader, General Ironsi. His efforts to eliminate political corruption and redefine the country's political boundaries met with stern opposition, and by May of 1966 he had been replaced in a bloody coup by a group of northern army officers, led by Lieutenant Colonel Gowon. Gowon's attempts to create twelve states out of

## The Politics of Population: Nigeria                    Box 6.8

Due to the ever-present tensions between the regions and ethnic groups of Nigeria, the question of regional population size has been a perennial issue of contention. In 1962 the government carried out a census to determine the correct distribution of political power and financial resources. This became a heavily contested issue, and the importance invested in the census was reflected in its results, and the reaction to those results. First, the census showed that the south had grown rapidly in size, to the point where it now surpassed the historically more populous north. Second, it quickly became clear that the figures for the eastern region were inflated. In response to this the north announced that it had overlooked 8 million people in its region, a number sufficient to restore its numerical superiority.

When the census was repeated a year later, the outcome was even more ridiculous. The results showed that the population had increased by over 80 percent since the last census ten years before, but still with a northern majority. Despite this incredible outcome, the north's political forces managed to secure official acceptance of the census, thus guaranteeing them higher levels of support from the federal government.

the four existing units resulted in a civil war with the breakaway republic of Biafra, a conflict that cost hundreds of thousands of lives and left a severe famine in its wake.

A series of coups followed the conclusion of the Biafran war, and Nigeria did not return to civilian rule until 1979. The man responsible for the eventual return to democracy was the then military ruler, General Olusegun Obasanjo. He has been identified as the one post-colonial leader who attempted to strengthen democracy and the political institutions of Nigeria rather than seeking to subvert them for narrower interests, and was to return to prominence later in Nigeria's history. Nonetheless, the Second Republic was short-lived, falling victim to similar problems of fraud, corruption, and abuse of power. The perennial problems of regionalism and tribalism persisted, despite the existence of new, more nationally based parties. On December 31, 1983, the military once again took over the country, following the discredited elections earlier that year and the eruption of ethnic violence in the west of the country, which had taken the lives of hundreds of Nigerians. Once again the military coup was widely welcomed as the only viable solution to the country's troubles, and once again the military, led by General Buhari, moved to punish those guilty of fraud and corruption. Though initially welcomed, these reprisals were soon perceived as unduly harsh and suspected of having an ethnic bias, promoting the interests of the northern peoples. Repression worsened as freedom of expression was curtailed, and economic hardship spread as the military government implemented policies of economic austerity. In August of 1985 the inevitable occurred, when a military coup pushed Buhari out of power. This coup, however, led by Major General Ibrahim Babangida, a northern Muslim, was to usher in a period of personal dictatorship and political repression hitherto unseen in Nigerian politics. Babangida remained in power until 1993, having survived for eight years and the most bloody coup attempt in the country's history. During that period he severely restricted political freedoms, ruled in an arbitrary manner, and subjected the Nigerian people to intense economic hardship. In 1993, after finally living up to his repeatedly delayed promise to deliver democracy, he nullified the results of an apparently free and fair election. The winner of that election, Moshood Abiola, was promised a fresh election, but Babangida's chosen successor, General Sani Abacha, arrested Abiola in June of 1994 and postponed the election. This seemed to mark the low point of Nigerian politics, as the Abiola regime pulled Nigeria into what Larry Diamond has referred to as **praetorianism**, meaning the complete ineffectiveness of pluralist democratic institutions.[2] Nonetheless, Abiola's government managed to drag the country further into disrepute and lawlessness with the 1995 political execution of human rights activist Ken Saro-Wiwa and eight of his co-workers.

Abacha himself died of a heart attack in June of 1998, and was replaced by his Chief of Defence Staff, Major General Abdusalam Abubakar. Abubakar came into power promising much the same as his military predecessors, a swift return to democracy. However, unlike his forerunners, Abubakar moved rapidly, creating a constitutional committee which would give the country a new constitution by the end of 1998. Furthermore, he promised to hand over power to elected civilians at the end of May 1999. On February 27, 1999, former military leader General Olusegun Obasanjo won the presidential election with nearly 19 million votes, compared to just over 11 million for his rival, Olu Falae, a former finance minister. Despite complaints that there was election fraud, it seems that there will finally be another transition to a democratic system in Nigeria. Whether or not it will last remains to be seen.

---

[2] Larry Diamond, "The Uncivic Society and the Descent into Praetorianism," in Diamond, Linz and Lipset, eds. *Politics in Developing Countries: Comparing Experiences with Democracy* (Boulder, CO: Lynne Rienner Publishers, Inc., 1995).

## Economy

Nigeria's economic development has been heavily handicapped by its political instability and arbitrary political rule. Its immense mineral wealth has been squandered through corruption, leading to the personal enrichment of its leaders, and poor economic management has resulted in an underdeveloped economy that faces a long uphill struggle before it returns to the right path.

This political instability, coupled with the regional and ethnic divisions and the wealth flowing from Nigeria's oil reserves, has given the country a complex political economy. In order to bind the country together the government, whether military or civilian, has been forced to use the allocation of state spending as a way of "buying off" regional and ethnic dissent. This has created a system of **patron-client relations** in Nigeria, which has compromised the effectiveness of political institutions and built up a strong opposition to reform of the economy. With the Organization of Petroleum Exporting Nations (OPEC) oil price hike in the 1970s (see Chapter 8), Nigeria received a huge windfall in foreign exchange earnings, and this surplus capital was quickly funnelled through the federal government, building up the education and social security systems (a positive response) but also increasing both the level of public sector wages and the overall role of the state in the economy, with the government heavily subsidizing public utilities.

The encouragement of poor economic management by the Nigerian government due to the oil boom of the 1970s came back to haunt the country in the 1980s, when oil prices fell internationally. Committed to expensive state spending programs, the government decided to borrow from international banks rather than reform the economy. This led to disaster, and in 1983 Nigeria was forced to go cap in hand to the IMF, seeking money and advice on how to bring about a structural adjustment in the national economy. While accepting part of the IMF's reform program, the Nigerian government, at this time civilian, refused to accept a key element, namely the devaluation of the Nigerian currency, the naira. This refusal to negotiate with the IMF over such a key aspect of reform brought about the denial of any official international credit, either from the IMF or from any other international organization or foreign government. What's more, commercial banks stopped lending to the country at around the same time, meaning that Nigeria went into deep economic and financial crisis.

This debt crisis resulted in severe economic hardship for large sections of Nigerian society and helped to bring about the end of the civilian regime under Shagari, and then the military government under Buhari. Under Babangida and authoritarian rule the government was able to implement its own structural adjustment program, which included wage cuts and a reduction in government spending. Babangida was able to achieve this economic stabilization and structural adjustment, which implied high costs for Nigeria's population, by making concessions in the political arena on human rights, and by outmaneuvring his opposition using nationalistic appeals. The reforms prepared the country for a much-needed return to both IMF loans and commercial bank borrowing.

The domestic support for the government's reform programs lasted only so long, however. As the decade wore on the nation's labour unions began to protest against structural adjustment and were joined by key figures such as General Obasanjo. In order to placate the opposition, the Babangida regime regularly overspent, giving out fiscal favours that to some degree quelled dissent, but resulted in persistent budget deficits.

In the 1990s Nigeria has continued to depend upon the international price of oil for its revenue, and, despite a short-lived oil price boom following the Persian Gulf War in 1990–91, has been hard hit by the progressively declining price of petroleum. In 1997 and 1998, when oil prices slid as low as $10 US per barrel, Nigeria was once again crippled by government deficits and foreign loans. The new civilian government faces an enormous challenge if it is to overcome these problems and put Nigeria on a steady path to development.

## Future Challenges in Nigeria

The future for Nigeria holds a dual challenge of political and economic reform. On the former issue the government must consolidate democracy by solidifying new political institutions and somehow overcoming the ethnic and regional divide that has torn Nigeria apart in the past. Human rights remains an issue to be watched, particularly from the perspective of the military. Connected to this last point, it is far from certain that the military has removed itself from an active role in the country's politics. Obasanjo, it must be remembered, is a general himself, and history indicates that if he fails to stabilize the country, there is a military alternative to civilian rule waiting in the wings.

On the economic side, Nigeria must diversify its economy, reducing its dependence on oil and seek to develop a strong industrial base if it is ever to achieve sustainable growth. Government finances require a complete overhaul, in order to reduce corruption and rationalize the fiscal outlook. International investors must be reassured that Nigeria is a stable country, and that conducting business is worth the effort if MNCs are ever to return to the country.

One last challenge that awaits Nigeria, as it does so many other countries in Africa, is the tragedy of AIDS (see Box 6.9). Nigeria has one of the highest levels of human infection in the world, with over 2.3 million people infected out of a population of 118 million (1997 figures). This is not just a personal and human tragedy, but also is a huge drain on a state's healthcare resources. Even with effective treatment of the disease itself, AIDS patients require constant monitoring and care if they are not to fall victim to some lesser illness now that their immune systems are so severely compromised. The spread of AIDS is accelerating throughout Africa and it seems it will be a long time before that spread is slowed.

## Africa and AIDS                                                Box 6.9

The continent that continues to be hardest hit by the spread of the AIDS virus is Africa. There the infection rate is rising daily, and there seems to be little that health authorities, both national and from international organizations such as the World Health Organization (WHO) can do to stop its spread. Part of the problem stems from a lack of education, part from cultural values preventing the use of condoms, and part from economic realities. In Africa many men are forced to travel far from their homes to find work, spending months away from their families at a time. While separated from their wives, these migrant workers will have sex, more often than not unprotected sex, with local prostitutes. Because so many men have sex with the same prostitutes, the rate of infection is very high indeed. These men then go back to their wives and families, to whom they pass on the disease.

### The Problem of AIDS (1997)

| Country or Region | Population | AIDS/HIV infection |
|---|---|---|
| W. Europe | 400 million | 480,000 |
| USA | 280 million | 820,000 |
| Mexico | 94 million | 180,000 |
| Mozambique | 18 million | 1.2 million |
| Kenya | 60 million | 1.6 million |
| Nigeria | 118 million | 2.3 million |
| Ethiopia | 60 million | 2.6 million |
| South Africa | 43 million | 2.9 million |

Source: World Health Organization.

## Summary

This chapter has introduced you to some of the myriad of challenges that face developing countries as they enter the twenty-first century. Mexico, China, and Nigeria share some elements of these challenges in common, such as the need to secure the support of key constituencies for economic reform, but at the same time they exist at different stages of development in widely divergent social, political, geographical, and economic settings. Part of the challenge for each of these countries, as for all LDCs, is to find their place in an increasingly interdependent world, and to seek out cooperative modes of development that harness the economic power of the developed states. They can only do this by understanding the nature of the international system, a system to which this book now turns.

## Self-Assessment Questions

1. Why do you think there are rich and poor countries in the world?

2. Why have some LDCs been able to achieve sustainable growth, while others have failed?

3. What is the link between political and economic development?

4. How important is democracy to political stability in your opinion, and why?

5. What should international organizations and foreign governments do to encourage democracy and respect for human rights?

## Further Reading

Krauze, Enrique, and Hank Heifetz, trans. *Mexico: Biography of Power: A History of Modern Mexico, 1810-1996.* New York: Harper Perennial Library, 1998.

Ellis, Stephen, ed. *Africa Now: People, Policies and Institutions.* Texas: Heinemann, 1996.

Hope, Kempe Ronald. *African Political Economy: Contemporary Issues in Development.* London: M.E. Sharpe, 1996.

Itoh, Fumio, ed. *China in the Twenty-First Century: Politics, Economy and Society.* New York: United Nations Publications, 1997.

Meier, Gerald M., ed. *Leading Issues in Economic Development.* Oxford: Oxford University Press, 1995.

World Bank. *World Development Report 1999-2000.* New York: Oxford University Press, 2000.

 Web Links

### Government of China
http://dir.yahoo.com/Government/Politics/By_Region/Countries/China/

### Government of Nigeria
http://dir.yahoo.com/Regional/Countries/Nigeria/Government/

### Government of Mexico
http://dir.yahoo.com/Regional/Countries/Mexico/Government/Politics/

### United Nations Development Program
http://www.undp.org/

### Human Rights Web
http://www.hrweb.org/

# CHAPTER SEVEN

# INTERNATIONAL POLITICS

## Chapter Objectives

At the end of this chapter you will be familiar with international politics as it relates to the study of politics in general. You will be able to:

- associate the field of international politics with political studies in general
- distinguish among the various approaches to international politics
- understand some basic concepts in international politics, including the nation-state, power, the international system, foreign policy, and interdependence
- comprehend the differences between the Cold War and the post-Cold War era
- recognize the importance of "change" in the post-Cold War era, and
- assess some of the contemporary issue areas in international politics.

This chapter is intended to introduce you to the substance and nature of international politics, one of the more prominent sub-fields of political studies. In some respects, the attributes of international politics are quite similar to those of domestic politics: actors compete in a structured environment for limited resources; several different types of actors relate with one another; and there is a very clear demarcation between those who have power, and those who do not. The main focus of analyzing international politics is to understand the allocation of public goods within the system and to explain the relationships among the main actors.

Although there are some clear similarities between domestic and international politics, it is necessary to examine the two levels separately, while at the same time recognizing that these levels are intertwined. International politics, then, introduces a new set of concepts and ideas that, while related to our basic notion of politics and political life, force us nonetheless to stretch the boundaries of relations to a global scale.

Chapter 7 will discuss some of the primary areas of interest for international politics (or international relations) specialists. To that end, its main area of analysis will be the nature of the nation-state, as well as the alternate approaches to the study of international politics, some of the main conceptual themes of the sub-field, the main structure of international politics, and finally, some of the issues facing those who study international politics.

# International Politics, International Relations, and the State

Just as politics affects our everyday lives, sometimes in ways that we do not necessarily notice, international politics influences many of our day-to-day activities. Simply watching the nightly news demonstrates to us, often in immediate and vivid detail, the surprising closeness of our global community. Elections, wars, sporting events, entertainment, even local weather broadcasts are available to us almost on demand. Indeed, it often confounds us why this information does not arrive sooner at our doorsteps, our radios and television sets, and increasingly, through our computer connections.

It is often said that we live in a "global village," where events on one side of the world have instant repercussions on the other. To a degree, this is true: the collapse of trading on a stock exchange in another part of the world, for instance, or news of the death of a prominent public figure, will surely have an effect—sometimes quite dramatic—on our more localized way of life. But we should be wary of phrases such as "the global village," because we are also constantly reminded of the ways in which we are divided from the rest of the world, even as we connect in a greater fashion with it. That is to say, identifying oneself with a larger community also means separating oneself from other communities. This is most evident in the "us versus them" mentality that frames so much of the substance of world affairs that we witness on a daily basis.

This, then, is one of the greatest paradoxes of the study of international politics: understanding an increasingly disparate, yet joined, world. Even as we learn more about relatively unknown parts of the world, or of different cultures and peoples, modern international politics is also still very much about identifying oneself and one's community, often at the expense of others.

In broad terms, "international relations" can be about almost any aspect of relations at the international level. In this sense, the 1972 Canada-Soviet hockey series, the Toronto International Film Festival, the Olympic Games, or travel tours arranged in one country and held in another are as much about "international relations" as are the G7 meetings, NATO deliberations with the former Soviet Union, or international trade agreements such as the North American Free Trade Agreement (NAFTA). **International relations,** in its strictest sense, therefore, is about all relations at the international level. However, it would be impossible to study all aspects of all types of relations in the international community. That would be an overwhelming task, and would provide very little understanding of the broader political relationship among countries. **International politics** is a more apt reference to our goals here: to study the decidedly political nature of relations at the international level. That stated, it should be kept in mind that those who study international politics are often referred to as international relations specialists; in fact, the sub-field is often called "international relations," though it is not about all types of relations. Although there is clearly a difference between the two terms, they are usually used interchangeably.

**Foreign policy** is the third term that should be clear in our minds before moving forward. Foreign policy, a term often used in the same manner as international politics, refers to the relationship states have to their external environment—policies created to govern state relations beyond national borders. So, if international politics is about the mutual relationship of two or more actors at the international level, foreign policy is essentially about the manner in which individual states present themselves to the international community. Foreign policy is policy; therefore, we are primarily concerned with the legislated, or legalistic, structure of a state's relations in the international system (see Fig. 7.1).

The history and current state of world politics do not make for a peaceful scene. Instead of nations and peoples living together in harmony, the world is

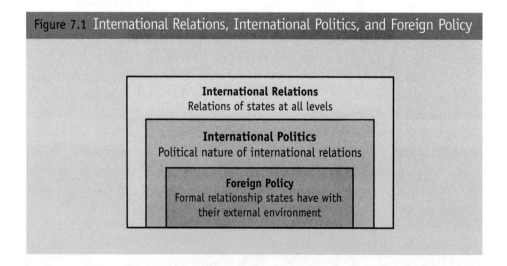

Figure 7.1 International Relations, International Politics, and Foreign Policy

**International Relations**
Relations of states at all levels

**International Politics**
Political nature of international relations

**Foreign Policy**
Formal relationship states have with their external environment

divided. The world drama has a cast of national and international actors at odds with one another, forever calculating what is good for themselves and then defining those ends in terms of universal justice and the common good of all humankind.

Given its influence and power in the world, it is not surprising that the **state** is the most important actor in international politics. The state, for international politics, is a recognized political unit with a defined territory and people, and a central government administration responsible for administering the state's affairs. States are considered to be **sovereign**, meaning that their rights of self-determination and authority may not be overridden by any other international actor, even the United Nations.

The modern notion of the sovereign state follows the collapse of the universalism of the Middle Ages. Medieval Europe shared a religion, a culture, a written language and, to a certain extent, political institutions: the Holy Roman Empire. The religious and political reforms of the sixteenth century shattered this universalism and created a political vacuum that allowed for the emergence and development of modern sovereign nation-states. Various political writers, including Grotius, Vattel, Machiavelli, and Bodin wrote in support of giving these new emergent states sovereign power and legitimacy. By the time of Montesquieu's *The Spirit of the Laws* (1789), the concept of sovereignty was well accepted in law and in practice. In its modern sense, sovereignty means a monopoly of power over territory, people, and resources.

The state (often in cooperation or conflict with other states) thus creates a boundary consisting of legal elements that prevent (within certain parameters) external interference and reinforce internal solidarity. Boundaries define the territorial extent of the jurisdiction of sovereign political-administrative units and are, therefore, legitimized by law and/or informal conventions agreed upon by the people of the society. Because boundaries retain their significance only if there is social and political agreement within the state about their value, it is to the state's advantage to influence public opinion to coincide with its objectives. By emphasizing patriotism and similarities within the state, and exaggerating the linguistic and cultural differences of outsiders, the state reinforces national territorial boundaries.

However, this relatively positive notion of emphasizing the distinctiveness of the state as a political unit is not always the manner in which governments assert and maintain their authority. In fact, a large number of states in the international system sustain their control over their citizens though the use of force. **Authoritarian** states are those that seek to preserve their authority through the direct use of threats and fear among citizens and groups. As you may recall from the earlier chapter on types of governments, **totalitarian** states, a variant of authoritarian regimes, also seek a fundamental reordering of societal values and belief systems to match the wishes of the rulers.

This is not to say that the state has always been considered worthy of its central role. Following the Second World, for example, and particularly with the emergence of the United Nations and a greater internationalization of economic activities, many scholars and politicians alike proclaimed that the nation-state was "on the way out." The state, after all, was in many ways considered responsible for the horrors of the great wars (World War I, 1914–1918; World War II, 1939–1945), as a result of fervent nationalism, and the belief by some that their states were superior to others. In reality, however, the prediction that the state would "go away" has been proved wrong. In the late 1990s, there were over 185 sovereign states in the international system, up dramatically from the roughly 50 states at the close of the Second World War. Nationalism, once thought to be on the decline, has been reinvigorated, and the perspectives and demands of these countries have considerably changed the focus and tone of world political and economic debate.

In sum, the state is clearly the central unit of analysis in international politics, though it is not without its challengers and doubters. International politics in the late twentieth century is an increasingly complicated set of interrelated relations and actors, with a wide variety of goals sought by states, and levels of interaction.

# The International System

In simple terms, an **international system** may be any grouping of two or more states that have organized and regularized relations with one another. In this strictest sense, then, Canada, the United States, and Mexico, as members of the North American Free Trade Agreement (NAFTA), form an international system. So do the member states of the European Union (EU), *La francophonie*, NATO states, or the Organization for African Unity (OAU). But we most often hear references to the "international system" as the entire globe, encompassing every state in the world. This "global" dimension, then, is the more common way that we may use the term, but it is not the only one.

The framework of the international system is one of the most important determinants of the ability of a state to achieve its goals. Units in the international system (predominately states, but also including other actors such as multinational corporations and international organizations) are distinguished and divided on the basis of their **relative power**, or the way that one state's

## NATO after the Cold War

Box 7.1

The North Atlantic Treaty Organization (NATO) was founded in the late 1940s as a way of uniting the countries of Western Europe and North America in the common struggle against communism and the Soviet Union. For 50 years NATO stood face to face with the Warsaw Pact, its eastern bloc counterpart, and defined security relations between Western nations. With the end of the Cold War in the late 1980s, several analysts predicted that NATO would be dissolved, now that its *raison d'être* had disappeared. The countries of Western Europe and North America, it was argued, would not be willing to pay the costs of a security organization that had become an anachronism.

In fact NATO, instead of becoming part of history, has grown in size and membership. In 1993 NATO invited Eastern European states of the former Warsaw Pact to join with them in the Partnership for Peace (PFP), an initiative designed to increase cooperation in political and military affairs throughout Europe, to augment stability and remove threats to the peace. The PFP received a favourable response from most former Warsaw Pact countries, with the notable exception of Russia. Russia saw PFP as a precursor to the expansion of NATO, something the Russian government claimed posed an unacceptable threat to its national security.

Despite Russia's protests the United States and NATO pursued expansion of the organization, and in 1997 the Founding Act on Mutual Relations Cooperation and Security between NATO and the Russian Federation was signed, creating the NATO-Russia Permanent Joint Council. The Council is intended to work towards cooperation and consensus-building between the Alliance and Russia. This cleared the way for the future incorporation of Eastern European states. This became a reality on the March 12, 1999, when the Czech Republic, Hungary, and Poland were welcomed into the Alliance. NATO now numbers 19 members, and has become the world's most important security organization.

With NATO actions in Kosovo in 1999, the role of peacekeeping was added to the organization's mandate. Though heavily criticized by many commentators, particularly in countries outside of Europe and North America, NATO justified its intervention in Kosovo as a way of protecting human rights and of preventing the conflict from escalating and potentially spreading to neighbouring states.

capabilities may be compared to those of another. The relative power of political actors in the international system is based on a state's function in the international system and the manner in which these functions may be differentiated from the functions of others. States that are militarily powerful, for instance, may have far more influence and effect in the international system than those states whose power is based on limited physical resources, because military power is more easily extended in the attempt to obtain objectives.

Although all political entities are part of the international system (and also of **sub-systemic** groupings, or those that do not include all members of the world community), we are still primarily members of individual political states rather than of the world community. The structures and processes used internally to arrive at decisions and to maintain stability are highly developed. On the other hand, few political actors are willing to cede the same degree of authority or legitimacy to global institutions and organizations—even the United Nations—out of concern that this would diminish the role for the state and the concept of state sovereignty.

Yet some regional sub-systems such as the European Union, NAFTA, and the Asia-Pacific Economic Cooperation (APEC) body are representative of a growing tendency in the international system not simply to hand power and authority over to non-state actors, but rather to work as a body of political entities—all the while retaining individual sovereign power—in order to achieve certain economic goals.

## Actors in World Politics

By now it should be fairly clear to you that there are several different types of actors that are important in international affairs. Though we deal primarily with nation-states in international relations, there can be no doubt that other **units of analysis** on the world stage are significant for our better understanding of international relations. And though we might designate some actors more prominent than others, it is nonetheless essential to have a grasp of the competing influences.

First, we should start with the state. As mentioned above, sovereignty is a consequential concept in international relations. That is because actors that have sovereignty—states—are given certain rights and responsibilities that others simply do not have. For instance, only nation-states are permitted to enter into formal legal treaties or to wage wars with other states. These privileges extend back hundreds of years to the creation of the first political systems, which were not always states. States today are still the most important actors in the international system because of what we call **structural anarchy**, which simply means that there is no political authority greater than the sovereign state in international affairs. States which exist in this condition of anarchy, where there is no "world government" (not even the United Nations), are ultimately responsible for their own behaviour within their borders.

Other actors, such as the United Nations, are **international governmental organizations** (IGOs). These actors are larger conglomerates of nation-states that have grouped together for a common purpose. For instance, the United Nations was formed in 1945 to deal with problems that simply could not be dealt with by individual states—international insecurity, global indebtedness, world hunger, and underdevelopment, for instance. Members of these IGOs do not give up their sovereignty, but agree to work with other states to come to common positions on these and other issues. And—significantly—they agree to abide by the decisions of the IGO, which means that, in exchange for group attention to common problems, the individual states do sometimes give up a bit of their independent actions for the common good.

Sometimes international institutions are formed by actors that are not governments. **Non-governmental organizations** (NGOs), such as the Red Cross, Doctors Without Borders, or Amnesty International, are groupings of like-minded organizations that all seek to work together on problems of a common nature, but without the direct input of governments in the decision-making process. This means that NGOs often have to work with governments, perhaps in the distribution of aid, for example, but the governments themselves are not part of the organization. NGOs are becoming an increasing presence in international affairs as a result of the growing nature of world problems that simply cannot be dealt with by states alone.

IGOs and NGOs are both **international organizations** (IOs). Another type of non-governmental actor is the **multinational corporation** (MNC). MNCs are unlike both IOs and states in that their constituency (that is, who they must answer to) are shareholders or members of a board. MNCs are international corporations that seek to make a profit, like any other corporation, but their arena is the globalized economy. MNCs are now one of the world's most important actors, since there are so many (over 80,000 "home" offices and affiliates worldwide), and because they have so much economic clout. Many MNCs are far more powerful than nation-states, and not just developing states. General Motors, for instance, has larger yearly sales than the entire **gross national product** (GNP, the total value of goods and services produced by a nation within its borders and abroad) of countries such as Finland and Hong Kong. This clearly shows the importance of these groups, especially when they invest in foreign economies, or negotiate with weaker states regarding access to local markets.

Finally, we cannot forget the influence and importance of people and groups. We think so frequently of states, institutions, and organizations, that we tend to forget that individuals often make a difference. Think, for example, of the influence of notable and well-known individuals such as the Pope, or the Dalai Lama, or Princess Diana. These people often can change the mindsets of millions of people, or even whole countries, based on the roles they play internationally, or the causes they take up. And groups of people, often short-lived, or unorganized, regularly have an effect as well. Student protest groups in China, or agricultural workers in Europe, may come together for a brief period of time, but in that time they may affect the way we view the world.

In conclusion, then, let us keep in mind the array of actors that regularly affect and influence the course of world affairs. Though in this chapter most reference will be to states, it is nonetheless critical to remember that there are several types of groups, with varying levels of influence and power, that consistently play a role in the international arena.

# Globalization

This is perhaps the best place to introduce a concept that we are no doubt familiar with, if only by name. We hear about **globalization** daily, but few of us really understand what the term means, or what its significance is for us and others. A basic definition was given by Hans-Henrik Holm and Georg Sørenson in their 1995 book, *Whose World Order? Uneven Globalization and the End of the Cold War*. They defined globalization as "the intensification of economic, political, social, and cultural relations across borders."

But this is a little too simple—it really tells us very little about the process of globalization, focusing instead on the outcome. Globalization is a process that has been underway since the post-World War II economic recovery of the European states, and has been driven primarily by economic interests, initially in the US, but later from all parts of the globe. Technology has clearly played an important role, too, and it would be remiss to ignore the role of states in encouraging, or at least not stopping, the process.

Let us begin with **economic globalization**. Corporations have sought out profit opportunities by expanding their production and sales to the international level, linking national economies together. In addition, groups of corporations have formed strategic alliances and joint ventures that have served

The process of globalization has brought the peoples of the world closer together than at any point in history. As this chapter explains, globalization has several dimensions: economic, political, and social/cultural. One of the key elements driving this globalization has been the rapid advance in technology, in particular in the area of communications. Not only are we able to communicate instantaneously with other individuals around the world, but we now also share the same news sources, watch the same television programs, enjoy the same sporting events. This is leading to the homogenization of culture.

This process, however, is desperately uneven. While millions of young people across Canada are plugged into the same culture as countless millions of their peers in the United States, Europe, and Japan, the vast majority of the youth in countries such as Mozambique, Cambodia, or Guatemala remain isolated from events transpiring as close as 10 kilometers away. Thus the distribution of wealth in the international system directly affects the intensity of the globalization process on a local level.

to integrate national markets. Furthermore, financial institutions have increasingly moved capital across national borders, engaging in lending, borrowing, and investment activities at hitherto unforeseen levels. This process has been driven by market forces, but has been encouraged by governmental actions. States have progressively removed barriers to the flow of goods, services, and capital across their borders, and the process of liberalization has thus boosted globalization.

The second aspect of this process can be seen in **sociological** and **cultural globalization**. In this sense, globalization refers to the emergence of a global society and of global norms. The first of these elements means that across the globe individuals are increasingly associating themselves not only with their local or national societies, but also with billions of other individuals around the world. To say that one was a "citizen of the world" used to be considered strange, but more and more it is accepted as normal. The emergence of global norms and cultural standards is also underway, as communications become easier and faster and people around the world exchange opinions and experiences. The international consensus over human rights that came about at the end of the Second World War was a major step forward in this process.

The political element is the last, and most controversial of these facets of globalization. **Political globalization** refers to the emergence of a political process that spans national borders, and that, increasingly, circumvents them entirely. This is not merely the process of international relations and diplomacy that has been a part of our political reality for hundreds of years. Rather, political globalization implies that the influences on policy-making at both national and international levels derive from many different sources, and involve actors that reach across the globe. One example has been the creation of non-governmental organizations that are represented in many different countries, such as Greenpeace and Amnesty International. Political globalization is tying national governments together through common pressures.

Globalization affects us all, but it affect some more than others, and the distribution of costs and benefits is far from equal. Individuals in some areas of the globe, in particular in the advanced capitalist democracies of North America, Western Europe, and Japan, are highly integrated into the process of globalization, taking advantage of high technologies and communications to maintain contact with the rest of the world. The increasing importance of the World Wide Web and e-mail in the everyday life of citizens in these countries has led some to speak of the creation of an "Internet society."

The economies and political systems of these countries are also profoundly affected by globalization. Many developing countries, however, and in particular the rural regions of these countries, seem relatively unaffected by advances in telecommunications and the growth of the Internet. The daily lives of citizens in these parts of the world are, nonetheless, affected by economic globalization, as the values of the goods they produce and consume, of their national currencies and thus of their personal wealth, are moved upwards or downwards according to the activities of global markets.

# Competing Approaches to International Politics

In addition to recognizable differences in perceptions of the world, there are also significantly different orientations to the study of world politics among scholars and political leaders. These orientations can be roughly divided into three basic groups: realism, liberalism, and Marxism. While these approaches can be separated for the purpose of discussion and analysis, in reality there are not neat lines of demarcation between each, and many scholars and political leaders will use one or more approach, depending on the political needs of the time.

## Power Politics: The Realist Approach

As a theory of international politics and standard for its conduct, realism extends far back in history. Over 2,000 years ago, Kautilya, Minister of the first Maurya Emperor of India, wrote, "The possession of power... in a greater degree makes a king superior to another; in a lesser degree, inferior; and in an equal degree, equal." This view, that world politics is a contest for power, has continued to dominate the thinking of most of the decision-makers who practise international affairs.

During most of the post-World War II period to 1970, realist theory was also the main theme of academic international relations theory. Probably the most influential realist theorist of recent times has been Hans Morgenthau, who defined politics as a "struggle for power." Morgenthau, like most realists, argued that human nature and societies are imperfect. Therefore conflict is an inherent danger. Given that reality, decision-makers should structure their polices and define national interest in terms of power. They should follow policies designed to maximize their power and should avoid policies that overstep the limits of their powers. Realists believe that political leaders can avoid war by not pursuing goals they do not have the power to achieve. It is necessary, therefore, to understand the goals and the power of your opponents, in order not to underestimate their abilities or threaten their vital interests.

Realism envisions the state as the key variable in the study of international politics. Other actors, such as international institutions or corporations, may become involved, but realists believe that the state will always wield the most power. Politics, for realists, is a struggle for limited resources in a competitive and non-cooperative environment.

Based on these views, realists advocate a relatively pragmatic approach to world politics, sometimes called **realpolitik**. This orientation argues that countries should practise balance-of-power politics. That is, diplomats should strive to achieve an equilibrium of power in the world in order to prevent any other country or coalition of countries from dominating the system. This can be done through a variety of methods, including building up your own strength, allying yourself with others, or dividing your opponents.

## Process and Cooperation: The Liberal Approach

Many scholars and policy-makers reject the idea that international affairs should or must be played simply according to the dictates of power politics. They suggest that the real world of political life demonstrates that cooperation is inevitable, because participants—states and otherwise—inevitably come to recognize that the **zero-sum game** of the world of the realists, where one has to lose in order for another to gain, is self-defeating and misdirected. Instead, liberalism suggests that the process attributes of the international system show us that politics may take place in a cooperative manner, though not without competition.

The liberal approach differs from realism in a number of ways. First, liberals do not believe that acquiring, preserving, and applying power is the essence of international relations. Instead, they argue that foreign policy should be formulated according to more cooperative and ethical standards. Second, the liberal approach also dismisses the charge by some realists that pursuing ethical policy works against the national interest; in other words, liberals suggest that ethical policy may in fact be in the national interest of states, rather than diametrically opposed to it. Third, the liberal approach believes that the world must seek a new system of order; they argue that it is imperative to find new paths to cooperation. Finally, in contrast to realists, liberals are prone to believe that humans and countries are capable of achieving more cooperative, less conflicting relations.

## Rejecting Realism: The Marxist Approach

In contrast to the liberal approach, which is reflective of the environment of the realists, the Marxist approach advocates a completely separate form of political interaction on the world stage. Arguing that the orthodoxy that bred realism also established the conditions of inequity and poverty worldwide, the Marxist approach concentrates, not on the political nature of the state, but on the economic nature of the process of interaction. Thus, the Marxists suggest that a more equitable distribution of ownership and goods would create an international political system of greater fairness and security.

There is some irony in the Marxist approach, since the pure communist ideals espoused by Marx himself at the end of the nineteenth century envisioned the end of the nation-state, which he saw as an instrument of the oppressors against the oppressed. It really was not until the 1920s that Vladimir Lenin considered the nature of the international system from a Marxist approach, actually employing the state in a critical approach that denied the state as a viable unit. Nonetheless, Lenin saw the imperialist tendencies of industrialized economies as the "highest stage" of capitalism and the most severe dimension of a fundamentally unequal system.

Therefore, political scientists and politicians who operate from this perspective believe that economic forces and conditions play a primary role in international relations. Some analysts in this general group study political structure and process from the perspective of the control and distribution of economic forces. For them, the economic base (the modes of production) determine the superstructure (the political, legal, cultural, and religious justifications, structures, and practices) which corresponds to a given economic system. They contend that a historically inevitable series of economic pressures and counter-pressures (dialectical materialism) will, and should, lead to the destruction of capitalism and the triumph of communism.

Often, however, world politics is based on **perception** rather than reality. Political developments are creations of the publics concerned with them. Whether events are noticed and what they mean depend on the observers' situations and the language that reflects and interprets those situations. A global economic or military problem, a political enemy, or a leader is both an entity and a signifier with a range of meanings that vary in ways we can at least partly understand. International politics is thus more than a matter of objective facts. It is a study of subjective judgments based on images of oneself and other international actors.

A final word on approaches here is necessary, before moving on to the nature of foreign policy and its determination. Although the study of international politics is largely analytical, the "scientific" dimensions of political science were reflected in a different approach to understanding international politics that gained influence after the Second World War. This "scientific school" of political science is interested in recurring patterns and causal relations of international behaviour. Those who follow this approach, also called the **behaviouralist** approach, often use quantitative methods to arrive at and prove hypotheses that will explain both why certain events have occurred and under what circumstances they might occur again. They also often use cross-cultural analyses to test whether similar or divergent causal patterns occur between different political systems as well as over time. (You will recall references to behaviouralism in earlier chapters.) Like realists, behaviouralists have little interest in advocating fundamental changes in the world system. Where they differ is that realists accept what is and often advocate that politicians should also accept and operate within the world of power politics. Behaviouralists, from their "value-free" or "scientific" perspective, are more disinterested in the good or ill of world politics. They tend to operate from a value-free posture, neither condoning nor condemning what is. They only describe what is and why and try to predict what will be. This value-free approach has been the source of some criticism of behaviouralism by those who contend that the problems and stakes of the world are too great to be studied dispassionately.

## Determinants of Foreign Policy-Making

Foreign policy comprises the key elements to understanding the international system. In order to explain and understand the structure of relations among states, it is necessary to understand the political nature within states. Thus, foreign policy determinants, and the decision-making that influences foreign policy, are central for our broadened comprehension of international politics in general.

In reality, the actions of the state in making foreign policy are determined by several factors, of which international law is only one (and not the most significant) dimension. A state's actions in the international arena are determined by several factors. Some of the more important are: power, domestic capabilities, tradition, ideology, and perceptions of the national interest. The reputation and strength of a state can be ascertained by reference to at least some of the following characteristics.

### Geography

Geography, in terms of size and location in the world, is always part of the power equation. Canada's size and location next to the United States means that our resources and friendliness will be of constant interest to the United States. Likewise the location and economic strength of Germany in the middle of Europe means that a divided Germany will likely continue for some time.

## Natural Resources

A country's natural resources play an important part in establishing the power of a state. Some countries are close to being self-sufficient in terms of critical resources; for example, South Africa. Others have to rely on imports in such critical areas as sources of energy and food. Some countries such as Japan and Korea are able to offset relative shortages of natural resources by basing their economy on "high technology," which is possible with a highly skilled labour force. Other countries, particularly underdeveloped countries, are under constant pressure to share or sell their resources at artificially low prices in order to receive other benefits.

## Population

Population is a major factor in determining the political, economic, and military power of a state. A very small population (particularly in relation to the size of the country) will prevent the state from being very powerful (unless the country occupies a strategic location and has other capabilities that offset its small population). On the other hand, a very large population that lacks an industrial base and suffers from food shortages will also lack the means required to exert power in the international world (see Fig. 7.2).

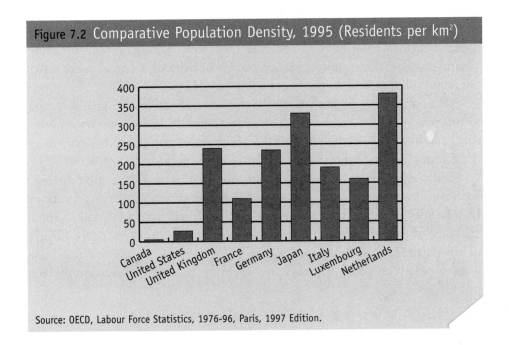

**Figure 7.2** Comparative Population Density, 1995 (Residents per km²)

Source: OECD, Labour Force Statistics, 1976-96, Paris, 1997 Edition.

## Technological Development

The level of technological development in general and in the specific area of military technology (when combined with the strength of the military) will also contribute to the state's relative position in the international community. In some respects, technological innovation has become one of the most important indicators of economic strength, as many of the states that have shown their ability to compete today, such as Japan, Taiwan, and Hong Kong, place a great deal of emphasis on technological innovation and strategically marketing a state's productive output within the world.

## Internal Structural Functional Development

The internal structural functional development of the state will also have its effect. This includes factors such as the type of political system and the degree of societal agreement about shared values and norms.

Such questions as the nature of groups participating in the decision-making processes, performance of the system maintenance function, and the extent of support for the system will all shape the state's behaviour in the international arena. History, prevailing political ideologies, and dominant perceptions of national interest will also contribute to the direction of the state's decisions. The experience of some countries' relations with each other has left them historical friends or enemies. For example, the history of relations between Russia and Germany makes it very difficult for these two countries to overcome traditional hostilities. Some countries have a long history of being "world powers" (for example, France and Great Britain), whereas other states are relative newcomers on the international stage.

Prevailing ideologies both from the outside and inside also give direction to foreign policy. As we have seen in earlier chapters, there are various pressures and influences in the political machinations of any state; this extends to the decision-making process and, in turn, foreign policy.

Finally, each and every state has some notion of what is in its best interest. Such notions transcend ideologies, elite behaviour, or any other considerations because they are embedded in the way of life of that particular polity. These are some of the main determinants of foreign policy operating independently of any particular decision or policy. Not all of these factors always determine a given policy outcome, but they are always a part of the decision-making process.

# Conflict Management and Resolution

Despite the frequency of conflict and its adverse effects in the international system, most activities of states are actually aimed at preserving or improving the conditions of international political life. Most actions of states within the international system are not the sort that occupy the front pages of newspapers; in fact, in contrast to the excitement of these events, the day-to-day operations of states are rather mundane: trade, diplomacy, and routine relations of states. Yet these regularized activities are in some respects an ongoing effort to mitigate conflict in the international system. This section, then, details some of the methods employed by states to regulate and manage conflict in the world.

## State Power and Influence

One of the most common methods of conflict resolution or achievement of state goals is the usage of state power. Regrettably, history is full of examples of how frequently states are prepared to use this method in negative ways. There are several ways in which power is used in a negative manner in international politics.

First, states use their power, in particular military power, to coerce others to do as they wish. Second, demands against other states are frequently made with the stated or understood threat of military intervention in the case of non-compliance with the threatening state's objectives. Third, states defend their sovereignty by threatening to use military force in protection of physical territory. Fourth, states threaten or use trade embargoes and physical blockades to influence the behaviour of other states.

However, there is another dimension to the use of state "power" as it pertains to conflict management and resolution. States often use their powers of influence, gained through respect and authority in the international system, to avoid conflict or avert it. Often powerful states will send representatives to negotiate with other states, sometimes in cases where the powerful state has no immediate relationship, as a means of obtaining settlement. In addition, states sometimes use the threat of their power to dissuade other states from taking actions that may be deemed detrimental to the international system.

## Diplomacy

Another tool of international conflict resolution is the use of diplomacy as a means of obtaining the desired state objectives. This is a process through which negotiators on behalf of their countries attempt to explain the position of their principles and/or attempt to secure agreements on issues ranging from nuclear disarmament, fishing rights, and weather services to cooperative economic development.

To this end, most countries have a large diplomatic service that interacts with the governments of the host countries on a continual basis. This style or technique of interstate interaction is undergoing a significant change. Increasingly, domestic political actors (presidents, prime ministers, and other senior public officials) involve themselves in direct negotiation, frequently conducted in public.

## International Law

The development and acceptance of international law as a means of conflict resolution and pursuit of international goals is yet another tool in reducing tensions. The developments in this area are taking place primarily in two areas: in substantive law, and in the development of processes and structures through which states interact and resolve disputes.

The law of nations develops as a result of custom, bilateral treaties, multilateral treaties and, to some extent, by rulings of arbiters, international organizations (courts), and the writings of jurists. The importance of international law is evaluated in radically different ways. Some states, predominately those powerful enough to ignore the concerns of others, at times ignore international law. Others view it as an instrument that should be generally observed, partly because it does not make excessive demands on the nation-states and partly because, where it interacts with the governments of the host countries on a continual basis, it is usually to the benefit of the states.

## International Organizations

The establishment of and participation of nations in international organizations is another means of arriving at cooperative international policies and contributes to the reduction (or containment) of conflicts. Although these organizations cannot be expected to avert all forms of conflict, international organizations provide a diverse yet integrated structure for systematic, standardized state relations in the international system.

There are a variety of international organizations in existence in the world today. They may be global, such as the United Nations; regional, exemplified by the Organization of American States (OAS), and the European Union (EU);

or specialized, including the International Monetary Fund (IMF), the World Bank, or OPEC. Some of these enjoy a high degree of success, others have only been partially successful.

# The End of World War II and the New World

The Second World War was an important watershed in international politics because it signaled the end of one era (the age of Empire and European domination) and brought about the leadership of the United States and the rise of international institutions to help regulate an increasingly complex international system. The end of the Second World War also initiated a wider understanding of the type of relations considered to be important, moving from the almost singular attention to security to a wider definition of social and economic considerations.

The end of the Second World War, and the period following it that came to be known as the "post-war" era, brought about major shifts in world economics, both in trade and monetary relations. The level of world trade had been gradually rising for several centuries, but after the war it greatly accelerated. In addition to non-political technological and economic factors, trade was encouraged by the belief that trade barriers had contributed to the economic collapse (world depression) that preceded and (some argued) helped cause the Second World War. As a result, and in their own interest, many countries agreed to remove tariffs and other trade restrictions. The result was the creation of the General Agreement on Tariffs and Trade (GATT) and later the World Trade Organization (WTO), which replaced the GATT. One result of increased trade, as well as other factors, is increasing **economic interdependence**: almost all countries have economies that rely on foreign markets and sources of supply.

Monetary relations were also considerably revamped at the end of the war, primarily at a 1944 conference at Bretton Woods, New Hampshire. The resulting monetary arrangements, known as the Bretton Woods system, were based on the gold standard and the strength of the American dollar. That system lasted until the early 1970s, when a number of factors, including the weakening of the dollar and the unwillingness of the United States to sell gold at a fixed (and no longer realistic) rate, brought the world to a new system of currencies that generally "float"; that is, currencies are exchanged on the basis of supply and demand conditions. The Bretton Woods structure also included the International Monetary Fund (IMF), which was designed to help stabilize currency exchange rates by loaning countries money to meet international currency demands, thereby keeping the supply and demand stable.

The drive to create institutions in the immediate post-war period was in large part in recognition of the causes of the Second World War itself. World leaders in 1944 were concerned that the lack of regulation, integration, and normalcy of economic and political relations during the 1930s led some states, such as Germany and Italy, to react to what they viewed to be a system balanced against them. Those who met at Bretton Woods felt that a new system of **multilateralism** (involving many states in a cooperative manner) was necessary to regulate and normalize a very fractious state of affairs. This was achieved through a systemic development of international organizations, institutions, and forums for deliberation that, it was hoped, would ameliorate any future conflict.

We can easily see, therefore, the way in which the end of the Second World War affected the international system. Indeed, the very functioning and purpose of relations among states radically altered after the war. However, perhaps the most important element of the post-war period was the emerging conflict between the United States and the Soviet Union: the **Cold War**—the strategic arrangement of states in the international system, and their respective quest for individual security.

Although the United States and the Soviet Union were united during the Second World War in their attempts to stop German imperialism under Hitler, it would be wrong to assume that both countries viewed the world in the same manner or had the same attitudes about its direction. Very quickly after the end of the war, both sides began their pursuit of independent goals for the international system. On the one hand, the Soviet Union envisioned a world united in socialism, with centralized and controlled economies that would seek to redistribute wealth in a more equitable manner. On the other hand, the United States and its allies sought an international environment marked by economic opportunity, political freedom, and international liberalism. These two antithetical approaches influenced all aspects of international politics during the post-war period.

This era was called the Cold War because it was marked by rhetorical hostilities by both sides that never erupted into violence or a "hot war" that involved the two countries fighting each other. Furthermore, the possession of great numbers of nuclear weapons by both sides, with sufficient power to destroy the world many times over, exacerbated the situation, and added to the sense of fear and distrust.

In brief, all aspects of international life—strategic, economic, cultural, and political—were deeply affected by the ideological divisions between the United States and the Soviet Union during the Cold War. Some aspects of global relations were more influenced than others, such as the way in which states sought military security through the forging of tight alliances with more powerful states. But even seemingly innocuous events like the Olympic Games were victim to the Cold War animosity; in 1980 the United States and most of its allies **boycotted** (a refusal to deal with another political community) the games, a decision mimicked by the Soviets in 1984, when the games were held in Los Angeles. The Cold War, simply put, was the primary influence in world politics at this time.

The Cold War had a number of different phases. Immediately following the Second World War, tensions between the two sides brought about what has sometimes been referred to as the "long decade" of the 1950s. The fifties were marked by the first detonation of a Soviet nuclear device in 1949 and the corresponding American doctrine to contain Soviet expansionism, followed in 1963 by the signing of the nuclear Limited Test Ban Treaty, considered by many to be the first real recognition by both sides that nuclear weapons escalation was out of control. The 1970s, on the other hand, were branded the decade of **détente** (a warming of relations), as the two sides sought a degree of *rapprochement* (reconciliation) with the other.

However, the election of Ronald Reagan in 1980 and his emphasis on a military build-up as a response to a perception of a Soviet threat ushered in what was called the "second" Cold War (in fact a continuation of the previous Cold War), and a return to colder and more remote relations, and a corresponding renewed fear of nuclear war. Finally, the election of Mikhail Gorbachev as General Secretary of the Communist Party of the Soviet Union in 1985, and his program of restructuring Soviet politics and economics, brought about the beginning of the end of the Cold War, which finally ended (symbolically, at least) with the collapse of the Soviet Union itself, and its formal demise at the stroke of midnight on New Year's Eve 1991.

Despite the changes to the international system after the end of the Cold War, a constant basic world reality is that the substantial majority of people and countries are poor. Since the vast majority of these countries are situated either near or below the equator, they have become known as the **South**. In contrast, world wealth is concentrated in a few industrialized countries that lie in the northern hemisphere (the **North**). Although the absolute economic (and related social) conditions of the South are improving slightly, the gap between the North and the South is widening at an alarming rate. Since the 1970s the

**less developed countries** (LDCs) have demanded a fundamental restructuring of the distribution of wealth and the end of trade and monetary policies that favour the North. The response of the North has been limited to date, and the question of Third World development and North-South relations will remain a perplexing and contentious aspect of international relations for years to come.

Compounding this increasing variance in economic opportunity is the more recent rise of the so-called **newly industrialized countries,** or NICs. Whereas we once had a fairly simple model of relative wealth in the international system—basically the highly industrialized Organization for Economic Cooperation and Development (OECD) member states and their partners versus the rest of the world—the relationship today is far more complicated. The past two decades have witnessed the rise of new, stronger economies, sometimes from states that were once considered "Third World." As a result of strategically positioning themselves in the international economic environment and liberalizing their economies, states such as Malaysia, Singapore, Taiwan, Hong Kong, Thailand, and even Brazil and Argentina, cannot be considered simply LDCs anymore. In addition, the very uneven progression of economies in the former Soviet bloc (the countries of Eastern and Central Europe) has left us with a number of different levels of economic and political development today.

Though certainly not exhaustive, the preceding discussion gives us some insights into the nature of change in the international system. Indeed, one of the constant features of any international system is the transformation and variance of relations among the primary units of analysis. Politics is naturally a dynamic force in social life, and this dynamism is perhaps no more evident than in the international system. The fundamental alteration of the international system with the ending of the Cold War is an illustration of this tendency for substantial change in international politics.

## The Post-Cold War Era

In 1988 then British Prime Minister Margaret Thatcher declared that "the Cold war is over." In hindsight, it may appear as though Thatcher was somewhat premature in her statement; after all, the Soviet Union existed until the end of 1991, and Central and Eastern Europe surely had not been integrated into the world political system to the degree they were even five years later. Yet, Thatcher's comment was not merely idle prognostication. In fact, she was responding to a series of events that had taken place in the early to mid-1980s that represented a truly new way of viewing the international system, and the bipolar animosity that prevailed for much of the Cold War.

Perhaps the most important event leading up to the end of the Cold War was the ascent of Mikhail Gorbachev to the position of General Secretary of the Communist Party of the Soviet Union; as the General Secretary and head of state of the Soviet Union, he was primarily responsible for the formation of Soviet foreign policy.

Immediately upon election, Gorbachev began a series of momentous structural changes in Soviet life and politics. Beginning with culture and gradually moving through to the realm of political rights, Gorbachev's *glasnost* (openness) and *perestroika* (restructuring) programs were intended to fundamentally alter the Soviet approach to political authority and control. Recognizing that the Soviets were earnest in their attempt to reformulate their relations in the international system, the American government—and others with it—took a series of unprecedented steps to engage and integrate the Soviet Union into the Western-led system of economics and political interaction.

## Human Security                                                           Box 7.2

Since the end of the Cold War the meaning of the term "security" has undergone significant change. Originally referring to the protection of civilians from external threats, security in contemporary discussions now includes such diverse issues as monetary stability, economic growth, disease control, human migration, and human rights.

In the late 1990s the Canadian Minister for Foreign Affairs, Lloyd Axworthy, seized upon a new concept in the international relations lexicon. Axworthy began to talk of "human security," a term that had first appeared in the 1994 UNDP Human Development Report. Underlying the concept is the claim that "since the end of the Cold War, security for the majority of states has increased, while security for many of the world's people has declined," and that traditional notions of defending national security are "insufficient to guarantee people's security."

The Canadian Department of Foreign Affairs and International Trade defines human security thus:

> In essence, human security means safety for people from both violent and
> non-violent threats. It is a condition or state of being characterized by
> freedom from pervasive threats to people's rights, their safety, or even their

lives. From a foreign policy perspective, human security is perhaps best understood as a shift in perspective or orientation. It is an alternative way of seeing the world, taking people as its point of reference, rather than focusing exclusively on the security of territory or governments. Like other security concepts—national security, economic security, food security—it is about protection. Human security entails taking preventive measures to reduce vulnerability and minimize risk, and taking remedial action where prevention fails.

The range of potential threats to human security should not be narrowly conceived. While the safety of people is obviously at grave risk in situations of armed conflict, a human security approach is not simply synonymous with humanitarian action. It highlights the need to address the root causes of insecurity and to help ensure people's future safety. There are also human security dimensions to a broad range of challenges, such as gross violations of human rights, environmental degradation, terrorism, transnational organized crime, gender-based violence, infectious diseases, and natural disasters. The widespread social unrest and violence that often accompanies economic crises demonstrates that there are clear economic underpinnings to human security. The litmus test for determining if it is useful to frame an issue in human security terms is the degree to which the safety of people is at risk."

Source: Department of Foreign Affairs and International Trade. "Human Security: Safety for People in a Changing World." [Online.] http://www.dfait-maeci.gc.ca/foreignp/humansecurity/secur-e.htm

In 1989 the Berlin Wall, which divided the city of Berlin in Germany, was taken down. This symbolic crumbling of the division between "East" and "West" was seen as a tangible signal that the ideological detachment of the Soviet- and American-led alliances was on its last legs. As a show of resolution to the warming of relations, the Soviet Union removed its military forces from Czechoslovakia and Hungary in 1990. And, beginning in August 1990, and continuing into 1991, the Soviet Union supported, at least in principle, the position of the American-led coalition force against Iraq after that country invaded the tiny state of Kuwait, setting off the events leading to the Gulf War of 1991. After an attempted *coup d'état* (the forcible replacement of a governing authority, usually through overt military means) by hard-line Communist supporters in late summer 1991, the Soviet Union appeared to have run its course. Acknowledging that his authority over the Soviet Union, and the Soviet Union itself, had declined to the point of inconsequence,

Gorbachev oversaw the formal demise of the Soviet Union, exemplified by the ceremonial removal of the old Soviet flag and its replacement with the new flag of the Russian federation on New Year's Eve 1991.

Although the full integration of the former Soviet states and the rest of the Central and Eastern European region had not been attained at the close of the twentieth century, it may clearly be stated that international politics is decidedly and monumentally different than the period of the Cold War.

Beginning with strategic affairs, the omnipresent fear of nuclear war, and the certainty that it would wipe out all life as we know it, has dissipated greatly. Although both the United States and the Russian Federation still possess nuclear weapons, these numbers are reduced from the height of the Cold War, and both sides have entered into a series of agreements to limit their continued production and use. Other nuclear weapons-possessing states—Great Britain, France, and China—have also demonstrated a commitment to the eradication of these weapons of mass destruction.

Furthermore, the continent of Europe is not divided as it was during the Cold War, and the massive military forces of the United States and the Soviet Union (along with their respective alliances) are not poised for potential conflict. Clearly, the strategic concerns of the Cold War are no longer as pressing, though some of their legacies still exist.

Economically, the end of the Soviet Union has permitted its limited involvement in global institutions. However, because most new states of the former Soviet "bloc" have not developed to the degree that they may be given full status membership, integration of these new economies has been a deliberate and constant process.

On a political level, the end of the tensions of the Cold War has permitted a new sense of openness and cooperation in the international system. Almost unimaginable to many observers of Cold War international politics, the former adversaries of the Soviet and American alliances have worked together to forge a different structure of relations, an unmistakable and distinct framework for international politics. Though it may not be said that all of the challenges of the Cold War are behind us (and in fact many new ones have emerged), the post-Cold War era appears to be undergoing constant change, reflecting elements of the past order, and recognizing a distinctive and emerging set of world relations.

| Box 7.3 | Ethnic Nationalism |
|---------|--------------------|

Since the end of the Cold War, many of the conflicts that have dominated the world's headlines have involved disputes and fighting between different ethnic groups. The conflicts in Bosnia-Herzegovina, Rwanda, Burundi, East Timor, and of course in Kosovo each concerned ethnic groups seeking self-determination and freedom from oppression by other ethnicities. Such conflicts led Harvard professor Samuel Huntington to argue in the 1990s that the next century would be dominated by what he called "the clash of civilizations."

The appearance of ethnic nationalism, however, does not always involve bloody conflict. The emergence of Quebec separatism, Scottish nationalism, and Welsh nationalism, for example, have to date meant heated political debate and constitutional reform. This is not to say that the demands of these nationalist groupings have been satisfied, but the pattern has been one of peaceful resolution of conflict, rather than more extreme measures.

One of the largest problems related to ethnic nationalism is that there are potentially thousands, if not tens of thousands, of ethnicities in the world. If each were allowed to form its own political unit, then the system of states that we currently know would be turned upside-down. Imagine a system made up of thousands of microstates—even European states such as Germany, France, and Italy would be broken up into several different units.

The consequences are immense for the stability of the international system, and for the institutions to which we have turned in recent history to provide stability and economic and political benefits. How could cooperation be organized among such a huge number of tiny states? More importantly, how could these states effectively provide for the economic and social well-being of their citizens? Would they be politically stable?

# International Challenges

## A Changing Set of East-West Relations

As outlined in greater detail earlier in this chapter, the legacy of the Cold War is a number of serious issues facing the primary actors in the international system today. Of these, responding to the new focus and nature of East-West relations is perhaps the most crucial. Though not framed in the same light as the "tensions" that were represented during the Cold War, the challenges fac-

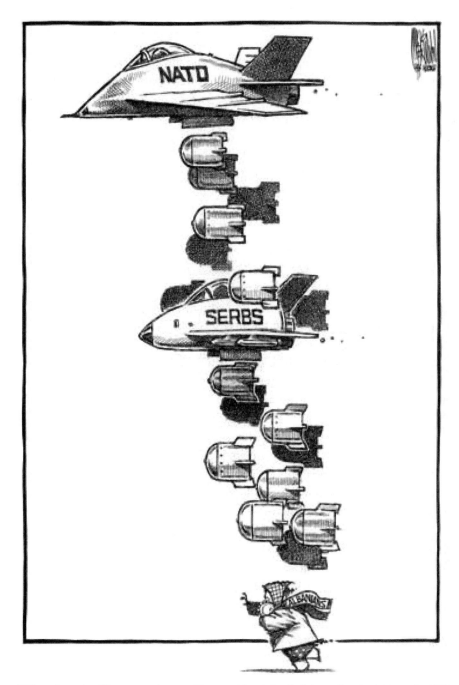

Military force is still very much an option used by states in international relations. In 1999, NATO air strikes in Kosovo were criticized as contributing to the plight of Albanian refugees, who were already being attacked by Serbian forces.

Bruce MacKinnon, The Chronicle Herald

ing states of the East and West are nonetheless significant and sometimes daunting.

Some of these daunting challenges include the integration of former Soviet bloc economies into the Western model of economic relations; continuing anxieties about the possible proliferation of nuclear weapons; conventional arms races in the Indian subcontinent, Middle East, and North Pacific; social change in the former communist states; democratization in socialist political systems; and concerns about political leadership and institutions in states undergoing tremendous systemic change.

## The North-South Debate

Poverty and regional disputes in the Third World are another challenge to global stability. Many observers consider the current international disparities of wealth allotment as simply unmanageable; in simple terms, over three-quarters of the people in the world cannot remain in such adverse conditions. A great deal of the globe's land mass and virtually all of three continents—South America, Africa, and Asia—are part of the South. Yet the world's wealth is badly apportioned. More than 77 percent of the world's people live in the South, yet they produce only 15.5 percent of the global Gross National Product (GNP). Conversely, this means that the less than 23 percent of the people who are fortunate enough to reside in the North command 84.5 percent of the world's wealth. Additionally, the people in the South collect only 19.6 percent of the world's export earnings and are cared for by only 9 percent of global expenditures on public health.

Nor is the future picture for many in the South optimistic. At least relative to the North, the socioeconomic plight of the South is not improving. Some indicators, such as literacy rate, physicians per capita, and life expectancy, show advances in Third World absolute conditions, but the general economic gap between North and South is widening. In the worst scenarios, absolute conditions are declining. Sub-Saharan Africa is a particularly depressed region. The rapidly rising population is overwhelming agriculture. Per capita food production in the region declined in 14 of 15 years between 1972 and 1987 and dropped by an ominous total of 20 percent during this period; this decline has been exacerbated in the 1990s. Illnesses ranging from traditional tropical diseases to AIDS ravage the region, average life expectancy is less than 50 years, and one of every five children dies before the age of five. In relative terms—and in too many cases in absolute terms—the rich are getting richer, and the poor are getting poorer.

## Nationalism

One of the seeming paradoxes of the post-Cold War era is that, despite the suggestions that the international system is somehow "shrinking," and citizens compose a form of "global village," the forces of identity, and the negativity that often accompanies severe affinities with identity, have created a condition of increased conflict and misunderstanding.

Nationality is essentially the identity one feels for a larger community of individuals, based on—but not necessarily reducible to—religion, race, culture, ethnicity, language, or even a form of government. When this identity takes on the role of a political movement to create a separate political unit, nationalism is born. In our contemporary international system, nationalist fervour in Eastern and Western Europe, the Middle East, Asia, and even North America, has led to constant challenges for political allegiance and unity.

## Environmental Concerns

Another challenge facing the international system concerns the environment, or what is sometimes called the "ecological crisis." This problem has two dimensions. First, many of the non-reusable resources are rapidly approaching exhaustion, and there is little evidence that the decision-makers are prepared to take a long-term view. Compounding that problem is the destruction of the environment. The quality of our land, water, and air is decreasing over time. Some predict that the damage to the natural environment has reached a point of no return and that through our own activities, even without any military conflict, life on planet Earth will cease to exist sometime soon.

Such assessments, although not universally accepted, carry with them the weight of a large proportion of the scientific community. This concern is increasingly being shared by public interest groups and political parties. However, the present state of the international system does not allow for positive redress of the situation at the global level.

International cooperation to meet environmental concerns has been slow. It is beset by a combination of related economic and political barriers. Less developed countries are often willing to accept environmentally damaging practices by local or multinational corporations in return for industrialization. Environmental controls are expensive, and to a degree, industrialization money flows to cheap production areas.

| Box 7.4 | Human Migration |
|---------|-----------------|

One of the challenges for states in the twenty-first century is to deal with the threat of mass human migration. The movement of huge numbers of people has been a threat to national governments for hundreds of years, as these new arrivals in a country absorb precious resources and contribute to political and economic instability. With the end of the Cold War, and the stability that it provided, Western European governments were forced to deal with the prospect of mass movements of citizens westward from the former Eastern bloc in search of a better life. With the Kosovo conflict in 1999, Albania faced the prospect of hundreds of thousands of Kosovars seeking shelter and refuge from the violence, a situation which cost Albania hundreds of millions of dollars, financial resources it could ill afford.

Human migration finds its starkest example on the southern border of the United States. In the states of California and Texas, in particular, the border with Mexico has been illegally crossed by millions of Mexicans and central Americans who seek employment and prosperity in "El Norte." This has drawn a vehement response from many US citizens in the southern states, who argue that illegal immigrants take away jobs and drain the social security and health systems. By way of response, the US government has erected high walls and fences and put in place border patrols to keep illegal aliens from entering United States territory. However, the activities of the so-called "coyotes," individuals who organize the illegal transport of immigrants into the US, continue to evade US restrictions. The coyotes, who charge hundreds of dollars for their services, routinely abuse, rob, and maltreat their human cargoes.

## Summary

In this chapter we have examined the formation and development of the modern international political system. Filling the gap created by the breakdown of the Holy Roman Empire, dominant states within Europe developed a body of conventions and laws to conduct interstate affairs. The prominence of and legitimacy of the nation-state is an important feature of the modern international world. Coupled with the sovereignty of the nation-state are important ideological, religious, and environmental concerns. These issues confound the ability of states to bring about solutions independently of each other and have led to the creation of international organizations through which international cooperation can be achieved. Although there are always examples showing a lack of cooperation and understanding between states, there is also evidence that increasing demands for international peace, a solution to the arms race, and addressing a global pollution problem are resulting in new avenues of cooperation between states.

## Self-Assessment Questions

1.  How might we distinguish among international politics, international relations, and foreign policy? In what ways do they overlap?

2.  How did the Cold War era following the Second World War shape and influence international politics?

3.  What are the prospects for developing states in contemporary international politics? Have conditions improved, or worsened, for developing states in the post-Cold War era?

4.  What are the primary approaches to understanding international politics, and how do they differ? What is the role of the state in each of these approaches?

5.  What are the prospects for growing "regionalism" in the international system? Do state actors have anything to fear in this regard? Why is the concept of state sovereignty held so strongly in the international system?

## Further Reading

Art, Robert C., and Robert Jervis. *International Politics: Enduring Concepts and Contemporary Issues.* New York: HarperCollins, 1996.

Dougherty, James E., and Robert L. Pfaltzgraff, Jr. *Contending Theories of International Relations: A Comprehensive Survey*, 3rd ed. Grand Rapids: Harper and Row, 1990.

Genest, Marc A. *Conflict and Cooperation: Evolving Theories of International Relations.* Toronto: Harcourt Brace Jovanovich, 1996.

Hauss, Charles. *Beyond Confrontation: Transforming the New World Order.* Westport: Praeger, 1996.

Holm, H.H., and G. Sørenson, eds. *Whose World Order? Uneven Globalization and the End of the Cold War.* Boulder: Westview Press, 1995.

Kegley, Charles W., and Eugene R. Wittkopf. *World Politics: Trend and Transformation*, 5th ed. New York: St. Martin's Press, 1995.

Morgenthau, H.J. *Politics among Nations: The Struggle for Power and Peace.* New York: McGraw-Hill, 1948.

## Web Links

Trade and Development Centre
http://www.itd.org/

North South Institute
http://www.nsi-ins.ca/

CNN special Cold War
http://www.cnn.com/SPECIALS/cold.war/

Nationalism Project
http://www.wisc.edu/nationalism/

Environment Links
http://dir.yahoo.com/Society_and_Culture/Environment_and_Nature/

## CHAPTER EIGHT

# STATES, WEALTH, AND POWER: THE POLITICAL ECONOMY OF THE INTERNATIONAL SYSTEM

## Chapter Objectives

This chapter will describe and explain:

- the major tenets of the most important theories and perspectives of IPE
- the link between wealth and power in the international system
- the development of international trade, production, and finance since the nineteenth century
- the growth of economic interdependence between states
- the connection between national and international economic and political processes
- the importance of international economic organizations

In this, the eighth and last chapter of the book, you will be introduced to an area of study that has grown remarkably in the last 30 years. International political economy became established as a sub-discipline of political science and international relations in the 1970s. Since then it has produced many of the insights that have been most important in advancing our understanding of the international system, of the dynamic relationship between politics and economics and, indeed, of politics itself. International political economy, or IPE as it is most commonly called, covers a vast area of political and economic activity and clearly demonstrates the intimate connection between national and international processes.

## What Is IPE?

As with our definition of political economy in general, IPE studies the interaction between politics and economics, between states and markets. Of course, in IPE we are looking at this interaction at the level of the international system. This does not mean that other levels of analysis are ignored. On the contrary, IPE explicitly recognizes that domestic and international actors and processes continuously interact. The most obvious example of this is the making of foreign economic policy.

A central aspect of international political economy is the examination of how the activities of, and distribution of power between, states and other political authorities affect the international economic system, and also how international economic processes and actors impact upon the activities and power of states. In this way it studies the interaction between the distribution of power and of wealth, and the intimate connection between economic and political power. Throughout history states have depended upon their economic capabilities to develop power and influence in other forms. The Spanish crown, for example, in the fourteenth and fifteenth centuries, depended upon the supply of gold and silver from its New World colonies to underwrite its military prowess. In the nineteenth century Great Britain built its primacy on its industrial leadership and dominance of international trade; and of course, the global predominance of the United States at the beginning of the twenty-first century is dependent on the continuing strength of its domestic economy.

The scope of international political economy is broad: IPE scholars study trade, finance, environment, business organization, and industrial policy, to name just a few areas of focus. What's more, the study of the international political economy encompasses the activities of many different actors, both state and non-state. The work of the International Monetary Fund, the World Bank, and of the World Health Organization fit equally well into the scope of IPE, as do the operations of IBM, Archers Daniels Midland (ADM), Exxon, and other major multinational firms. Of particular importance and interest is the study of the interaction between different kinds of actors, and studying the balance of economic power among them. In international financial affairs, for example, there has been since 1945 a fundamental shift in power and influence away from states and towards private financial actors such as banks and securities firms. What's more, there has been a changing balance of power within the financial sector, with securities firms and mutual funds and insurance companies now rivalling banks for influence. The changing relations among the actors that have an impact on the shape of the international economic system is a primary concern of IPE.

## The Perspectives of IPE

As we established back in Chapter 2, political economy as a discipline is dominated by three major perspectives, the liberal, Marxist, and nationalist perspectives. However, we must also be aware of another perspective that is becoming more and more important, and that is increasingly being seen as a mainstream perspective. Gender-based analysis is becoming a central perspective in IPE. Promoted initially by feminist writers but now employed by political economists across the political spectrum, gender-based analysis focuses on a key issue in political economy, namely, the distribution of costs and benefits in the system, in this case between the genders. For this reason the **gender perspective** is included here alongside the more traditional approaches to IPE.

The liberal perspective on IPE is guided by the central concerns of liberal ideology, both political and economic. It is concerned with the free functioning of markets, increased individual freedom, and progress in the form of increased wealth. It is also concerned with the issue of international cooperation between states, particularly, but not exclusively, in the area of trade. Through cooperation states can reduce the distorting effects of tariffs and duties and create institutions that set up rules for international economic intercourse. They can also rescue the international economic system in times of trouble, as did the International Monetary Fund during the Asian crisis of 1997-98. The central focus of the liberal perspective, however, is to remove the state as much as possible from the economic sphere, in order to increase the role played by the market in issues of distribution, competition, and pricing.

Marxists, on the other hand, have quite a different outlook on the international system. They view the international capitalist economy as a tool of oppression whereby the controllers of capital exploit the labouring classes. This perspective is extended to states: for Marxists the international economic system is one in which the wealthy, powerful states exploit their poorer, weaker counterparts. As we saw in Chapter 6, the challenges of development are many for LDCs, but Marxists see the structure of the international system as one of the major hurdles standing in the way of true development. The major concern of Marxist international political economists, therefore, is to analyze the unequal conditions of the international economy, and to study the exploitation of certain groups by others. It is important to remember that for most Marxists analysis of the exploitative nature of the international system goes hand-in-hand with a commitment to change it.

Nationalists see the international economy as an arena in which states are involved in a constant battle for survival, at least, and supremacy, at best.

International economic relations, therefore, are viewed in a competitive light, with states striving to surpass each other not only in their levels of productivity, growth, and power, but also in the benefits that each gains from economic intercourse. Nationalists call for an expanded role for the state so that it can manage its external economic relations to the best advantage. Mercantilism is the best example of a nationalistic approach to international political economy, for it sees the state directing its foreign trade according to the principle of maximization of state power. A good historical example of economic nationalism at work is Nazi Germany in the 1930s. Under Adolph Hitler and his finance minister Schacht, the German government manipulated its trade and financial relations with other states so that German state power was increased.

The final perspective that should be noted at this point is gender analysis. Like Marxists, gender analysts study the differential costs and benefits derived from the international political economy by different groups. For gender analysts, however, the most important groups are not class-based, but gender-based. Though for many years this was not a mainstream perspective, it has in recent years joined those mentioned above as a central mode of analysis. Its utility is quite clear. The process of industrialization, integral to most LDC development strategies, affects men and women in dramatically different ways. While men shift their economic activities from agriculture to industry, it is quite common for women to be left to take care of the home and children, as well as domestic agricultural production. Another example is the growth in the international sex trade and sex tourism. These economic activities rely on the exploitation of female (and often child) labour while producing huge economic rewards for a small group of (usually) male organizers (see Box 8.1).

These four perspectives on IPE allow us to view the international economic system from different points of view, and each perspective should be seen as useful in its own way. As we will see, the history of the international political economy in this century alone is a mixture of growth, liberalizaton, state control, and exploitation of the weak by the powerful. The competing perspectives on IPE, therefore, should not be seen as mutually exclusive. Rather, we should use them to ask interesting and important questions about the international economic system, questions such as:

- Which are the most important actors in the international economic system?

- Who gains from an economic relationship, and how much?

- Who pays the costs of an economic process?

## Gender and the *Maquilas*    Box 8.1

In the last quarter of the twentieth century a number of LDC states allowed the creation of what came to be known as *maquiladora* (meaning "assembly") zones or *maquilas* in their countries. These zones hold a special status for they allowed foreign corporations to come in, produce goods, and then export them back to their home country duty free. *Maquilas* became an important source of employment and income to these economies, and further increased the level of inter-dependence between developed and developing economies.

However, these zones, though they provide employment and wages that are generally higher than those available locally, are a mixed blessing. Many companies operating in *maquilas* tend to hire women in the assembly plants, on the justification that female labour is better suited to the work involved and also that it is generally cheaper than the male equivalent. This in itself is problematical, but women in the *maquilas* face a range of other challenges.

Sexual harassment is one. Local governments tend to leave foreign producers alone when they operate in these zones, and so regulation and enforcement is often weak. Management levels are generally dominated by men, some of whom are foreign, and there have been many documented cases of managers sexually harassing. or even raping female employees. A second area of rights abuse has been compulsory pregnancy testing. Before a women is hired, and periodically during her employment, she must face pregnancy tests. If she is discovered to be pregnant, she will not be hired, or if already employed, will be fired. The *maquilas* pose a challenge for state policy-makers, women's rights action groups, and gender analysts, and raise the issue of gender relations within the new international production structure.

- How are bargains struck between important actors?
- What are the conditions under which cooperation takes place?
- Is the role of the state increasing or decreasing?

## The Link between Domestic and International Factors

In every area of political science and political economy it is important that we understand all of the major factors impacting on an event, process, or actor.

In studying the international political economy it is essential because the international economic system is made up, not of monolithic units that are independent from each other or from third parties, but rather of states and firms, labour unions, and individuals that each depend upon a specific local, national, or regional economic, social, and political environment for their existence. Thus, to understand how a Canadian firm operates in the international economic setting, we also have to be aware of the challenges, obstacles, and incentives it faces within Canada. This is because it will primarily be Canadian authorities (local, provincial, and federal) that regulate the largest part of a Canadian firm's activities. But of course the story of the relationship between domestic and international factors does not end there. When the same Canadian firm seeks to invest in a foreign country (an international activity) it will have to negotiate with the foreign government concerned, as well as the trade unions, consumers groups, and suppliers in that country.

Domestic politics has its most direct and important impact on the international economic system in the formulation of **foreign economic policy**. Here, at the national level, domestic interest groups and other constituencies, from both within government and without, lobby and apply pressure to the government and the bureaucracy to influence the shape and direction of a state's policy. One of the clearest examples is in foreign trade. Domestic producers can lobby either for protection from international competition (if they are not internationally competitive in their production and pricing) or for increased openness, so that they will be allowed to compete on a level playing field in international markets (if they are competitive by international standards). This lobbying can be aimed at securing barriers that protect national producers (such as a **duty** applied to a good when it enters the country, thus raising its price), or at negotiating free trade deals with other states and regions. In the 1960s and 1970s, the United States steel industry successfully lobbied the US government for protection from foreign producers. The US government imposed very high **tariffs** on foreign steel entering the United States, which raised its price and made domestically produced steel more competitive.

But such lobbying also takes place in less obvious circumstances. Exporters often lobby the government of a country to bring down the value of the national currency. This, they argue, will lower the price of their exports by international standards, thus making the exports more competitive. Importers would lobby against such a depreciation in the value of the national currency because it would make the goods that they import more expensive. Investment firms, and investors' organizations often lobby the government to negotiate international agreements that will make it possible to invest freely in foreign countries, while labour unions and poverty action groups often lobby against such liberalizaton of international investment rules (see Box 8.2).

Another link between domestic and international levels is worth mentioning here. Because the world's national economies have become more and more interdependent since 1945, what appears to be a purely domestic economic decision can have far-reaching and profound effects on individuals, firms, and governments in other parts of the world. Nowhere is this more true than in the economy of the United States. Let us imagine that the Federal Reserve (the United States central bank) decides to combat high inflation by dramatically raising interest rates (see Chapter 3). This could be a purely domestic decision that will likely dampen economic activity in that country by making it more expensive for consumers and producers to borrow money. However, it will also encourage investment into the United States as foreign investors look to take advantage of the higher rates of interest. This will mean two things:

## The MAI and the Internet                                              Box 8.2

In the mid-1990s the advanced industrialized economies came together to draft an agreement that would create an international set of rules for international investment. The Multilateral Agreement on Investment (MAI) was promoted by the member countries of the Organization for Economic Cooperation and Development (OECD) to be a means of giving certainty to the business of foreign investment for both investors and the recipient countries.

Opponents of the deal saw things rather differently. Poverty action groups, labour unions, and social activists argued that the MAI was merely a way of prising open the economies of developing states and forcing them to accept investment from the owners and managers of capital in the industrialized states on terms that were much more favourable to the latter. They further claimed that implementation of the MAI would only increase the level of dependence of developing on developed states.

The campaign against the MAI took many different forms, but one which made it a protest campaign of the 1990s was the way in which activists used the World Wide Web as a medium for dispersing information, rallying support, and challenging the OECD. Canadian private citizens in particular became heavily involved in protesting the MAI. By informing and then pulling together public opposition, these groups were able to apply sufficient pressure to their national governments to force the OECD to drop the MAI in 1998.

money leaving other economies and the governments responsible for those economies raising their interest rates to stem the exodus. In turn, economic activity in those countries will be slowed down. The cumulative effect of these decisions will be that the world economy slows down, as producers slow production, and consumers slow their levels of consumption. In this case a purely domestic decision would have deeply felt consequences across the globe.

But it is not just in the powerful states that domestic politics have an international effect. In Mexico in 1994 the political instability that was caused by a rebellion in the southern state of Chiapas and two political assassinations combined with the end of a presidential term (*sexenio*) to lead to increased investor nervousness. This came after several years of heavy foreign investment in the country, and contributed to the deep financial crisis that hit Mexico in December 1994. This crisis not only affected Mexico, it also drove down stock markets and currency values in other Latin American economies through what came to be known as the **tequila effect**.

## Economic Interdependence

Much of the story of the development of the international economy contained in this chapter is the story of growing **interdependence** between states. The term *interdependence* refers to the mutual, but not necessarily equal, dependence between states. It can take an economic, political, environmental, or security form, but it always implies that actions and policies taken in one national political or economic system will have effects on other states in the international system.

An excellent example of interdependence can be found in the relationship between the United States and Canada. These two states have maintained peaceful relations since 1812, and their economies have become highly interconnected. It is natural to think of Canada as being dependent upon the US, because it is clearly the less powerful partner in the relationship. But it would also be fair to say that the US is dependent upon the Canadian economy for a large part of its well-being. We must remember that the US-Canada trading relationship is the largest in the world, that many thousands of citizens of both countries work in the other country, that production processes extend North-South just as much as they do East-West, and that the environmental effects of economic activities in each state affect the other.

Interdependence, however, does not merely take the bilateral form that we see in the US-Canada relationship. It also applies to the interactions within and between regions, and between groups of states. The international finan-

## Natural Resources and the Canadian Economy    Box 8.3

We tend to think of Canada as an advanced industrialized, or even a post-industrial state. Those who live in major urban centres are surrounded by the services industries, by financial institutions, and in some cases, by heavy industry such as automobile production. Yet Canada still depends of natural resources for a significant part of its Gross Domestic Product (GDP), and of its foreign export earnings. By the mid-1990s natural resource industries such as mining and petroleum, forestry, agriculture, and fishing were responsible for approximately 7–8 percent of Canadian GDP but almost 60 percent of total exports.

As many of us know, Canada's fishing industry is currently going through a period of severe adjustment as the government tries to rescue fish stocks and to turn fishing into a sustainable resource industry. Though not as urgent, the problem of sustainability haunts all natural resource industries in Canada, as environmental degradation and exhaustion of supplies threaten their ongoing profitability.

**Employment By Sector, 1997**

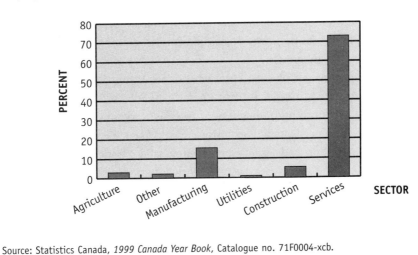

Source: Statistics Canada, *1999 Canada Year Book*, Catalogue no. 71F0004-xcb.

cial system, as will be discussed below, perhaps more than any other area of the global economy, has tied national economic systems together through flows of capital and currency trading.

## International Economic Cooperation

The second half of the twentieth century saw unprecedented levels of economic cooperation between the great powers. The growth in international trade and finance, coupled with the emergence of new technologies and new markets in developing countries, pushed the industrialized states towards ever higher levels of interdependence. It would be easy to think that this happened spontaneously, that the growth in international markets was a natural phenomenon. Yet we must remember that states and other forms of political authority played a central role in increasing global economic intercourse.

Essential to the growth of interdependence were international organizations and institutions. To manage interdependence, and in many cases to propel it forward, the powerful states of the international economy created

---

**Box 8.4**

## Trade Diplomacy—Team Canada

At the end of the twentieth century a majority of states in the international economy were looking to exports as the main source of economic development. This was especially so for Canada. Federal and provincial governments sought to promote export industries as a way of earning foreign currencies and of providing a boost to economic growth.

The federal government of Jean Chretien was not content merely to encourage Canadian exporters. Instead, it came up with the idea of engaging in active trade diplomacy, of launching trade missions to various regions of the world seen as crucial to the future of Canadian exporters. "Team Canada" involved the Prime Minister and Minister of Trade, a number of provincial premiers, and important members of the Canadian private sector. These last participants came from a number of different sectors, including the natural resource, industrial, financial, and education sectors. The goal of the mission was to visit several key export markets in a region, such as Latin America, and sign deals and agreements securing future sales.

This clear mix of politics with business, of the state with the market, proved highly successful. In Mexico in January of 1998, the Team Canada mission resulted in the signing of 91 commercial deals, worth a total of $230 million. The mission is especially important to small and medium-sized enterprises (SMEs), who find it difficult and expensive to develop their own export networks. In the case of the mission to Mexico, over 90 percent of deals were signed by SMEs.

international institutions and **international organizations** (IOs) that facilitated the signing of multilateral agreements. Organizations such as the IMF and World Bank, the General Agreement on Tariffs and Trade (GATT), and the World Trade Organization (WTO) were all designed to increase levels of cooperation between states in order to maximize the beneficial effects of interdependence and to minimize the probability of conflict.

But why are such institutions so important to international economic cooperation? Could states not just sign bilateral agreements and manage the international economy without the help of international organizations? The answer is that maybe they could, but history has shown that cooperation is more likely and more productive when IOs are used to promote it. IOs perform many functions that contribute to the efficiency and probability of cooperation, such as providing a forum for negotiation and setting out definite rules and processes that make negotiation and the deals that emerge from it more predictable and reliable. IOs also tie states into longer-term patterns of cooperation, which means that each individual state is less likely to cheat on a deal (which would cause it to miss out on the potential benefits of such deals in the future). IOs can help to monitor and verify the implementation of international agreements, which helps to reassure negotiating parties that deals will be respected. All of these facets, of course, apply not only to the international economy but also to other areas of interstate interaction. But they have proven particularly important in the management of the international economy since 1945.

Below is a short list of important international economic organizations and their functional areas:

- International Monetary Fund (IMF)—international monetary cooperation, balance of payments stability, financial aid, technical aid

- World Bank—lends money to developing countries for development projects, usually in the long term

- Bank for International Settlements (BIS)—also known as the central bankers' bank, arranges loans for central banks and encourages central bank cooperation

- International Labour Organization (ILO)—created in 1919 to improve working conditions around the world by setting minimum standards, providing technical assistance, and promoting the development of labour unions

- World Trade Organization (WTO)—created in 1995 as a forum for promoting free trade between nations in goods and services.

| Box 8.5 | The Great Crash of 1929 |
|---------|-------------------------|

Because the last few years of the twentieth century were marked by recurrent financial crises in the developing world, we tend to think of this phenomenon as something that is relatively modern, and that affects the economies of LDC states. However, financial crisis has in fact been much more common in the developed world and has a long history, going back at least to the nineteenth century.

The most famous crisis of them all occurred in 1929, in the United States. New York had by then replaced London as the world's most important financial centre, and was closely linked to the international economy through a system of loans and credits. The financial markets in New York, however, were prone to what analysts have variously called "manias," "euphoria," or "irrational exuberance," meaning that money would pour into the market periodically, according to what the latest trend in investment might be. Similarly, when attitudes and perceptions changed, money would be rapidly withdrawn from the markets, causing "panics" and "crashes."

This turbulence was seen repeatedly throughout the 1920s, famously with the case of Florida real estate in the mid-20s. But the biggest crash was to come in 1929, when an inflated stock market began to slip, setting off a panic that ruined thousands of stockbrokers and bankrupted hundreds of thousands of investors. The stories of this period are now classic—brokers and investors leaping from the upper floors of office blocks rather than face bankruptcy, individuals selling assets worth thousands for dollars (such as cars) for only a hundred dollars, just to try to get hold of cash to settle their debts.

But the effects of the 1929 Crash were not just felt by individuals involved in the market. It caused a massive contraction of credit, as banks called in loans, shrinking the economy and forcing many firms to either lay off workers or close down completely. Internationally, it interrupted the flow of capital from New York to debtor countries, causing economic and financial crises there. What followed was the Great Depression in the United States, and the world economy began a slippery slide towards economic conflict and then war.

# The World Trading System

Enter any supermarket, department, or hardware store today and you will find the shelves stocked with goods from all over the world. The average consumer can now eat mangoes in any season, including mid-winter (providing you are willing to pay the price), and choose from an array of home electronics made and assembled all over the world. International trade by the beginning of the twenty-first century has brought an unprecedented level of consumer choice to our society. Trade, however, does not have merely economic effects. It can be a source of cultural contact between peoples, and is often responsible for the transmission of new ideas, concepts, and technologies. Indeed, throughout history trading routes have linked distant peoples together. The ancient Phoenicians brought goods from the eastern Mediterranean to the shores of the British Isles, thus linking the two peoples together through trade. African peoples who would never see each other's homelands were connected by trade routes that stretched for hundreds, even thousands of miles.

International trade is often credited with creating employment, increasing consumer choice, introducing new ideas and cultural ideals, and contributing to economic efficiency. Indeed, there is a lot of evidence to support each of these claims. But international trade is not an issue on which everyone agrees, with all the players simply accepting the great benefits to be gained from liberal trading policies. Just as trade creates employment, it has been known to destroy jobs in economies and industries that are not competitive by international standards, either in terms of their pricing or their quality. When such economies and industries are exposed to open international competition, they simply cannot maintain profitability, and may be forced to cut production and lay off workers if they are to survive. At times such as these, workers and producers alike call for **trade protection** from the government, seeking either subsidies to supplement their income, or protective tariffs to reduce the price advantage of foreign goods.

Equally controversial is the cultural aspect of international trade. As mentioned above, its proponents argue that trade introduces new ideas and norms to closed societies, thus contributing to mutual understanding between states and peoples. However, trade can also be accused of contributing to the spread of dominant cultures at the expense of traditional values and norms. The spread of American products throughout the world, for example, has not been value-free. All one has to do is look at the packaging of a breakfast cereal box to realize that US culture is transmitted by the most unobtrusive means. And trade, of course, does not refer merely to manufactured goods or foodstuffs. Books, films, and music are also included within the sphere of international trade, as well as technology in the form of computers and software, for example. Faced with the overwhelming choice presented by goods from the industrialized states, it is very difficult for most traditional cultures to compete, particularly in the eyes of young people.

## The Growth of Trade since 1846

International trade as we know it today, with rapid transportation of goods from one side of the world to the other, with extremely low levels of government involvement and taxation, is a very recent development. High levels of growth in international trade have usually followed periods of rapid economic development, and it was really only in the nineteenth century that the modern concept of international trade began to take shape. When it did, its development depended heavily on three factors: ideology, domestic political decisions, and the exercise of state power in the international system. The first factor, ideology, concerned the growing acceptance of Adam Smith's ideas on **free trade**, first published in the eighteenth century. Smith's ideas were truly revolutionary, since prior to his work *The Wealth of Nations*, mercantilism (see Chapter 2) had been the dominant approach to international trade. Smith's argument was that free trade brought benefits in terms of efficiency, cost, and the division of labour. The second factor affecting the acceptance of international trade, domestic politics, concerned the effects of industrialization. As Great Britain went through the Industrial Revolution and its economy became the most developed in the world, British producers needed to secure cheap supplies of food for their workers, so that they could keep wages low. Pressure from these British industrialists caused the government of that country to liberalize its food policy in 1846 by repealing the **Corn Laws**, which had regulated the trade in corn, one of the most basic foodstuffs. This action led to the liberalizaton of Britain's agricultural trade, which in turn set the stage for that country opening its borders to all kinds of products from producers throughout the world.

When Great Britain did so, other nations reciprocated, though not to the same degree, and the overall result was a dramatic growth in the level of world trade, particularly among the European countries and their present and former colonies in Africa, India, and the Americas. Even when other states did not reciprocate fully in opening up their economies to trade, Britain still allowed their goods to enter with low tariffs. Britain was able to do so because its economy had become so much larger than other states', and thus the relative costs of such a policy were low. In order to maintain international trading routes, however, mere openness was not enough. The British navy, at the time the largest in the world by a wide margin, used its predominance to keep sea routes open and unmolested so that goods could travel unimpeded from one part of the world to another. The transportation of goods was also greatly helped by British (and to a lesser degree German) investment in railway systems around the world.

The growth in international trade that went along with British economic and naval predominance continued until the early years of the twentieth century. With the First World War, and the destruction that it wrought on European economies, trade would not regain its pre-WWI levels until long after the Second World War. One of the lessons of this period was that trade and peace were inextricably linked. Clearly, in a world where political and military relations between the Great Powers were unstable, it was very difficult for trade to flourish. However, some (liberal theorists) have also argued that high levels of trade between states helps maintain peace. Their logic is that if states depended on each other for their economic well-being, they would be unwilling to go to war as that would mean sacrificing the benefits of trade. Others have argued that the historical example of the First World War proves that even states that have high levels of trade between them (such as Britain and Germany at the end of the nineteenth century) will go to war with each other if they are rivals for military, economic, and cultural dominance.

## The GATT

The end of the Second World War saw the emergence of the United States as an economic and military superpower. From this position of dominance, the US decided to shape the international economic system through the creation of institutions and organizations aimed at international economic management. In the area of trade the institution that emerged was the **General Agreement on Tariffs and Trade** (GATT). Though originally intended only as a temporary arrangement, the GATT became the world's permanent trade regime when the Havana Charter, a treaty aimed at creating an International Trade Organization (ITO), failed to be approved by the United States Congress. The GATT was designed to promote several values held to be central by the United States and its allies, including:

- **Multilateralism**: that decisions would be taken in consultation with all members, and in their interests
- **Reciprocity**: that the liberalizaton of trade would be beneficial for all parties concerned
- **Non-discrimination**: that no members of the GATT could be excluded from the benefits that one member state extends to another
- **Free trade**: free trade was seen as promoting efficiency, prosperity, and peace.
  The GATT came into operation in 1947 and until 1995 remained the world's

trading regime. As an organization it proved incredibly successful in opening up international trade between the developed countries, and in particular in reducing tariffs between them. However, the GATT system did not benefit all states in the international system equally. The communist bloc countries, of course, were excluded, but so were many developing countries whose industrial sectors were not sufficiently competitive to benefit from free trade, and most did not become members until the 1980s. A large number of LDCs chose to stay outside of the GATT rather than accept the principles outlined above, opting for policies of protectionism and state control of industries to aid rapid growth.

One of the major reasons why LDCs did not join the GATT system until the second half of the 1980s was that the achievements of the GATT in liberalizing trade were limited in one very important way. Until the late 1960s, the system focused on manufactured goods, leaving aside agricultural trade and commodities, traditionally two of the most difficult areas to liberalize. Agriculture and raw materials, of course, were two areas in which many LDCs had a comparative advantage and thus it could be said that the GATT's operations were biased in favour of the developed states.

In response to these inadequacies of the GATT system, the developing states attempted to set up a rival organization for international trade in the 1960s. Under the auspices of the United Nations, the **Committee on Trade and Development** (UNCTAD) was created in 1964. As its name suggests, UNCTAD attempted to link the issues of trade and economic development directly, speaking to many of the developing states' concerns about agriculture and commodities. However, though the creation of the committee was a great achievement, the developed states refused to allow it to replace the GATT, opting instead to make small, conciliatory changes to that system to placate LDCs.

Despite the deep economic recessions that hit the industrialized states in the 1970s and early 1980s, international trade has continued to grow rapidly, slowing its rate of growth in the late 1990s only because of the financial and economic crises that hit Asia, Russia, and Brazil. Indeed, the growth in world trade has consistently outpaced the growth in the global economy as a whole, and continues to be a provider of employment in many parts of the world.

## The WTO

The GATT was largely responsible for much of this growth from 1947 to 1995. In that year it was replaced as the world's trading regime by the **World Trade Organization** (WTO). The GATT was not discarded, but rather became part of a more formal international organization. During the **Uruguay Round** of GATT negotiations, which began in 1986, the world's most important trading nations agreed to overhaul the trading system and create a permanent international organization that is much more ambitious than the GATT was ever intended to be. The WTO has a legal status matching that of the other major international economic organizations such as the IMF and World Bank, and places trade at the top of the international economic agenda, alongside monetary and financial affairs.

Indeed the WTO is one of the most important international organizations today, dealing with all aspects of trade, from manufactured goods to commodities, environmental aspects of trade to intellectual property and from agriculture to trade and development. One of the key achievements of the WTO has been to institute a system of **dispute resolution**, by which trading disputes between member states can be resolved by an impartial tribunal, thus preventing such disputes from becoming too political or controversial, in theory at least (see Box 8.6).

## China and the WTO                                           Box 8.6

China's rapid economic industrialization and economic development since the 1970s has brought the country to a central position in the international system. Yet China remained, until the end of 1999, on the outside of the world's most important trading regime, the WTO. For many years the United States government had argued that China was not ready to enter the organization, claiming that Chinese trading practices remained a far cry from the norms enshrined in the regime. At times the US also used the terrible human rights record of the Chinese government as an excuse to prevent Chinese accession. In 1999 the two states clashed over whether China should be admitted as a developing economy (which would entail easier terms of admission) or as a developed economy. Clearly China could only be classified as a developing economy in 1999, but the United States claimed that the size and rate of growth of the Chinese economy merited its classification as developed. The 1999 US bombing of the Chinese Embassy in Serbia during the Kosovo campaign served to further worsen relations between the two governments.

However, by the Fall of that year the situation seemed to be improving. The two countries had once again agreed to sit down and discuss the issue of Chinese classification within the WTO, and the Seattle summit of the WTO in November promised to see calls from several WTO members, including Japan, for Chinese admission.

## Present and Future Challenges for Trade

Even so, trade has not become a controversy-free area of the international political economy. Many LDC states continue to see the structure of the trading system as a reflection of the power and success of the developed states, and are pressing the WTO for greater concessions that would spur growth in their economies. The link between trade and environmental issues remains a vital area for research and political action. But the two biggest challenges for the future of the international trading system lie in the hands of the world's largest economies.

The first of these concerns the growing **regionalism** that has become a feature of the world economy since the 1980s. The emergence of regional free trade blocs, most importantly in Europe and North America, provides an alternative to international trade for the world's largest economies. Naturally this means that they have a fall-back option in the event that the WTO fails to maintain the current healthy state of global trade, which in turn provides a test of their commitment to maintaining that system. The countries of the **European Union** (EU) and **North American Free Trade Agreement** (NAFTA) have shown a distinct tendency over the last decade to trade more and more within their respective blocs, a trend which some see as threatening international trade. In fact these fears may be exaggerated, as the level of interregional trade continues to grow; it is just that intra-regional trade is growing at a faster rate (see below).

The second challenge for the future of the world trading system lies in the conflict between these two regions. It is important to remember that the European and North American (and in particular US) conceptions of economic liberalism are far from identical. Europeans have traditionally seen a more expanded role for the state in the economy and are more comfortable with free trade taking a back seat to political and social concerns. The 1999 disputes between the US and EU over hormones in beef and the international trade in bananas (see Box 8.7) are but two examples where the interests and ideals of these two economic giants have begun to clash.

# The Political Economy of International Production

Production, as the element on which all the other elements depend, is the most basic facet of the political. What we produce as individuals, firms, and nations to a large extent determines not only our wealth, but also our power and sta-

## The US-EU Banana Dispute

Box 8.7

Though the United States and European Union are highly interdependent, this does not mean that their relations are trouble-free. In 1999 the United States accused the EU of distorting the international trade in bananas by giving preferential access to the European market to banana producers from select developing countries. This, the US argued, went contrary to the rules and principles of free trade protected by the World Trade Organization (WTO), which enforce the principle of non-discrimination between WTO members.

The accusation was based on fact. In 1975 the EU (then known as the EC or European Communities) set up the Lome Convention, an agreement with certain African, Caribbean, and Pacific (ACP) states giving them access to the European marketplace at preferential tariff levels. The stated goal of the Lome Convention was to aid LDCs in their economic development. Bananas were one commodity included under the convention.

The United States brought the issue before the Dispute Settlement Mechanism of the WTO, which judged against the EU. This meant that the European Union was forced to dismantle its system of preferential access and grant the same privileges to all outside banana producers, or to none at all.

Why did the United States force this issue? The stated goal of the US was to promote and protect the principle of free trade in the world economy. A closer examination of the issue, however, suggests that the United States government was promoting the interests of US corporations that produced bananas in countries outside of the Lome Convention, countries such as Mexico and Brazil. These corporations wanted equal access to European markets as the producers based in the ACP states, producers of largely European origin. This series of events showed once again that the link between states and markets, public and private actors remains a major force in shaping international trade.

tus in political and economic systems. Of course, production is also the most fundamental element of the political economy because the other economic elements, such as trade and the accumulation of capital, are shaped and determined by what is produced, and how much. Karl Marx recognized the importance of production when he argued that political and economic power derive from control over the means of production (meaning factories and industrial plants).

Throughout most of human history, production has been organized on a local basis, with small cottage industries predominating. This began to change in the seventeenth and eighteenth centuries, when the Industrial Revolution created large firms producing for national (and to a lesser extent, international) markets. At the same time, improvements in communications and transportation created the right conditions for the integration of production processes on a national basis.

The nineteenth century saw the internationalization of trade, but not of production. While raw materials were transported across great distances to be used in national production processes, production itself remained rooted at the level of the nation-state. It was only in the second half of the twentieth century that production took on an international dimension. With the expansion of US firms into first Europe, and then Asia, national production processes began to be integrated, in turn drawing together national economies. Indeed it was the spread of US **multinational corporations** (MNCs) that began a process that has led to the globalized production we see today.

## The Product Cycle

One of the most important links between production and power lies in the theory of the **product cycle**. This theory explains the development of production as connected to the life of the product itself. In political economy it can also be used to help explain the distribution of power and wealth in the system.

In the **first phase** of the cycle, that is, when a product is new on the market and is being produced by a small number of firms, production tends to be concentrated in the wealthy, industrialized countries, where there is a concentration of wealth, consumers, technology, and production facilities. In this stage the corporations of these countries tend to hold a **monopolistic** or **oligopolistic** position, thus controlling both supply and pricing. So in the early and mid-nineteenth-century Britain led the product cycle, producing the first wave of manufactured goods and exporting them to the rest of the world through the system of free trade that was promoted by the British government. Later in the nineteenth century, new production processes (based in steel and electricity) tended to be located in countries such as the United States and Germany, which had by then developed their economies through rapid industrialization and accumulation of capital. For both Britain in the early to mid-nineteenth century, and the US and Germany in the later part of the century, being on the cutting edge of production and new technologies translated into wealth and political power in the international system.

In this century we can see a similar shift in the locus of the first phase of the product cycle. While the United States has led the product cycle for most of the century, Japan benefited from the manufacture of new products and technologies in the 1970s and 1980s, particularly those based in electronics and high technology. This process led many analysts to argue that Japan would become the next leader of the international economy, and possibly of the international system as a whole.

In the **second phase** of the product cycle there is a diffusion of the technologies required for the manufacture of the product, and thus production spreads from the countries of the first phase to their foreign competitors in other advanced countries. This does not mean that the market becomes any more competitive, rather that the successful firms from the first phase now engage in production in other countries. In the **third phase** the location of production shifts again, this time from the advanced to the less developed economies. In this third stage the LDCs benefits from their lower wage rates and export their goods and materials around the world. It is in this third phase that production becomes truly integrated at the international level as firms produce different components for a product in different parts of the world.

Product cycle theory is, of course, far from being a complete explanation of the link between states and production, and leaves much to be desired as an explanation of the globalization of production. However, it does give us an idea of the process by which manufacturing spreads throughout the world, and of the competitiveness inherent in international production.

## The Globalization of Production since 1945

In 1945 one country dominated world production: the United States. With the economies of Europe and Japan in ruins, the US was the only large economic system producing the goods necessary for post-war rebuilding and economic recovery. This meant that US producers found themselves in the enviable position of facing minimal competition from firms in other states. Not only did this allow them to make huge profits in the early post-war years, it also encouraged a process by which US corporations invested directly in European and Asian economies, setting up productive capacities there rather than merely exporting from their US base. Helping this internationalization of US producers was the strength of the dollar, which was also in great demand from European and Asian nations. Because there was such a strong demand for the dollar, US firms were able to invest in foreign economies very cheaply, as the governments of those countries tried to gather dollars from every source possible.

As US firms set up production facilities in various countries around the world, their production became "multinational," and the era of the multinational corporation (MNC) was born. MNCs are simply firms whose productive and management activities take place in several different countries. The main advantage of multinational production is, of course, economies of scale, whereby mass production can be organized for huge numbers of consumers spread across many different nations. The post-WWII period saw a dramatic rise in this kind of production, and by the 1960s, US MNCs had been joined by European and Japanese competitors, and later by MNCs from developing states (such as CEMEX, a Mexican cement producer).

By the 1970s, some academics and policy-makers had begun to ask serious questions about the power and influence of MNCs, particularly with reference to their relations with LDC governments. Raymond Vernon even wrote of states facing a situation which could best be described as "sovereignty at bay," where governments were increasingly challenged by large MNCs. The reasoning behind this claim was simple: throughout the post-war period MNCs had grown so large that their economic and technical resources matched or even dwarfed those available to many LDC governments. What's more, with developing states desperate for foreign investment, MNCs found themselves in a strong bargaining position in their negotiations with LDCs. To make matters worse, even if a state secured investment from a foreign MNC, the corporation could always withdraw or divest from that country if the level of rewards did not remain satisfactory.

Such negotiating power enabled MNCs to negotiate preferential conditions for their investments, securing tax breaks and cheap access to labour and raw materials. More sinister, however, was the suggestion that MNCs were engaging in political activities within their host states, designed to manipulate the democratic process so that the political and economic preferences of the firm were promoted. A famous example of such interference in domestic affairs concerned a US telecommunications corporation, ITT, in Chile in the 1970s, when the firm conspired to bring down a Marxist government that threatened its interests.

Other concerns about the influence of MNCs related to their close relationship with their home country (i.e., their nation of origin) governments. Though there is little evidence to support it, the accusation has been made that MNCs sometimes act as agents of their home country's government in foreign countries. Either through espionage, political activities, or economic dependence, MNCs have the potential to advance the interests of their home country at the expense of the host.

There is more evidence that home country governments defend the interests of their MNCs abroad. During the 1960s and 1970s leftist governments in LDCs began nationalizing foreign enterprises as part of their attempts to institute command economies. The US Congress has passed several acts that punish foreign governments if they expropriate the economic interests of US citizens. Such legislation was designed to force foreign governments to reconsider the costs and benefits of nationalizing US corporations operating in their territory. Since the mid-1980s and the beginning of the domination of neoliberal approaches to economic management throughout the world, the use of such drastic measures of home country support for MNCs has declined.

**The Integration of Production** The internationalization of production has not only seen firms producing goods in many different geographical locations. The actual process of production has become internationalized. This means that automobiles, televisions, computers, and a host of other products are not made in a single country, but assembled from parts manufactured in many different countries. General Motors, for example, has integrated its vehicle production process not only on a North American basis, but worldwide. The significance of integrated production processes is immense, for it facilitates the transmission of corporate management techniques and strategies, and technologies, and links workers and consumers across the globe.

## The OPEC Oil Crisis

One area of international production that remains central to the world economy is the production of oil. Because so many of our means of production, transportation, and energy generation depend directly or indirectly on petroleum products, oil continues to affect the health of the international economy as a whole. For many years the international oil industry was dominated by what came to be known as the **Seven Sisters**, that is, the seven largest oil companies in the world. Since the early twentieth century they had controlled oil supplies and prices, manipulating the market to their advantage. However, in 1960 five of the world's most important oil-producing states—Iran, Iraq, Kuwait, Saudi Arabia, and Venezuela—came together and formed the **Organization of Petroleum Exporting Countries** (OPEC). OPEC was designed to strengthen the hand of the oil producers, and to strengthen the international price of oil and thus their revenues.

A dramatic change occurred in 1973. During that year, OPEC and the major oil companies failed to come to a lasting agreement on the price of oil, and the fourth Arab-Israeli war began, driving up the market price of oil. The oil-

The OPEC oil crisis of 1973 posed a deep challenge to both the stability of the international political economy and to the dominance of the Western industrialized states within the system. Though the oil price rise of the early and late 1970s was only a temporary deviation from the historical pattern of low petroleum prices, it showed how a group of developing states, working together, could stand up to the developed world and win significant concessions. Today oil continues to be a key commodity, both for those states that produce it and those that consume it. It is central to the development paths of each of the states we saw in Chapter 6, and remains the single most important energy source for all economies around the world.

producing states soon realized that they possessed the power to control the supply and thus the price of oil in the world marketplace, a power that had once belonged exclusively to the Seven Sisters. The price of oil rose from $2.48 per barrel at the end of 1972 to $11.65 per barrel a year later. For the next five years, OPEC would manipulate the supply and the price of oil, consistently raising the price and bringing these states enormous revenues. The net result was a massive transfer of capital from the oil-importing states to the OPEC countries.

A second major price rise took place in 1979 and 1980. With the joint developments of the Iranian revolution and the onset of the Iran-Iraq war, the supply of oil was threatened, for between them these two states were responsible for 10 percent of global oil supplies. This second shock to the international oil market forced prices as high as $41 per barrel, bringing still further transfers of wealth from the industrialized states to OPEC.

The effects of these oil price rises on the international political economy should not be underestimated. First, states that previously had played only a secondary role in global politics acquired a significance that made them major players. Saudi Arabia, in particular, became a state of primary importance as it was the central country in OPEC. Second, the dramatically higher oil prices contributed to the growing problem of inflation in the advanced industrialized states as prices for almost all goods were pushed higher. Third, the transfer of capital from the advanced industrialized states to OPEC members resulted in an enormous inflow of funds into the international financial system (see Fig. 8.1). This took place because many OPEC states were earning more from oil than they could possibly spend on economic development and infrastructure, so they deposited the surplus into international banks. Much of this money was funnelled to other developing states and contributed to the debt crisis in the 1980s (see below).

Unfortunately for OPEC, the situation of the 1970s proved unique, and oil prices began a long-term downward trend in the 1980s. The reasons for this were several: new producers, less demand from the industrialized states as they found alternative energy sources in response to higher prices, and tensions within OPEC that complicated coordination of production levels. By the late 1990s oil prices had fallen to 20-year lows, and OPEC states were forced to accept large cuts in production in order to bring prices up again.

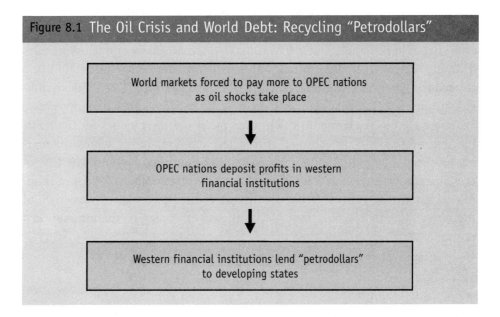

**Figure 8.1** The Oil Crisis and World Debt: Recycling "Petrodollars"

# The International System of Money and Finance

While the international production system is responsible for the tangible goods that we consume every day, both it and the international trading system depend upon the global system of money and finance for their ability to function. The **international financial system** and **international monetary system** can be compared to the root system of a plant: just as the invisible roots provide minerals, nutrition, and moisture to a plant, so the financial system provides currency and credit to the international economy. Without a reliable and steady supply of loans and investment, the international economy would soon wither and die.

International finance, contrary to popular conceptions, is nothing new. In the fifteenth and sixteenth centuries Italian banks lent huge sums of money to the monarchs of Europe for the purposes of exploration, personal enrichment, and war. The City of London emerged as the dominant financial centre of the nineteenth century, channelling funds to traders, investors, and governments throughout the world. Money and finance has always been central to the development of the international economy, and the health and stability of the two systems have always been intertwined.

## What Is the International Monetary System?

For international economic intercourse to be feasible and efficient, it is necessary to have either a global currency, that is, one form of money acceptable in every national economic system, or to have internationally agreed-upon rules dictating the relative values of national currencies. In former times gold performed the function of a global medium of exchange, being acceptable to individuals and governments all over the world. In modern times two alternative systems have emerged, one in which states agree upon set values for their currencies in terms of other national currencies, and a second in which the market has been left to decide the relative values of national monies. The first of these systems is known as a **fixed exchange rate system**, the second as a **floating exchange rate system**. Debates continue to the present day over which of these two systems provides more stability and efficiency to the international economy.

## What Is the International Financial System?

Very closely connected to the monetary system is the international financial system, the means by which capital and funds are moved from one national economy to another. The financial system is made up of the financial transactions that take place between states, international financial institutions such as the IMF and World Bank, banks and other private financial institutions and corporations, and individuals. Throughout history the level of political control over the international financial system has varied, from almost complete control in the 1940s and 1950s, to dominance by private financial actors at the beginning of the twenty-first century. The international financial system is fundamental to the international economy because without it surplus capital in one part of the globe could not be assigned to those parts of the world where it can be put to good and profitable use. A badly functioning financial system not only compromises economic efficiency, it also restrains economic development.

## The Bretton Woods System

In June of 1944, with the end of the Second World War close at hand, the governments of the Allied powers met at a resort in **Bretton Woods**, New Hampshire, in the United States to discuss the future of the international economy. The economic planners who met there, particularly those from the United States and Great Britain, were determined to avoid the mistakes of the interwar years, which had seen high levels of economic nationalism and competition between states, a situation which had eventually led to war. Foremost in their minds was the determination to promote free trade and to avoid the kind of financial crisis that had taken place in 1929.

For the Bretton Woods planners, the solution lay in creating a system of fixed exchange rates and putting heavy controls on private banks and other financial institutions so that their role in international finance would be limited. In the place of private banks, The American and British representatives created the International Monetary Fund and the International Bank for Reconstruction and Development (World Bank). The first of these institutions was designed to oversee the international monetary system, enforce a regime of fixed exchange rates, and lend money to states experiencing balance of payments difficulties. The second institution was created to provide funding for the reconstruction of Europe after the destruction of the Second World War and for programs of economic development in the Third World.

This left very little space for private institutions to play a role in international finance, and in the years following 1945 private finance remained largely national, international finance being dominated by the IMF and World Bank, but more importantly in this period, by government-to-government loans in the form of **bilateral aid**. This system of fixed exchange rates and public international finance lasted for a period of 25 years, bringing both stability and unprecedented levels of global economic growth. During this period the flow of finance obeyed distinctly political purposes, with interstates loans being used to strengthen friendly regimes and to buy the support of governments in the Cold War struggle.

In August of 1971, however, this situation changed. The US government of Richard Nixon made a unilateral decision that the Bretton Woods system no longer served the interests of the United States, and the US abandoned the system of fixed exchange rates. Despite months of negotiations, a rules-based alternative could not be found, and from 1973 onwards the world's major currencies have been floating, that is, their values have been decided by the activities of global currency markets. This new arrangement is sometimes referred to as a **non-system**, because of the absence of clearly defined rules determining relative currency values. The transition represented an abdication of power by political authorities over one of the most important areas of economic management, and can be seen as a part of wider trend towards less state control over the economy.

Currency markets are made up of banks and other financial institutions that buy and sell national currencies according to the demand for their use, and the relative values of these currencies is determined by such demand. If, for example, demand for the French franc is high because international investors wish to invest in the French economy or because French exports have become very successful, then the relative value of the franc will rise. If, on the other hand, the French economy is going through a recession and has become uncompetitive by international standards, then traders are likely to sell the franc and its relative value will fall.

Even before the system of fixed exchange rates had broken, private finance was beginning to break free from the controls instituted at Bretton Woods in 1944. First, European banks succeeded in evading national regulatory control by lending money denominated in currencies other than that used in the national economy. Such practices gave private banks the freedom to engage in international lending without the interference of national governments (see Box 8.8). Secondly, private banks, in particular those of the US, had gradually expanded their operations outside of national markets in response to the

## Foreign Aid and Tied Aid

Box 8.8

In the post-World War II period the advanced industrialized states began a system of bilateral aid, lending money to developing states in the form of economic or military assistance. This system replaced the private flows of capital that had been a feature of the nineteenth century and interwar years. Foreign aid became a crucial source of income for many states, and throughout the 1960s, '70s, and '80s there were calls for aid to be increased.

But foreign aid is not simply the transfer of money from one national government to another. It can take many forms, such as material (food, grain, emergency supplies, or military equipment), loans at preferential rates, or sometimes grants. Often, aid comes with a commitment on the part of the recipient to fulfil some responsibility to the donor state. During the Cold War this commitment was most commonly to support the foreign policy goals of either the Soviet Union or United States, thus involving the LDC in the ideological conflict.

At others times, aid has been "tied" in other ways. Frequently, loans given to LDCs by a developed state can only be used to purchase goods from producers in that state. Therefore, the developed country government is providing an economic stimulus to its own economy by lending money to the LDC, while at the same time making interest on its loan. Another example is the donation of some form of high-technology machinery to a developing country. Though the machinery is given free of charge, maintaining the equipment will require both expertise and parts from the donor state. In these ways and others, aid can actually become a drain on the economic resources of the recipient state.

growth of MNCs and their need for capital. These two developments propelled the growth of private international finance, and helped to create the system we have today.

Another factor in the globalization of finance was the role played by technological advance, in particular in the area of communications. The development of satellite communications allowed the transmission of information and funds from one side of the world to another at the touch of a button. This made the transfer of capital instantaneous, and gave banks and investors the ability to seize upon opportunities whenever, and wherever, they occur.

However, by speeding up international finance in this way, technological and other advances have also threatened the stability of the international financial system. It is now possible for billions of dollars to be moved from

Floating currency exchange rates often lead to weakened currency values. In 1998 the Canadian dollar was worth 68 cents relative to the American dollar.

John Larter, Calgary Sun

one national economy to another very rapidly, and this has contributed to a number of the deep financial crises witnessed at the end of the twenty-first century (see below).

It was not only technology and the drive for profits that caused the internationalization of finance. States, too, played a central role. Particularly in the 1980s and 1990s, Western governments began to remove regulations restricting foreign competition in national financial markets, as well as regulations restricting the activities of banks and other financial actors. This **deregulation** of finance was undertaken because it matched both the liberal ideology and the economic goals of leading states such as Britain and the US. By the late

## The Euromarkets

Box 8.9

In the 1950s, the government of the Soviet Union faced a problem. It needed to maintain US dollar reserves in banks outside the Soviet Union for use in buying exports, and commodities in particular. However, to place the money in United States banks would risk the US government freezing the money and thus cutting the Soviet state off from its deposits. Instead of risking this eventuality, the Soviet government persuaded a French bank to provide a bank account for it denominated in US dollars. The bank's cable address was EUROBANK, and thus were born Eurodollars and the Euromarkets.

A Eurodollar is simply a dollar held in a bank account outside of the US. The process can be copied with other national currencies, to produce Europounds, Eurofrancs, Euroyen, etc. The bank does not have to be in Europe for the currency to become a Eurocurrency.

The advantage for banks in providing such accounts was that they were able to evade the regulations of national authorities who chose to regulate only transactions conducted in the national currency of that country. This meant that huge amounts of capital were released from the control and supervision of national regulators, and this money was free to flow around the world as the bankers saw fit.

Today the Euromarkets continue, but have become much more complex. It is not only possible to set up a bank account in a currency other than that of the country where the bank operates, it is possible to borrow money, conduct bond releases, swaps and options in Eurocurrencies. This growth in the complexity and size of international finance contributed greatly to the process of deregulation that took place in the 1980s and 1990s, and also, some claim, to the growing instability of global finance.

twentieth century national financial centres such as London, New York, and Tokyo were actively competing among themselves for the business of finance, and one advantage which could be offered by a financial centre was that its level of restrictions and controls were lower than its competitors.

But the new system of money and finance that replaced the Bretton Woods system was not without its problems. Crisis has plagued international finance since the 1980s, and it is only at the turn of the century that states are attempting to reform the international financial system to prevent and moderate the effects of financial crises.

## The Latin American Debt Crisis

In the 1970s, after the end of the Bretton Woods system and the relaxation of many national restrictions on foreign lending, banks in the advanced industrialized economies, in particular in the US, began looking to developing economies as an outlet for the capital that had been deposited with them. Developing countries offered potentially very high profits for the banks, as they were rapidly industrializing and were willing to pay higher interest rates than borrowers in developed markets.

Of course not all developing states were targets for bank loans. Most African states, and some in Asia, were not regarded as having the right economic conditions to merit large transfers of capital. The area of the globe that benefited most, however, from this trend in the 1970s was Latin America, a region that was rapidly developing and showed immense potential. Latin American countries that exported oil in particular, such as Mexico, were prime candidates for loans as the price of oil was soaring due to the OPEC crisis.

The flow of loans to Latin America in the 1970s and early 1980s was truly immense, reaching between 150 and 200 billion dollars by 1983. This would not necessarily have become a problem, if the money received through these loans had been invested wisely by the recipient governments and corporations. Instead, much of the inflow of capital was wasted in the form of economically non-viable projects and corruption. In addition, Latin American states' economic growth slowed at the end of the 1970s due to a number of factors, including declining commodity prices, and thus their ability to meet debt interest payments was reduced. The only way these economies were able to continue making debt payments was by accepting more money from the financial institutions to whom they were already heavily indebted.

The combination of these factors brought about a situation in which several Latin American states found themselves unable to make their debt payments. In 1982 the Mexican government announced that it would not be able to make the interest payments on its debt, and the **Debt Crisis** had begun. This led to a crisis of confidence on the part of the banks, who then refused to lend any further money to economies in the region. This abrupt cut-off of new finance to Latin American countries meant that they could not meet their own debt obligations, thus deepening the crisis.

It took many years to find a solution to this crisis. The International Monetary Fund acted as a coordinating agency, bringing together both creditors and debtors, but was unable to come up with anything more than stop-gap measures between 1982 and 1989. It was only in that year, through a debt reduction plan proposed by US Treasury Secretary Brady, that a lasting solution was discovered. In the meantime many years of economic growth were lost, and investor confidence in the region was put on hold.

## The New International Finance and the Crises of the Late 1990s

With the ending of the Latin American Debt Crisis at the end of the 1980s, a new era in international finance began. This was to be a period in which banks faced stiff competition from other kinds of financial institution (such as mutual funds companies, in which thousands of individuals pool their investments and the company invests the total amount), and international capital became much more mobile. The increased size and mobility of international capital proved to be both a blessing and a curse for the system. On the positive side it enabled huge sums of capital to move rapidly around the globe to take advantage of investment opportunities. On the negative side of things, however, this increased mobility meant that billions of dollars could be withdrawn from a national economy in a matter of hours.

Such was the case in Mexico in December 1994. Following a political crisis and rapidly worsening economic situation, the Mexican government devalued the national currency, the peso, causing both Mexican and foreign investors to pull their money out of the country. This precipitated a deep economic crisis in the country, one that took several years to resolve. The managing director of the IMF, Michel Camdessus, called the Mexican crisis the "first financial crisis of the twenty-first century" because it involved millions of investors and enormous, immediate capital flight, unlike the Latin American Debt Crisis of the 1980s.

The Mexican crisis was followed, three years later, by similar crises in a number of Asian economies. Beginning in Thailand in July of 1997, the crisis spread throughout the region, a phenomenon that had deep effects not only on the region, but on the world economy as a whole. In addition to Thailand, countries such as Indonesia and South Korea, long considered economic powerhouses, were reduced to petitioning the IMF for loans to allow them to restructure their economies. In 1998, economic and financial crises followed in Russia and Brazil, and national policy-makers in the wealthy states were forced to recognize that the international financial system was facing deep problems. As this book is being written, the search for a new "International Financial Architecture" continues.

# The G7/8 and Leadership in the International Political Economy

We often hear talk of "leaders" and the exercise of "leadership" in the international economy, but few of us question what that leadership is, or why it is necessary. By leadership in the international economy we are generally referring to actions by one, or a group of states that provide some good to the system that would not otherwise be provided. In recent years we have come to think of leadership as providing effective responses to problems or crises facing the international economy, such as the financial crises that struck Asia and Brazil in the late 1990s. Such responses may take the form of providing financial assistance to economies in crisis, formulating new rules for international finance, or opening up a domestic market to absorb exports from distressed economies.

For most of the post-WWII period we have been accustomed to thinking of the United States as the only leader of the capitalist world. Indeed, from 1945 to the 1960s the US was able to manage and guide the Western system with little help from its allies. However, beginning in the mid-60s the United States was forced to seek the help of Europe and Japan in providing stability to the system through the coordination of economic policies. This necessity became even more pressing following the end of the Bretton Woods system and the oil crises of the 1970s, and the ensuing turbulence in the world economy. In November 1975, the US and five other major economic powers (France, Britain, Germany, Japan, and Italy) came together in Rambouillet, France, to discuss the major political and economic challenges facing their countries (see Table 8.1). In 1976, in San Juan, Puerto Rico, these six states were joined by Canada to form the Group of Seven (G7).

Since 1976 the G7 has become one of the most important organs of world economic management, coordinating macroeconomic policies and national positions in fora such as the IMF. In the mid-1980s the G7 played a central role in attempting to restore stability to international currency markets through coordinated central bank interventions, but the importance of the grouping would grow in the 1990s. The G7's response to the financial crises that struck Mexico, Asia, Russia, and Brazil determined the longevity of these crises and the future shape of the international financial system. Though the reform of that system is far from complete, all important decisions concerning its future must first be approved by the G7.

The G7, however, is not only concerned with economic issues. In 1998 the seven members were joined by Russia to form the G8, a forum whose aim is

| Table 8.1 Member States in the G8 | |
|---|---|
| **Year of entry** | **Country** |
| 1975 The "Library Group" | Britain |
| | France |
| | Germany |
| | Japan |
| | United States |
| 1976 The Group of Seven (G7) | Italy |
| | Canada |
| 1998 The Group of Eight (G8) | Russia |

to achieve improved coordination of policy responses to the world's most pressing challenges, such as environmental degradation, nuclear proliferation, or regional conflicts. However, though Russia claims equal membership in this group alongside the countries of the G7, the most important economic decisions are still taken separately through the mechanism of the G7.

## The Transition from Third World to Emerging Markets

As we saw in Chapter 6, political economy in the developing world exhibits many of the same, but also some very different, qualities as that in the advanced industrialized states. It is important to remember that, though we tend to concentrate on the world's largest economies in the study of IPE, developing countries both outnumber the developed states and are on average growing economically at a much faster rate. By the year 2020 it is projected that the developing world will be responsible for almost 50 percent of world exports, and LDC markets will absorb an ever-growing percentage of exports from ACDs. Already some industries, such as the global alcohol and spirits business, for example, sell more than 50 percent of their worldwide production in LDCs.

Just as important as this overall growth is the emergence of key states in the developing world. These are states such as China, Brazil, Mexico, and Indonesia, states that have grown rapidly and have become increasingly interdependent with the economies of the advanced capitalist states. They have become important destinations for capital, and large exporters of both raw materials and manufactured goods. For these reasons and others, by the 1990s analysts, and in particular investors, had come to call such countries **emerging markets**, recognizing their coming of age in economic terms. This was an immense change in perception since the mid-1980s, when the "Third World" seemed to be mired in perpetual economic underdevelopment.

The rise of these economies has meant a re-evaluation of the nature of the international economy. In 1997 Jeffrey Garten wrote of the impact of the "Big Ten" emerging markets and how they would change the distribution of power in the international economy. Garten argued that the shift in economic power towards the 10 largest emerging markets will necessitate a redefinition of US foreign policy. One country above all, of course, is having and will continue to have a dramatic impact on the state of the world economy. The People's Republic of China, it is predicted, will become the world's largest economy at some point in the first half of this century, surpassing the United States. In preparation for this structural change in the international system, those states that currently dominate the global economy (in particular the US) are attempting to engage the Chinese government and augment the level of interdependence between them and the Chinese economy through increased investment and trade levels.

## Economic Regionalism

Much of this chapter has described the factors leading to the internationalization, or as some would put it, the globalization of the world economy. There can be little doubt that, since 1945, national economies have become more and more interdependent, and that trade, production, and investment have moved far from their predominantly national basis at that time. But the globalizing trend has been matched in recent years by another tendency, that towards economic development based on geographic regions, or **economic regionalism**. This chapter has already discussed the concerns over the regionalization of trade, but the same trend can be observed in both finance and production, too.

In Europe, Asia, and North America investment flows and production patterns are more and more based on the region. This development has taken place for several reasons. First, in Europe and North America the logic has been to take advantage of the free trade arrangements in place, and to produce goods within these regional markets. Another rationale has been to take advantage of lower wages in other economies in the region. This has been a driving force behind the regionalization of investment and production in Asia and North America.

This process, liberal economists predict, will lead to the economic enrichment of these regions, but in particular of the poorer countries within them. Within NAFTA Mexico is currently benefiting from very high levels of foreign direct investment, a phenomenon which stems from the combination of its access to the US market and its comparatively low wage levels. This should lead, in the long term, to a more highly developed Mexican economy and, it is hoped, a higher standard of living for Mexicans. Less orthodox analysts of the situation, however, claim that the trend towards economic regionalism is resulting in the exploitation of the cheap labour and natural resources of poorer nations, something that will keep them in an inferior position to the economies of the advanced industrialized states.

# Summary

The international political economy that surrounds us today at the beginning of the twenty-first century is one that is almost unrecognizable from the system that was created at the end of the Second World War. The role of private actors has increased dramatically, and the level of interaction between states has reached levels unseen since before the First World War. Trade and financial flows continue to grow, both within and between regions, and advances in the fields of communications and transportation have made the world seem much smaller than it once did.

Yet many of the fundamentals of IPE remain the same. State power still matters, and the powerful continue to write the rules of the game and thus shape the international economic system. Efficiency and competitiveness remain primary goals of states, as they seek to retain an edge over their rivals (and friends). Many of the question marks that haunted the beginning of the post-war international economy have returned today. How much freedom should states grant to private finance? What should be done to assist the poorer nations of the world? What is the role of the state in economic management?

The international economy remains highly dynamic, and in a state of constant flux. Our study of it tells us much about the nature of political economy, about the interaction between politics and economics, states and markets. The development of the international economy in the early years of this century will bring new forces to the fore, and substantial transformations, many unforeseen. We can hope to understand the political economy of our own nation only if we take into account the system of which it is a part.

## Self-Assessment Questions

1. What have been the major forces behind the growth in international trade since 1945?

2. What is the balance between political authorities and market actors in the world economy today?

3. Why do gender issues matter in IPE?

4. What is the role of negotiation and cooperation in the international economy?

5. Why does the international financial system tend towards crisis?

## Further Reading

Gilpin, Robert. *The Political Economy of International Relations*. Princeton: Princeton University Press, 1987.

Spero, Joan, and Jeffrey A. Hart. *The Politics of International Economic Relations*. New York: St. Martin's Press, 1997.

Stubbs, Richard, and Geoffrey Underhill, eds. *Political Economy and the New Global Order*. New York: Oxford University Press, 1999.

Frieden, Jeffry, and David A. Lake, eds. *International Political Economy*. New York: St. Martin's Press, 1999.

 ## Web Links

**Bretton Woods Conference**
http://www.chebucto.ns.ca/Current/P7/mess.html

**International Monetary Fund**
http://www.imf.org/

**Word Bank (IBRD)**
http://www.worldbank.org/

**G8 Online**
http://www.g8online.org/

# Glossary

**Agricultural revolution** period in history (around 4000 BC) during which organized agricultural practices emerged, eliminating the need for mobility and permitting the rise of civilization.

**Analytical approach** perspective that views politics as an empirical discipline, rather than a science. The basis of this approach is that politics cannot be broken down into parts, and must be viewed as a aggregate.

**Anarchism** approach that is concerned with the primacy of the individual, in which outside interference in people's lives, especially by government and the state, is minimized.

**Anomic interest group** ad hoc interest groups that do not have a standard organized composition; these groups are formed to deal with short-term issues.

**Anti-dumping** surcharges placed on imported goods that are priced lower than they are in their country of production.

**APEC** Asia-Pacific Economic Cooperation —a group for promoting open trade and economic cooperation among Asia-Pacific economies.

**ASEAN** Association of South-East Asian Nations—a group devoted to peace, security, progress, and prosperity in the South-East Asian region.

**Associational interest group** interest group closely related to particular political objectives.

**Autarky** condition of complete self-sufficiency and isolation from the rest of the system.

**Authoritarianism** political system requiring absolute obedience to a constituted authority.

**Authority** the power or right to force obedience.

**Behaviouralism** perspective that concentrates on the "tangible" aspects of political life, rather than values; objective was to establish a discipline that was "scientific" and objective.

**Bicameral** legislative or parliamentary body with two assemblies.

**BIS** Bank for International Settlements— also known as the central bankers' bank, it arranges loans for central banks and encourages central bank cooperation.

**Body politic** nation or state constituted as a united body.

**Boycott** consolidation of refusal to enter into or continue social or commercial relations with a political system.

**Bretton Woods agreement** post-World War II system of fixed exchange rates and heavy controls on private banks and other financial institutions so that their role in international finance would be limited.

**Budget** sum of money available or needed for a given period of time.

**Bureaucracy** division of government responsible for carrying out public policy, and staffed by public employees.

**Cadre party** parties that are created and directed by a small elite group; tend to control much power within legislatures.

*Camarillas* Mexican patron-client relationships.

**Campaign** organized movement to raise awareness concerning political platforms leading up to elections.

**Capitalism** economic system where production and distribution of goods rely on private capital and investment.

**Catch-all party** parties that are formed to attract a wide variety of support across diverse ideologies and perspectives.

**CCP** Communist Party of China.

**Centralization** concentration of power in a single body, usually the principal government.

**Checks and balances** system of inspection and evaluation of different levels and branches of governments by others.

**Cold War** a period of rhetorical hostility not marked by violence that existed between the alliance systems centred around the United States and the Union of Soviet Socialist Republics (USSR). Most often referenced to the period from 1945–1991.

**Colonization** process of establishing colonies abroad, where people of one political community are forcibly subjected to the rule of another dominant country.

**Communism** political theory based on the writings of Karl Marx and Friedrich Engels that espouses class conflict to form a system where all property is publicly owned, and each citizen works to his or her own best ability and is compensated equitably.

**Comparative advantage** classical economic theory that suggests that every individual in a system ought to work towards his or her personal maximum potential to serve the interests of the larger society.

**Comparative approach** method of political analysis that compares different systems of political authority based on system type, time period, or form of leadership.

**Comparative politics** a sub-field of political studies that examines politics using the comparative approach.

**Competition** basic tenet of capitalism, which holds that economic production and exchange in society must be based on the free contention by many actors for market share and advantage.

**Competitive party system** electoral system found in liberal democracies where political parties are permitted to compete with one another for support from the electorate.

**Confederalism** political system of divided powers where added power is given to the non-central governments, and limited authority and power is conferred on the central government.

**Conflict resolution** process in domestic or international affairs where antagonism (either existing of potential) is sought to be reconciled through the use of mediation and negotiation.

**Congress** legislative chamber of government in the some governments, including the United States.

**Consent** legitimate compliance or voluntary agreement given by citizens to political authorities for decision-making.

**Conservatism** political perspective that seeks to conserve the best of what has come before for future generations and is concerned with maintaining political and social traditions and customs.

**Constituencies** territorial or geographical localities (ridings) represented by a politician chosen through the electoral process.

**Constitution** composition of fundamental laws and principles upon which a political system is governed.

**Constitutional authority** legitimate power given to an institution of government by the constitution of a nation state.

**Corn Laws** 1846 set of laws regulating the trade in corn, one of the most basic foodstuffs at that time.

**Corporatism** approach to governance that entails close cooperation and coordination among government, business, and labour in the expectation that such activity will bring more stability to the political economy.

**Countervail** surcharge placed on an imported good to offset a subsidy provided by the exporting country.

*Coup d'état* forcible replacement of a governing authority, usually through overt military means.

**CPSU** Communist Party of the Soviet Union.

**DC** Developed country.

**Debt crisis** financial predicament that began in the early 1980s resulting from the inability of developing countries to repay the massive loans from developed countries, international institutions, and private banks.

**Decentralization** process whereby power and authority is taken from the central government and conferred on non-central (for example, state, regional, or provincial) governments.

**Decision-making process** mechanism or pattern of relations involving different levels of government where determinations and judgments regarding the governance of political system are made (sometimes referred to as the "black box").

**Decolonization** process where political authority and independence are relinquished to territories once controlled externally by another political system.

**Deficit** excess of liabilities over assets within a specified time period (budget year).

**Delegated authority** situation where some powers may be given to sub-national authorities by the national government in a unitary system.

**Democracy** political system based on the principle that governance requires the assent of all citizens through participation in the electoral process, articulation of views, and direct or indirect representation in governing institutions.

**Dependency theory** related to structural theory, which argues that the structure of the international economic system was such that close integration into that system would not benefit the economies of the developing world.

**Depression** extended period of economic, industrial, and financial decline.

**Détente** a warming of relations; closely related to the period of enhanced relations between the United States and the Soviet Union in the 1970s.

**Developed world** industrialized nations, including western Europe, North America, Japan, Australia, and New Zealand that are part of a structurally integrated system of global capitalism.

**Devolution** political system where some authority is given to regional governments, but the power to oversee, dismiss, or entrench these authorities is still held by the central government.

**Direct democracy** political system where citizens are directly involved in the decision-making process.

**Duty** payment levied on the import, export, manufacture, or purchase of a good or service.

**Empirical** analysis based not on concepts and theory, but on what can be observed or experimented with.

**Enumeration** the process of determining the number of individuals eligible to vote in a constituency.

**Environmentalism** political ideology based on the notion that modern economic systems are the main dilemma for nature; it also views modern industrialism as a hierarchical system that restricts human freedom.

**Equalization payments** compensation given to more needy regions in a political system in order to create a general state of parity.

*Estados Unidos de Mexico*  United States of Mexico.

**Exchange system**  mechanism to regulate currencies and currency trading; may be a fixed exchange rate system, or a floating exchange rate system.

**Executive**  usually the top level of government, or the leader. Maintains leadership for the entire political system, and often reflects the leadership and preoccupations of the dominant political party.

**Fascism**  ideology that holds that the nation should be organized within by the state, with an unquestioned authority (national leader); in practical terms this means extreme authoritarianism, and the will to use force, indeed violence, to ensure order and compliance.

**Federalism**  form of governance that divides powers between the central government and regional governments; often, particular roles and capacities are given to the regional governments.

**Feminism**  an ideology based on a set of demands concerning the status of women in every aspect of human life; "equal rights for women."

**First-past-the-post**  electoral system (simple plurality) where the winner receives the most (but not necessarily a majority of) votes.

**First World**  industrialized nations, including Western Europe, North America, Japan, Australia, and New Zealand that are part of a structurally integrated system of global capitalism.

**Fiscal policy**  the balance between spending and taxes set out by a government in a "fiscal" budget year.

*la francophonie*  international organization of francophone countries.

**Free trade**  international trade among political systems unimpeded by restrictions or tariffs on imports or exports.

**FTA**  Free Trade Agreement (Canada-United States).

**G8**  Group of Eight (formerly G7—Group of Seven) major economic actors: United States, United Kingdom, France, Germany, Canada, Italy, Japan, Russia.

**GATT**  General Agreement on Tariffs and Trade.

**GDP**  gross domestic product—total value of goods and services produced in a country in one year.

*Glasnost*  openness—Mikhail Gorbachev's initiative to open up the political system in the former Soviet Union in both domestic and international affairs.

**Globalization**  the intensification of economic, political, social, and cultural relations across borders.

**GNP**  gross national product—total value of goods and services produced in a country in one year plus total of net income earned abroad.

**Government**  the institutions and people responsible for carrying out the affairs and administration of a political system.

**Great Leap Forward**  Chinese program of economic policies designed to revolutionize rural production by replacing private ownership of land with communes, in which all agricultural production was to be sold to the state.

**HDI**  Human Development Index—method used by United Nations to determine relative level of development in a country.

**Hegemony**  international political system marked by leadership by one country with inordinate capability to uphold and protect the system.

**Historical materialism**  principle that holds that human development could be understood by studying history and analyzing the economic processes within it.

**IBRD** International Bank for Reconstruction and Development (World Bank)—lends money to developing countries for development projects, usually in the long term.

**Ideology** set or system of ideas that form the basis of a political or economic system and provide guidance and direction for political leadership.

**IGO** International governmental organization.

**ILO** International Labour Organization—created in 1919 to improve working conditions around the world by setting minimum standards, providing technical assistance, and promoting the development of labour unions.

**IMF** International Monetary Fund—facilitates international monetary cooperation, balance of payments stability, financial aid, and technical aid.

**Indirect democracy** political system of representation where citizens elect a delegate to act on their behalf.

**Industrial revolution** period during late eighteenth century and early nineteenth centuries of rapid development of industrial potential and output, starting in the United Kingdom, and spreading through Europe and North America; led to massive population of urban centres.

**Industrialization** process whereby countries improve and strengthen their industrial capability and production.

**Industrialized nations** nations including Western Europe, North America, Japan, Australia, and New Zealand that are part of a structurally integrated system of global capitalism.

**Infant technology** technological development that is protected due to its new and innovative advantages.

**Innovative economy** an economic system that emphasizes knowledge-based research and development sectors.

**Inputs** information inflows (from both domestic and international environments) within a political system.

**Interdependence** "mutual dependence"; a method of measuring dependent relationships among countries, based on the level of sensitivity and vulnerability one country has to another.

**Interest groups** groups in a political system that seek either to alter or maintain the approach of government without taking a formal role in elections or seeking an official capacity in government.

**International anarchy** condition where there is no "world government"; the sovereign nation-state is the highest authority in the international system.

**International political economy** IPE; political and economic activity on an international stage that demonstrates the intimate connection between national and international processes.

**International politics** relations of a political nature that exist at the international level.

**International system** a system of two or more actors that interact regularly using established processes in given issue areas in the global arena.

**International relations** all relations at the international level.

**Interwar period** years 1919–1939 between the First and Second World wars.

**Invisible hand** Adam Smith's notion that economic forces left on their own would lead to maximum efficiency and economic growth over time as they engaged in competition against each other; benefits to society as a whole exist without political interference.

**ISI** Import Substitution Industrialization—aimed at developing a domestic industrial base by keeping out imports of certain manufactured goods and investing in their production on a national level.

**Judicial review** power of the courts to interpret the constitution, varying from the ability to resolve disputes between levels of government in federal systems to the ability to annul legislative and executive actions outright.

**Judiciary** judicial (courts) level of governance.

**Justice** state of affairs involving the maintenance of what is morally right and fair.

*Keiretsu* vertical integration of large industrial groups in Japan where independence in decision-making and production is retained by individual industries and businesses while at the same time permitting like-minded groups to bind together to influence the policy process.

**Kuznets Effect** economic formula that demonstrates that, as a country develops economically, income distribution will become more unequal before it becomes more equal.

*Laissez-faire* "to let be"—economic theory that suggests that a reduction in political control will benefit the economic system.

**LDC** less developed countries.

**Legislature** legislative body of a political system with the responsibility to make laws.

**Legitimacy** what is lawful, appropriate, and proper, and conforms to the standards of a political system.

**Levels of analysis** approach to political studies that suggests that accurate analysis must be inclusive of international, domestic, and individual arenas of interaction.

**Liberal democracy** political system based on freedom and individual liberty, and on the principle that governance requires the assent of all citizens through participation in the electoral process, articulation of views, and direct or indirect representation in governing institutions.

**Liberalism** view of politics that favours liberty, free trade, and moderate social and political change.

**Liberty** freedom from despotic control.

**Lobbying** method that business/interest groups use to apply direct pressure to the executive, legislative, and bureaucratic branches of government.

*Los Pinos* the Mexican equivalent of the White House.

**MAI** Multilateral Agreement on Investment.

**Majority government** government by the party that received a majority of seats in an election.

**Market** social environment—domestic or international—that permits the exchange of goods and services for sale or purchase.

**Mass party** parties that are organized in society at large, rather than within government, and have public influence through power of membership, rather than in the hands of a small minority elite.

**Mature technology** a technology that is generally available to anyone, and is not protected for its innovation or breakthrough potential.

**Media** main means of mass communication, through print, and television and radio broadcasting.

**Military coup** seizure of government through the use of military force.

**Militia party** party systems with a centralized leadership system; they are often led by martial leaders, and are frequently found in one-party systems.

**Ministerial responsibility** Principle in parliamentary systems that requires members of the political executive, both individually and as a group, to remain accountable to the legislature.

**Minority government** government by the party that received the most, but not a majority of, votes in an election.

**MNC** multinational corporation.

**Monarchy** form of government with monarch as head of state.

**Monetary policy** the management of the money supply and interest rates.

**Monopoly** exclusive control of trade in a commodity or service.

**Multilateralism** integration or coordination of policies or decision-making by three or more nation-states.

**Multinational corporations** corporate bodies that operate in more than one country.

**Multi-party system** competitive party system with more than two parties.

**NAFTA** North American Free Trade Agreement, involving Canada, the United States, and Mexico.

**Nation** groups of persons who share an identity that is based on, but not limited to, shared ethnic, religious, cultural, or linguistic qualities.

**Nationalism** political movement, based on national identity, to create a political state; may also be interpreted as a strong feeling of patriotism.

**NATO** North Atlantic Treaty Organization.

**NGO** Non-governmental organization.

**NIC** Newly industrialized country.

**Non-associational interest group** interest group not closely related to, or not connected with, particular political objectives.

**Non-tariff barriers** (NTB) imposing national content requirements on certain products or applying quotas to their import.

**Non-zero-sum game** political or economic situation where whatever is gained by one side may be also gained by the other; cooperative behaviour that results in a net change for all parties, though not always in an equitable manner.

**NORAD** North American Aerospace Defence Agreement, between Canada and the United States.

**Norms** standards of interaction, customary patterns of behaviour.

**North** industrialized nations including Western Europe, North America, Japan, Australia, and New Zealand that are part of a structurally integrated system of global capitalism.

**OAS** Organization of American States.

**OECD** Organization for Economic Cooperation and Development.

**Oil shocks** events in 1973 and 1979 that saw the dramatic increase in price of oil by the OPEC nations.

**Oligopoly** condition of limited competition among a small number of providers or producers.

**One-party system** political system where only one political party is allowed to form the government, or compete in elections.

**OPEC** Organization of the Petroleum Exporting Countries.

**OSCE** Organization for Security and Cooperation in Europe.

**Outputs** final decisions made in the decision-making process.

*Pareto optimal* economic or social arrangement deemed to be efficient if one individual or group in society can be made better off without making any other individual or group worse off.

**Parliament** legislature in Westminster form of government.

**Party** group of individuals engaged in the attempt to control government through the election of their members.

**PEMEX** *Petroleos de Mexico*—Mexico's national oil company.

*Perestroika* restructuring; the process put into place by Mikhail Gorbachev as leader of the Soviet Union to reorganize the administration of that political system.

**PLA** China's People's Liberation Army.

**Pluralism** society where several disparate groups (minority and majority) maintain their interests, and a number of concerns and traditions persist.

**Policy** laws or principle of performance adopted by a government.

**Political action committees** conglomerations of several interest groups to more effectively influence the decision-making process.

**Political business cycle** when governments seeking re-election spend freely towards the end of their terms of office, in an effort to buy votes.

**Political culture** set of attitudes, beliefs, and values that underpin any political system.

**Political economy** approach that views political and economic spheres as harmonious and mutually dependent perceptions of the world; relationship between people, government, and the economy.

**Political participation** taking a part, share, or interest in the political process.

**Political philosophy** search for understanding of things political and political systems; attempt to explain the significance of political phenomena in order to improve our understanding of politics and to better design solutions for the problems that mark human life and society.

**Political system** conglomerate of numerous political structures that work together to drive the political aspects of social interaction.

**Political theory** system of ideas regarding political behaviour based on a set of principles that is independent of what is to be analyzed; that which may be "tested" in political analysis.

**Politics** the governance of social units, allocation of power and responsibility, and relationship among political actors in society.

**Polity** the form or process of organized government; can mean a state, or it can refer more generally to a collection of individuals in a community that have a political relationship with one another.

**Portfolio investment** acquisition of shares (stocks) in a corporate actor for the purpose of profit; does not imply ownership.

**Post-behaviouralism** approach that attempted to reconcile the problems encountered by behaviouralism by allowing for values and ideology in its analysis.

**Post-Cold War** period following the end of the Cold War, generally accepted to have begun in 1992 with the formal dissolution of the Soviet Union on December 31, 1991.

**Post-Industrial Revolution** term sometimes used to describe the process whereby developed economies increasingly have come to focus on the necessary components of a high-technology, or high-value, economy.

**Post-War order** political arrangement settled upon by industrialized countries after the Second World War.

**Power** ability to achieve goals in a political system, and to have others do as you wish them to.

**Praetorianism** ineffectiveness of pluralist democratic institutions.

**PRC**  People's Republic of China.

**Presidential system**  system of government originating in the United States that places power in the presidential executive with a series of checks and balances of power among the institutions of government.

**Pressure group**  groups in a political system that seek to either alter or maintain the approach of government without taking a formal role in elections or seeking an official capacity in government.

**PRI**  *Partido Revolucionario Institucional* (Institutional Revolutionary Party of Mexico).

**Product cycle**  theory explains the development of production as connected to the life of the product itself.

**Progress**  advancement in society towards a better and improved state of affairs; an integral element of liberal political theory.

**Progressive taxation system**  system of taxation based on income.

**Proportional representation**  electoral system where seats are designated according to the parties' popular vote; uses country as a whole in order to institute proportions between votes allotted for all the parties.

**Protectionism**  tendency of countries to safeguard their own economic sectors or industries using tariffs, quotas, or other forms of trade and investment legislation.

**Public administration**  management of public affairs and government by politicians and public servants.

**Public goods**  wealth and resources that are present in a political system.

**Public opinion**  citizen participation in the form of expressing viewpoints in public discourse.

**Public policy**  laws or principles of performance adopted by a government that affect a political system.

*Rapprochement*  "reconciliation" or a warming of relations between normally antagonistic actors.

**Realism**  view that world politics is a contest for power; human nature and societies are imperfect; conflict is an inherent danger, and the state is the key variable in the study of international politics. For realists, politics is a struggle for limited resources in a competitive and non-cooperative environment.

**Realpolitik**  pragmatic approach to world politics; countries should practise balance-of-power politics and strive to achieve an equilibrium of power in the world in order to prevent any other country or coalition of countries from dominating the system.

**Recession**  temporary decline in economic productivity or affluence.

**Reciprocity**  complementary or mutual behaviour among two or more actors; view that liberalzation of trade would be beneficial for all parties concerned if cooperative policies were pursued.

**Regionalism**  process of economic or political integration in a defined territorial area.

**Regulation**  economic or political policies that are subject to restrictions by political authorities.

**Relative power**  method of distinguishing the comparable strength of a political unit by contrasting it with another.

**Repatriation**  to restore or bring back to a native land.

**Representation**  the act of standing for the views of others; election of a representative to symbolize the collective view of all constituents.

**Republic**  political unit where supreme power is held by the people or elected representatives of the people.

**Rights** socially acceptable, morally correct, just and fair privileges granted to members of a political community.

**Sanctions** penalties or rewards given to a political authority to coerce (or preserve) their behaviour according to accepted norms of conduct.

**Second World** classification of countries that were part of the closed system of communism; Soviet Union and its allies during the Cold War.

**Security dilemma** conception in world politics that states are both protected by the existence of states, and threatened by them.

**Self-interest** belief that political actors will behave in order to serve their own concerns.

*Sexenio* six-year term for the Mexican presidency.

**Simple plurality** electoral system (first-past-the-post) where the winner receives the most (but not necessarily a majority of) votes.

**Social sciences** scientific study of human society and social relationships.

**Socialism** economic and political theory of society that holds that citizens should own the means of production, exchange, and allocation.

**Socialization** process whereby individuals act in a social manner; creation of social and political authority and rules to regulate behaviour so as to permit operation of social units.

**Sound-byte** tendency of the mass media to seek short snippets of observations from commentators in order to package news in a more condensed form.

**South** categorization of less developed nations that are not part of a structurally integrated system of global capitalism.

**Sovereignty** recognition by other political authorities that a government is legitimate and rightful for a political community.

**Stagflation** negative economic period of inflation without related rise in demand or employment; high unemployment coupled with high inflation.

**State** a recognized political unit with a defined territory and people, and a central government administration responsible for administering and considered to be sovereign.

**Structural-functionalism** approach that focuses on the role of political structures and their functions in society.

**Sub-systemic** below the level of the nation state.

**Suffrage** granting of the right to vote.

**Supply and demand** amounts available and required in economic systems that affect pricing and value of goods and services.

**Supply side economics** economic theory whose expectation is that by minimizing taxes and the role of government, private investment will rise, and growth will be stimulated; this will in turn raise revenue for government by allowing individuals and corporations to retain—and likely spend—more money than they otherwise might have.

**Surplus** what is left over when requirements are met.

**Sustainable development** model of economic growth that seeks to use renewable resources so as not to destroy the environment in which human beings have to live.

**Systems theory** approach that views politics as a system of interaction, binding political structures such as government to individual action; argues that politics is a dynamic process of information flows and responses that encompasses political institutions, groups, and individuals.

**Tariff** a duty placed on a particular category of imported or exported goods or services.

**Technical state** a political and economic system that emphasizes knowledge-based research and development sectors.

**Terrorism** use of violence and fear by individuals and organized groups to achieve political goals.

**Theory** premise or set of ideas that may be tested and is based on a set of principles that are independent of what is to be applied to the theory or test.

**Third World** largely Cold War categorization of less developed nations that are not part of a structurally integrated system of global capitalism.

**Throughputs** system of analysis, investigation, options, and decision-making housed in the government of the system itself.

**Totalitarianism** authoritarian political system that controls not only most social interaction, but is also marked by a desire by the government to force its objectives and values on citizens in an unlimited manner.

**Two-party system** competitive party systems marked by two competing parties.

**Typology** study and interpretation of political classifications.

**Tyranny** the harsh and arbitrary exercise of authority.

**UN** United Nations.

**UNCTAD** United Nations Committee on Trade and Development.

**Undeveloped world** categorization of less developed nations that are not part of a structurally integrated system of global capitalism.

**Unicameral** legislative or parliamentary body with one assembly.

**Unitary systems** political systems that concentrate political authority and power within one central government, which is singularly responsible for the activities of the political unit, both domestic and foreign.

**Values** principles, standards; what an individual or community esteems as meaningful.

**Welfare state** political system that creates the means for individual protection and quality of life, such as healthcare, employment insurance, pensions, social programs for the elderly, children, and unemployed.

**Westminster system** British model of parliamentary representative government.

**WTO** World Trade Organization—created in 1995 as a forum for promoting free trade in goods and services between nations.

**WTO** Warsaw Treaty Organization (defunct).

**Yoshida Doctrine** post-war Japanese political and economic policy to establish a more non-interventionist role in international affairs, support the United States as hegemonic in the global system, deepen links with the Americans; and focus on the domestic economy of Japan as a means of reassembling power and influence.

**Zero-sum game** political or economic situation where whatever is gained by one side is lost by the other, so the net change is always zero.

# Index